China Watching

China is the most rapidly and dramatically changing society in the world. Consequently, China Watchers have never been in higher demand to analyze and interpret it for multiple audiences. This book assesses the scholarship of China Watchers from Europe, Japan and the United States over the last decade in three specific areas: the Chinese economy, Chinese domestic politics, and China's foreign relations and national security. Contributions from leading experts in the field contrast the different research foci, methodologies and conclusions that are drawn by Sinologists regarding the complexities of contemporary China. Debates such as the sustainability of China's economic growth, the prospects for political change, the degree to which China constitutes a "threat" to the world with its heightened international profile and military modernization, and other issues are all hotly debated among China Watchers worldwide. *China Watching* provides a unique insight into the world of China studies as well as China itself, and will appeal to those with an interest in Chinese politics, economics, foreign policy and security studies.

Robert Ash is Professor of Economics with reference to China and Taiwan at the School of Oriental and African Studies (SOAS), University of London.

David Shambaugh is Professor of Political Science and International Affairs and Director of the China Policy Program at the George Washington University. He is also a Nonresident Senior Fellow in the Foreign Policy Studies Program at the Brookings Institution.

Seiichiro Takagi is Professor at the School of International Politics, Economics, and Business at the Aoyama Gakuin University in Japan. He is also a Senior Fellow at the Japan Institute of International Affairs.

China Watching

Perspectives from Europe, Japan and
the United States

Edited by
Robert Ash
David Shambaugh
Seiichiro Takagi

Routledge
Taylor & Francis Group

LONDON AND NEW YORK

First published 2007
by Routledge
2 Park Square, Milton Park, Abingdon, Oxon OX14 4RN

Simultaneously published in the USA and Canada
by Routledge
270 Madison Ave, New York, NY 10016

Routledge is an imprint of the Taylor & Francis Group, an informa business

© 2007 Editorial selection, © Robert Ash, David Shambaugh, and Seiichiro Takagi; individual chapters, © the contributors

Typeset in Times by
HWA Text and Data Management, Tunbridge Wells
Printed and bound in Great Britain by
Antony Rowe Ltd, Chippenham, Wiltshire

British Library Cataloguing in Publication Data
A catalogue record for this book is available from the British Library

Library of Congress Cataloging-in-Publication Data
China watching : perspectives from Europe, Japan and the United States / edited by Robert Ash, David Shambaugh and Seiichiro Takagi.
    p.   cm. (Routledge contemporary China series)
Includes bibliographical references and index.
1. China–Economic conditions–Bibliography–Catalogs. 2. China–Politics and government –Bibliography–Catalogs. 3. China–Foreign relations–Bibliography–Catalogs. 4. China–Foreign public opinion, European–Bibliography–Catalogs. 5. China–Foreign public opinion, Japanese–Bibliography–Catalogs. 6. China–Foreign public opinion, American–Bibliography–Catalogs. I. Ash, Robert F. II. Shambaugh, David L. III. Takagi, Seiichiro, 1943– IV. Series.
Z3108.A5C445 2006
[HC427]
016.95105'9–dc22   2006017820

ISBN10: 0–415–41396–6 (hbk)   ISBN13: 978–0–415–41396–1 (hbk)
ISBN10: 0–415–41397–4 (pbk)   ISBN13: 978–0–415–41397–8 (pbk)
ISBN10: 0–203–96775–5 (ebk)   ISBN13: 978– 0–203–96775–1 (ebk)

Contents

Contributors

Robert Ash is Professor of Economics with reference to China and Taiwan at the School of Oriental and African Studies (SOAS), University of London. Since 1999 he has been Director of the SOAS Taiwan Studies Program, and he is currently an Associate Dean in the Faculty of Law and Social Sciences. From 1986 to 1995 he was Head of the Contemporary China Institute at SOAS; and in 1997–2001 he was Director of the EU-China Academic Network. He has held visiting research and teaching positions in Australia, Hong Kong and, most recently, at Fondation des Sciences-Politiques (Sciences-Po) in Paris. He has written or edited 13 books on China, and over 30 articles and book chapters, as well as some 150 other reports and shorter papers. His publications embrace a wide range of topics relating to the social and economic development of China, as well as the economies of Hong Kong and Taiwan.

Richard Baum is Professor of Political Science at UCLA and past Director of the UCLA Center for Chinese Studies. He is author or editor of eight books, including *Burying Mao: Chinese Politics in the Age of Deng Xiaoping* (1996). A frequent consultant and media commentator on Chinese politics and foreign relations, he has contributed over 100 articles to scholarly and popular journals. He is currently writing a book on the perils and pitfalls of China watching.

Jean-Pierre Cabestan is Senior Researcher at the French National Center for Scientific Research (Centre National de la Recherche Scientifique). He is attached to the Institute of Comparative Law of the University of Paris I. He is also associate researcher at the Asia Centre, Paris. His most recent publications include *Chine-Taiwan: la guerre est-elle concevable? La sécurité extérieure de Taiwan face à la menace de la Chine populaire* (Paris: Economica, 2003); and (with Benoît Vermander) *La Chine et ses frontières: La confrontation Chine-Taiwan* (Paris: Presses des Sciences-Po, 2005). He has also published numerous articles and contributions in English on China's political system and reform, Chinese law, the relations across the Taiwan Strait and Taiwanese politics.

Tomoyuki Kojima is Professor of Political Science and International Affairs, and Dean of the Department of Policy Management, at Keio University. He specializes in Chinese domestic politics and foreign relations, as well as the international relations of East Asia. His most recent books are *Restructuring China* (Tokyo: Toyo Bunko, 2006) in English, *The Rise of China* (Tokyo: Ashi Shobo, 2005) in Japanese, and *China with Power and Prosperity* (Tokyo: Ashi Shobo, 2003) in Japanese.

Kay Möller is Senior Research Associate at the Stiftung Wissenschaft und Politik (German Institute for Security Studies and Politics) in Berlin, Germany. His principal research interests are the security problems and cooperation in the Western Pacific, and China's foreign relations. His most recent book is *Die Aussenpolitik der Volksrepublic China, 1949–2004* (The Foreign Policy of the People's Republic of China (2005)).

Hideo Ohashi is Professor of Development Economics and East Asian Studies at Senshu University. He was a Research Fellow at the Mitsubishi Research Institute during 1984–1989, the Consulate-General of Japan in Hong Kong during 1989–1991, and the Japan Institute of International Affairs during 1992–2001. His research focuses on economic development of Greater China, economic relations between Japan and East Asia, and political economy of Asia-Pacific economic cooperation. His publications in Japanese include *U.S.– China Economic Friction* (1998), *Comparative International Development* (co-authored 2000), *Globalization of China's Economy* (2003), and *Contemporary Chinese Economy* (2005).

Penelope B. Prime is Professor of Economics in the Department of Economics and Finance at the Coles College of Business, and Director of the China Research Center, at Kennesaw State University, Atlanta, Georgia. She specializes in international economics and development with a research focus on China's economy and business environment. Her articles have been published in a number of economics journals, including *Applied Economics, Economic Development and Cultural Change, Growth and Change*, and *Change and Business Economics*. She also serves on the editorial boards of *China Economic Review* and the *Indian Journal of Economics and Business*.

David Shambaugh is Professor of Political Science and International Affairs, and Director of the China Policy Program, at the George Washington University. He is also a Nonresident Senior Fellow in the Foreign Policy Studies Program at the Brookings Institution in Washington, D.C. Professor Shambaugh specializes in Chinese domestic politics, foreign relations and national security affairs, as well as the international relations of the Asian region. He is a consultant to many government and private sector institutions, and is involved in various forms of public education. His most recent books are *Power Shift: China and Asia's New Dynamics* (edited 2005), and *The Odyssey of China's Imperial Art Treasures* (co-authored 2005).

Seiichiro Takagi is Professor at the School of International Politics, Economics, and Business, the Aoyama Gakuin University. He is also a Senior Fellow at the Japan Institute of International Affairs. Professor Takagi specializes in

Chinese domestic politics, foreign relations and national security affairs, as well as international relations in the Asia-Pacific region. He is a member of the Japan Committee of the Council for Security Cooperation in the Asia-Pacific (CSCAP) and a board member of the Program for International Studies in Asia (PISA), an international academic NGO based at the George Washington University. His recent books are *China's Post-Cold War Diplomacy and the Asia-Pacific* (edited, 2000), and *South Asian Security* (co-author, 2006), both in Japanese.

1   Introduction

*Robert Ash, David Shambaugh, and
Seiichiro Takagi*

Periodically it is useful to take stock of the state of a scholarly field and profession. While this volume does not claim to be comprehensive in its scope or definitive in its assessments, it nonetheless offers a useful window into the state of research and publication on contemporary China in Europe, Japan, and the United States. On balance, the assessments contained in this volume attest to the fact that the field is doing a good job of keeping up with and interpreting fast-changing developments in China, and that the international "state of the field" can be judged to be healthy and growing. While this overall judgment applies, the state of the field in these different nations and regions is uneven.

The chapters that follow in this volume provide an authoritative introduction to the state of international contemporary China studies today. Regrettably, they do not include assessments of the field elsewhere in Asia, Canada, or Oceania, nor in China itself. Chinese studies in Australia and Canada have always been particularly robust, and the field has made important new strides in Asia in recent years (particularly in South Korea, Singapore, India). Chinese studies in Latin America and South Africa have also begun to develop during the past decade. Despite the fact that this volume does not include assessments of contemporary China studies in these regions, the examination of China studies in America, Europe, and Japan does capture the main trends in the field internationally. The main temporal focus is limited to studies published since 1990 or so, although a few of the chapters range back further in time. The disciplinary focus is limited to economics, politics, and foreign/security affairs. This necessitates the omission of much valuable work in other disciplines and subject areas, such as Chinese society, culture or the humanities. But we hope and believe that the disciplinary sample contained in these chapters capture the state of the field in three principal areas of social science research on China.

What makes this book unique is its international and comparative character. Previous assessments have been undertaken on contemporary China studies in the United States,[1] United Kingdom,[2] Canada,[3] France,[4] Germany,[5] Scandinavia,[6] and Vietnam,[7] and there also exist a number of functional studies of different sectors and disciplines.[8] But, to date, there has only been one attempt at a cross-national assessment. This was done by the Universities Service Centre (USC) in Hong Kong to commemorate its thirtieth anniversary in 1993. It included contributions on Britain, France, northern Europe, Japan, North America, and Russia.[9] While an interesting survey of Sinological trends in these different parts of the world, the USC effort was not well-focused. This volume attempts to bring greater comparative perspectives to bear, by tightly focusing on three subject areas and three countries/regions (in the case of Europe). The chapters were originally presented at the conference "Overseas Studies of Contemporary China," convened at Fudan University in Shanghai in November 2005, but have been subsequently updated and thoroughly revised (several times) for publication in this volume.

Highlights of the Volume

Chinese Economic Studies

The watershed events in China at the end of the 1970s and the fundamental readjustment of domestic priorities away from Mao's ideological preoccupation with class struggle towards the imperative of economic growth were bound to have a major impact on overseas perceptions of, and interest in, the Chinese economy. All three contributors to this section refer to the dramatic expansion in research and publications that have taken place in Europe, Japan and the United States in recent years. In order to make her task manageable, Penelope Prime deliberately restricts her focus to articles that have appeared in refereed economics journals since 1995. Statistics cited in all three chapters demonstrate how far and how fast the field has moved on since the late 1960s, when an authoritative study of Chinese economic studies throughout the world saw fit to refer to the work of a mere 19 authors (17 of them based in the U.S.!).[10]

Intellectual, practical and historical forces have both encouraged and facilitated this explosion in scholarly activity, although their relative importance has sometimes differed in the three countries (regions) represented in this volume. Professor Prime uses a number of theoretical economic issues, as well as other "puzzles" posed by China's experience under reform, as a framework within which to offer a rigorous commentary and analysis of trends in North American research on the Chinese economy. She makes the important point that the perceived *success* of China's economic reforms, not least *vis-à-vis* the more halting performances of the former Soviet Union and – at least until recently – India, goes some way towards explaining what has at times resembled an obsession with the Chinese experience. The most obvious manifestation of China's economic success has been the rapid and sustained nature of its GDP growth. Hence, Prime's focus on the contributions made by U.S.-based economists towards understanding the nature, level and sources of post-1978 growth in China.

The speed of China's recent economic growth is a fundamental issue on which the U.S. academic community has yet to agree, and Prime draws attention to varying degrees of skepticism with which official Chinese growth estimates have been received. In the end, however, the more important question relates to the sources of growth and the relative contributions of physical increases in inputs, improvements in the efficiency with which they are used and the introduction of more effective technologies. Prime's review of work in this regard is a further salutary reminder of the considerable uncertainty that surrounds the debate about the basis of Chinese economic growth. It also highlights the need for caution in merely extrapolating from previous growth trends in order to predict China's future growth trajectory. Nor does the work of U.S.-based scholars offer unambiguous evidence of growth *convergence*. The important conclusion that emerges from this part of Prime's analysis is that while the work of the U.S. China economy-watching community has contributed much to our understanding of China's recent growth, plenty of questions still await answers.

Institutional factors – ownership and privatization, fiscal and financial reforms, market integration – define the second set of issues which Penelope Prime investigates through the prism of U.S. scholars of the Chinese economy. She acknowledges the orthodoxy that effective institutions are likely to benefit growth and efficiency. Interestingly, however, out of her review emerges the finding that empirical studies conducted by U.S.-based scholars highlight the mixed, even "contradictory," impact of institutional reform in China upon growth and efficiency.

History and geographical propinquity lend a distinctive flavor to studies of the Chinese economy undertaken in Japan. Hideo Ohashi observes that Japan's economic well-being is highly sensitive to China's economic performance, as a result of which the study of the Chinese economy in Japan has become "internalized" almost to the extent of being made a part of the study of the domestic Japanese economy. It is a commonplace in both North America and Europe that their economic fates are increasingly linked to events in China. But in neither case is the relationship as personalized as it is for Japan, almost 80,000 of whose citizens now live and work in China. The emergence of China specialists working in government and the corporate sector reflects the close engagement by both these constituencies in economic developments taking place in China.

Ohashi also makes an interesting distinction between a tendency by the Japanese academic China-watching community to focus on China's domestic economic issues – for example, inter-sectoral resource flows, employment and migration, fiscal decentralization and income inequality – while research by Japanese non-China specialists focus on the external dimensions of China's economic development (especially those, such as the performance of small and medium-scale enterprises (SMEs) or the prospects for current realignment, that impinge on Japan). Ohashi notes that the basis of the former group's work on domestic issues lies in empirical investigations conducted through fieldwork conducted in China. It is not clear whether this tendency towards on-the-spot research is more common among Japanese than among North American scholars (it is almost certainly more common than among their European counterparts) although there is little doubt that individual Japanese scholars travel more frequently to China than those based in the U.S. or Europe. As Ohashi seems to imply, this methodology is another distinctive characteristic of Japanese work on the Chinese economy.

Ideological factors have also shaped Japanese studies of the Chinese economy to a much greater extent than they have in Europe and the United States. Ohashi distinguishes between the explicitly ideological thrust of such studies before the 1980s and the more "empirical" tendency that has more recently characterized them. Communism's collapse and its abandonment as an ideology driving economic change contributed most to this change of mindset. But the removal of restrictions of statistical reporting also played a significant role, making possible a more accurate and realistic assessment of economic conditions in China. Ohashi notes that the release of statistical information has also made possible the involvement of economists lacking specific expertise on China in the study of the Chinese economy. A feature of the Japanese scene that has no real parallel, at least in terms of numerical significance, in Europe or the United States is the participation in Chinese economic studies of Chinese nationals living and working in Japan. So significant is this involvement that Ohashi argues that most Japanese work on the Chinese economy should be regarded as a "collaborative" effort. Without wishing to overstate the case, cultural and linguistic affinities have no doubt helped to nurture the close Sino-Japanese professional relationship. Equally, the lack of such affinities has clearly contributed to what Ohashi describes as the "aloofness" of Japan's China economy-watchers from the international community of scholars in the West – although it is largely the role of English as an international *lingua franca* that prevents one from noting the aloofness of Western scholars from the Japanese academic community.

Cultural and linguistic barriers have also been serious obstacles to the emergence of an integrated, let alone unified "European," approach to the study of the Chinese economy. Ash suggests that these and other impediments remain major challenges to both the promotion of collaborative cross-country economic research on China and also the dissemination of scholarly work undertaken by Europeans within the boundaries of their own countries. Until very recently, European scholars of the Chinese economy were more likely to interact with their Asian and North American counterparts than they were with colleagues working elsewhere in Europe. Happily, as Ash shows, this is a situation that in recent years has at last begun to change, thanks to major institutional initiatives, such as the establishment in Amsterdam of the International Institute for Asian Studies (IIAS) and the pan-regional Europe-China Academic Network (ECAN), which operated from 1997–2001 and, after a five-year hiatus, was resurrected in 2006.

Ash surveys the development of Chinese economic studies in Europe from the 1960s to the present day from both national and individual perspectives. His analysis shows, perhaps predictably, the disproportionate contributions to the field made by scholars in France, Germany, the United Kingdom and – albeit to a lesser extent – Holland. In Scandinavia, the study of contemporary China has grown quite rapidly in recent years, although the focus has been more on political and security issues than on the economy. In Southern Europe, notably Spain and Portugal, scholarly interest in the Chinese economy is a more recent phenomenon.

For these reasons it is difficult to identify a characteristically "European" approach towards the study of the Chinese economy. There are, however, emphases and themes that appear to recur. As in Japan, but less so in the United States, economic studies of China by Europeans have been driven more by empirical than by theoretical concerns. Ash's chronological approach also serves to highlight the strong generational component that attaches to the evolution of such studies. Traditional Sinology has a long history in many European countries – a tradition that may at times have impeded efforts to engage in contemporary studies. But in France, Germany and the U.K., by the 1960s a small number of scholars were already engaged in work that offered valuable insights into the rationale and impact of economic policies in the first decade of the Mao era. Not all of this early work was by trained economists. In France, in particular, the writings of the first outstanding generation of contemporary China scholars – Lucien Bianco is a prime example – addressed political issues. But their political analysis of events such as the revolution in the Chinese countryside proved to be a fertile soil in which others' *economic* analysis of, for example, agricultural policies in the 1950s could take seed. Indeed, the political economy tradition is one which has characterized much European work on the Chinese economy, even if the latest generation of economic analysts of China are far better equipped with theoretical and econometric tools than their forbears ever were.

Ash concludes his overview of European studies of the Chinese economy by acknowledging the considerable progress that has been made in improving understanding of the process of economic change in China, both before and after 1978. But he is also at pains to emphasize that there is no room for complacency. The speed and complexity of the changes taking place in China highlight the importance of ensuring adequate funding provision – in both public and private sectors – to maintain and strengthen the momentum of progress. The diversity of intellectual and cultural traditions in Europe also offers a unique opportunity to engage in cross-border collaborative research on the Chinese economy. In terms of understanding the wider significance of economic events unfolding in China, such efforts would not only be to the further benefit of Europe itself, but would complement research being undertaken in Japan, the United States and elsewhere.

Chinese Political Studies

The second section of the volume examines studies of domestic Chinese politics. Jean-Pierre Cabestan of the French National Center for Scientific Research (CNRS) surveys European studies of Chinese politics. Although his findings indicate that such studies have developed and grown in recent years, Cabestan also observes that European scholars of Chinese politics remain limited in number – especially when compared with those in the United States, Japan, or Australia (South Korea alone may contain as many specialists on Chinese politics as there are in the whole of Europe). He also notes that European scholars of Chinese politics tend to be much more general in their research foci compared with those in Japan or the U.S., although he suggests that there is a degree of over-specialization in the latter two countries. He also notes different emphases in choice of research subjects and theoretical approaches of European scholars and their counterparts in the U.S. and

Japan, with Europeans seemingly more interested in the politics of social policy and governance issues.

European scholars of domestic Chinese politics continue to be concentrated in the U.K., France, and Germany, with a scattering of specialists in the Benelux and Scandinavian countries. By contrast, with one exception in Italy, he identifies no specialists in the Mediterranean states and only three in Central Europe (in the Czech Republic and Poland). Cabestan reflects on some of the reasons for the relative dearth in numbers of specialists or their lack of specialization. Among those to which he draws attention are: the narrowness of national job markets in European countries; pressures to publish in native languages and national markets (rather than in English and international publications); the lingering impact of classical Sinology, which emphasizes history and the humanities, rather than embedding area studies within social science disciplines; lack of government demand for relevant expertise because of very limited strategic interests in Asia; low government financial support and dearth of private sector resources for the field; and the departure of some notable scholars to universities in America, Australia, and Hong Kong.

Despite these problems, Cabestan notes that the study of Chinese politics has increased in quantity and improved in quality, and he argues that the community of European scholars working in this field has become increasingly integrated into the global network of specialists on contemporary Chinese politics. Despite relative improvements over the past, there remains room for improvement. A noteworthy characteristic of contemporary China studies, as discussed above, remains the *lack* of interaction and collaboration among China specialists around the world. Moreover, because a large number of Europeans tend not to publish in English or in the main scholarly journals (*The China Quarterly, The China Journal, Journal of Contemporary China, China: An International Journal*), their work is not well known outside of the continent. The best vistas into European (particularly French) work on Chinese politics is the English-language version of *Perspectives Chinoises* (which Bonnin established and Cabestan further developed), and the Dutch-published *China Information*.

The main part of Cabestan's chapter provides a very useful overview of the various European researchers and institutions involved in contemporary China studies, particularly politics. The survey lists the names and research foci of many scholars who are otherwise invisible outside of continental Europe (the same may be said of some of the European scholars of the Chinese economy referred to by Ash). One notices that a gradual generational change is underway, particularly in Britain and France, and that some Chinese *émigré* scholars have also entered the field (albeit far fewer than in North America).

In terms of specific subjects of research in Chinese politics, Cabestan argues that the European oeuvre both has its own unique features, while also revealing similarities to those studied in other parts of the world. European scholars do appear more interested in certain subjects, he argues: governance issues, nationalism, the prospects for civil society and democracy, and human rights. They seem less interested in institutions, the policymaking process, and political economy topics. He also notes the rising interest in Taiwan studies across Europe.

Tomoyuki Kojima's chapter offers an overview of publications on Chinese domestic politics in Japan in recent years. Kojima offers some sharp observations and criticisms of the sub-field of Chinese politics in Japan. He begins by noting that there is no tradition in Japan for such introspective "state of the field" assessments and, as a result, Japanese China watchers have little comparative or detached perspective on their work. Some of Kojima's judgments also echo those of Takagi and Ohashi in their chapters. For example, all three Japanese contributors note the considerable insularity of the Japanese China studies community. Part of this insularity is due to linguistic issues, given that few Japanese scholars of China have been trained in English-speaking countries and do not publish in English publications, but it is also due to an intellectual insularity that reflects lack of exposure and awareness of topics and methodological approaches used by China watchers elsewhere in the world.

Kojima also takes the sub-field of Chinese politics in Japan to task for several other failings and problems (in his view). He notes that Japanese scholars of Chinese politics have long been too politicized in their work, i.e. that studies of China were intimately wrapped up with the politics of Sino-Japanese relations and Japan's broader China policy. Accordingly he calls for the depoliticization of academic research work on China, and notes that this problem is less severe in the most recent decade than it was in the first four decades of the PRC. He also points out that Japanese China scholars have too readily accepted the language, analytical frameworks, and conclusions of the Chinese government and scholars in China. As such, they often fall into the "propaganda trap" of Chinese political terminology (*tifa*) and too readily and easily accept the Chinese government's judgments on various events, e.g. the arrest of the "Gang of Four," the June 4 "rebellion," the "Three Represents," etc. Kojima thus calls on his colleagues for greater analytical detachment and "value-free research" in their work.

Kojima also notes, as does Takagi, that Japanese studies of Chinese politics are largely atheoretical and excessively descriptive. Very few scholars, he notes, attempt to adopt theories generated in political science and to test hypotheses accordingly. This observation may again speak to the insularity of Japanese China watchers, as so few were trained in Western political science, and it may well reflect how the field is taught in major Japanese universities. Hence, Kojima calls for more theory-informed research and more comparative case studies. In a seeming contradiction, he also notes the dearth of empirical case studies carried out by Japanese scholars on China, and how few actually carry out field research *in situ* over extended periods of time or conduct interviews with Chinese officials or the public. Japanese scholars seem content to do their research from Japan, using various published Chinese sources, combined with quick single or multi-day trips to China. He does note that this is beginning to change with the ascent of a new generation of scholars who are more interested in the politics of social issues, but it is still not the norm to conduct field research by actually living in China for sustained periods.

Kojima is also critical of some other characteristics of the field in Japan. He observes that Japanese specialists on contemporary Chinese politics are excessively concerned with short-term events rather than longer-term trends – thus not easily distinguishing scholarship from pseudo-journalism or intelligence analysis. Part of this tendency, he claims, is due to the aforementioned penchant to conduct research from published and Chinese media sources rather than on-site investigation: the "easy topics," he claims. Again, he calls for longer-term perspectives, longer-term research projects, longer-term research stays in China, and deeper data collection. Kojima also calls for less attention to the study of the *structure* of Chinese political institutions and greater focus on the *process* of policymaking and implementation, and he notes that a small handful of scholars, particularly Mori Kazuko and Tang Liang, have begun to do so. He also notes that some members of the "younger generation," such as Zhao Hengwei, have begun to look beyond the party and state to examine state-society relations and the political implications of social change and stratification in China. While he does not comment on it, Kojima's review does point up the important impact that *émigré* scholars from China are having on the field of Chinese politics in Japan. Finally, Kojima's chapter elucidates the main institutional centers of contemporary China studies in Japan.

Richard Baum's assessment of the study of Chinese politics in the United States is presented historically. He begins with recollections on the "birth of the field" of "Communist China Studies" in the 1950s, and traces the key individuals and institutions that shaped and inspired the field. He notes the importance of U.S. government support during the Cold War and of the initiatives of the Ford Foundation, Carnegie Foundation, and the Joint Committee on Contemporary China of the Social Science Research Council and American Council of Learned Societies. He also writes of the difficulties which this "first generation" faced in carrying out research at a time when China itself was off-limits. Despite the impediments, Baum credits this generation with having produced a number of major, path breaking studies.

The "second generation" came of age and cut their professional teeth during the period of the Cultural Revolution. Much of their work was conducted under the auspices of a handful of major university programs in the United States – many catalyzed by the funding initiatives noted above – while field research was carried at the Universities Service Centre in Hong Kong and, to a lesser extent, on Taiwan. Baum also draws attention to the divisive impact of the Vietnam War on this generation of American China hands.

The opening of China after 1972, but particularly following the normalization of diplomatic relations in 1979, was a great boon to the field. For the first time American scholars could carry out research *in situ* on the mainland. Armed with advanced language training and social science research tools acquired in the top graduate schools, this generation fanned out across China – living in cities and villages, interviewing in bureaucracies, delving into libraries and archives, and traveling the country. They thereby acquired a first-hand "feel" for China, absent among its "first generation" predecessors, which was every evident in their studies and work. Such direct access to China necessarily altered the research foci of scholarship – generally away from elite and national-level issues to intermediate and local level subjects. The outpouring of books and articles from this generation has revolutionized the field of study of Chinese politics.

June 4, 1989 was, of course, a major interruption for many American scholars – logistically and intellectually – but it was temporary. Most returned to do work in China by 1992. Baum notes, however, that June 4 did affect the tone and subject matter of political studies, giving rise to what he describes as a new wave of "revulsion scholarship." A simultaneous trend was the new interest in civil society – sparked largely by the translation into English of Habermas' work. Baum also points out that it was during this period that large numbers of *émigré* scholars entered the field, although they also experienced numerous political difficulties and pressures in carrying out research in China (including arrest and imprisonment).

Professor Baum observes that a new "fourth generation" of scholarship has now emerged in the form of scholars whose work focuses on issues of political economy. This changed emphasis, he suggests, has its negative potential side-effects. In particular, Baum laments the exaggerated emphasis on methodology, as a result what were formerly *tools for* research have now become (he argues) the *object of* research among American political scientists studying Chinese politics. Hence his conclusion that *procedure* has trumped *analysis* – with deleterious consequences for understanding what should really be the object of study: China itself.

Foreign Relations and Security Studies

The third section examines studies of Chinese foreign relations and security affairs. Although these are related subjects, in many countries they are pursued by different communities of scholars and specialists: with a few exceptions, researchers of China's foreign relations tend not to engage in the study of Chinese security affairs and vice versa. Indeed, the study of Chinese military and security affairs is a rather specialized cottage industry, and is largely confined to the United States and a handful of specialists outside the U.S. (Ellis Joffe in Israel, Srikanth Kondapalli in India, Nan Li in Singapore and You Ji in Australia). As Kay Möller's contribution makes evident, there is a real paucity of expertise on Chinese security and military affairs in Europe. Japan has a similarly small community of specialists. The United States remains, by far, the main repository of research in this sub-field.

Kay Möller's chapter begins by noting (as does Cabestan) the strong residual effects of traditional European Sinology. This tradition stunted the integration of China area studies into the social sciences – and vice versa – and maintained a strong humanistic orientation in research. But, as both Möller and Cabestan note, the barriers have eroded over time, and increasing attention has been directed to Chinese domestic politics and international relations. Möller discusses, in particular, the development of Chinese foreign policy studies. His chapter begins by cataloguing the extant community of researchers in Europe who specialize in this area. It is not a large community, but it has grown from the handful of experts that existed only two decades ago. It is currently scattered among universities in the U.K., Germany, and Scandinavia – with government-affiliated research institutes in Britain, Belgium, France, Germany, and Italy also housing a number of Chinese foreign policy specialists.

Following his institutional survey, Möller examines the principal debates in which European scholars have engaged since the mid-1980s. He delineates two broad periods: 1985–1996, when emphasis was placed on analyzing the "strategic triangle" and "multipolarity"; and 1997–2005, during which the subject of "China's rise" has animated discussions. He also draws attention to a secondary interest in Chinese multilateral diplomacy, which began in the late-1990s. Möller further distinguishes between several schools of analysis that are currently evident in European debates. He refers to these as the "China threat school," the "China nuisance school," and the "China engagement school." The first draws on neo-realist theory and emphasizes China's growing attributes of power. The second emphasizes China's internal "structural deficits" that supposedly constrain China's external behavior. The third, which he claims to be representative of mainstream majority opinion, does not take China's relative strength or weakness as its starting point, but is premised on the need to deal pragmatically with China. Möller also identifies a strand of constructivism from international relations theory among some scholars, whom he terms "cultural relativists." Through his emphasis on the numerous internal problems that beset China and that will ultimately act as a brake on its external relations, Möller himself seems to position himself in the "China nuisance school."

The chapter by Seiichiro Takagi examines Japanese studies of China's foreign and security policies. Given that so few foreign China specialists read Japanese books and journals, with even fewer Japanese scholars publishing in English, this chapter provides a real window into a universe of research and discourse closed to the rest of the world. The chapter is largely a critical literature review of Japanese writings on these subjects.

Like Kojima, Takagi notes the difficulty of providing a survey of Chinese studies, or a sub-set thereof, in Japan. He notes the dearth of such surveys in the past, citing only one on China's economic diplomacy, published in Japanese. Only one other exists in English, the aforementioned survey by Tanaka Kyoko of Japanese research on China's economy and foreign trade.[11] It seems that Japanese scholars do not readily engage in state-of-field surveys, and are uneasy about publicly evaluating their colleagues' work – a cultural predisposition against the "constructive criticism" norm so prevalent in the West. But Takagi notes that the sheer volume and disparate nature of publications in Japan also militates against undertaking such an exercise. He also notes that there is no Japanese equivalent to *The China Quarterly* or its peer journals, as a result Japanese scholarship on China is published in a very diverse group of journals and newspapers. He also draws attention to the narrow boundary that exists between scholarship and journalism in Japan.

Takagi first surveys Japanese studies of the history of the PRC's foreign relations. Various Japanese scholars are active in this area, all of whom make extensive use of international archival materials – for example, those made available through the Cold War International History Project (CWIHP) based at the Woodrow Wilson International Center for Scholars in Washington, D.C. In this category are studies undertaken by Japanese scholars of China's diplomacy during the Korean and Vietnam Wars, and the 1958 Taiwan Straits, as well as of U.S.–China *rapprochement*, and China–Japan normalization of relations.

Takagi next identifies a number of overview and integrated studies of Chinese foreign policy, and goes on to examine an area that has been of particular interest to Japanese scholars: China's relations with other major powers. He shows that Japanese scholars (including Takagi himself) have been at great pains to explore and explain Chinese concepts of "strategic partnerships" and the "New Security Concept." Japanese analyses have also drawn a lot of attention to shifting Chinese perceptions of world order – in some cases (such as Okabe and Mori), quite critically probing the bases of Chinese perceptions. As in Europe and the United States, the notion of a "China threat" has been prevalent within Japanese foreign policy and security circles, as well as among Japanese journalists and the public. Takagi describes and reviews the studies, and their authors, that have asserted this theory, and he makes clear the considerable impact that it has had in Japan. Some Japanese observers have stressed China's military buildup; others have highlighted the economic and energy dimensions of the "China threat."

Takagi also examines studies of bilateral U.S.–China and China–Japan relations, as well as trilateral ties among the three. He notes that the latter has become a hot topic in Japan in recent years. A smaller number of scholars have investigated other bilateral relationships, such as those with Russia, North and South Korea, and ASEAN.

In his concluding observations, Takagi highlights a number of characteristic features of Japanese studies of China's foreign relations and security. He notes, for example, the almost complete absence of theorizing about, or hypothesis testing of, China's external behavior, as well as of materials drawn from interviews with Chinese officials, and/or members of Chinese research institutes and universities. He also observes a preoccupation among Japanese scholars to take words seriously in order to identify the true meaning of terms like "strategic partnership." Takagi's hope is that Japanese scholars will in the future broaden their research to embrace more topics in greater depth, and to undertake more collaborative research projects with Chinese scholars.

The final chapter in this section is by David Shambaugh, in which he surveys the state of American studies of China's foreign relations and military/defense/ security policies. Shambaugh notes that – against the background of China's rising global influence, military capabilities, and the vagaries of Sino-American relations – these areas of study have expanded rapidly in the U.S. during the past decade. Curiously, Shambaugh finds that those who work on China's foreign relations tend not to research China's military and security policies. This may reflect the special expertise needed to analyze the latter subjects, although it also reflects the proclivities of university-based scholars. For various reasons, there are few incentives for university-based scholars or graduate students in political science to pursue the study of Chinese military or security affairs; as a result, it has been left to think tanks, consultancies, and the intelligence community. The outcome is that only a handful of academics have investigated the Chinese military.

Shambaugh's chapter begins with a discussion of the composition, and research orientation, of the communities of specialists active in researching China's external relations and military/security. He observes that the varied nature of the "consumers" of such studies and their different research orientations goes some way towards shaping not only the research questions that are posed, but also sometimes the conclusions that are reached. Further, academics and those working in Washington think tanks or consultancies follow distinctive approaches in terms of their research methodologies, data sets, arguments, and style of presentation. Researchers of the Chinese military/security who work in think tanks or consultancies, which do contract research for the Department of Defense or intelligence agencies, have dominated this field.

Shambaugh goes on to survey books written by American China specialists on China's foreign relations, published since around 1990. He distinguishes eight general categories that capture the main research foci: edited compendia and synthesized overviews (including textbooks); studies of "China's rise"; histories of CCP foreign policy; histories of China and the Cold War; the foreign policy making process; Chinese perceptions of international affairs in general, and the United States in particular; China's roles in international institutions and regimes; and China's bilateral and regional relationships. The corpus of research and published work contained in these eight categories define a burgeoning and academically healthy field. Work is theoretically informed and not just descriptive, field research opportunities are manifold, data are plentiful, and opportunities for collaborative work are abundant. Nonetheless, there remains unfulfilled potential: new directions to be pursued, new subjects to be explored, new data to be tapped into, and new empirical and policy-related questions to answer.

In the next section, Shambaugh's survey of studies of the Chinese military (PLA) and security also notes the considerable progress that has been made in recent years. In many ways, this sub-field has become a bona fide area of research during the past decade or so. Prior to that time, the few analysts published on this subject. But a combination of factors – the steady modernization of the Chinese military, the emergence of "crises" (for example, in the Taiwan Strait during 1995–1996), and the rapidly growing demand for information by the U.S. government, Congress, journalists, and the public – has, since the mid-1990s, served as a catalyst to the field. Much security-related published work exists either in the form of journal articles (not included in Shambaugh's survey) or in edited volumes. The latter category includes the proceedings of an annual series of conferences on the PLA, many of which have become benchmarks in the field. Shambaugh also draws attention to a second category of "comprehensive studies" – monographs that cover the spectrum of China's military organization, capabilities, behavior, doctrine, etc.

There is, finally, a third and general category, comprising specialized studies of various aspects of Chinese military and security affairs. This grouping is usefully disaggregated into eight separate sub-categories, focusing on the following issues: the use of force; strategic culture; the military-industrial complex; arms control policies and behavior; individual armed services (ground, air, naval, and missile forces); perception studies; civil–military relations; military diplomacy and U.S.–China strategic relations. In addition to reviewing published work of each of these issues, Shambaugh makes suggestions for future research.

In conclusion, Shambaugh avers that Chinese foreign and security policy studies are alive and well in the United States. Increased demand for information and informed analysis in these areas, driven by public and private sector interests, will continue to drive the field. The influx of Chinese *émigré* scholars into the field has been, and will continue to be, a major bonus. Publishers are also beginning to show a greater interest in publishing books on these subjects, reflecting growing public demand for informed analysis and comment. But Shambaugh also warns against complacency, arguing that there is still room for more cross-fertilization between these two sub-fields, as well as greater contact among American, Asian, and European specialists, and between Americans and their counterparts in China.

Looking Ahead

We hope that readers will enjoy each of the subsequent chapters in this volume. Taken together, they offer a window through which to view the state of contemporary China studies in three principal regions/countries of the world at the beginning of the twenty-first century. The Epilogue offers some concluding observations by the Editors.

Overall, this volume is testimony to the impressive quality of international research on, and knowledge about, contemporary China. This emerges all the more forcefully, when set against the challenge of studying a country that remains a perpetual puzzle and that houses a society and economy undergoing rapid and profound change in all dimensions. No nation in the history of the world has experienced such rapid and comprehensive change as China has undergone during the last two or three decades. To stay abreast of such changes and to analyze their implications for China's domestic and external policies are, by any standards, key challenges in themselves – but to knowledgeably *explain* them to multiple audiences beyond the academic community is an increasing task of China scholars worldwide (see Epilogue).

Notes

1 See Bruce Dickson (ed.), *Trends in China Watching: Observing the PRC at Fifty* (Washington, D.C.: Sigur Center for Asian Studies, 1999); David Shambaugh (ed.), *American Studies of Contemporary China* (Washington, D.C. and Armonk, N.Y.: Woodrow Wilson Center Press and M.E. Sharpe, 1993); John M. H. Lindbeck, *Understanding China: An Assessment of American Scholarly Resources* (New York: Praeger, 1971); Tai-chun Kuo and Ramon H. Myers, *Understanding Communist China: Communist China Studies in the United States and the Republic of China, 1949-1978* (Palo Alto, CA: Hoover Institution Press, 1986); Ramon H. Myers and Thomas A. Metzger, "Sinological Shadows: The State of Modern China Studies in the United States," *Washington Quarterly* (Spring 1980); Andrew Nathan, "Americans Look at China: The New Optimism and Some Historical Perspectives," in *China's Crisis* (New York: Columbia University Press, 1990); Edward Friedman, "In Defense of China Studies," *Pacific Affairs* (Summer 1992); Richard Wilson, "China Studies in Crisis," *World Politics* (January 1971).

2 For official perspectives, see *Report of the Inter-Departmental Commission of Enquiry on Oriental, Slavonic, East European and African Studies* (a.k.a. *The Scarborough Report*) chaired by the Earl of Scarborough (1945); *Report of the Sub-Committee on Oriental, Slavonic, East European and African Studies* (a.k.a. *Hayter Report*), chaired by Sir William Hayter (1961); *"Speaking for the Future" – A Review of the Requirements of Diplomacy and Commerce for Asian and African Languages and Area Studies* (a.k.a. *Parker Report*), submitted by Sir Peter Parker to the Chairman of the University Grants Committee (1986); Higher Education Funding Council for England (HECFE), *Review of Chinese Studies* (1999); Universitas, *An Evaluation of HEFCE's Chinese Studies Initiative* (2005). See also T.H. Barrett, *Singular Listlessness: A Short History of Chinese Books and British Scholars* (London: Wellsweep, 1989); Owen Lattimore, *Britain's Opportunity in Asian Studies* (London: SOAS, 1970); Christopher Howe FBA, *The China Business: From the Great Leap Forward to the World Trade Organization – Can Academics Keep Up?* (London: SOAS, 2003); David Shambaugh, "Observations on a New Generation of China Scholarship," *Bulletin of the British Association of Chinese Studies* (1988).

3 Graham E. Johnson, "True North Strong: Contemporary Chinese Studies in Canada," *The China Quarterly*, No. 143 (September 1995).

4 Lucien Bianco, "French Studies of Contemporary China," *The China Quarterly*, No. 142 (June 1995).

5 Herbert Franke, *Sinology at German Universities* (N.P.: F. Steiner, 1968).

6 Kjeld-Erik Brodsgaard, "Contemporary China Studies in Scandinavia," *The China Quarterly*, No. 147 (September 1996).

7 Mark Sidel, "The Reemergence of China Studies in Vietnam," *The China Quarterly*, No. 142 (June 1995).

8 In addition to chapters by Gold, Kane, Prime, Halpern, Ross and Godwin in Shambaugh (ed.), *American Studies of Contemporary China*, op. cit., see, for example, Walter Galenson, "The Current State of Chinese Economic Studies," in U.S. Congress Joint Economic Committee, *An Economic Profile of Mainland China* (Washington D.C.: Government Printing Office, 1967); Chalmers Johnson, "What's Wrong with Chinese Political Studies?" *Asian Survey* (October 1982); Andrew Walder, "Chinese Communist Society: The State of the Field," *Issues & Studies* (October 1982); Harry Harding, "Competing Political Models of the Chinese Political Process: Towards a Sorting and Evaluation," *Issues & Studies* (February 1984); Harry Harding, "The Study of Chinese Politics: Toward a Third Generation of Scholarship," *World Politics* (January 1984); Elizabeth Perry, "State and Society in Contemporary China," *World Politics* (July 1989); Symposia on Chinese Politics in *The China Quarterly* (September 1994); Lowell Dittmer and William Hurst, "Analysis in Limbo: Contemporary

Chinese Politics Amid the Maturation of Reform," *Issues & Studies*, Nos. 38-39 (2003-2004); Yanjie Bian, "Sociological Research on Reform-Era China," ibid.; Jack Williams, "Geographers and China," ibid.; Yu-Shan Wu, "Chinese Economic Reform in a Comparative Perspective: Asia vs. Europe," ibid.

9 Kuan Hsin-chi (ed.), *The Development of Contemporary China Studies* (Tokyo: Center for East Asian Cultural Studies of UNESCO, Toyo Bunko, 1994); reprinted in *Asian Research Trends: A Humanities & Social Sciences Review*, No. 4 (1994). An earlier effort was undertaken by Eugene Wu, "Studies of Contemporary China Outside the United States," *Harvard Library Bulletin*, Vol. 18, No. 2 (1970). Also of relevance is the symposium "China, China Studies, and *The China Quarterly*," *The China Quarterly* (September 1996).

10 See Walter Galenson, "The Current State of Chinese Economic Studies," op. cit.

11 Tanaka Kyoko, "Research in Japan on China's Economy and Foreign Trade, 1978-1992," in Kuan Hsin-chi (ed.), *The Development of Contemporary China Studies*, op. cit.

I. Studies of China's Economy

2   Studies of China's Economy in Europe

Robert Ash

To undertake a comprehensive analysis of European studies of the Chinese economy is beyond my competence. Indeed, the field has advanced so rapidly, that the task is probably beyond that of any single person. In trying to make sense of the contemporary Chinese economy,[1] it is often argued that a regional approach is more meaningful and offers more useful insights than one that seeks to focus only on national trends. Trying to encapsulate the "European" study of Chinese economic studies presents a similar dilemma. Europe's identity as a political unit has grown much stronger in recent years. But it is still far from being a unified, let alone uniform, entity. Defining Europe even in a geographical sense is difficult enough. For the last 500 years, we have wrestled with whether or not Russia should be included as part of Europe. At the moment, the question of Turkey's admission to the European Union is a major topic of debate. I should make clear therefore that the European thrust of this chapter is overwhelmingly orientated towards Western European countries.

There is also a practical challenge that confronts any attempt to embrace Europe. Unlike the United States and Japan, Europe rejoices in a large variety of languages, most of which have shared roots, but not always from the same family. Unlike Professor Walter Simon – a great British Sinologist of the past – my own European linguistic expertise is sadly lacking,[2] perhaps reflecting that curiously English trait that assumes that anyone one meets is bound to speak English.[3] I can pick up a book in French with a reasonable expectation of understanding it, and many years ago I flirted briefly with Italian and Russian. But having at school chosen between Ancient Greek and German in favor of the former, my acquaintance with the German language derives mainly from odd words and phrases picked up from listening to the songs of Schubert and Mahler.[4]

In addition to linguistic barriers, political and economic interests have also influenced the nature and direction of studies of contemporary China in Europe. Until less than 20 years ago, Europe was divided by the Cold War. Beneath this political division ran ideological currents which effectively separated Western and Eastern Europe, and had serious implications for the activities of universities and research institutions – above all, in Russia and its Soviet bloc satrapies. In Western Europe, different historical traditions have meanwhile made themselves felt. Not least, the imperial pasts of countries which had a colonial presence in East and

Southeast Asia – especially Britain, France and the Netherlands – have colored cultural and historical approaches towards Asian Studies (China included). In addition, as Thomas Kampen has observed *à propos* of European China Studies, "... other conflicts ... between modern and classical scholars, social scientists and historians, and ... leftists and rightists" have had their own impact.[5] To such differences may be added familiar tensions between area studies advocates and defenders of disciplinary expertise.[6] Most recently of all, the emergence of business and management studies has added yet another weft to the tapestry of Chinese economic studies.[7] This complex matrix of influences and traditions is part of the background against which the evolution of European studies of contemporary China needs to be set.

Awareness of personal linguistic inadequacies, as well as of the complicated and often confusing nature of European Sinology, has dictated the structure of this chapter. In researching it, I have been struck too by the sheer scale of intellectual activity that has come to characterize European study of the Chinese economy. These are all formidable constraints. Accordingly, the scope of the chapter is defined by two simple aims. The first is to provide a quite broad survey of European research and publication activity on the contemporary Chinese economy.[8] The second is to highlight the work of some of the actors – both institutional and individual – that have been and are still engaged in such study. In short, the remit is wide, but the treatment is necessarily selective. It does not provide a complete listing of what has been accomplished in the European field of Chinese economic studies, let alone offer a comprehensive evaluation of published work. *Caveat lector!*[9]

The Study of the Contemporary Chinese Economy: A Brief Note on its Origins

The first overview of contemporary Chinese economic studies of which I am aware was written by Walter Galenson almost 40 years ago.[10] At that time, the systematic study of post-1949 China's economy was still in its infancy. The problems of learning a difficult language apart, the formidable obstacles that confronted the academic investigation of economic conditions in China were an additional major impediment. Since the end of the 1950s, no statistical economic indicators of any importance had been published by the Chinese government; references to China's economic development were strongly impregnated with political and ideological comment; and fieldwork visits to China were impossible. Because of such constraints, young Western scholars who wished to conduct doctoral research on the contemporary Chinese economy had little choice but to confine their studies to the period between 1949 and the late 1950s.

In his study, Galenson divided the field of Chinese economic studies into eight major categories, as follows:

- national product and income;
- population and labor force;

- agriculture;
- industry and handicrafts;
- trade and commerce;
- prices, money and banking;
- wages, living standards, labor incentives;
- planning, investment and management.

Today, each of these has spawned a major literature of its own in English (let alone other European languages), typically running into many dozens of books, and an even larger number of journal articles and chapters in books.[11] By contrast, back in the late 1960s Galenson identified just *nineteen* (sic) scholars and analysts whom he regarded as having made a significant contribution to the field under all eight categories taken together. It is noteworthy that only two of these were not American, or anyway based in the United States.[12] Of the two scholars who were not from the United States, one was Japanese (Shigeru Ishikawa), whose early work focused on Chinese national accounting concepts and associated methodology. The other was a British economist (Kenneth R. Walker), who was in the early stages of what was to be a lifetime's study of China's agricultural development. Walker was the sole European representative of Chinese economic studies included in Galenson's overview.[13]

From today's perspective, it is difficult to imagine conditions characterized by a "dearth of serious analysis,"[14] such as (according to Galenson) defined Western studies of the contemporary Chinese economy in the second half of the 1960s. The fact that Chinese economic studies were at least 15 years behind the study of the Soviet economy highlights the scale of the challenge facing analysts at the time. Indeed, there was a note of something akin to panic in Galenson's concluding remarks, which, against the background of the problems he had already set out, defended the validity of a second-best approach by academics towards Chinese economic studies:

> Scholars are reticent to speak out unless they are absolutely certain of their facts. This is normally a good rule, but for those who are seriously concerned with China, its relaxation may be in order for the present. The boundaries of our current knowledge should be made clear, lest mere speculation be taken for proven reality. But if speculation there must be – and the present intense curiosity about China guarantees that it must – there is a case for urging those who are best informed to participate in the public discussion notwithstanding the many doubts that they may have about the validity of their present conclusions."[15]

The rest of this chapter will show how far we have advanced since the late 1960s, and, in particular, how European scholars and professional analysts have contributed to such progress.

The Institutional Framework of Contemporary Chinese Studies in Europe

In the early 1990s the number of "active China experts" in Europe – some 2,000 – was estimated to be no fewer than in Japan and the United States.[16] In interpreting such comparisons, it is important to keep in mind the stronger Sinological tradition that has existed in Europe, compared with the other two countries.[17] Among American and Japanese specialists, a significantly higher proportion has always been involved in studying *contemporary* China than in Europe. This is by no means to devalue European studies of contemporary China. For one thing, the European Sinological tradition has much of value to impart to the study of contemporary China, including its economy.[18] For another, there can be no doubt that the study of contemporary China has expanded rapidly in recent years. In short, compared with the situation described in the previous section, Chinese economic studies in Europe are blooming as never before.

EACS, IIAS, and EIAS

Major on-going challenges facing European scholars and others engaged in the study of China include how to disseminate knowledge of their activities, how to bring relevant researchers and scholars together, and how to promote cross-country collaborative research within Europe. For many years, the annual conference of the European Association of Chinese Studies (EACS) was the only mechanism for bringing together European researchers and scholars of China. Although intended to be all-embracing,[19] EACS conferences have in fact displayed a strong orientation towards traditional Sinology. For example, at the most recent (Fifteenth) EACS Conference, held in Heidelberg (Germany) in August 2004, only three of the eleven rubrics under which the conference was organized addressed truly contemporary issues relating to China's social, economic, and political development.[20]

The somewhat traditional focus of EACS highlights the significance of more recent institutional initiatives, expressly designed to focus on contemporary issues. Thus, the International Institute for Asian Studies (IIAS), established in 1994 and based in Leiden and Amsterdam, is a post-doctoral research center, which seeks to promote national and international inter-disciplinary and comparative research into human and social science-related issues in Asia. Its intended facilitating role is well expressed at IIAS's website:

> The IIAS acts as an international mediator, bringing various parties together. In keeping with the Dutch tradition of transferring goods and ideas, the IIAS works as a clearinghouse of knowledge and information. This entails activities such as providing information services, constructing international networks, and setting up international cooperative projects and research programmes. In this way, the IIAS functions as a window on Europe for non-European scholars and contributes to the cultural rapprochement between Asia and Europe.[21]

To date, IIAS's involvement in research on the Chinese economy has been fairly modest. However, the 2004 Annual Report notes that since 2003 the focus of IIAS research has shifted towards "the humanities and social sciences," including economics.[22] It also reveals that one of the fellows hosted under the IIAS program during 2004 was sponsored by the Chinese Academy of Social Sciences (CASS). Notwithstanding the Dutch bias towards its former imperial heartland of Southeast Asia, IIAS offers a useful framework in which individual and collaborative work on the Chinese economy can be conducted in the future.

The European Institute for Asian Studies (EIAS), based in Brussels, describes itself as "a research and policy think-tank that analyzes political, economic and security relations between the European Union and Asia."[23] In pursuit of its aims, EIAS organizes open workshops and conferences, as well as more specialized closed briefings (e.g. for EU policy makers and Members of the European Parliament). It promotes research, which it publishes as *EIAS Briefing Papers*, and it issues a regular bi-monthly newsletter (*Eur-Asia Bulletin*), which is intended to be a vehicle for analysis and the expression of viewpoints. A recent publications initiative has been the institution of a series of *EIAS Briefing Papers*. The *policy thrust* is a noteworthy feature of EIAS activities. It is also noteworthy that EIAS has been selected by the European Commission as the institution to coordinate the second five-year operation of the European China Academic Network (ECAN), a pan-regional network of contemporary China scholars. Starting in January 2005, the EIAS also joined Nomisma (a leading European research center) in a study focusing on East Asian cooperation (with special reference to China's related role) and its implications for EU member states.[24] A significant part of this study addressed economic and socio-economic issues arising out of China's transition towards a market-orientated economy.[25] Following the completion of this study, in June 2005 a two-day workshop took place in Brussels, where experts considered the study's findings. This meeting generated a major publication, including a paper on China's economic reform prospects.[26]

EIAS and IIAS are two of the seven member institutions of the European Alliance for Asian Studies (a.k.a. the "Asia Alliance"), which was set up in 1997.[27] The Alliance now comprises institutional members representative of nine European countries – Belgium, Denmark, Finland, France, Germany, the Netherlands, Sweden, Spain and the United Kingdom. As its name indicates, its area remit is broad. But a particular goal that it seeks to fulfil is to encourage and facilitate "border-transcending" research on *contemporary* issues.[28]

ECAN

From the narrower perspective of contemporary China studies, even more significant than the IIAS, EIAS, and Asia Alliance initiatives, was the aforementioned creation, in December 1996, of the Europe-China Academic Network (ECAN).[29] Both public policy concerns and academic considerations informed the perceived need to establish a network of China specialists within the European Union. On the one hand, the rapid expansion since the mid-1990s of relations between China and

EU member states, not least, in the economic sphere, underlined the increasingly important role of China in Europe's future external relations. On the other hand, an awareness of the highly fragmented and compartmentalized nature of national academic and professional expertise on contemporary China among EU member states highlighted the desirability of instituting a framework in which closer contact between China-related research communities in Europe could be facilitated. Implicit in the setting up of ECAN was the hope that the new institutional framework would exploit synergies, previously untapped, in order to help fulfill two major goals: first, to enhance collaboration between academic and other research institutions and individuals in Europe; second, to use related expertise in order to help inform EU policy-related issues on China. ECAN also administered the EU-China Research Fellowship Fund (ECRFF), which provided financial support to young academic researchers on contemporary China by facilitating fieldwork and archival visits to China, Hong Kong and Taiwan.[30]

Through its conferences, workshops and publications, ECAN was instrumental in encouraging and facilitating analysis of a wide range of economic issues relating to contemporary China. Its first book, based on a small workshop held in Hamburg (Germany), addressed questions of economic security, as they affected China.[31] From the premise of economic security having become a key determinant of regional stability, scholars from Denmark, France, Germany, the Netherlands, Spain and Turkey examined key priorities confronting China in this area in an attempt to anticipate future major policy shifts. A noteworthy feature of the book was the inclusion of a long discussion paper, originally prepared by Unit I-2 (Policy Planning) of the Directorate General I (External Relations) of the European Commission.[32] Published, as it was, some five years before the now pre-eminent emphasis on sustainability and China's embrace of a new "scientific development" concept, articulated by Chinese leaders Hu Jintao and Wen Jiabao, this paper was quite prescient in drawing attention to the implications for economic and social reform contingent on the maintenance of a growth-maximization strategy.

Economic issues were to the fore in each of the volumes arising out of the four annual conferences organized by ECAN, and published, initially, by Curzon Press[33] and later by RoutledgeCurzon.[34] These conference volumes exemplify, but by no means exhaust, the range of expertise on the Chinese economy that had emerged in Europe since Galenson's inclusion of a single European in his 1967 review. They are also pointers to the kinds of issues on which European analysts have focused their attention, as well as to those thought by the conference organizers to have particular relevance to European policy-makers *vis-à-vis* China. These issues, as revealed by the four ECAN volumes, may be arranged for convenience under the following headings, which are not analytically mutually exclusive:[35]

- China's regional and international economic relations;[36]
- sectoral issues;[37]
- economic security issues;[38]
- social and socio-economic issues.[39]

With the renewal of ECAN in early 2006, and the awarding of the contract to EIAS as the institutional center of the network (notwithstanding that ECAN incorporates other partner institutions across Europe), scope is afforded to revitalize both the network and contemporary China studies across the European continent.

ECARDC

A European organization whose work has made a major contribution to understanding China's agricultural and rural development is the European Conference on Agriculture and Rural Development in China (ECARDC).[40] The focus of ECARDC is deliberately multi-disciplinary, embracing not only the purely economic dimensions of development in the Chinese countryside, but also its implications for wider political and social development. Its associated ECARDC Network provides a forum for the discussion and dissemination of information among "scholars, development agencies, international donors, and professionals in development aid."[41] For the purposes of this chapter, the outstanding feature of ECARDC lies in the four rich conference volumes generated by its conferences.[42] To my mind, these volumes have been under-regarded by scholars and others interested in China's agricultural and rural development (by any standard, key determinants of China's future economic and social trajectories). Through the contributions of both young and established scholars drawn from countries in Western Europe,[43] they track the main social and economic trends in the Chinese countryside in a way that is comprehensive, detailed and carefully-considered. Many of the papers derive from fieldwork in China undertaken by the authors, and a significant number have a regional, including sub-provincial micro focus.

In a short space, it is impossible to do justice to the wide range of topics that are embraced by these four volumes. The evolution of China's rural policy is captured in the differing thrusts of the various volumes. For example, the first two volumes (1990 and 1992) show a much greater preoccupation with purely farm and agricultural-related issues than those published more recently (1998 and 2002), in which more attention is focused on rural, non-agricultural development – especially rural industrialization, the role of township and village enterprises, and that characteristically Chinese phenomenon of "rural urbanization" – including its financial and institutional rationale.[44] Social welfare and environmental issues also assume increasing prominence over time, as do questions relating to labor and employment, rural migration and gender. Taken together, the four volumes are an expression of the impressive breadth of European expertise on all major aspects of China's agricultural and rural development.

European Journals on Contemporary China: A Brief Note

In the face of increasing competition from new journals, a European periodical – *The China Quarterly* (*CQ*) – has maintained its pre-eminence in the journal literature on China throughout the world.[45] There is a widespread presumption that articles published in *CQ* are dominated by American authors. Analyzed in terms of authors' nationalities, this turns out to be correct. But a simple comparative statistical analysis, conducted in 2003 by then Editor Richard Louis Edmonds, offers interesting insights into the changing profile of article topics and authors between 1969 and 2002.[46] It reveals that between 1969 and 2002, the proportion of all articles categorized as "political studies" fell from 79 percent to 58 percent, while the share of "economics" articles rose dramatically from a mere 4 percent to 25 percent. No less striking, the same comparison showed that during the same period the proportion of authors from the U.S. had fallen from 77 to 44 percent, while the European share had risen from 14 to 32 percent.[47] Even if these figures are not wholly representative, they do appear to highlight a major expansion in European engagement in contemporary China (including economic) studies. Meanwhile, each issue of *CQ* contains a "Quarterly Chronicle and Documentation" (compiled by this author), which offers, *inter alia*, straightforward reportage – deliberately, not critical analysis – of important economic developments that have occurred in China in the previous three months. Where appropriate this is supplemented by translations of key Chinese policy and other official documents.

Of the newcomers to the journal literature on contemporary China, one European periodical deserves mention within the particular remit of this chapter. It is *China Perspectives*, which began publication in 1995.[48] Originally intended as a vehicle for the expression of comment and analysis undertaken by the French Centre for Research on Contemporary China,[49] it continues to be an important outlet, especially for French analysts and scholars – as such, testifying to the vibrancy of contemporary Chinese studies in France – but has also become a desirable platform for scholars elsewhere in Europe and further a field to set down analysis and express their views. Its focus on current issues is one of its hallmarks. In the economic field, this last was strikingly demonstrated in two "Special Editions" of the journal devoted to the economic and other implications of China's WTO accession in November 2001,[50] mainly written by European authors.[51] In general, *China Perspectives* has played an outstanding role as a forum for the expression of European views on contemporary Chinese economic,[52] as well as other issues.[53]

National Perspectives

In this section I try to suggest the range of academic activity – in terms of experts, expertise and subject matter – in contemporary Chinese economic studies in Western European countries (or groups of countries). For reasons of space, the treatment is necessarily selective and I make no claim to its representativeness.

France

Writing in 1995, Lucien Bianco referred to the recent "maturing" of French contemporary Chinese studies from the perspective of some 30 years previously, when the field had simply not existed in France.[54] Bianco is one of a number of major French figures of an older generation – Marianne Bastid-Bruguière, Marie-

Claire Bergère, Jean Chesneaux, Jacques Guillermaz and Jean-Luc Domenach are others – who can now be seen as the original driving forces behind French studies of contemporary China. Of these, two – Bergère and Bianco[55] – have made major contributions to understanding the origins and process of economic and political-economy development in modern China.

Bergère's first major monograph,[56] based on her Ph.D. thesis, sought to highlight the role of the bourgeoisie as the main driver of China's economic modernization in the first decades after the fall of the Qing Dynasty. A previous paper by Bergère[57] had already focused on Shanghai, and this great metropolis was at the center of her detailed analysis of the economic dynamism which she detected at work in China's pre-1949 modern industrial sector. Significantly, however, Bergère's early monograph does not suggest that the same modernizing influences were felt in other parts of China's economy (most notably, the farm sector). The "Shanghai theme" is a recurring one in Bergère's work, and it is one to which she has returned in her most recent – and arguably finest – book,[58] which examines the vagaries of Shanghai's history as a node of capitalistic development since 1842. It deserves saying, however, that Bergère's work on the Chinese economy and political-economy by no means ignores truly contemporary developments.[59]

Like that of Bergère, Lucien Bianco's research and publications span the 1949 historical divide. His best known early work was his *Les origines de la revolution chinoise, 1915–1949*,[60] which focused on peasant discontent – viewed as the product of social, political, and demographic factors – at the heart of the rural malaise that ultimately precipitated Mao's revolution and the coming to power of the Chinese Communist Party. Forty years on, this book repays careful re-reading and remains a classic exposition of the sources and potency of rural-based social revolution. The apotheosis of Bianco's preoccupation with China's peasantry is his most recent book – *Peasants Without the Party*,[61] which in 2003 was awarded the Joseph Levenson Book Prize on Modern China. This volume is a collection of 13 chapters, published in various journals and books between 1970 and 1999. Its central theme is, once again, the origins, nature, and impact of peasant unrest and conflict,[62] as shown in China's rural history during the twentieth century. Although the emphasis is on pre-1949 history, Bianco also considers peasant resistance under the PRC and the increased incidence of collective violence by peasants since the 1980s.

Younger generations of French scholars and analysts of the contemporary Chinese economy have emerged quite forcefully in recent years. The published work – in English and French – of Claude Aubert stands on its own as an important *oeuvre* on China's rural, and especially agricultural, development.[63] His analysis of China's agricultural problems is outstanding for the meticulous research – often derived from on-the-ground fieldwork – and statistical analysis which it embodies. It is also wide-ranging. Aubert has been closely involved with ECARDC activities and his work can be sampled in three of the ECARDC volumes. One of these is a *tour d'horizon* of economic and institutional problems confronting Chinese agriculture after a decade of reform.[64] Two others are more micro orientated, examining grain farming – an agricultural sub-sector to which Aubert has devoted much attention – and meat and dairy production.[65] Aubert's expertise as an agronomist, as well as an economist, lends his work rare authority.

Thierry Pairault is someone else whose work has embraced China's rural sector,[66] but, as an early co-edited publication indicates, [67] whose interests have also extended to other areas of the Chinese economy.[68] In an early book,[69] Pairault addressed industrial policy issues under the impact of the early economic reforms. Subsequently, his focus shifted towards China's regional development.[70] More recently still, he has published a detailed analysis of the relationship between educational attainments, educational financing and economic growth in China in the 1990s.[71]

The work of François Gipoloux has tended to focus on China's external economic relations,[72] but is of special interest for its attempt to place China's experience in a broader Asian regional context.[73] In this last respect, comparative analysis of regional and sub-regional development policies conducted by Gipoloux offers an original and innovative approach towards China's foreign trade and FDI inflows.[74] He is also the author of numerous papers, which investigate from a more "orthodox" perspective issues relating to China's foreign trade, FDI inflows and their impact, WTO accession and its implications, and technology transfer.[75]

I will end this selective survey with a few short comments on the work of other scholars merely to underline the richness and diversity that today characterizes academic activity in France in contemporary Chinese economic studies. One who comes to mind is Jean-François Huchet,[76] an economist who has written and published, *inter alia*, several insightful papers on China's industrial reforms.[77] Another – albeit a political scientist by training – is Jean-Louis Rocca,[78] who has conducted in-depth research on unemployment, employment and social welfare policies in China (including their social and economic impact). His work is strongly embedded in fieldwork conducted in Shanghai, Sichuan, and Northeast China.[79] A third young scholar is Gilles Guiheux, based at CEFC in Hong Kong, the focus of whose work has been private entrepreneurship in China.[80] Finally, mention should be made of Antoine Kernen (University of Lausanne), whose work on unemployment and social security issues in China has overlapped with that of Rocca;[81] and of Françoise Lemoine (Centre d'Études Prospectives et d'Informations Internationales [CEPII], Paris), who has published widely on a range of economic issues facing China, with an emphasis on the foreign trade sector.[82]

Germany

Although Sinology has a history of about a century in Germany, as a field of academic investigation it contracted during the first half of the twentieth century, and only revived and expanded to embrace the study of contemporary China in the postwar period. Since then it has expanded steadily and by the 1990s there were an estimated 20 universities in Germany, Austria and Switzerland which included Sinology in their curricula. As elsewhere in Europe, *contemporary* Chinese studies have assumed increasing importance, and related research and teaching are pursued in a significant number of academic and research institutions. Of these, the Freie Universität Berlin (Free University of Berlin), and the Universities of Bochum (Ruhr-Universität Bochum), Cologne (Universität zu Köln), Duisburg (Universität Duisburg-Essen), Hamburg (Universität Hamburg, Fachbereich Orientalistik, Asien-Afrika-Institut, Abteilung für Sprache und Kultur Chinas), Heidelberg (Ruprecht-Karls-Universität Heidelberg, Sinologisches Seminar), Munich (Ludwig-Maximilians-Universität München, Institut für Ostasienkunde – Sinologie), Trier (Universität Trier) and Tübingen (Eberhard-Karls-Universität Tübingen) are the most important. Two other German-speaking academic institutions are the Universities of Vienna (Universität Wien, Institut für Sinologie) in Austria, and Zürich (Universität Zürich, Ostasiatisches Seminar), Switzerland.

Willy Kraus was a pioneer of Chinese economic studies in Germany,[83] and his study of China's economic and social development between 1949 and the first years of reform was, at the time of its publication, the most detailed general analysis then available.[84] For some reason – perhaps the detail was found to be excessive – it never received the attention it deserved, although it remains a useful source and text for teaching. Kraus was also one of the first scholars to examine the resurgence during the first reform decade.[85] It too remains a valuable research source.

Another German scholar of an older generation – Wolfgang Klenner – has a rich list of publications on China, as well as other parts of East Asia (notably Japan).[86] His work is mainly orientated towards China's external economic relations, and focuses on trade and FDI-related issues.[87] Klenner's work is characterized by its strong theoretical underpinnings, as well as insights derived from many years of close acquaintance with China. His work is less well known than it should be, no doubt because so much of it has been published only in German.

Much of the work undertaken by or on behalf of the Institut für Asienkunde (Hamburg) has similarly been published in German, and therefore had less widespread exposure than it deserves. But two IFA staff members, whose work on China's economy has more frequently appeared in English, are Margot Schüller and Heike Holbig.[88] Schüller's research gains much from her background as an economist; it also reflects extensive use of Chinese-language materials. Her work is quite wide-ranging, although in recent years it has tended to focus on the regional and global implications of China's economic engagement in the international economy.[89] Heike Holbig is less easily pigeonholed. Her training at the University of Heidelberg was in Chinese studies and economics, but her publications have ranged across both economic and political issues in China.[90] A recent chapter which nicely brings together her dual expertise analyzes developments in the private sector of the Chinese economy from the perspective of the entrepreneurial involvement of CCP members.[91] The analysis here is subtle and offers valuable insights into the relationship between changes in the structure of party membership, especially through the admission of capitalists – private entrepreneurs – to the CCP, and efforts to strengthen party leadership in accordance with China's changing socio-economic circumstances.[92]

Sebastian Heilmann is best known as a political scientist working on China, most of whose published work has appeared only in German. However, not unlike Heike Holbig, in a recent article he has investigated the impact of entrenched political structures on China's economic reform through an analysis of the impact of "pervasive government interference and cronyism" on China's financial sector.[93] Heilmann's article is a fine example of an exercise in political economy, written by someone who is primarily a political scientist.[94]

A German scholar, whose most recent book is one of the most outstanding contributions to contemporary China studies in recent years, is Thomas Scharping.[95] Scharping's research has focused on demographic issues in China and his previous published work on this critically important dimension of China's social and economic development,[96] is a minor self-contained literature in its own right. His latest book is a comprehensive and painstakingly researched survey and analysis of Chinese population policies between 1949 and the most recent census in 2000.[97] It addresses every aspect of the complex issues that have faced China's family planners, including sensitive questions relating to fertility controls and China's abnormal gender ratio. Over the years, the study of China's population has generated a number of outstanding books and other contributions,[98] and Scharping's most recent volume fully deserves to be set alongside these.

Markus Taube is an economist with wide-ranging research interests that embrace both theoretical and applied dimensions (including institutional economics, the economics of multinational enterprises and foreign direct investment) with reference to developing countries and economies in transition.[99] The regional foci of his work are China and Southeast Asia. A good example of Taube's application of new institutional economics to China can be found in an article published in 2002, which analyzes the role and impact of property rights structures that have characterized rural township and village enterprises.[100] Like other of his German academic colleagues, Taube's published work also investigates China's emerging role in the international economy. For example, an important recent contribution analyzed China's trade with European countries under the impact of post-1978 reform.[101]

The "Low Countries" (Belgium and the Netherlands)

Belgium does not have a strong tradition of China studies, although mention may be made here of the work of Sylvain Plasschaert.[102] For most of his professional academic life, Plasschaert's research was far removed from questions relating to China, but in more recent years his attention has increasingly turned towards contemporary Chinese economic issues (especially those that relate to the impact and implications of China's integration into the global economy). He has, however, published relatively little.

As Director of EIAS in Brussels, Willem van der Geest has also recently become increasingly involved in contemporary China studies, including issues related to the economy and foreign trade. Van der Geest is an economist by training, and his work has focused on questions of international development, although his regional foci have been Africa and South Asia. A review of his publications since 1997 reveals one journal article,[103] and two refereed conference papers on topics related to the Chinese economy.[104]

In contrast to its neighbor, the Netherlands has a strong tradition of Sinology and has also developed strength in contemporary China studies. An outstanding Dutch scholar is Eduard Vermeer,[105] whose work has focused almost exclusively on China from both historical and current perspectives. The thrust of his work on contemporary Chinese economic issues has been directed towards environmental problems, as well as the rural economy and agriculture. His research is heavily based on personal fieldwork, but also makes use of data collected through national and local surveys.

Within a single paragraph, it is impossible to do justice to the variety of Vermeer's publications (overwhelmingly in English, but also in Dutch and Chinese), which span almost 30 years. In the most recent past, much of his research has been on institutional dimensions of China's rural reforms, such as the development of shareholding cooperative systems and associated property rights issues.[106] A significant contribution to the literature on China's environmental problems was a conference paper he published on industrial pollution policies.[107]

Someone who is not Dutch, as far as I know, but whose work is most usefully associated with contemporary Chinese economic studies in the Netherlands, is Peter Ho.[108] His name has already appeared in this chapter in the context of the activities of ECARDC, of which he has been an energetic advocate. Like Vermeer, Ho concerns himself mainly with China's rural sector. In particular, he is the author of a path-breaking study of China's land problems and related policies, especially as they relate to ownership and property rights,[109] and the editor of a rich collection of papers on land issues.[110] The changing institutional framework in which land – cropland, grassland, forest and even wasteland – is used and owned is the source of bitter disputes, and Ho's monograph is a very important contribution to the related literature. Its scholarship is unrivalled,[111] and it promises to remain a standard source for many years to come.

Scandinavia and Nordic Countries (Denmark, Finland, Norway and Sweden)

Exactly as Lucien Bianco described French studies of contemporary China, so Kjeld-Erik Brødsgaard once similarly observed that until the 1960s, contemporary China studies in Scandinavia were "largely an unknown phenomenon".[112] Today, the field is quite well established, with centres of study in Copenhagen (Denmark), Stockholm and Lund (Sweden), Helsinki and Turku (Finland), and Bergen and Oslo (Norway).[113]

The most senior Danish academic researcher on contemporary China is Kjeld-Erik Brødsgaard.[114] Interestingly, his doctoral dissertation addressed economic issues,[115] although his post-doctoral research and publications have focused more on China's domestic politics (especially party affairs).[116] From time to time, however, his interests have shown an economic orientation, and his current research includes analysis of China's integration in the global economy, and the relationship between state, party, and the changing business environment in China (both from a national perspective and regionally, through the experience of Hainan.[117]

Among other Danish scholars are Flemming Christiansen[118] and Jørgen Delman.[119] Both have worked extensively on China's agricultural and rural problems.[120] Stig Thøgersen, works primarily on educational questions, although he has occasionally researched domestic political affairs.[121]

The first chair of East Asian studies was established in Finland (University of Helsinki) as recently as 1987. For the time being, Finnish studies of the Chinese contemporary economy remain in their infancy. The foci of such work are the University of Turku and, especially, the Swedish School of Economics and Business Administration (Hanken) in Helsinki, where the late Oiva Laaksonen undertook and published research on the modern Chinese economy.[122]

Work on the contemporary Chinese economy in Sweden has primarily taken place at the Center for Pacific Asia Studies (CPAS) in Stockholm, and at Lund University. Established in 1984, CPAS has overseen a significant research and publications program, including monographs, journal articles and working papers (including some in Swedish). Among CPAS English-language publications is a collection of papers on China's market-orientated economic reforms.[123] At Lund University, the most significant contribution to contemporary Chinese economic studies has probably been the work of Jon Sigurdson, whose research has increasingly focused on technological management in China and its (China's) emergence as a technological superpower.[124]

In case this brief résumé suggests a dearth of activity in Scandinavia, it deserves stating that contemporary Chinese studies, taken as a whole, have grown significantly in the region in recent years. My impression is, however, that the focus of such work has been more on political and security issues, as well as China's international relations, than on economic questions.

Southern Europe (Spain and Portugal)

Spain[125] and Portugal[126] are relative newcomers to contemporary China studies. Since its establishment in 1992, the Centro de Estudios de Asia Oriental in Madrid – the principal focus of Spanish studies on contemporary China – has made one of its major goals the training of young social scientists in East Asian studies. To date, the most important work on the Chinese economy is that of Leila Fernández-Stembridge.[127] Her work has focused on labor, employment and migration issues.[128] Some research on contemporary China is also undertaken at Real Instituto Elcano de Estudios Internacionales y Estratégicos and Universidad Complutense (both in Madrid), although I have been unable to identify any published work in English relating to China's economy.

United Kingdom

Towards the beginning of this chapter, I cited a survey of contemporary Chinese economic studies written by Walter Galenson, in which just one European scholar was cited – Kenneth R. Walker.[129] Some 40 years on, the situation has improved markedly: as this chapter has demonstrated, there is now a significant research establishment of European academic and professional analysts engaged in research on the Chinese economy. Sadly, however, the field has expanded quite slowly within the U.K., and it is telling that in 1999 a report on Chinese Studies in the U.K. issued by the Higher Educational Funding Council for England (HEFCE) highlighted the "lack of capacity in the U.K. to respond to the challenge posed by the rapidly growing role that the PRC is playing in the spheres of diplomacy, culture and business."[130] A survey of returns arising out of the 1996 "Research Assessment Exercise" (RAE), one of several quality assessment exercises carried out on a regular basis in British universities, revealed that 400 people out of 57,000 active researchers in British higher education institutions (a mere 0.7 percent) had cited works relating to China. In turn, only a tiny proportion of the publications of these 400 researchers were concerned with the contemporary Chinese economy.[131]

One of the points of emphasis in the HECFE report was the disappointing scale of activity in Chinese Studies in the U.K., compared with that in some other European countries.[132] Hence, the conclusion that "… the scale of the U.K. effort in research and scholarship in this field [Chinese studies] lags well behind that achieved by some European and other Western countries trading with China." It was against this background that HEFCE called for a reorientation of Chinese Studies in the U.K. towards language acquisition and "studies of contemporary China in the social sciences," and provided annual funding of over £1 million in order to strengthen such studies. The impact of this initiative is reflected in the expansion of postgraduate training in contemporary Chinese studies that has taken place in recent years.[133] It remains to be seen to what extent this will generate a corresponding expansion of higher-level research and publications on contemporary China, including the economy.

Kenneth Walker is widely regarded as the founder of modern Chinese economic studies in Britain, a field which he subsequently dominated until his premature death in 1989.[134] Walker was a leading figure in the international academic community of scholars of contemporary China. As I have written elsewhere, Walker's publications "constitute a uniquely consistent and authoritative account of the economic development of Chinese agriculture during the first four decades of the People's Republic."[135] The foci of his work were threefold: first, the institutional parameters of agricultural development between the 1950s and 1980s (with particular reference to collectivization in the 1950s,[136] the role of the private sector during the Mao period,[137] and the rationale and impact of *decollectivization* in the 1980s[138]); second, the long-run performance of the all-important grain sector[139] (including a posthumously published analysis of grain production and consumption under the impact of the Great Leap Forward[140]); and third, the impact of post-1978 reforms on economic diversification of the rural sector – a paper which also captures the provincial dimensions of agricultural and rural development which preoccupied Walker and was a recurring theme in his work.[141] During his academic career of almost 40 years, Walker supervised the Ph.D. dissertations of only three students, all of whom subsequently pursued academic careers in contemporary Chinese economic studies, mostly based in the U.K.

The first of these was Christopher Howe,[142] who, despite having retired a few years ago, remains actively engaged in research. For many years, his work focused exclusively on the Chinese economy; subsequently, his research emphasis shifted towards Japan, Hong Kong, and Taiwan; today, it embraces economic development in all four regions. Howe's early publications were concerned with labor market and employment issues.[143] They were among the earliest attempts to investigate the scale and determinants of urban employment during the period of the First Five-Year Plan, and to analyze the rationale and impact of wage policies up to the early Cultural Revolution period. His work on China's labor problems was mainly based on an impressive array of Chinese-language materials (both provincial newspapers and economic journals).[144] More than 30 years after their publication, these two books still offer important insights into the evolution of urban wage and employment policy in China between the 1960s and early 1970s. From the 1980s, Howe's published work on China was strongly colored by his research concerns with Japan, Hong Kong, and Taiwan. Accordingly, the thrust of much of this work was analysis of China's foreign trade and, in more general terms, China's emerging role in regional foreign economic relations.[145] At the time of writing, he is completing a study of China's energy sector, co-authored with Dr Tatsu Kambara (Institute of Energy Economics, Tokyo).

Some would regard the lack of single-authored general surveys and analyses of China's post-1949 or post-1978 economic development as a curious feature of contemporary Chinese economic studies.[146] From this perspective, reference should be made to Howe's "Guide"[147] to the Chinese economy, which following its publication in 1978 was probably the most widely-used textbook on China's economic development under Mao Zedong. Noteworthy too are two collections of translated Chinese documents on policy-related economic issues in China.[148] Recent years have seen the appearance of a number of collections of articles and chapters from journals and books already in print that focus on China's economic development. But attempts to tell the same story through the medium of Chinese-language materials (official documents and other writings by Chinese analysts) are much rarer, and offer distinctive and insightful perspectives lacking elsewhere in the published literature. As one reviewer put it, the 2003 volume provides "a vivid insider's view of the thinking and analyses that led China to abandon central planning and seek to establish a market economy."[149]

The second of Kenneth Walker's three Ph.D. students was Robert Ash,[150] whose first degree was in Sinology and who came to the study of economics through a subsequent postgraduate degree and doctoral research. For many years, the almost exclusive focus of his research, no doubt reflecting Walker's influence, was China's agricultural development (especially the performance of the grain sector).[151] In more recent years, however, his interests have embraced a much wider range of issues, including population, employment and migration, industrial performance, and China's foreign economic relations (including cross-border trade and investment).[152]

The final member of the trinity of Walker's research students is Peter Nolan.[153] Nolan is a prolific writer – the author of 16 books and monographs, and 40 book chapters and journal articles. The range of his research interests defies simple categorization.[154] Much of his early work was driven by political economy concerns.[155] More recently, following his appointment at the Judge Business School (Cambridge University), his focus has shifted towards in-depth analysis, backed by detailed sectoral case studies, of industrial policies and performance in China under the impact of reform.[156] This work derives from the China Big Business Programme (CBBP), inaugurated and managed by Nolan at the Judge Business School in Cambridge. Through case study research, the CBBP seeks to assess the effectiveness of policies designed to facilitate the transformation of large-scale Chinese companies into globally competitive entities. The CBBP is also noteworthy for bringing together academics and non-academics – in the latter case, representatives of both government and the corporate business sector in China and the EU – in order to investigate industrial policy-related issues. The CBBP and its associated publications offer valuable, not to say unique insights into the interaction between China and the global business revolution in the late twentieth and early twenty-first centuries.

The remarkable breadth of Nolan's interests and expertise are apparent from a glance at his publications. Noteworthy in this respect is his comparative study of the Russian and Chinese economies in transition,[157] a book which was the first serious attempt to compare systemic reform in the two countries and provoked controversy that has lasted to the present day. That a number of his recent books have been published in Chinese-language versions testifies to the seriousness with which his views are regarded in China.

Someone of Chinese nationality, but who is now an established member of the British academic community is Laixiang Sun.[158] His "field site" is China and his work has ranged over a very wide range of economic and business-related issues, published in English and Chinese. Someone else who, like Sun, publishes in Chinese and English is Dic Lo.[159] Much of Lo's work has a strong political economy thrust.[160] His more strictly economic-orientated research has focused on two major areas: first, China's industrial sector (above all, the restructuring of its state-owned industries);[161] second, China's foreign trade and the impact of FDI inflows on the Chinese economy.

A scholar who deserves mention here is the late Gordon White (d. 1998), much of whose work had a strong political economy thrust. As an author, White was even more prolific than Nolan, publishing 14 books, 9 monographs, and about 100 articles – most of them on China. His legacy of publications represents a major contribution to the literature of economic reform and transition. In particular, it highlights the progressive decline of the state's economic control (and associated central planning mechanisms) in favor of much a greater role in economic management and guidance over production and distribution for enterprises and markets.[162]

Of a younger generation, Chris Bramall's primary research interest lies in the growth of the post-1978 Chinese economy, with a particular focus on the contribution that some aspects of the Maoist legacy have made to such growth.[163] Bramall explored some of these issues in his first short monograph on Sichuan,[164] but developed them in much greater detail in his first full-length book (published in English and later in a Chinese-language translation).[165] It offers an original and provocative account of the development record of the Maoist regime – not least, in terms of its argument that the weakening of private and CCP-based interest groups was a significant factor facilitating the post-1978 reallocation of resources from inefficient heavy industries to more efficient sectors of the economy. Embodied in the analysis are two controversial hypotheses: the first is that a state-led development strategy may achieve more than one based on capitalist mechanisms; the second is that China's success under the impact of early reform also derived from favorable political and institutional conditions, not necessarily replicable in other transition economies. In Bramall's most recent book,[166] these themes reappear, but are placed in a new analytical framework that re-evaluates and extends the role of the "developmental state" in the Chinese context.

Within the youngest generation of scholars of contemporary China working in the U.K., I will mention just one: Rachel Murphy.[167] Her work on rural–urban migration and other rural–urban interactions is not primarily economic in its orientation, but has nevertheless offered rich insights into the economic challenges that China currently faces. The findings of her fieldwork, undertaken as part of her Ph.D. research (University of Cambridge, 1999), were published in a fine first book.[168] In it she analyzes the impact of labor outflows and – a truly original contribution – *return* flows of people, skills, and capital on rural wealth and inequality, land distribution and farm production, and rural industrialization. Murphy is the most recent recipient of the "Gordon White Prize," awarded for the most original article to appear in *The China Quarterly* (in her case, during 2004).[169]

Conclusion

The European scene, as it relates to the study of the contemporary Chinese economy, offers plenty of room for optimism. Economic studies of China have expanded steadily in recent decades, and there now exists a body of expertise working in academic and research institutions that compares favorably with any other part of the world. In many European countries, programs are in place to enhance the provision of such expertise in order to respond to the challenges posed by the emergence of China as a global economic power. Increasingly, it seems that European governments acknowledge the special – even unique – place that China fills in the international community. As the 1999 UK HEFCE Report, to which reference has already been made, observed, "whatever the need for expertise in relation to the Pacific Rim countries more generally, the needs in relation to China [are] of a different order in their scale, complexity and priority."[170]

Nor has the response to the rise of China been felt only in national terms. Also significant has been the contribution made by trans-national European institutions, such as ECAN, EIAS, and IIAS. One hopes that the role of such bodies in promoting research on the Chinese economy and facilitating the exchange of ideas within relevant European professionals will be not only maintained, but also strengthened.

There is, however, no room for complacency. As trading and investment links between China and Europe – whether on an individual country basis or through some collective means, such as the EU – grow, so the needs of industry and commerce will also expand. If these needs are to be met, it is incumbent on universities and research institutions to respond in the following areas:

- to provide specialists who possess both academic expertise and "hands on" experience of China's economic organization, management, and decision-making processes;
- to generate a database of specialists and information, capable of responding to the emerging economic challenges associated with China's continued social and economic development;
- to put in place an institutional framework through which expertise and information can be made available effectively and in a timely fashion;
- to establish postgraduate teaching and research programs that can nurture graduates equipped with appropriate linguistic and business-related skills.

As Europeans, we may feel a degree of self-satisfaction that recent decades have seen modest progress made towards fulfilling these goals. But the more important message is that there is still much to be done.

Notes

1 In this chapter, I generally take "contemporary" to refer to very recent developments in China, although I occasionally follow a more relaxed definition that embraces pre-1949 developments.

2 Hugh Baker (another British Sinologist) tells the story of Harry Simon (*another* British Sinologist and the son of Walter) coming across his father reading a book in Hungarian and asking him how many European languages he could read. Walter thought for a while and replied, "Well, all of them, I suppose." See David Arnold and Christopher Shackle (ed.), *SOAS Since the Sixties* (London: School of Oriental and African Studies, 2003), p. 167.

3 More often than not, they do! As Herbert Franke observed in 1997, "… English has become the *lingua franca* of Chinese studies … Nothing shall be said against the preponderance of English … but it should not lead to us to a neglect of scholarly productions written in [European] languages other than English." Described in Franke, "In Search of China: Some General Remarks on the History of European Sinology," in Ming Wilson and John Kayley (eds), *Europe Studies China: Papers*

from an International Conference on the History of European Sinology (London: Han-Shan Tang Books, 1995), p. 20.

4   Musically-minded Sinologists will know that Mahler's supreme achievement – *Das Lied von der Erde* (*Song of the Earth*) – derives its inspiration and its words from the poems of Chang Tsi, Meng Kao-yen, Wang Wei and, especially, Li Po!

5   Thomas Kampen, "China in Europe: A Brief Survey of European China Studies at the Turn of the Century," *China Review International*, Vol. 7, No. 2 (Fall 2000), pp. 291–5.

6   As someone whose first acquaintance with China was through a degree in Chinese language and literature, and who subsequently wandered almost accidentally into social sciences, my sympathy and attachment incline towards area studies.

7   The decline of economics and rise of business and management studies is a notable feature of recent curricular developments in British and European schools and universities.

8   For reasons of expertise and space, I have mostly omitted consideration of work that falls within the remit of business and management studies.

9   To any European colleague whose work on the Chinese economy I have ignored or unfairly neglected, I unreservedly apologize.

10 Walter Galenson, "The Current State of Chinese Economic Studies," U.S. Congress Joint Economic Committee, *An Economic Profile of Mainland China*, originally published by the U.S. Government Printing Office (Washington D.C.) and subsequently reprinted by Frederick A. Praeger Publishers in 1968. See pp. 3–13.

11 On my bookshelves, I have counted 51 *books and monographs* on post-1949 agricultural and rural development, almost all of which have been published since 1970. This is in addition to the much greater number of articles on the same topic that have been published during the same period.

12 Those from the U.S. to whom Galenson made reference were: John S. Aird, John Lossing Buck, Kang Chao, Chu-Yuan Cheng, Owen L. Dawson, George C. Ecklund, Alexander Eckstein, John P. Emerson, Charles Hoffman, William G. Hollister, Ta-Chung Liu, Leo A. Orleans, Dwight H. Perkins, Peter Schran, Anthony Tang, Yuan-li Wu and K.C. Yeh. I wonder how many of these are on the reading lists of today's students of the Chinese economy!

13 There is an interesting historical counterpoint to the U.S. dominance of contemporary Chinese studies: "Up to 1939 … Chinese studies in the US were largely dominated by Europeans. Prior to World War I the Columbia Professor of Chinese was Friedrich Hirth … When in May 1937 a group of Sinologists published a memorandum on the necessity to promote Chinese studies, the document was signed by George A. Kennedy, Ferdinand Lessing and Peter A. Boodberg. Among these Kennedy had a Ph.D. from Berlin University, Lessing was a German immigrant and Boodberg had a Russian background (he never applied for US citizenship)," as described in Franke, "In Search of China", op. cit., p. 16.

14 Galenson, op. cit., p. 12.

15 Galenson, op. cit., p. 13.

16 In 1998 the International Institute for Asian Studies (IIAS) in Leiden (The Netherlands) published a far-from-exhaustive directory of European *Asianists* that listed some 5,000 researchers and scholars. See IIAS, *Guide to Asian Studies in Europe* (Richmond: Curzon Press, 1998). The European Association of Chinese Studies (EACS) has a membership of around 700. EACS is a non-political association that seeks, through its biennial conference and newsletter, to provide a forum in which to discuss and explore all fields of scholarly activity relating to Chinese studies throughout Europe.

17 Those who are interested in exploring the origins and development of European Sinology should read Ming Wilson and John Kayley (eds), *Europe Studies China*, op. cit. For a wonderfully lively account of the history of *British* Sinology, see T.H.

Barrett, *Singular Listlessness: A Short History of Chinese Books and British Scholars* (London: Wellsweep, 1989); and for valuable insights into the development of German Sinology, see Helmut Martin and Christiane Hammer (ed.), *Chinawissenschaften – Deutschsprage Entwicklungen* (Hamburg: Mitteilungen des Instituts für Asienkunde, 1999).

18 A characteristically provocative and insightful attempt to posit an integration of aspects of China's past with its future economic, social, and political trajectory is that of Peter Nolan in his *China at the Crossroads* (Cambridge: Polity Press, 2004), esp. chapter 3.

19 The conference seeks "to present the best and most innovative of recent research across the spectrum of Chinese Studies from archaeological to political science approaches, from phenomena in the distant past to those of the present day, from China's global interaction to local developments; [and] to foster exchange and cooperation across national and disciplinary, methodological and generational borders …" (see EACS Conference website at http://www.uni-aas.si/eacs/conferenceinfo).

20 The three in question were: Modern History and Society, Women and Gender Studies, and Contemporary Economy and Society. Of these, only the last-named was wholly orientated towards contemporary issues. The remaining panels were: Linguistic and Languages (Classical and Modern), Literature (Classical and Modern), Pre-Modern History and Society, Art and Archaeology, Religion and Philosophy, Teaching Chinese Language, Performing Arts, and Other. The sixteenth EACS Conference will take place in Ljubljana, Slovenia in Aug.–Sept. 2006. As of end Jan. 2006, three roundtable sessions have been confirmed, all on "traditional" topics (Chinese and Western Formal Logic, Qing History, and Jesuit Studies).

21 See http://ecardc.org/iias/show/id=41312 (accessed on 28 Jan. 2006).

22 Recent IIAS Annual Reports can be accessed via the IIAS website. At the time of writing, the 2004 Report is the most recently available.

23 From the home page of EIAS, available at http://www.eias.org/ (accessed on 28 Jan. 2006). EIAS's remit extends to 26 Asian countries in the Middle East, and South, Southeast and East Asia.

24 The full title of the study was *Economics and Politics of East Asian Co-operation and China's Role in the Process: Opportunities and Challenges for the EU.*

25 These include macroeconomic regulation (including monetary and exchange rate policies), trade and services liberalization, especially in relation to China's WTO membership, China's regional economic integration (incl. the emergence of FTAs), SOE restructuring and privatization, banking reform, demographic trends and labor market policies, social security provision, etc.

26 R. Ash, "The Long-Term Outlook for Economic Reform in China."

27 The origins of the Asia Alliance lie in the "Nordic-Netherlands Strategic Alliance," whose membership consisted of IIAS and the Nordic Institute of Asian Studies (NIAS). In 1998, the re-named Asia Alliance welcomed the Institut für Asienkunde (Institute for Asian Studies) (IFA), based in Hamburg (Germany) to its ranks; and in 2000 and 2001 two other institutions – EIAS and the Paris-based Centre d'Études et de Recherches Internationales (Center for International Studies and Research) (CERI) – also joined. The most recent additions to membership of the Asia Alliance are the Centro de Estudios de Asia Oriental (Centre of East Asian Studies) (CEAO) in the Universidad Autónoma de Madrid (Spain), and the School of Oriental and African Studies (SOAS) (London, U.K.).

28 For further information about the Asia Alliance, see its website at www.asia-alliance. org.

29 ECAN was funded by a grant from the European Commission. Funding ceased in 2001, but was revived in 2006.

30 Through the ECRFF scheme, 24 young scholars from Denmark, Finland, France, Germany, Italy, the Netherlands, Spain and the U.K. undertook fieldwork and archival research visits, mainly in China.

31 Werner Draguhn and Robert Ash (ed.), *China's Economic Security* (Richmond: Curzon Press, 1999).

32 Katja Afheldt (in collaboration with S. Weyand and M. Gago de la Mata), "Economic Security: the EU's Stake in a Sustainable Development in China," in Werner Draguhn and Robert Ash (ed.), *China's Economic Security* (Richmond: Curzon Press, 1999). pp. 163–232.

33 Robert Ash (ed.), *China's Integration in Asia: Economic Security and Strategic Issues* (Richmond: Curzon Press, 2002).

34 Heike Holbig and Robert Ash (eds), *China's Accession to the World Trade Organisation: National and International Perspectives* (London: RoutledgeCurzon, 2002); Kjeld-Erik Brødsgaard (ed.), *China's Place in Global Politics: International, Regional and Domestic Challenges* (London: RoutledgeCurzon, 2002); Taciana Fisac and Leila Fernández-Stembridge (eds), *China Today: Economic Reforms, Social Cohesion and Collective Identities* (London: RoutledgeCurzon, 2003).

35 Nor were the authors exclusively – although they were mainly – European. It is, however, with the European contributors alone that I am concerned here.

36 See especially Christopher Howe, "The Changing Asian Environment of China's Economic Development: The Perspective from Japan (with particular reference to foreign direct investment and industrial re-structuring)," and David Wall, "China and the World Trade Organisation," both in Ash (ed.) *China's Integration in Asia*, op. cit., pp. 3–38 and pp. 39–55; Christopher Howe, "Development and International Integration", Angelos Pangratis, "The EU and China: Economic Giants," and Robert Ash, "Does the Chinese Economy Matter?" all in Brødsgaard and Heurlin (eds), *China's Place in Global Politics*, op. cit., pp. 70–78, Hans-Friedrich Beseler, "The EU-China Negotiations: Breaking the Deadlock," Margot Schüller, "The Impact of China's WTO Accession on International Trade and Capital Flows", Françoise Lemoine and Deniz Ünal Kesenci, "The Impact of China's WTO Accession on EU Trade," Michael Yahuda, "China's Future Role in the WTO: 'Developing Country', 'Regional Economic Power', 'New Economic Superpower'?" all in Holbig and Ash (eds), *China's Accession to the WTO*, op. cit., pp. 3–19 and pp. 229–319.

37 E.g. Peter Nolan, "China and the WTO: the Challenge for China's Large-Scale Industry", Martin Posth, "The Automobile Sector," Jürgen Oberg, "The Telecommunications Sector," Hans-Jörg Probst, "The Insurance Sector," in Holbig and Ash (eds), *China's Accession to the WTO*, op. cit., pp. 43–136.

38 Nikos Alexandratos and Jelle Bruinsma, "Asia's Food and the World", Claude Aubert, "Food Consumption and Food Production in China: Statistical Uncertainties, Educated Guesses, and Reasoned Optimism", and Mehmet Ögütçü, "China and Asia: Growing Energy and Geopolitical Concerns," all in Ash (ed.), *China's Integration in Asia*, op. cit., pp. 76–134.

39 Ku Hok-bun and Elisabeth Croll, "Social Security: Rights and Contracts in a Chinese Village," Ash (ed.), *China's Integration in Asia*, op. cit., pp. 169–87; Flemming Christiansen, "Will WTO Accession Threaten China's Social Stability?", Holbig and Ash (ed.), *China's Accession to the WTO*, op. cit., pp. 176–92; Leila Fernández-Stembridge, "Stabilising Potential Instability: Re-employment in Today's China," Jean-Louis Rocca, "Old Working Class, New Working Class: Reforms, Labor Crisis and the Two Faces of Conflicts in Chinese Urban Areas", Brian Hook, "The Development of the Urban Housing Market: Social Implications", all in Brødsgaard and Heurlin (eds), *China's Place in Global Politics*, op. cit., pp. 55–119.

40 ECARDC is a cooperative framework of European and Chinese institutes that specialize in the study of China's agricultural and rural development. It comprises nine institutions, as follows: Centre for Development Studies, Groningen University

(Groningen, The Netherlands), College of Agricultural and Rural Development, China Agricultural University (Beijing, China), Institut National de la Recherche Agronomique (INRA) [National Institute of Agronomical Research] (Paris, France), Institute for Chinese Studies, Oxford University (Oxford, U.K.), Institute of Agricultural Economics, Chinese Academy of Agricultural Sciences, (Beijing, China), Nordic Institute for Asian Studies (Copenhagen, Denmark), Rights Practice (London, U.K.), Rural Development Institute, Chinese Academy of Social Sciences (CASS) and School of Humanities, University of Greenwich (London, U.K.).

41 From the ECARDC website: www.ecardc.org (accessed on 28 Jan. 2006).

42 The most recent ECARDC conference ("China's Agricultural Transition: Balancing Rural–Urban Relations") was held in 2004; the next will be co-organized by the Rural Development Institute (CASS) and took place in China in 2006 under the title "China's Agricultural Transition: Balancing Rural-Urban Relations." The conference volumes so far published are: Jørgen Delman, Clemens Stubbe Østergaard and Flemming Christiansen (eds), *Remaking Peasant China: Problems of Rural Development and Institutions at the Start of the 1990s* (Aarhus, Denmark: Aarhus University Press, 1990); E.B. Vermeer (ed.), *From Peasant to Entrepreneur: Growth and Change in Rural China* (Wageningen, Netherlands: Centre for Agricultural Publishing and Documentation [Pudoc], 1992); Flemming Christiansen and Zhang Junzuo (eds), *Village Inc.: Chinese Rural Society in the 1990s* (Richmond, Surrey: Curzon, 1998); Peter Ho, Jacob Eyferth and Eduard B. Vermeer (eds), *Rural Development in Transitional China: The New Agriculture* (London and Portland, OR: Frank Cass, 2004).

43 The following European institutions and countries have been represented in the four ECARDC volumes: Institute of Asian Affairs (Hamburg, Germany), Institute of Social Studies (The Hague, Netherlands), INRA (Paris, France), Catholic University Nijmegen (Netherlands), Free University of Berlin (Germany), Hohenheim University (Stuttgart, Germany), Queen's University of Belfast (Northern Ireland, U.K.), and the Universities of Aarhus and Copenhagen (Denmark), Bologna (Italy), Bremen, Göttingen, Munich, Osnabrück and Technische Universität Berlin (Germany), Leiden and Wageningen (Netherlands), Leeds, London [London School of Economics], Manchester and Oxford (U.K.), and Uppsala (Sweden)

44 E.g. see Wolfgang Taubmann, "The Finance System and the Development of Rural Towns," Örjan Sjöberg and Zhang Gang, "Soft Budget Constraints in Chinese Rural Enterprises," both in Christiansen and Zhang (eds), *Village Inc.*, op. cit., pp. 48–65 and 103–21); and Jacob Eyferth, Peter Ho, and E.B. Vermeer, "The Opening-up of the Chinese Countryside" and Maria Edin, "Local State Corporatism and Private Business," both in Eyferth, Ho, and Vermeer (eds), *Rural Development in Transitional China*, op. cit., pp. 1–17 and 278–95).

45 *CQ* was established in 1960 with financial support from the Congress for Cultural Freedom, and subsequently the Ford Foundation. By the end of 2006, it will have published 188 issues.

46 R.L. Edmonds, "The Growth of Contemporary China Studies and *The China Quarterly*," *Issues and Studies*, Vol. 38, No. 4 and Vol. 39, No. 1 (Dec. 2002/Mar. 2004), pp. 320–6.

47 However, these figures reflect only two issues (one each from 1969 and 2002), one of which was expressly devoted to China–Europe relations. On their representativeness, see Edmonds, p. 321, fn. 3.

48 Its French-language "sister journal" – *Perspectives Chinoises* – had already been in publication for three years. See Jean-Pierre Cabestan, "China Perspectives and Perspectives Chinoises," *Issues and Studies*, Vol. 38, no. 4 and Vol. 39, no. 1 (Dec. 2002/Mar. 2004), pp. 340–3. For a brief comment on another European journal – *China Information* – which has devoted some coverage to economic issues, but whose coverage tends to be more historical, see Tak-Wing Ngo, "Putting Information

on China in Perspective: *China Information," Issues and Studies*, Vol. 38, no. 4 and Vol. 39, no. 1 (Dec. 2002/Mar. 2004), pp. 337–9.

49 Centre d'études français sur la Chine contemporaine.

50 *China Perspectives*, Nos. 40 and 41 (March–April 2002 and May–June 2002).

51 For European scholars' comments on the economic dimensions of China's WTO accession, see esp. Antoine Kernen, "State Employees Face an Uncertain Future," and Andreas Oberheitmann, "Energy Production and Related Environmental Issues in China" *China Perspectives*, No. 40; Jean-François Huchet, "China's Economic Wages on the WTO: Realities, Myths and Unknown Factors," Eric Sautedé, "Telecommunications in China: Towards a Post-WTO Shock Therapy?" and Claude Aubert and Li Xiande, "Agricultural Underemployment and Rural Migration in China: Facts and Figures," *China Perspectives*, No. 41.

52 Another long-standing European journal of contemporary China – *China Aktuell* – has been published on a bi-monthly basis since 1972, and contains articles on current economic and other developments in China. These papers are overwhelmingly written in German by German scholars. A noteworthy feature of *China Aktuell* is its "Documentation" section and "Data Supplement." which contain factual economic information and statistics.

53 I have deliberately excluded from consideration commercially-orientated periodicals intended to provide companies with information that may assist them in their professional operations in China. No doubt periodicals of this kind exist these days in most, if not all, EU member states. One such example is the *China-Britain Business Review*, published in London by the China-Britain Trade Group, which carries "features on industry sectors and Chinese regions as well as news about the latest developments in the Chinese economy and legal issues relevant to British companies" (www.cbbc.org/the_review/).

54 Lucien Bianco, "French Studies of Contemporary China," *China Quarterly*, No. 142 (June 1995), pp. 508–20. As Bianco put it, "[Until the 1960s] most Sinologists [in France] either carried on the ... philological tradition or concentrated on philosophy, religion, classical literature and ancient history. Few were happy to see the sacred field encroached upon by modern historians, whose secular interests they deemed closer to those of reporters than of scholars. Furthermore the tiny bunch of 'barbarians' comprised mostly historians, not political scientists, economists or sociologists, and so they were interested in the century that preceded the Communist takeover (1840 to 1949), not in contemporary China as such" (p. 508).

55 Pigeonholing scholars is of course hazardous, and historians – even some political scientists – will claim Bergère and Bianco as their own. By the same token, it is only fair to point out that although Domenach is regarded primarily as an historian and analyst of China's and Asia's politics and international relations, his work also has an economic dimension – most notably in his *Aux origines du Grand Bond en Avant, Le cas d'une province Chinoise 1956–1958* [*Origins of the Great Leap Forward: A Single Provincial Case Study, 1956–58*] (Paris: École des Hautes Études en Sciences Sociales, 1982). (*A propos* of European studies of Mao's second adventure – the Cultural Revolution – reference may usefully be made here to a very recent work by another French scholar: Michel Bonnin, *Génération perdue: Le mouvement d'envoi des jeunes instruits à la campagne en Chine, 1968–1980* (Paris: Éditions de l'École des Hautes Études en Sciences Sociales, 2005).) Another book, co-edited by Domenach and François Godement, which touches on economic issues in China and elsewhere in Asia, is *Communismes d'Asie: mort ou metamorphose* (Paris: Edition Complexe, 1994).

56 *The Golden Age of the Chinese Bourgeoisie, 1911–1937* (Cambridge: Cambridge University Press, 1989).

57 "The 'Other China': Shanghai from 1911 to 1949," Christopher Howe, *Shanghai: Revolution and Development in an Asian Metropolis* (Cambridge: Cambridge University Press, 1981), pp. 1–34.
58 *Histoire de Shanghai* (Paris: Libraire Arthème Fayard, 2002). An extended review of Bergère's book by Christopher Howe can be found in *CQ*, 184 (Dec. 2005), pp. 952–8.
59 Other published work by Bergère that relates to China's economic development includes *L'économie de la Chine populaire* (Paris-La Haye: Mouton, 1968), "The Chinese Bourgeoisie," D. Twitchett and J.K. Fairbank (eds), *The Cambridge Economic History of China, Vol. 12, Republican China* (Cambridge: Cambridge University Press, 1983), "Shanghai Capitalists and the Transition from Nationalist to Communist Regime (1948–1952)," Marta Dassù and Tony Saich (eds), *The Reform Decade in China* (London: Kegan Paul International, 1992), "La Chine après Deng Xiaoping: développement économique et accomplissement nationaliste," *Tiers-Monde*, No. 147 (July–Sept. 1996).
60 Originally published in 1967 by Editions Gallimard (Paris), an English translation (*Origins of the Chinese Revolution, 1915–1949*) appeared under the imprint of Stanford University Press in 1971.
61 *Peasants Without the Party: Grass-roots Movements in Twentieth-Century China* (Armonk, NY: M.E. Sharpe, 2001).
62 Including peasant resistance to tax and rent payments, the impact of food shortages, the role of *xiedou*, etc.
63 Aubert is an agronomist working at INRA in Paris.
64 "The Agricultural Crisis in China at the End of the 1980s," Delman, Østergaard and Christiansen (eds), *Remaking Peasant China*, op. cit., pp. 16–37.
65 "Problems of Agricultural Diversification: Some Aspects of Animal Husbandry and Grain Utilisation in China," Vermeer (ed.), *From Peasant to Entrepreneur*, op. cit., pp. 105–28; [with Lai Xiufang] "Grain and Meat in China: Agricultural Development in Two Counties in Henan and Jiangxi," Christiansen and Zhang (eds), *Village Inc.*, op. cit., pp. 123–58.
66 Former Director and now Senior Researcher, Centre National de la Recherche Scientifique (CNRS), and at the École des Hautes Études en Sciences Sociales (EHESS), both in Paris.
67 E.g. see his *Dazhai recupéré: la politique économique rurale au début des années 1970* (Paris: Publications Orientalistes de France, 1978).
68 E.g. see Stefan Feuchtwang, Athar Hussain, and T. Pairault (ed.), *Transforming China's Economy in the Eighties*, Vol. 1, *The Rural Sector, Welfare and Employment*; Vol. 2, *Management, Industry and Urban Economy* (London: Zed Books, 1988).
69 *Politique industrielle et industrialisation en Chine* (Paris: La Documentation Française, 1983).
70 "Développement et dynamiques provincials," Alexandre Fur, Pierre Gentelle, and T. Pairault (eds), *Economie et regions de la Chine* (Paris: Armand Colin, 1999).
71 "Initial training and economic development," *Chinese Perspectives*, No. 36 (July–August 2001), pp. 5–16. The same issue contains an article by Marianne Bastid-Bruguière on "Educational Diversity in China."
72 Senior Researcher at CNRS and former Research Director of the French Centre for Research on Contemporary China (CEFC), Hong Kong.
73 He has also published a more general account of China's post-1978 economic development: see his *La Chine vers l'économie de marché: la longue marche de l'après-Mao* (Paris: Nathan, 1993), and a detailed examination of the "Hundred Flowers Movement" and its implications for factory management in China (*Les Cents Fleurs à l'usine: Agitation ouvrière et crise du modèle soviétique en Chine: 1956–57* [Paris: Éditions de l'École des Hautes Études en Sciences Sociales, 1986]).

74   The following are representative of Gipoloux's work in this regard: "The Network of Port-cities in China and the formation of an Asiatic Mediterranean Sea," Bert Edström (ed.), *Interdependence in Asia Pacific* (Stockholm: University of Stockholm Press, 2001), pp. 27–51; "Hong Kong, Taiwan et Shanghai, plate-formes logistiques rivals du corridor maritime de l'Asie de l'est," *Perspectives chinoises*, No. 62 (Nov.–Dec. 2000), pp. 4–12; "Firm and Port-City Networks in East Asia: Can Chinese Coastal Cities Find Their Place in the Fabric of Intra-Asiatic Trade," in Susan Strange (ed.), *Globalisation and Capitalist Diversity: Experiences on the Asian Mainland* (Florence: The Robert Schumann Centre, European University Institute, 1997), pp. 213–27; *Regional Economic Strategies in East Asia* (Tokyo: Maison Franco-Japonaise, 1994); etc.

75   E.g. "China's Economic Development and the WTO Membership Issue," F. Snyder (ed.), *Regional and Global Regulation of International Trade* (Oxford: Hart Publishing, 2002), pp. 181–92; "Declining Trend and Uneven Spatial Distribution of FDI in China," Lau Chung-ming and Jianfa Shen (eds), *China Review 2000: The People's Republic of China in the New Millennium* (Hong Kong; Chinese University Press, 2001), pp. 285–305.

76   Huchet is based at Université Rennes II and has a research attachment at EHESS.

77   E.g. "The Hidden Aspect of Public Sector Reforms in China's State and Collective SMEs in Urban Areas," *China Perspectives*, No. 32 (Nov.–Dec. 2000), pp. 37–48; "Concentration and the Emergence of Corporate Groups in Chinese Industry," *China Perspectives*, No. 23 (May–June 1999), pp. 5–17; and "The 'Achilles Heel' of the Economic Reforms: Financing China's Companies," *China Perspectives*, No. 20 (Nov.–Dec. 1998).

78   Rocca is a Research Fellow at the Centre d'Etudes et de Recherches Internationales (CERI), Paris; he is also a Visiting Professor at the People's University, Beijing.

79   See "'Three at Once': The Multidimensional Scope of Labor Crisis in China," Rocca and Françoise Mengin (ed.), *Politics in China: Moving Frontiers* (New York and Basingstoke: Palgrave Macmillan, 2002), pp. 3–30. (Mengin herself is an outstanding French political scientist, much of whose work has focused on Taiwan and China in the context of Greater China.)

80   The most recent example is "The Revival of Family Capitalism: a Zhejiang Entrepreneur," *China Perspectives*, No. 58 (March–April 2005), pp. 22–31.

81   Kernen and Rocca are the co-authors of "The Social Responses to Unemployment and the 'New Urban Poor'," *China Perspectives*, No. 27 (Jan.–Feb. 2000), pp. 35–51.

82   E.g. "The Impact of China's WTO Accession on EU Trade" (co-written with Deniz Ünal-Kesenci), Holbig and Ash (eds), *China's Accession to the WTO*, op. cit., pp. 251–82.

83   Kraus was Professor Emeritus of East Asian Economic Studies at the Ruhr University, Bochum (Germany). Remarkably, his work embraced a wide range of topics and spanned several countries and regions (including Afghanistan, Japan, and the Pacific-Basin).

84   *Economic Development and Social Change in the People's Republic of China* (New York: Springer, 1982).

85   His *Private Unternehmerwirtschaft in der Volksrepublik China: Wiederbelebung zwischen Ideologie und Pragmatismus* was first published in 1989 under the imprint of IFA. In 1991 an English translation appeared under the title *Private Business in China: Revival Between Ideology and Pragmatism* (London: Hurst & Co.).

86   Klenner is Professor of Economics in the Departments of East Asian Studies, and of Economics and Business Administration at Ruhr-Universität Bochum. He was formerly Head of the China Department at the HWWA Institute for World Economics in Hamburg (HWWA-Institut für Wirtschaftsforschung) and Counsellor to the PRC Planning Commission for Economic Reform.

87   E.g. "China's Economic Growth and Transformation: Effects on the World Economy," Frank-Jürgen Richter (ed.), *The East Asian Development Model: Economic Growth, Institutional Failure and the Aftermath of the Crisis* (London: Macmillan, 2000).

88   Dr Schüller and Dr Holbig are both Senior Research Fellows at IFA.

89   E.g. "The Impact of China's WTO Accession on International Trade and Capital Flows," Holbig and Ash (eds), *China's Accession to the WTO*, op. cit., pp. 229–50. See also her "Cross-Strait Economic Interaction: The Role of the Business Community as a Driving Force for Bilateral Economic Relations," in Günter Schucher and Margot Schüller (eds), *Perspective on Cross-Strait Relations: View from Europe* (Hamburg: Institut für Asienkunde, 2005), pp. 89–112.

90   Holbig and I were co-editors of an ECAN conference volume *China's Accession to the WTO: National and International Perspectives*, op. cit.

91   "The Party and Private Entrepreneurs in the PRC," Kjeld-Erik Brødsgaard and Zheng Yongnian (eds), *Bringing the Party Back In: How China is Governed* (Singapore: Eastern Universities Press, 2004), pp. 239–68.

92   An article with a more overtly political thrust, but which also touches on economic questions is Holbig, "The Emergence of the Campaign to Open up the West: Ideological Formation, Central Decision Making and the Role of the Provinces," *China Quarterly*, No. 178 (June 2004), pp. 335–57.

93   "Regulatory Innovation by Leninist Means: Communist Party Supervision in China's Financial Industry," *China Quarterly*, No. 181 (March 2005), pp. 1–21.

94   Heilmann has a M.A. and Ph.D. in Political Science. He is Professor of Comparative Government and Political Economy of China at Trier University. See also Thomas Heberer, "Strategic Groups and State Capacity: The Case of Private Entrepreneurs," *China Perspectives*, No. 46 (March–April 2003), pp. 4–14.

95   Scharping is Professor of Modern China Studies at the University of Cologne.

96   E.g. (ed.), *Floating Population and Migration in China: The Impact of Economic Reforms* (Hamburg, 2000); (ed.) *The Evolution of Regional Birth-Planning Norms, 1954–97* (2 Vols.) (Armonk, NY: M.E. Sharpe, 2000).

97   *Birth Control in China, 1949–2000: Population Policy and Demographic Development* (London: RoutledgeCurzon, 2003).

98   Perhaps the first was Ping-ti Ho, *Studies on the Population of China, 1368–1953* (Cambridge, MA: Harvard University Press, 1959). There followed several long and detailed papers on post-1949 demographic change by John S. Aird, the first of which was *The Size, Composition, and Growth of Mainland China's Population* (Washington, D.C.: U.S. Bureau of the Census, 1961). Aird's high standard of analysis was maintained by his successor, Judith Banister (e.g. see *China's Changing Population* (Stanford, CA: Stanford University Press, 1987).

99   Taube is Professor of Economics for East Asian Economies and China, and Director of the East Asia Institute at Gerhard Mercator University Duisburg-Essen.

100 "Stability in Instability: China's TVEs and the Evolution of Property Rights," *Asien*, July 2002, pp. 59–66.

101 "Economic Relations Between the PRC and the States of Europe," *China Quarterly*, No. 169 (March 2002), pp. 78–107. See also Taube, "Transatlantic Economic Competition and Cooperation with China in the Post-WTO Era," available at the website of the German Council on Foreign Relations (DGAP), www.dap.org.

102 Plasschaert is an Emeritus Professor at the University of Leuven (Belgium), where he has taught courses on the economy of China.

103 "Bringing China into the Concert of Nations: An Analysis of its Accession to the WTO," *Journal of World Trade*, Vol. 32, No. 3 (June 1998).

104 "Economic Transition I: China – A Model for Gradualism?" (2003); and "China's Accession to the World Trade Organisation: Impact on Global Trade Balances" (1999).

105 Vermeer is Associate Professor of Modern Chinese History at Leiden University. He was a founder member of ECAN, co-edits *China Information*, and is an Honorary Lecturer at Beijing University.
106 E.g. see "Development of the Shareholding Cooperative System and Property Rights in China," E.B. Vermeer and Ingrid d'Hooghe (eds), *China's Legal Reforms and their Political Limits* (London: Curzon Press, 2002), pp. 123–56; "Shareholding Cooperatives: A Property Rights Analysis," Jean Oi and Andrew Walder, *Property Rights and Economic Reform in China* (Stanford, CA: Stanford University Press, 1999), pp. 123–44. Also "Zhongguo xinxingde nongcun zuzhi" [New Forms of Rural Organization], Zhang Minjie (ed.), *Xifang zhuanjia wei Zhongguo jingji zenduan* [Western Experts' Diagnoses of China's Economy] (Changchun: Changchun chubanshe, 1999), pp. 140–52.
107 "Industrial Pollution in China and Remedial Policies," *China Quarterly*, No. 156 (Dec. 1998), pp. 952–84.
108 Ho is Professor of International Development Studies and concurrent Director of the Centre for Development Studies at the University of Groningen.
109 *Institutions in Transition: Land Ownership, Property Rights and Social Conflict in China* (Oxford: Oxford University Press, 2005).
110 (Ed.) *Developmental Dilemmas: Land Reform and Institutional Change* (London: Routledge, 2005). On a narrower, but allied topic, see also Ho, "The Clash Over State and Collective Property: The Making of the Grassland Law," *China Quarterly*, No. 161 (March 2000), pp. 348–95.
111 A glance at Ho's bibliography attests to his use of an extraordinarily rich array of Chinese-language materials – this in addition to information derived from personal fieldwork.
112 Brødsgaard, "Contemporary China Studies in Scandinavia," *China Quarterly*, No. 147 (Sept. 1996), pp. 938–61. Much of the content of this section is based on Brødsgaard's article.
113 I am not, however, aware of any major publication on the contemporary Chinese economy by Norwegian scholars. I apologize if I have overlooked any such work.
114 Brødsgaard is Director of the Asia Research Centre at the Copenhagen Business School.
115 *Readjustment and Reform in the Chinese Economy, 1953–1986* (Copenhagen: University of Copenhagen, 1989).
116 E.g. (ed. with Zheng Yongnian), *The Chinese Communist Party in Reform* (London: Routledge, 2005); (co-ed.) *Bringing the Party Back In*, op. cit.; (ed. with Zheng Yongnian), *The Chinese Communist Party in Reform* (London: Routledge, 2006); "Institutional Reform and the *Bianzhi* System in China," *China Quarterly*, No. 170 (June 2002), pp. 361–86.
117 See "Central-Regional Relations in Mainland China: The Case of Hainan," in Robert Ash, R.L. Edmonds, and Wu An-chia (eds), *Perspectives on Contemporary China in Transition* (Taipei: Institute of International Relations, 1998), pp. 26–57. Also "Regional Disparities in China," in Draguhn and Ash (eds), *China's Economic Security*, op. cit., pp. 1–18.
118 Formerly at the University of Aarhus, Christiansen now works in the Department of East Asian Studies, University of Leeds (U.K.).
119 Delman is Director of the Nordic Institute of Asian Studies (NIAS).
120 E.g. Christiansen, Østergaard, and Delman (eds), *Remaking Peasant China*, op. cit.
121 E.g. *Secondary Education in China after Mao* (Aarhus: Aarhus University Press, 1990).
122 *Management in China during and after Mao in Enterprises, Government and Party* (Berlin: Walter de Gruyter, 1988).

123 George Totten and Zhou Shulian (eds), *China's Economic Reform: Administering the Introduction of the Market Mechanism* (Boulder, CO: Westview Press and CPAS, 1992).

124 E.g. "A New Technological Landscape in China," *China Perspectives*, No. 42 (July–Aug. 2002), pp. 37–53.

125 The most important Spanish center of Chinese studies is the Centro de Estudios de Asia Oriental, [Centre for East Asian Studies] at Universidad Autónoma de Madrid. Research on contemporary China also takes place at the University of Barcelona.

126 The first ever master's program in Chinese Studies was inaugurated at the University of Aveiro in Nov. 1998. Two years later, a second program was instituted. The Aveiro program has two tracks, one of which focuses on business and international relations (including China's foreign relations, economic development, Chinese business, and domestic politics and government). All the courses are taught in English.

127 Fernández-Stembridge is Professor of the Chinese Economy, Centre for East Asian Studies, Universidad Autónoma de Madrid. She is currently based in Beijing, where she is a Project Manager on an EU-China trade project.

128 E.g. "Stabilising Potential Instability: Re-employment in Today's China," Fisac and Fernández-Stembridge (eds), *China Today*, op. cit., pp. 55–76.

129 See above, p. 6.

130 See www.lang.ltsn.ac.uk/resources/goodpractice.aspx?resourceid=131 (accessed 28 Jan. 2006).

131 Moreover, as the report observed, "[t]he works cited were diverse, ranging from studies in Chinese language and culture to reports on engineering projects …," ibid.

132 Thus, "[a]ccording to the database of the IIAS in Leiden, the UK currently has 88 listed specialists working in the China field in some branch of social studies, history or business studies. This compares with 174 in the Netherlands; 173 in Germany; 138 in France; and, remarkably given their lack of a historic connection, 42 in Spain". However, these data are not comprehensive and therefore unreliable for purposes of accurate comparisons.

133 Postgraduate masters courses on China are offered at the Universities of Cambridge, Durham, Edinburgh (with Glasgow and Aberdeen), Leeds, LSE, Oxford, SOAS, Sheffield, Sussex and Westminster. New programmes are being introduced at the Universities of Bristol, Manchester, and Nottingham.

134 For a brief portrait of Kenneth Walker – the person and academic – see Robert Ash, "Introduction," in Robert Ash (collected and ed.), *Agricultural Development in China, 1949–1989: The Collected Papers of Kenneth R. Walker (1931–1989)* (Oxford: Oxford University Press, 1998), pp. 1–8.

135 Ibid.

136 See "Collectivisation in Retrospect: The 'Socialist High Tide' of Autumn 1955–Spring 1956," originally published in *China Quarterly*, No. 26 (April–June 1966), pp. 1–43.

137 *Planning in Chinese Agriculture: Socialisation and the Private Sector, 1956–1962* (London: Frank Cass, 1965).

138 "Chinese Agriculture During the Period of the Readjustment," *China Quarterly*, No. 100 (Dec. 1984), pp. 783–812.

139 See esp. *Food Grain Procurement and Consumption in China* (Oxford: Oxford University Press, 1984).

140 (Ed. Ash), "Food and Mortality in China During the Great Leap Forward, 1958–1961," Ash (ed.), *Agricultural Development in China*, op. cit., pp. 106–47.

141 "Forty Years On: Provincial Contrasts in China's Rural Economic Development," *China Quarterly*, No. 116 (Dec. 1988), pp. 592–633.

142 Christopher Howe's entire academic career was spent at SOAS, where, on his retirement, he was Professor of Chinese Business Management. Formerly, he was

Head of the Contemporary China Institute (SOAS) and Professor of Economics with Reference to Asia, University of London.

143 *Employment and Economic Growth in Urban China, 1949–1957* (Cambridge: Cambridge University Press, 1970); *Wage Patterns and Wage Policy in Modern China, 1919–1972* (Cambridge: Cambridge University Press, 1973); "Labor Organization and Incentives in Industry, Before and After the Cultural Revolution," Stuart Schram (ed.), *Authority, Participation and Cultural Change in China* (Cambridge: Cambridge University Press 1973), pp. 223–56.

144 E.g. *Jihua Jingji, Jingji Yanjiu, Xinhua Yuebao.*

145 E.g. see "China's International Trade: Policy and Organisational Change and Their Place in the 'Economic Readjustment'" (with Y.Y. Kueh), *China Quarterly*, No. 100 (Dec. 1984), pp. 813–48; "Direct Investment and Economic Integration in the Asia-Pacific: The Case of Taiwanese Investment in Xiamen" (with Qi Luo), David Shambaugh (ed.), *Greater China: The Next Superpower?* (Oxford: Oxford University Press, 1995), pp. 94–117; "China, Japan and Economic Interdependence in the Asia-Pacific Region," Christopher Howe (ed.), *China and Japan: History, Trends, and Prospects* (Oxford: Oxford University Press, 1996), pp. 98–126.

146 There are exceptions. An outstanding one, which falls outside the scope of this Eurocentric chapter is Carl Riskin, *China's Political Economy: The Quest for Development since 1949* (Oxford: Oxford University Press, 1987), which, however, extends only into the early post-1978 reform era.

147 *China's Economy: A Basic Guide* (London: Paul Elek, 1978).

148 (With Kenneth R. Walker), *The Foundations of the Chinese Planned Economy: A Documentary Survey* (Basingstoke: Macmillan, 1989); (with Y.Y. Kueh and Robert Ash), *China's Economic Reform: A Study with Documents* (London: Routledge Curzon, 2003).

149 Lucian Pye in *Foreign Affairs* (Sept.–Oct. 2003).

150 Ash is Professor of Economics with reference to China and Taiwan at SOAS. He was Director of the Contemporary China Institute (SOAS) between 1986 and 1995, and of the Europe-China Academic Network (ECAN), 1997–2001. He is also Director of the Taiwan Studies Program at SOAS.

151 E.g. "Agricultural Policy Under the Impact of Reform," in Y. Kueh and R. Ash (eds), *Economic Trends in Chinese Agriculture: The Impact of Reform* (Oxford: Clarendon Press, 1993), pp. 11–45; "China's Agricultural Reforms: A Twenty Year Retrospective," in Chien-min Chao and Bruce J. Dickson (eds), *Remaking the Chinese State: Strategies, Society and Security* (London and New York: Routledge, 2001), pp. 76–100.

152 "The Cultural Revolution as an Economic Phenomenon," in David Goodman and Sebastian Heilmann (eds), *Was the Chinese Revolution Necessary? Interpreting Fifty Years of the People's Republic of China* (London: Routledge Curzon, 2002), pp. 124–58; "Does the Chinese Economy Matter?" in Kjeld-Erik Brødsgaard and Bertel Heurlin (eds), *China's Place in Global Geopolitics: International, Regional and Domestic Challenges* (London: RoutledgeCurzon, 2002), pp. 32–59; "China's Regional Economies and the Asian Region: Building Interdependent Linkages," in David Shambaugh (ed.), *Power Shift: China and Asia's New Dynamics* (Berkeley, CA: University of California Press, 2006), pp. 96–131.

153 Nolan is the Sinyi Professor of Chinese Management at the Judge Business School, University of Cambridge, and Fellow of Jesus College, Cambridge. He is the Founder and Chairman of the China Big Business Programme at the Judge Business School.

154 At the Judge Business School website, Nolan's research interests are listed as follows: big business; globalization; developing countries; poverty and migration; economic development; the transition of former planned economies; comparative development in China and India; Chinese agriculture; system change in China and the former USSR; poverty, famine, inequality and migration; restructuring large global firms in the epoch of the global business revolution; the transformation of large Chinese firms

since the 1980s; the evolution of China's system of political economy; the interaction between Chinese and global firms in the epoch of the global business revolution.

155 A good early example is his *The Political Economy of Collective Farms: An Analysis of Post-Mao Rural Reforms* (Cambridge: Polity Press, 1988). See also the collection of essays: *State and Market in the Chinese Economy: Essays on Controversial Issues* (Basingstoke: Macmillan, 1993).

156 To date, the culmination of this work is Nolan's massive study, *China and the Global Business Revolution* (Basingstoke: Palgrave, 2001). See also the accompanying summary volume *China and the Global Economy: National Champions, Industrial Policy and the Big Business Revolution* (Basingstoke: Palgrave, 2001). Also relevant are *Coca-Cola and the Global Business Revolution: A Study with Special Reference to the EU* (Cambridge: Judge Institute of Management, 1999); and *Indigenous Large Firms in China's Economic Reform: The Case of Shougang Iron and Steel Corporation* (London: SOAS, Contemporary China Institute, 1998). See also a collection of essays, *Transforming China: Globalisation, Transition and Development* (London; Anthem Press, 2004).

157 *China's Rise, Russia's Fall: Politics and Economics in the Transition from Stalinism* (Basingstoke: Macmillan, 1995). Nolan's comparative interests were apparent early in his career, his first publication, co-authored with T.J. Byres, being *Inequality: India and China Compared, 1950–1970* (Milton Keynes: Open University Press, 1976). Distributional issues were also central to his first publication devoted solely to China: *Growth Processes and Distributional Change in a South Chinese Province: The Case of Guangdong* (London: SOAS, Contemporary China Institute, 1983).

158 Sun is Professor of Chinese Business and Management at SOAS. He concurrently holds visiting posts at the International Institute for Applied System Analysis (IIASA) in Austria, as well as in the Chinese Academy of Sciences and at Beijing University.

159 Lo is a Senior Lecturer in the Department of Economics at SOAS. Since April 2005, he has divided his time between London and Beijing, where he is Director of the Centre of Research in Comparative Political Economy at Renmin University of China.

160 E.g. "Globalisation and Comparative Political Economy: Of Efficiency, Efficient Institutions and Late Development" [in Chinese], *Zhengzhi jingjixue pinglun* (Review of Political Economy), No. 7 (2004), pp. 55–72.

161 E.g. see *Market and Institutional Regulation in Chinese Industrialisation, 1978–1994* (Basingstoke: Macmillan, 1997).

162 See *Riding the Tiger: The Politics of Economic Reform in Post-Mao China* (Basingstoke: Macmillan, 1993); and (with Jude Howell and Shang Xiaoyuan) *In Search of Civil Society: Market Reforms and Social Change in Contemporary China* (Oxford: Oxford University Press, 1995).

163 Bramall is a Senior Lecturer in the School of East Asian Studies, University of Sheffield.

164 *Living Standards in Sichuan, 1931–1978* (London: SOAS, Contemporary China Institute, 1989).

165 *In Praise of Maoist Economic Planning* (Oxford: Oxford University Press, 1993).

166 *Sources of Chinese Economic Growth*, 1978–1996 (Oxford: Oxford University Press, 2000).

167 Murphy is a Senior Lecturer in the newly-established Centre of East Asian Studies at the University of Bristol.

168 *How Migrant Labour is Changing Rural China* (Cambridge: Cambridge University Press, 2002).

169 The title of the article was "Turning Peasants into Modern Chinese Citizens: Population Quality Discourse, Demographic Transition and Primary Education," *China Quarterly*, op. cit.

170 www.lang.ltsn.ac.uk/resources/goodpractice.aspx?resourceid=131, op. cit.

3 Studies of China's Economy in Japan

Hideo Ohashi

Located in the center of the traditional world order, throughout its imperial history China had an enormous impact on neighboring countries. Japan itself has been influenced by the Middle Kingdom since earliest times. In particular, during Japan's modern history, the perceived importance of its policy towards China divided Japanese public opinion. China's changing status had obvious implications for Japan. From the mid-nineteenth to the mid-twentieth century, China was semi-colonized by imperialist forces and faced almost continuous dislocation from internal and external uprisings and wars. Starting in 1949, the People's Republic of China embarked on a three-decade experiment of socialist industrialization, which did not, however, generate unambiguous economic success.

At the end of the 1970s, China's development strategy shifted from autarkic Maoist self-reliance to policies of reform and opening up, and in the early 1990s the economy entered a phase of high growth. The economic rise of China has attracted international attention, not least because it represents the highest and most sustained economic growth by one of the biggest economies on the globe. Throughout this period Japan has maintained close economic relations with China, which is likely to become Japan's largest trade partner in the near future.[1] The Japanese economy, making full use of the opportunities offered by China's economic growth, is in the process of recovery from prolonged recession in the 1990s, and is therefore very sensitive to China's economic fluctuations. Sino-Japanese economic integration means that Japanese studies of the Chinese economy fall within the orbit of domestic, as well as foreign studies: in other words, such studies have become part of the study of Japanese economy because of the latter's expansion to China. This we might call the "internalization of foreign study."

The purpose of this chapter is to review recent studies of China's economy in Japan.[2] The first part is an overview of publications on China's economy in Japan. In the second section, I highlight current trends in the study of China's economy in Japan and review several important studies published in Japan – most of them in the past decade. The final section examines the study of China's economy in the context of economic fusion between Japan and China.

General Views of the Japanese Publications on China's Economy

Books on China's Economy

As Japanese interest in China's economy has grown, Japanese publications on it have rapidly increased. My search under "China's economy" on the Amazon. co.jp website revealed 1,801 titles, as of August 31, 2005.[3] This highlights the many books on the Chinese economy that are currently in print in Japan,[4] although book-length academic studies on the subject are still fairly limited in number.

Most of the books in print fall into one of the following categories:

1 Introductory books for general readers who have little experience or knowledge of China. Often containing many illustrations, most of these are written in a popular style. There even exist comic-strip versions of Chinese classics and famous novels, which are very popular among young readers in Japan.

2 Practical guides to doing business in China. Some of these are guides to personal investment in China's stock, currency, and real estate markets; others are corporate business guides, which explain trade, direct investment and joint venture procedures, and China's taxation system.

3 Lectures on business management. Business people in Japan show great interest in accounts of personal experiences in setting up subsidiaries and manufacturing plants in China. Some Chinese classics are also very popular among Japanese business people, who hope to gain valuable insights for their business operations from reading *Sunzi* or the *Saga of Three Kingdoms*.

4 Reports and reportage by journalists and non-fiction writers. Recent distinguished analysis in this category has highlighted the importance of a number of issues in China. Yoshikazu Shimizu has reported on the serious discrimination against Chinese peasants;[5] Hideya Yamamoto has also drawn attention to various serious challenges facing China, including the rural situation and problems of AIDS, the environment, and the judiciary.[6] These books, usually well-documented and often supplemented with in-depth interviews, shed timely light on critical issues in China. However, they suffer from a lack of systematization and analytical rigor.

5 Essays condemning China. Reflecting deteriorating bilateral relations between Japan and China, sensational essays seeking to criticize China are also increasing in number. They tend to exaggerate structural weaknesses in China, provoke ill-feeling against China, and voice disapproval of the Japanese government's policies toward China. In particular, inefficiency in offering official development assistance (ODA) to China has frequently been a target for criticism. Most of these books do not deserve serious comment, but they do command a significant audience within Japan.

In addition to these books, there exist Japanese translations of Chinese and English publications on China's economy written by leading economists and specialists in China and the United States. These are also highly rated in Japan.

If books falling in the above mentioned categories were excluded, academic books and other systematically-written factual books on China's economy would not exceed 100 titles – that is, less than five percent of the 1801 titles searched.

Articles and Papers on China's Economy

The scale of the literature is so vast that it is almost impossible to review in their entirety articles in general magazines, as well as papers in academic journals, that relate to China's economy.[7] According to the MAGAZINEPLUS – Japan's largest database of periodical indexes of the National Diet Library, containing 6.7 million articles and papers published in Japan since 1975 – there 5,040 articles and papers on the Chinese economy which appeared between 1980 and the first half of 2005.[8]

Figure 3.1 shows the annual number of articles and papers on China's economy published in Japan. These have increased rapidly in recent years. The time-series graph also reflects the rise of China in the world economy and the deepening economic relationship between Japan and China. Interestingly, the profile shown in Figure 3.1 mirrors that of graphs showing the bilateral trade volume between China and Japan,, and the number of Japanese residents in China.

Fluctuations in the number of articles and papers reflected changes in economic conditions in China. When China's economy was booming, they increased in number. In the mid-1980s, China experienced an unprecedented consumption

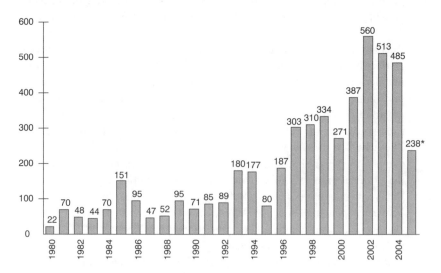

Figure 3.1 Number of Articles and Papers on 'China's Economy' in Japan (1980–2005*)
  * From January to June 2005 (Source: The MAGAZINEPLUS database, accessed on August 31, 2005)

boom, during which Japan exported a great many consumer durables to China. In the 1990s, after Deng Xiaoping's southern tour, China's economic growth accelerated still further, leading Japanese and international organizations to predict that China would become the world's largest economy in the coming century. In the late 1990s, Japanese big business increasingly transferred their production bases to China, and small and medium-sized enterprises (SMEs) followed suit. Hong Kong's handover and the Asian financial crisis also stimulated Japanese interests in China. More recently still, China's accession to the World Trade Organization (WTO) triggered a flood of Japanese investment in China. At the end of the twentieth century, the perception of China as an economic threat prevailed in Japan. At the beginning of the twenty-first century, it dispersed like mist as China's economic growth contributed to Japanese economic recovery and the Japanese began to regard China as an opportunity. In short, during the last two decades an increasing number of articles have put forward contrasting views on China. Some have sought to alert Japan to prepare to meet the economic threat of China; others have advocated seizing the opportunities afforded by China's economic growth.

Contributors to academic journals are less influenced by the current fashion, and more likely to give priority to their personal academic interests. In general, however, the number of academic publications has increased, partly because the number of contributors has also been rising rapidly. As China's economic growth has accelerated – and with it, China's influence in the global economy – so in addition to China specialists, general economists who are not China specialists, have taken an increasing interest in China and started to contribute papers on China's economy to academic journals.

This chapter does attempt a comprehensive review of Japanese studies of China's economy.[9] It focuses mainly on academic books, and a number of more general books that have influenced Japanese perceptions of the Chinese economy. Important academic studies, including doctoral dissertations, are usually published in book form in Japan. Moreover, in the academic community of Japanese social sciences, the publication of such studies in book form is more favorably regarded than contributing papers to leading international journals. Needless to say, since the papers are highly specialized, their potential readership is limited – and there is therefore little opportunity to publish these commercially. Authors cannot avoid seeking subsidies from funding organizations to enable them to publish their papers in book form, or to rewrite them in such a way as to make them acceptable to a more general readership.

Changes in the Study of China's Economy

From Ideology to Empiricism

Until the end of the 1970s, Japanese studies of the Chinese economy were part of on-going ideological debates. However, during the 1980s, ideological arguments gradually gave way to more empirically-based studies. More recently still, the study of China's economy has been totally "liberated" from Marxist and Maoist legacies. Marxist and Maoist – anti-Maoist too – scholars have played dominant roles in the study of the Chinese economy in Japan. Most of them belonged to the Marxian school of economics, and some of them acted in accordance with Marxist and Maoist (anti-Maoist) principles. Since the civil war between the Chinese Communist Part (CCP) and the Kuomintang (KMT), the CCP and the Japanese Communist Party (JCP) have maintained sometimes friendly, sometimes hostile, mutual relations. Scholars close to the JCP took a friendly attitude towards China until the Cultural Revolution. However, after the split between the two parties, they published a series of essays that were critical of China. The JCP finally restored relations with the CCP in 1998. But because of its members' repeated apostasy, Japanese readers have taken little notice of their publications.

In addition to Marxist and Maoist (and anti-Maoist) scholars, a considerable number of "progressive" intellectuals expressed pro-Marxist, pro-Maoist and anti-American sentiments. They were fundamentally critical of Japan's modernization after the Meiji Restoration and felt strong sympathy with the Maoist development model. But as China shifted its development strategy from one of Maoist self-reliance to reform and opening-up in the late 1970s, their ideal Maoist model became far removed from the reality of China. As a result, their readership gradually contracted.

Marxism's pre-war opposition to Japanese ultra-nationalism and imperialism gave it strong legitimacy and wide acceptance in Japan after the war. Marxism had a major impact on social sciences, and the Marxist theorem dominated Japanese economics. In the mid-1970s an OECD survey on social science policies in Japan made the following points.[10] First, as of the mid-1970s, more than 70 percent of social scientists could be considered Marxist, and they held a dominant position in economics as well as the other social sciences in Japan. Second, the main results and thinking of social science research were little used by policy-makers: the memory of widespread intervention by the pre-war government in academic life made social scientists extraordinarily cautious about becoming involved in policy processes and led them distance themselves from the government. Third, economics was divided into two schools: the Marxist camp and the school of modern economics (the latter chiefly imported from the United States in the post-war period), between whom there was unfortunately, little sound dialogue.

Three decades after publication of the OECD report, Marxian economics remains influential in economic studies in Japan, despite considerable changes affecting the social sciences (including the study of the Chinese economy). After the communist bloc collapsed in the early 1990s, the popularity of Marxian economics also declined in Japan. Furthermore, following the apparent volte-face in China's development strategy and economic policies, the release of much new information (including economic statistics) enabled foreigners to obtain a much better understanding of China's reality. As a result, most of Japanese Marxist economists have learned to conduct empirical studies of China's economy, although they continue to display different perspectives from those of the modern economists.

During the period of ideological debates on China, Shigeru Ishikawa charted his own course and undertook important empirical work. His book (1990), which exemplified the level of Japan's scholarship in development studies, clarified the customary economy of China and other Asian countries and showed how it differed from the market economy assumed by neo-classical economists.[11] His endorsement of the market economy was manifested in the form of Japanese intellectual support for market-oriented economic reform in Vietnam.[12] Indeed, there is a sense in which China's experience of economic reform was transplanted to Vietnam by way of Japanese scholars.

Value-free academic studies have been repeatedly criticized in Japan because of their alleged lack of a sense of realism and failure to understand social demands. It is often argued that social scientists should concentrate on analyzing current affairs, but even a historical event can have far-reaching implications for current economic life. For example, notwithstanding its historical focus, Wu Xiaolin's investigation of "Third Front" Construction under Mao Zedong sought to shed new light on the Third Front Strategy through its use of newly released materials in China. Through his study of the Third Front, Wu Xiaolin cannot fail to be conscious of current economic disparities between coastal and interior regions, and the rationale of the development strategy in the west of China.[13] Perhaps unlike their academic colleagues in history, social scientists should consider the implications of past events for the present day.

A New Generation of Scholars

Empirical studies have mostly been conducted by a new generation of scholars. The release by the Chinese authorities of so many economic statistics has lowered the technical barriers that previously prevented non-China specialists from participating in the study of China's economy. With their entry into the field, China studies have expanded to include more scholars. The new participants comprise the following groups.

First, Japanese students with expertise in economics are increasingly engaging in the study of China's economy. In the past, China studies mainly involved scholars who had majored in Chinese, history, geography, and agriculture – or, during the post-war period, journalists. Even today, China specialists tend to be drawn from an area studies background, although most of them have also received academic training in a social science (e.g. political science, sociology and international relations). Students majoring in economics who wish to undertake Chinese economic studies face a considerable challenge. They need to acquire expertise in basic theoretical and applied economics, in addition to which they must also study the language, culture, and history of China if they are to understand properly its economy (to which Western economic theories cannot easily be applied). Despite this intellectual burden, as China's status in the world economy has risen, many students majoring in economics have involved themselves in studying China's economy.

Second, a number of leading economists, who have little experience of studying China and have never been regarded as China specialists, have become actively interested in the Chinese economy. In the pre-reform period, such scholars were hesitant of becoming involved in Chinese economic studies because of the strong ideological complexion of debates on China. Once this ideologically-driven period had ended, they adopted a more proactive stance in such studies. China's economic growth was one source of fascination. In addition, China itself was eager to learn from Japan's post-war economic development. At first, government economists of the then Economic Planning Agency (EPA), Ministry of International Trade and Industry (MITI), and Ministry of Finance (MOF) visited China and informed their Chinese counterparts of Japan's post-war development experience. In particular, some elderly economists, who had spent some of their early years in China and felt a sense of shame for Japanese wartime activities, offered their intellectual assistance to China. A Japan–China study group, headed by Saburo Okita and Ma Hong, was set up to facilitate intellectual exchanges between the two countries. Economists at major universities in Japan also established academic exchanges with Chinese scholars at universities and institutes under the Chinese Academy of Social Sciences (CASS).

Out of such bilateral academic exchanges, Ryutaro Komiya and Ryoshin Minami – two noted and distinguished Japanese economists – published epoch-making books.[14] Following extended stays in China in the 1980s, they undertook comparative studies of Japanese and Chinese economic development. Ironically, the work of these non-China specialists became the first Japanese standard textbooks on the Chinese economy. Toshio Watanabe – another non-China specialist who had specialized in the economic development of the newly industrializing economies (NIEs) and the Association of Southeast Asian Nations (ASEAN) – also conducted pioneering work on China.[15] One outcome of the shifts in their research foci is that a number of the students of these leading economists have also become engaged in the study of China's economy.

New academic associations, such as the Japan Association for Chinese Business Management and the Japan Research Association for China's Economy, were established in 2000 and 2002. The leading academic associations involved in the study of the Chinese economy have been the Japan Association for Modern China Studies and the Japan Association for Asian Studies, established in 1951 and 1953. However, these bodies include China specialists in political science, international relations, sociology, and anthropology. By contrast, the newly established academic associations focusing exclusively on China's economy comprise economists, as well as non-China specialists who are interested in China from comparative viewpoints.

Third, *Chinese* students and scholars now take a leading part in Chinese economic studies in Japan. An increasing number of Chinese students choose Japan as their most favored destination for overseas study. In 2003, the number of foreign students in Japan reached 100,000 for the first time – a target set by the Nakasone administration in the 1980s. Among these, Chinese formed the largest group – by 2004 numbering 77,713 students, or 66 percent of 117,302 foreign students.[16] The participation of Chinese students and scholars who are closely acquainted with Chinese affairs and have expertise in economics (including the Japanese economy) has enriched the study of Chinese affairs in Japan. Chinese students form the largest group at top graduate schools of economics and presented papers at principal academic associations in Japan. They have also found jobs at universities and major research institutes (think tanks) in Japan, and in 2003 leading Chinese scholars founded the Society of Chinese Professors in Japan (SCPJ)[17] – an organization comprising scientists and engineers as well as social scientists that promotes interdisciplinary study groups to examine Japan–China bilateral cooperation in such areas as transportation and environment.

Government and Business Interests in China

As the Japanese government and business sector have taken an increasing interest in China's economy, economists within these communities have emerged as China specialists. In addition to the work of individual scholars, government and business now also promote research on the Chinese economy. Japanese government agencies have long reported the main economic indicators of the United States and European countries in their publications for the general public. Nowadays, they also carry the same indicators for China and the NIEs. China, as well as the United States and European countries, is included in the economic outlook and forecasts made by the Japanese government, financial institutions, and research institutes.

Shortly after the normalization of diplomatic relations between Japan and China, Japanese government agencies and related organizations, including the Ministry of Foreign Affairs, the Japan External Trade Organization (JETRO), the Japan–China Economic Association, and the Japan Association for the Promotion of International Trade took the lead in the study of the Chinese economy. Following the Japanese government's decision to offer ODA to China in 1980 and the subsequent emergence of Japan as top donor country to China, other government agencies participated in the study of China's economy on a large scale. The Overseas Economic Cooperation Fund (OECF) in charge of yen loans, the Japan International Cooperation Agency (JICA) offering technical asistance, and the Export–Import Bank of Japan (JEXIM) supplying trade credit and loans have engaged extensively in economic and industrial information-gathering through feasibility studies for their projects in China. In 1999 OECF and JEXIM were merged to form the Japan Bank for International Cooperation (JBIC), after which research was conducted by the JBIC Institute (JBICI), which succeeded the Research Institute for International Investment and Development (RIIID) of JEXIM and the Research Institute for Development Assistance (RIDA) of OECF. JBICI publishes a research review and research papers. The former has its origins in RIIID's research review and focuses on industry and business, including Japanese foreign direct investment (FDI), research and development (R&D), and financial and capital markets in China.[18] The latter, similarly descended from RIDA, addresses issues related to infrastructure, energy, and environment in

China.[19] Japan was the biggest donor country in the world from the mid-1980s to the late 1990s, and China is still one of the largest recipient countries of Japanese ODA. Japanese government agencies that oversee ODA have also used their ample research resources to engage intensively in the study of the Chinese economy.

China's attainment of sustained high economic growth rates in the 1990s had a significant impact on the Japanese economy. Japanese economic agencies – for example, the Ministry of Finance (MOF), the Cabinet Office (former EPA), the Ministry of Economy, Trade and Industry (METI or former MITI), and the Bank of Japan (BOJ) – began to hold regular dialogues for policy coordination with their Chinese counterparts, and embarked on wide-ranging studies of China's economy. These agencies have their own research institutes: the Policy Research Institute (PRI) for the MOF, the Economic and Social Research Institute (ESRI) for the Cabinet Office, the Research Institute of Economy, Trade and Industry (RIETI) for the METI, and the Institute for Monetary and Economic Studies (IMES) for the BOJ. These bodies regularly publish their own periodicals, which include work on China's economy, and organize research projects on China, with contributors and research fellows drawn from among government and private sector economists, university scholars, and experts in specific research fields.[20]

Government economic agencies have their own officials in the Japanese Embassy and consular offices, and JETRO offices in China and Hong Kong, where they gather basic information and consult with their Chinese counterparts. These agencies have representatives stationed in international financial centers, such as New York and London; with China's growing prominence in the world economy, representation has been extended to China. Their representative officials, having worked in China for some years, become China specialists in their agencies. Atsuo Kuroda (Hong Kong) investigated industrial agglomeration in advanced areas in China – the Pearl River Delta, the Yangzi River Delta, and Bohai (Beijing-Tianjin) Region.[21] From nationwide research trips, Toshiya Tsugami analyzed private entrepreneurial initiative in China.[22] Through their monitoring work in Beijing, Yasushi Onishi and Osamu Tanaka examined economic policy-making processes in China.[23] Through involvement in the Asian financial crisis in Hong Kong in the late 1990s, Yoshihisa Onishi considered the currency exchange adjustment, convertibility of *Renminbi*, the liberalization of capital flows, and financial reform in China.[24] As government officials, all of these are well acquainted with government activities, policy-making processes, and bureaucratic behavior. Because their publications are implicit comparative studies between Japan and China, their analysis is also accessible to general readers in Japan.

In the business community, major financial institutions, trading companies, manufacturing firms, big business groups and industrial associations also have their own research institutes – the Nomura Research Institute, the Mitsubishi Research Institute, the Mizuho Research Institute, the Japan Research Institute, the UFJ Research Institute, the Fujitsu Research Institute, etc. – which post timely research papers on their web sites. Alongside the U.S., the Chinese economy has become a major focus of their research activities. Most leading Japanese research institutes have Chinese economists in charge of China's economy.[25]

New Trends in the Study of China's Economy

Encouragement of China Studies

Economic information (especially economic statistics) newly released by the Chinese authorities have enabled Japanese economists with little previous experience of China to undertake fully-fledged research on China's economy. As a result, non-China specialists are now actively engaged in the study of the Chinese economy. Translating Chinese economic data and statistics into Japanese and presenting them in visual form to Japanese readers, the *China Information Handbook*, edited by Nijuichi Seiki Chugoku Soken, has contributed to the dissemination of Chinese economic information in Japan.[26]

Databases covering China's statistics have become very useful tools of economic analysis. Japan's major research institutes and research departments of big business mostly subscribe to the online database of the CEIC Data Company Ltd., a leading Hong Kong-based provider of macroeconomic, industrial, and financial time-series data, which aggregates data from 500 primary sources, including national statistical offices, central banks and financial exchanges in Asia. The online database facilitates current economic analysis on China by making available up-to-date information.

Although economic statistics have become plentiful, there are many pitfalls in their use which can undermine analysis of the Chinese economy. China's economic statistics have been based on different concepts from those of Western countries. As a member of most major international economic and financial organizations, China regularly submits estimates of the main economic indicators to them. In 2002 China joined the General Data Dissemination System (GDDS), established by the International Monetary Fund (IMF) in the late 1990s to help enhance the accuracy and reliability of economic statistics, promote standardization, and improve data accessibility. Even so, it is very difficult to understand the correct concepts of economic data, the coverage of data categories, the changes of categories over time, and the international comparability of economic data. The *Glossary of China's Economic Statistics and Law*, edited by Reiitsu Kojima, addresses these issues and has thereby helped reduce misuse of China's economic statistics.[27]

The rapid increase in research funds has also encouraged the study of China's economy in Japan. Throughout the 1990s the growing ODA budget promoted the study of developing economies. With government support, many universities established more graduate schools and undergraduate departments majoring in international relations, foreign aid, and development studies. Newly established graduate schools and departments at universities were also successful in attracting students majoring in international and development studies.

The government's policy goal to realize a nation built on intellectual property has also facilitated an increase in grants-in-aid scientific research. Most research funds have been allocated to science and engineering projects, although social scientists have also received a tiny part of expanded research funds. China studies do not require expensive laboratory equipment or costly experimental instruments, and many China specialists used government research funds to conduct field research in China. An important recent (1996–1999) large-scale research project on China, supported by grants-in-aid scientific research of the Ministry of Education, was entitled "Structural Change in Contemporary China." More than 80 China specialists participated in this project, the main research results of which were published in 2000–2001 in eight volumes of collected papers, covering economy, politics, history, society, environment, and international relations of contemporary China.[28]

New Approaches

Quantitative Analysis

Newly released economic statistics have enabled Japanese economists to use the standard tools of economic analysis in order to study the Chinese economy. The pioneer study edited by Hiroshi Onishi and Go Yano provides microeconomic analysis of enterprise reforms and macroeconomic analysis of economic management, focusing on finance, energy, environment, and regional disparities.[29] This study, based mainly on the work of non-China specialists was path-breaking in its use of econometric tools, such as the concept of production frontier, international input-output tables, and computable general equilibrium (CGE) models. Quantitative analysis has undoubtedly blazed a new trail in the study of China's economy, although many China specialists are skeptical about the use of Chinese economic statistics and show some discomfort in the face of the simplified logic and technical complexity of quantitative analyses.

Kenjiro Otsuka, Naoki Murakami, and Liu Deqiang have also pioneered the application of standard economic tools to the study of China's economy.[30] They recognize that while Chinese statistics show high economic growth, the spread of consumer durables, and the rise of private enterprises, it is still difficult to understand the complicated mechanism of economic growth in China. Focusing on steel, machine tools, and apparel industries, they seek to provide statistical verification of their hypotheses through production function analysis based on publicly available data and the result of their own questionnaire surveys conducted in Chinese enterprises and factories. Their findings suggest the following conclusions. In the steel industry, retained profits, the contract management responsibility system and the product mix have had positive effects on productivity. In machine tools industries, enterprises with high rates of purchasing parts and components from outside tend to be more efficient, which implies that they have benefited from specialization and scale advantages. In apparel industries, there are wide variations in resource allocation and productivity according to different ownership. State-owned enterprises (SOEs) tend to pay more wages above workers' production contributions, while township and village enterprises (TVEs) pursue more rational management thanks to the prevailing ethos of profit maximization. China specialists have endorsed procedures of hypothesis verification and accepted as persuasive the conclusions of these empirical case studies. From this perspective, such studies may be said to have introduced rigorous scientific methods to Japanese study of the Chinese economy.

New Economic Data

Empirical studies are wholly dependent on economic data and statistics. The study of labor migration in China has, for example, raised the level of analysis thanks to the publication of detailed data from population censuses. Newly released data have encouraged Japanese economists and non-China specialists to embark on the study of China's economy and thereby to estimate and compile new economic data series.

The input-output (I-O) table is a very useful tool for an economic analysis of China's industrial structure. China's National Bureau of Statistics published I-O tables for 1990, 1992, 1995, 1997 and 2000 on the system of national accounts (SNA) basis.[31] Considering the huge physical extent of China, its increasing regional disparities and unbalanced economic growth, and its regionally divided markets, it is necessary to compile I-O tables at different regional levels. Some provincial I-O tables have been already published by regional statistical offices,[32] but the national economy cannot be wholly covered since some provinces have never openly published such tables. The study edited by Shunichi Ichimura and Wang Hui-dong, which provides an inter-regional I-O table for 1997, therefore represents a path-breaking study of China's economy.[33] In Japan, the Institute of Developing Economies (IDE) has compiled Asian international I-O tables on the basis of international technical cooperation to assist Asian countries in compiling their I-O tables.[34] Based on this experience, IDE also published China's interregional I-O tables of 2000.[35] By using these tables, studies edited by Nobuhiro Okamoto have described inter-regional trade, characteristics of regional markets, differences in regional industrial structure, and flows of inputs and outputs of enterprises in specific regions in China.[36] A comparison of the interregional I-O tables for 1997 and 2000 makes it possible to understand how economic growth spilled over from coastal to interior regions and to appreciate the increasing dependence of interior regions on coastal industries. The interregional I-O table is a very useful analytical tool, but compiling it requires much time, and even the latest I-O tables cannot fully reflect China's current regional and industrial structure. The inevitable time lag of several years is probably the main reason why economists have avoided using such tables.

During the 1990s, China improved the statistical system by making it compatible with the SNA, and in 1998 the People's Bank of China published the flow of funds for 1992. Today, the Bank provides time series data of the flow of funds, which Tang Cheng has used to undertake an empirical research study of China's household behavior.[37] In this, he has clarified the factors that have contributed to Chinese households' extraordinarily high savings rate, highlighting structural changes in savings and shedding new light on the effects of high savings on excessive investments and economic overheating in China in the 1990s.

Securitization of state assets may be the most acceptable way of reforming the SOEs in China. Listing on the stock exchanges at home and abroad has enhanced transparency and disclosure of the SOEs, and corporate reports of listed companies have made available valuable industrial and corporate data. Using these corporate data, Shinichi Kawai examines the attributes of corporate governance of listed companies in China,[38] on the basis of which he reaches the following conclusions: Large-scale corporations generally have smaller rates of shares in circulation; and membership of the board of directors at the general shareholders meeting is mainly decided by a major shareholder – usually the parent company. As a result, the parent company provides a majority of the directors. It is therefore almost impossible to separate ownership from management. Kawai concludes that China's listed companies are significantly shaped by their former guise as SOEs. Securing general shareholders' interests and establishing an independent board of directors is the greatest challenge to the corporate governance of listed companies in China.

Collaborative Research

A number of Japanese and Chinese scholars are involved in collaborative research projects. The interregional I-O tables compiled by Ichimura and Wang (see above) resulted from a five-year collaborative research project between the International Centre for the Study of East Asian Development (ICSEAD) and the State Council's Development Research Center (DRC). In collaborative research, Chinese colleagues are first-hand sources of information for their Japanese counterparts, and without their assistance, it would be almost impossible to conduct fieldwork in China.

The study group headed by Shigeaki Uno and Zhu Tonghua was a pioneering model for Japan–China collaborative research projects.[39] This group sought to identify the origin of the indigenous development model in rural industrialization induced by TVEs, making reference to Fei Xioatong's well-known fieldwork in Sunan (southern Jiangsu). It also made an interesting comparison between indigenous development patterns represented by TVEs in China and the so-called 'one village, one product' campaign, designed to encourage villagers in Oita in Japan to generate their own specialty products.

The study group headed by Katsuji Nakagane is another example of Japan–China collaborative research.[40] With the assistance of Chinese colleagues, this group undertook intensive fact-finding fieldwork in rural villages in China, on the basis of which it analyzed the allocation of farm land, income distribution, labor migration, rural finance, and grain sales.

Japanese studies of the Chinese economy owe a considerable debt to Chinese scholars and their work. In this sense, most Japanese studies on China's economy may be classified as collaborative research.

Fieldwork

In the post-reform period foreign scholars have been allowed to conduct fieldwork in China, and a number of Japanese scholars have engaged in such activity. The most outstanding work in this regard has been produced by Mitsuhiro Seki and his colleagues, whose fact-finding results have been published in a series of books.[41] A number of doctoral theses written by Chinese graduate students in Japan are also based on their fieldwork.[42] The results of such fieldwork provide valuable records of Chinese economic conditions in a specific location at a specific point in time. However, the selection of research is not always on the basis of rational criteria. Chinese graduate students tend to select their home towns and other familiar places as sites for their research, making use of personal connections with local government officials and enterprise executives when they plan the detailed designs of their fieldwork. They often also apply hypotheses based on their fieldwork to the entire Chinese economy, even though their case studies can only represent the local conditions of their specific research sites.

Questionnaire survey is another valuable basis of fieldwork. Although some commercial-based market surveys have been conducted at various levels, foreign scholars still face restrictions in undertaking questionnaire surveys in China. In order to avoid these limitations, Japanese business organizations such as the JETRO send out questionnaires directed solely to Japanese residents and subsidiary companies in China. In academic circles, Hiroshi Sato, Kazutsugu Oshima and Hiroyuki Kato have characterized migrant workers on the basis of questionnaire and interview surveys with employees of a Japanese company's subsidiary factory in Guangdong.[43] They have also conducted similar surveys in Wuxi, Wenzhou, and other fast-growing cities in the Yangzi River Delta.

Group Study

China studies have been primarily dependent on individual efforts of scholars. But as the scope of China studies becomes more specialized and diversified, group studies, or "organized" research, are gradually becoming more popular. A good example of this approach has been the publication of the encyclopedia on contemporary China, to which more than 200 China specialists contributed.[44]

The publication (1989–1990) of a six-volume series of collected papers on China written by leading Japanese scholars and edited by Iwanami Shoten embraces politics, economy, society, history, literature, and international relations. The economic volume in this series was edited by Kazuo Yamanouchi and includes chapters on China's economic development in the context of development theories, comparative study of economic reforms between China and Russia, analysis of agricultural production, the development of rural organizations, industrialization, urbanization, and external economic relations.[45] As mentioned above, the University of Tokyo Press published eight-volumes of collected papers on China in 2000–2001, arising from the research project, "Structural Change in Contemporary China." The economic volume edited by Katsuji Nakagane embraces the transitional process, role of government, fiscal and financial reform, market integration, distribution of goods, income disparities, corporate governance, unemployment, and globalization.[46] The two volumes edited by Yamanouchi and Nakagane have different perspectives on China's economy: the former consists of papers dealing with economic sectors, while the latter is a collection of papers highlighting the *functional* aspects of the Chinese economy.

Each chapter of the economic volume edited by Nakagane has been developed into a new eight-volume series of books on contemporary China's economy, published by the University of Nagoya Press.[47] They address the topics in which China specialists in Japan currently take the greatest interest.

As China studies become even more specialized and diversified, China specialists have tended to shift from being generalists to becoming experts in specific areas, sectors, and issues of the Chinese economy. Two books edited by Tomoo Marukawa contain a wide range of review papers devoted to specific industrial policies and developments in China.[48] Interestingly, the contributors are primarily China specialists rather than industrial economists. The growing interest in China and the increasing number of China specialists lead to a natural "division of labor" amongst them.

Main Topics Researched

General Study

China specialists have taken the lead in producing general studies of China's economy by deciphering institutions, describing policies, and evaluating performance. They have also published a number of textbooks on China's economy. In the 1980s, the content of such books differed from author to author, reflecting their individual and unique viewpoints. However, as China's development converges toward a market economy, the content of recent textbooks on the Chinese economy has become much more standardized.

In the 1990s China's economy and reform process underwent fundamental changes: from shortage to surplus economy, from inflation to deflation, from initiation to institutionalization of a market economy, from gradual to comprehensive reform, from decentralization of decision-making to macroeconomic management, from incentive to production to rule-making of the market. As a result, most recent textbooks address the following issues: market transition, macroeconomic management, financial reform, technological progress, privatization, unemployment, income distribution, social safety net, corruption, environment, and globalization.[49]

Resource Flow

In the early post-reform period, a heated debate arose over resource flows between the agricultural and industrial sectors. This debate was closely related to the changing pattern of capital accumulation in China. The consensus view saw

China's capital accumulation in the pre-reform period as a process whereby an agrarian surplus was transferred through the state coffers to heavy industries.[50] It emphasized the government's compulsory purchasing system of agricultural products from peasants and the price scissors between agricultural and industrial products. This institutional framework was the basis of the one-way resource flow. After the government instituted agricultural reforms at the end of the 1970s that raised the purchasing prices of agricultural products, dismantled the people's communes, and revitalized independent farm household production and distribution in agriculture, it became impossible to squeeze any surplus from the agricultural sector. As a result, the government lost control over the mobilization of agricultural resources, and industry had to accumulate capital for investment and development from within its own boundaries.

Katsuji Nakagane offered a counter-argument to this orthodoxy.[51] He argued that it was almost impossible to verify the nonequivalent exchange between agricultural and industrial products, and suggested that it was not agriculture, but light industry, that generated a surplus for heavy industrial investment in China. That is, capital accumulation was achieved by transferring a surplus created in light industry to heavy industry. His study represents a modern economist's antithesis to the traditional Marxian interpretation of capital accumulation in China being based on inter-sectoral resource flows.

Labor Migration

Industrialization is usually accompanied by labor migration from the agricultural to the industrial sector, and from rural to urban areas. Since China is a labor-surplus economy, there should be an "unlimited supply of labor." Throughout the post-reform period, massive labor migration has taken place, although there are still rigid institutional impediments that deter peasants from migrating into cities. Many studies have therefore applied the dualist models proposed by pioneers of development economics – for example, W. Arthur Lewis, John C. Fei, Gustav Ranis, Dale W. Jorgenson, and Michael P. Todaro – to China's labor-surplus economy.[52] Japanese China specialists began their investigations with reviews of the institutional changes affecting labor migration, after which they conducted fact-finding field surveys of labor migration.[53] Some of these case studies have indicated that some fast-growing regions in the Pearl River Delta and the Yangzi River Delta had already passed the transitional turning point between a labor-surplus and a labor-shortage economy, as a result of which exerted upward pressure on wages spurred huge labor immigration into the modern sector.

The next analytical stage of such studies was to identify the determinants of migration. Through regression analyses, most studies showed both macroeconomic and microeconomic determinants of migration. The former include spatial income and growth differences, geographical distance to the destination, human networks based on territorial connection and blood relations, and size of the informal sector; the latter include farm size, agricultural income, the number of workers at home, their age, and education and skill level. The studies of labor migration also addressed the post-emigration impact on agricultural productivity, farm household consumption and investment behavior in rural areas, as well as post-immigration effects on labor supply and demand, wage levels, and unemployment rates in *urban* areas.[54]

Income Disparity

Income disparities generated by rapid economic growth are regarded as one of the most serious problems facing China. Hiroshi Sato is an expert in this field, and his work reviews current studies on income distribution and summarizes current economic differentials in China, as shown by the time-series data and the use of standard analytical tools to measure inequality; the coefficient of variation, Gini coefficient, Theil entropy measure and Atkinson index.[55]

In addition to historical legacies, the shift in China's development strategy has influenced economic disparities. Balanced growth represented by Maoist egalitarianism led China to the Third Front initiative. By contrast, unbalanced growth implied by Deng Xiaoping's proposal to "allow some people and areas to get rich first" encouraged a strong coastal bias in development. In the face of widening income gaps in recent years, the latest Japanese studies have embraced analysis of poverty and *sannong wenti* (the three problems of agriculture, rural villages, and peasants) in China. They highlight the lack of investment in agriculture, institutional impediments to migration, unequal tax burdens on farmers, and the absence of social security provision for them. They also show that asset accumulation triggered by the reform of house ownership and privatization of state-owned assets is another source of income disparities in China. Meanwhile, success in stock market deals and in booming industries (especially real estate and information technology (IT)) has given birth to the "new rich" in China. Japanese studies of income differentials also included research on rent-seeking activities and corruption in China.[56]

Market Economy

China is in transition to a market economy. How to transform the current economic system into a market economy is the central theme of economic reform in China. Unlike other developing countries, however, China and other transitional economies seek to fulfill two goals needed for a market economy. One is to transform itself from an underdeveloped state to a developed market economy; the other is to move from being a planned system to becoming a market economy – the process of de-socialization. Shigeru Ishikawa has pointed out that underdeveloped market economies have generally lacked social division of labor, infrastructure for distribution of goods and services, and rules and institutions for market exchanges.[57]

From the premise of the supposed dualistic nature of China's economy, Hiroyuki Kato has attempted to measure the points of economic "marketization" in China in the post-reform period on the basis of criteria that differentiate between planned versus market economy, and traditional versus modern economy.[58] His work also focuses on regional disparities between urban–rural and coastal–interior areas, and suggests that different levels of "marketization" have accelerated the process of widening regional differences within China. Part of his argument is that growth of the private sector, labor migration, foreign trade and capital, and regional development policies are also likely to have contributed to regional differences in "marketization" and income disparities in China.

China's economy has frequently been compared with a "lordship" economy. Wang Baolin addresses the "divided" nature of markets in China, examines macro- and microeconomic factors that have inhibited national market integration. He has also undertaken a cost–benefit analysis of the behavior of local governments' in the "divided" markets in China.[59]

Finally, fiscal decentralization is another important theme in the study of China's economy.[60] Many Japanese studies have sought to decipher the institutional changes affecting behavior of the fiscal system in the post-reform period. However, others view fiscal decentralization as a major *political* theme in the context of central–local relations in China.[61]

Study of China's Economy in the Context of Japan–China Economic Integration

Close Relations Between Japan and China

China is a very familiar place to most Japanese. China receives a lot of media attention in Japan, and it has become one of the favorite destinations for Japanese weekend visitors (including high school students, many of whom make excursions to China). Economic exchanges between Japan and China have also rapidly expanded in recent years, not least as Japanese companies transfer their manufacturing plants in order to reduce production costs, subsequently exporting their products back to Japan. Since the recession, most Japanese have become accustomed to low-priced and high-quality products made in China. There is also an increasing number of Japanese business persons and their families living in China. As of October 1, 2004, 73,405 Japanese residents were recorded as living in China – more than half of them in Shanghai and the Yangzi River Delta. Until the early 1990s, opportunities to stay in China were few and limited mainly to diplomats, media correspondents and their families. The experience of the large number of Japanese who now live in China will have a great influence on Japanese perceptions of China in the long run.

Close economic exchanges between Japan and China have raised bilateral relations to a new stage of economic integration. For economists in government and business circles, whose interest in China is greater than ever before, the Chinese economy is not just an object of foreign economic studies, but has become an integral part of the Japanese economy and a formative influence on its economic growth. Their comment on the Japanese economy cannot fail to take account of economic conditions in China.

The Rise of China and Economic "Threat"

Increasing imports from China have put immeasurable pressure on Japan's industrial adjustment. Throughout the "lost decade" of the 1990s, bankruptcies and unemployment increased and the hollowing-out the Japanese industries proceeded unabated. A deflationary spiral set in – which is now considered to have been a major cause of prolonged recession. As Haruhiko Kuroda and Masahiro Kawai have indicated, there were some suggestions in Japan that China was "exporting" deflation.[62] Many blamed Japan's economic difficulties on the rise of China, and various Japanese industries, especially those long protected by the government, perceived China to be an economic "threat." These sentiments were organized into powerful political pressure, which, in April 2001, induced the Japanese government to adopt protective measures against a few agricultural imports from China.

Although huge inflows of cheap Chinese products gave Japanese industries major opportunities to reform less efficient sectors and create more value-added industries, there was a tendency to attribute rising unemployment to industrial hollowing-out in Japan. There was intense competition for local investment areas in Japan and foreign countries. Although most Japanese firms retained their headquarters in Tokyo or other Japanese business centers, many domestic plants were closed and transferred abroad. In this way, Japanese FDI impacted negatively on the local economies of some parts of Japan.[63]

Sadao Nagaoka argues that the declining weight of manufacturing industries in Japan's industrial structure reflects their growing productivity and decreasing resource input.[64] Technology transfer of Japanese industries to China certainly has enhanced the competitiveness of China's industries, and many Japanese industries have expressed concern about the so-called "boomerang effect." However, the economic growth that technological progress has triggered in China is likely to offer Japanese industry new trade opportunities, and Nagaoka concludes that arguments about the supposed hollowing-out of Japanese industry lack a basic understanding of economics.

Kyoji Fukao and his colleagues seek to demonstrate that the gains from Japan's resource and market-development-related FDI exceed the losses of its export-substitution and import-expansion-related FDI to East Asia.[65] They estimate the loss of domestic manufacturing jobs due to Japan's export-substitution and import-expansion-related FDI to East Asia to have been 577,000 during 1987–1998.[66] Unemployment in textiles and clothing, electronics, and telecommunication equipment industries was particularly serious during that period. Their studies also show that overseas resource and market-development-related FDI created 514,000 new domestic jobs during those years, almost offsetting the rise in unemployment from other sources.

For many Japanese, the perceived economic "threat" from China was partly derived from a loss in confidence in Japan's economy, and partly from jealousy of China's economic success. Some leading Japanese critics have also argued that the possibility, or even likelihood, of China collapsing under the pressure of serious structural strains issues raises the spectre of a different kind of "threat" from China.[67] One of the primary purposes of academic studies of the Chinese undertaken by economists is to correct misconceptions where these are based on faulty economic reasoning.[68]

Such issues remain controversial with academic and journalistic circles. What is, however, is that China's economic growth has contributed to Japan's economic recovery. In addition to export-manufacturing industries, China's growing demand has revived a number of Japanese industries, including steel, oil refining, shipping and shipbuilding, all of which were previously regarded as "structurally-depressed industries" in Japan. This ray of sunshine piercing the clouds of a stagnant economy has led many Japanese to realize that the rise of China is not a "threat," but an opportunity. A well-known Japanese consultant's advocacy of closer ties with China has, for example, exerted a more positive influence of Japanese perceptions of China.[69]

The "Natural" Expansion of the Japanese Economy to China

Foreign Trade and Investment

Apart from a number of fact-finding surveys, Japanese studies of China's foreign trade and investment are limited.[70] China specialists in Japan seem to have been more interested in China's domestic economy than in its foreign economic relations. However, *non-China* specialists have begun to undertake in-depth studies on Japan–China bilateral economic relations, set against the "natural" expansion of the Japanese economy to China. Most of these analyses indicate that, considering relevant factor endowments, China's industrial and trade structure remains distorted and argue that China is most competitive in labor-intensive industries.[71] A more significant finding is that Japan and China have mutually complementary economic ties.[72]

China's foreign trade can be also observed against the backcloth of the FDI-trade nexus that exists in East Asia – a nexus that has changed East Asian development patterns. According to the traditional foreign trade theories of Ricardo and Hechscher-Ohlin, a difference in production technology or factor endowments encourages international exchange of tradable goods. However, traditional foreign trade theories do not allow for the FDI-trade nexus. FDI has the ability to transfer production factors or managerial resources overseas in such a way as, eventually, to change the factor endowments of recipient countries – thereby enabling developing countries to catch up rapidly with advanced countries in certain industries through the absorption of such factors and resources. In this way, FDI can create opportunities for international trade.

China has been successful in attracting FDI since the mid-1990s. Cheap labor and a huge domestic market have been the main determinants of foreign capital flows to China. From the perspective of foreign investors, however, agglomeration of industries has become a new determinant of FDI activities in China. Foreign investors stand to benefit from technical external economies, reductions in transaction costs, and scale advantages associated with industrial clusters in China. More concretely, agglomeration of industries offers an excellent investment environment, continuity of local governments' policies towards FDI, easy information exchange and local procurement, and technological spillover. Agglomeration of industries can induce new FDI inflows. Fragmentation of entire manufacturing process into smaller production blocks increases FDI and intra-industry trade in East Asia. Reduction in service link costs of transportation and communication between production blocks also accelerates the further fragmentation of manufacturing process. China has also succeeded in attracting these fragmented production blocks. Fragmentation of the manufacturing process into production blocks builds up multiple export production networks throughout East Asia. A number of manufacturers place China in the center of these export production networks in East Asia. New foreign trade theories are typically embodied in China's foreign trade and investment.[73]

China has assumed a very positive attitude towards the idea of free trade agreements (FTA).[74] As intra-regional trade grows, East Asian economies are increasingly being caught up in a process of de facto integration.[75] China seems to regard the political and diplomatic effects of FTAs, while Japan has tended to see FTA as an important means of facilitating domestic structural reform. Assuming that Japan can overcome that most controversial problem of liberalizing its agricultural market, Japanese scholars suggest that a FTA embracing ASEAN plus Three (Japan, China, and Korea) promises to generate the greatest gains and form the most efficient trade system in East Asia.[76]

SMEs and Regional Economy

SMEs are by far the most important destination of Japanese FDI in China. Investment in final assembly industries in China is usually backed up by affiliated suppliers of parts and components, most of which are SMEs. At the same time, Japanese SMEs have relocated their manufacturing bases to China in order to survive in a deteriorating business environment. Moreover, Japanese FDI has negatively impacted on some local regional economies in Japan, in which most of the SMEs have deep roots.

In the wake of closures of SMEs in Japan and the establishment of new factories in China, Japanese industrial and regional economists specializing in SMEs have changed their research sites from Japan to China. As mentioned above, a series of studies undertaken by Mitsuhiro Seki and his colleagues constitute outstanding research outcomes in this field. SMEs have played an important role in Japan's economic development, and the Japanese government has implemented comprehensive policy measures in order to promote them. China too has become interested in the developmental role of SMEs and associated policies – not least in the context of privatization of SOEs. Japanese economists consider SMEs to be important actors in China's economic development, and the Japanese government has also offered cooperation in promoting such enterprises.[77] Through wide-ranging fieldwork in regions in which the market dominates, Tetsuya Komagata's work illustrates the critical roles of SMEs in transition, employment, industrial development and regional economic development in China.[78]

The study of Tetsushi Sonobe and Kenjiro Otsuka represents an ideal fieldwork model, which also makes a theoretical contribution to development economics.[79] Through its fieldwork, the study is a comparative study of industrial clusters in apparel, motor cycle, general machinery, and printed circuit board industries in Japan, China, and Taiwan. The fieldwork is reinforced by scientifically-based hypothesis formulation, followed by statistical verification based on corporate data and the results of questionnaire surveys conducted at local enterprises and factories. In terms of economic theory, the study links the work on spatial economics by Fujita, Krugman, and Venables,[80] and that on endogenous development by Schumpeter. By contrast, the results of other fieldwork conducted in the post-reform period are mostly fact-finding reports that lack the insights that reference to the disciplinary literature on economics would have provided. Meanwhile, arguments about spatial economics are highly specialized and lack any sense of reality. In this sense, the study of Sonobe and Otsuka can be regarded as an accessible and balanced book that benefits from the academic rigor with which the authors have approached their subject.

Business Administration

China is described as the "workshop of the world" and it has become a major destination to transplant Japanese-style management. Most studies by Japanese scholars majoring in business administration with an interest in the study of China's economy address the indigenous management system of Chinese enterprises and suggest ways in which their productivity can be enhanced.

A book edited by Takahiro Fujimoto and Junjiro Shintaku is a unique study that focuses on differences in product architecture.[81] Industrial products based on the modular product architecture – typical examples are computers and other IT devices – are currently dominant in manufacturing industries. They consist of self-fulfilling parts and components, and the interface between them is very simple. Since these parts and components are highly standardized, they can be purchased in open markets at reasonable prices. Although they are based on high technology, they can be easily assembled by unskilled labor because of their standardization and the simple interface between them. China's manufacturing industries specialize in modular products, with high-tech parts and components being labor-intensively assembled in China (modular products require a sizable labor input even if they are classified as high-tech products). Thus, Kenichi Yasumuro suggests that the revolution of product architecture has transformed China into the "factory of the world" and thereby contributed to its economic success.[82] But although China is successful in manufacturing modular products, it still lags behind other industrial economies in basic industries, labor quality, and management systems.[83]

Currency Realignment

China has been under pressure to revalue the *renminbi*. However, neither the Japanese government nor business seems to expect China to take an immediate action to revalue the *renminbi*, since revaluation would affect the Japanese economy in the long run. Revaluation might benefit Japanese exporting industries, but it would hurt Japanese distributors who are heavily dependent on China in their merchant procurement. Japanese manufacturers are engaged in local production on a large scale in China and most of their products are exported back to Japan. Unlike the United States and European countries, Japan does not require the revaluation of *renminbi* in order to curb a flood of Chinese exports. Japan is much more concerned that revaluation would show down China's economic growth, on which the Japanese economy is increasingly dependent.

C.H. Kwan took the lead in a trilateral research project on currency realignment between Japan, China, and the United States.[84] Interestingly, Chinese scholars tend to emphasize the advantages of revaluation of the *renminbi*. It is often argued that revaluation would damage exports, FDI inflows, employment, and generate exchange speculation in China. However, the equilibrium exchange rate would lead to more effective resource allocation, independent monetary policy, greater purchasing power, and a reduction in trade surplus. In the short term, revaluation might regulate massive inflows of "hot money," curb inflationary pressure, and prevent a property bubble. In the long term, the aim should be to use the gradual adjustment of the exchange rate to create an economy driven by domestic demand and consumption.[85]

Yoshihisa Onishi and Masaru Yoshitomi recognize the significance of currency realignment, and suggest that China should reinforce the domestic banking system, with its considerable burden of nonperforming loans, before it adjusts the exchange rate.[86] In the absence of comprehensive financial reform, revaluation would not serve to enhance China's economic efficiency. Furthermore, Sayuri Shirai has expressed doubts about the argument that the *renminbi* has been undervalued.[87] It is true that in the face of huge inflows of Chinese products. the National Association of Manufacturers (NAM) indicated that the *renminbi* was undervalued by 30–40 percent.[88] According to Shirai, however, principal theories used to estimate the equilibrium exchange rate – including asset, investment-saving (I-S), purchasing power parity (PPP) and fundamentals approaches – failed to demonstrate that the *renminbi* has deviated considerably from the equilibrium exchange rate. As the IMF suggested, "it is difficult to find persuasive evidence that the *renminbi* is substantially undervalued."[89]

Conclusion

Japanese China specialists who have taken the lead in the study of the Chinese economy are quite independent from the mainstream discipline of economics. They have tended deliberately to resist the uncritical application of European and American-derived frames of reference to the study of China's economy.

Emphasizing the diversity of Chinese society, they have resisted making sweeping economic generalizations. They have also preferred to study parts of the Chinese economy rather than treating China as an integrated economic entity.

The rise of China has greatly impacted on the international economy and finance. Whereas open macroeconomists and econometricians play dominant roles in the study of China's international economic and currency issues, China specialists in Japan tend to confine themselves to fieldwork-based study of economic history, institutional development, and regional economies in China. The former seek to generalize an economic phenomenon, while the latter are more likely to emphasize specific and detailed dimensions of China's economy. This does not reflect division of labor, but rather the compartmentalization of the two approaches, between whom there is little constructive dialogue. As Katsuji Nakagane has put it,[90] since China has become an "ordinary country" in the post-reform period, it has become appropriate to employ general economic models and standard analytical tools to study the Chinese economy. One implication of this is that China specialists should acquire some minimum knowledge of economics.

Japanese China specialists also remain aloof from foreign scholars who specialize on the Chinese economy. They are willing to promote and participate in academic exchanges with Chinese scholars because most of them have studied in China and are good Chinese speakers. But – mainly because of language barriers – they have little dialogue with China specialists in the United States and Europe. In Japan, there is a big domestic market for China studies. Although the number of academic works on the Chinese economy is still limited, there is an expanding market for the study of China's economy among businessmen and journalists. The Japanese language as a key technical barrier has restricted the participation of foreign scholars in this big "domestic" Japanese market. Against this background, there are few incentives for Japanese China specialists to submit their papers to leading international journals, although they show real interest in the latest studies of the Chinese economy published abroad.

There are also different views about China's economic future among Japanese China specialists. Optimists emphasize the potential for continued sustained economic growth, while pessimists tend to highlight what they regard as intractable structural issues facing China. Extremist views apart, most Japanese China specialists could be described as being "cautious optimists." They reject exaggerated views of China as a "threat," but they do not overstate the rise of China. They are, however, likely to regard deteriorating environmental conditions and wasteful resource consumption as new "threats."[91] Paradigm changes in economic doctrines and strategies in China have fundamentally shaped Japanese study of the Chinese economy. Now that we have entered the twenty-first century, closer bilateral economic relations – even economic fusion – between Japan and China are shifting the lead role in Japanese studies of the Chinese economy from China specialists to non-China specialists.

Notes

1 Greater China (mainland China plus Hong Kong) has already become the largest trading partner of Japan. Most Japanese exports to Hong Kong are re-exported to China.
2 This chapter deals exclusively with Japanese studies of mainland China's economy and does not include Japanese studies of the economies of Hong Kong, Macau, Taiwan, or overseas Chinese.
3 Japan's leading booksellers have their own online bookstores. Among them, Amazon. co.jp has the most comprehensive and well-organized online book catalogue, and constitutes the de facto "Books in Print" in Japan.
4 In addition, books on "China's industry" and "China's market" number 186 and 95 titles respectively.
5 Yoshikazu Shimizu, *Chugoku Nomin no Hanran* (*Rebellion of the Chinese Peasants*) (Tokyo: Kodansha, 2002).
6 Hideya Yamamoto, *Honto no Chugoku wo Shitte Imasuka* (*Do You Know the Realties of China?*) (Tokyo: Soshisha, 2004).
7 At the same time, it is very difficult to distinguish articles of general magazines from papers of academic journals. Indeed, there is little difference in quality between the best essays of quality magazines and papers in academic journals.
8 In addition to MAGAZINEPLUS, we also made reference to the Periodical Index (http://opac.ide.go.jp/newlist/indexab.php), a database to cite articles of major social science periodicals received by the Institute of Developing Economies (IDE) Library, Japan's largest specialist library dealing with developing economies.
9 *Ajia Keizai*, a monthly journal of IDE, published special issues featuring review articles on area studies and development economics in Japan in 1969, 1978, 1986 and 1995. For a more comprehensive review of the study of China's economy in Japan, covering academic books and papers published in 1986–1994, see Kyoichi Ishihara, "Chugoku: Keizai/Keizaishi" ("China: Economy and Economic History"), *Ajia Keizai*, Vol. 36, No. 6/7 1995.
10 OECD, *Social Sciences Policy: Japan* (Paris: Organization for Economic Cooperation and Development, 1977).
11 Shigeru Ishikawa, *Kaihatsu Keizaigaku no Kihon Mondai* (*Basic Issues of Development Economics*) (Tokyo: Iwanami Shoten, 1990).
12 Shigeru Ishikawa and Yonosuke Hara (eds), *Betonamu no Shijo Keizaika* (*Market-Oriented Economic Reform in Vietnam*) (Tokyo: Toyokeizai Shinposha, 1999).
13 Wu Xiaolin, *Motakuto Jidai no Kogyoka Senryaku: Sansen Kensetsu no Seiji Keizaigaku* (*Industrialization Strategy in Mao's Era: Political Economic Study on the Third Front Construction Program in China*) (Tokyo: Ochanomizu Shobo, 2002).
14 Ryutaro Komiya, *Gendai Chugoku Keizai: Nicchu no Hikaku Kosatsu* (*Contemporary China's Economy: Comparative Consideration between Japan and China*) (Tokyo: University of Tokyo Press, 1989); and Minami Ryoshin, *Chugoku no Keizai Hatten: Nihon tono Hikaku* (*Economic Development of China: Comparative Study between Japan and China*) (Tokyo: Toyokeizai Shinposha, 1990).
15 Toshio Watanabe, *Nishi Taiheiyo no Jidai: Ajia Shin Sangyo Kokka no Seiji Keizaigaku* (*Western Pacific Age: Political Economy of Asian New Industrial States*) (Tokyo: Bungei Shunju, 1989).
16 The figures are based on the statistics of the Ministry of Education posted on the web site of the Japan Student Services Organization. Accessed on August 31, 2005 at http://www.jasso.go.jp/kikaku_chosa/ryugaku_chosa/gaiyou_16.html.
17 For details, visit the SCPJ web site at http://www.fromorient.com/cpj.
18 http://www.jbic.go.jp/japanese/research/report/review/index.php.
19 http://www.jbic.go.jp/japanese/research/report/paper/index.php.

20 As the main results of the research projects at these research institutes, see Koichi Hamada (ed.), *Sekai Keizai no Naka no Chugoku* (*China in the World Economy*) (Tokyo: NTT Shuppan, 2003); Motoshige Ito (ed.), *Nicchu Kankei no Keizai Bunseki* (*Economic Analysis of Japan-China Relations*) (Tokyo: Toyokeizai Shinposha, 2003), and C.H. Kwan (ed.), *Jinmingen Kiriage Ronso: Chu Nichi Bei no Rigai to Shucho* (*Debate on the Revaluation of Renminbi: Interests and Arguments among China, Japan and the United States*) (Tokyo: Toyokeizai Shinposha 2004).

21 Atsuo Kuroda, *Meido in Chaina* (*Made in China*) (Tokyo: Toyokeizai Shinposha, 2001).

22 Toshiya Tsugami, *Chugoku Taito* (*Rise of China*) (Tokyo: Nihonkeizai Shinbunsha, 2003).

23 Yasushi Onishi, *Chugoku Zaisei/Zeisei no Genjo to Tenbo* (*Current Status and Prospect of China's Fiscal and Tax Regime*) (Tokyo: Okurazaimu Kyokai 2004); and Osamu Tanaka, "Chugoku Keizai Seisakushi, 1996–2004: Zaisei Kinyu wo Chushin ni" ("Economic History of China, 1996–2004: Fiscal and Monetary Policy"), *PRI Discussion Paper Series*, No.05A–09, 2005.

24 Yoshihisa Onishi, *En to Jinmingen* (*Yen and Renminbi*) (Tokyo: Chuokoron Shinsha, 2003).

25 They play very important roles in explaining the current economic issues in China to the general public and businesspersons in Japan. For example, see C.H. Kwan, *Chugoku Keizai Kaikaku Saishusho* (*China's Economic Reform at the Final Stage*) (Tokyo: Nihonkeizai Shinbunsha, 2005).

26 Nijuichi Seiki Chugoku Soken (ed.), *Chugoku Joho Handobukku 2005* (*China Information Handbook 2005*), Tokyo: Sososha, 2005. The first edition of *China Information Handbook* was published in 1987. The *Handbook* was edited by Mitsubishi Research Institute until 2002.

27 Reiitsu Kojima (ed.), *Chugoku Keizai Tokei/Keizaiho Kaisetsu* (*Glossary of China's Economic Statistics and Law*) (Tokyo: Institute of Developing Economies, 1994).

28 The collected papers of "Structural Change in Contemporary China" published by University of Tokyo Press include the following volumes. Kazuko Mori (ed.), *Volume 1: Taikoku Chugoku eno Shiza* (*Outlook on China as a Great Power*), 2000, Katsuji Nakagane (ed.), *Volume 2: Keizai – Kozo Hendo to Shijoka* (*Economy – Structural Change and Market Economy*), 2000, Shigeo Nishimura (ed.), *Volume 3: Nashonarizumu – Rekishi karano Sekkin* (*Nationalism – Historical Approach*), 2000, Satoshi Amako (ed.), *Volume 4: Seiji – Chuo to Chiho no Kozu* (*Politics – Central-Local Relations*), 2000, Masaharu Hishida (ed.), *Volume 5: Shakai – Kokka tono Kyosei Kankei* (*Society – Symbiotic Relations with the State*), 2000, Reiitsu Kojima (ed.), *Volume 6: Kankyo – Seicho eno Seiyaku to Naruka* (*Environment – Restraints on the Growth?*), 2000, Kazuko Mori (ed.), *Volume 7: Chuka Sekai – Aidentiti no Saihen* (*Chinese World – Realignment of Identity*), 2001 and Kyoko Tanaka (ed.), *Volume 8: Kokusai Kankei – Ajia Taiheiyo no Chiiki Chitsujo* (*International Relations – Regional Order in the Asia-Pacific*), 2001.

29 Hiroshi Onishi and Go Yano (eds), *Chugoku Keizai no Suryo Bunseki* (*Quantitative Analysis of China's Economy*) (Kyoto: Sekai Shisosha, 2003).

30 Kenjiro Otsuka, Naoki Murakami, and Liu Deqiang, *Chugoku no Mikuro Keizai Kaikaku: Kigyo to Shijo no Suryo Bunseki* (*Microeconomic Analysis on China's Economic Reform: Quantitative Analysis on Enterprise and Market*) (Tokyo: Nihonkeizai Shinbunsha, 1995).

31 China published I-O tables on the material product system (MPS) basis until the early 1990s.

32 At provincial level, Wang Zaizhe drew up I-O tables for Shanghai for 1987, 1990, 1992 and 1995, and analyzed exports/imports and outward/inward shipments of goods in Shanghai. See Wang Zaizhe, *Chugoku no Chiiki Seicho: Chiiki Renkan to Seifu no*

Yakuwari (*Economic Growth in China: Regional Linkage and the Role of Government*) (Tokyo: University of Keio Press, 2001).

33 Shunichi Ichimura and Wang Hui-dong (eds), *Chugoku no Chiikikan Sangyo Renkan Bunseki* (*Interregional Input-Output Analysis of the Chinese Economy*) (Tokyo: Sobunsha, 2004). China also published the 1997 interregional I-O tables in 2005. See Guojia Xinxi Zhongxin (ed.), *Zhongguo Quyu Touruchanchubiao* (*Interregional Input-Output Table in China*) (Beijing: Shehui Kexue Wenxian Chubanshe, 2005).

34 IDE, *Asian International Input-Output Table 1990* (Tokyo: Institute of Developing Economies, 1998) and IDE, *Asian International Input-Output Table 1995* (Chiba: Institute of Developing Economies, 2001).

35 IDE, *Multi-regional Input-Output Model for China 2000* (Chiba: Institute of Developing Economies, 2003).

36 Nobuhiro Okamoto (ed.), *Chugoku no Chiikikan Sangyo Kozo I* (*Interregional Industrial Structure in China I*) (Chiba: Institute of Developing Economies, 2002) and *Chugoku no Chiikikan Sangyo Kozo II* (*Interregional Industrial Structure in China II*) (Chiba: Institute of Developing Economies, 2003).

37 Tang Cheng, *Chugoku no Chochiku to Kinyu: Kakei, Kigyo, Seifu no Jissho Bunseki* (*Savings and Finance in China: Empirical Analysis of Household, Enterprise, and Government*) (Tokyo: University of Keio Press, 2005).

38 Shinichi Kawai, *Chugoku Jojo Kigyo: Naibu Shihaisha no Gabanansu* (*Listed Companies in China: Governance by Internal Control*) (Tokyo: Sodosha, 2003).

39 Shigeaki Uno and Zhu Tonghua (eds), *Noson Chiiki no Kindaika to Naihatsuteki Hattenron: Nicchu Shojochin Kyodo Kenkyu* (*Modernization in Rural Area and Indigenous Development: Japan-China Collaborative Research on the Small Cities and Towns in China*) (Tokyo: Kokusai Shoin, 1991).

40 Katsuji Nakagane (ed.), *Kaikaku Igo no Chugoku Noson Shakai to Keizai: Nicchu Kyodo Chosa ni yoru Jittai Bunseki* (*Agrarian Society and Economy in the Post-Reform China: Japan-China Collaborative Survey*) (Tokyo: Tsukuba Shobo, 1997).

41 The books written by Mitsuhiro Seki include *Gendai Chugoku no Chiiki Sangyo to Kigyo* (*Regional Industries and Enterprises in Contemporary China*) (Tokyo: Shinhyoron, 1992); *Chugoku Kaiho Seisaku to Nihon Kigyo* (*China's Open-up Policy and Japanese Industries*) (Tokyo: Shinhyoron, 1993); *Chugoku Choko Ryuiki no Hatten Senryaku* (*Development Strategy of the Yangze River Delta in China*) (Tokyo: Shinhyoron, 1995), *Chugoku Shijo Keizaika to Chiiki Sangyo* (*Market-Oriented Economy and Regional Industries in China*) (Tokyo: Shinhyoron, 1996); *Shanhai no Sangyo Hatten to Nihon Kigyo* (*Shanghai's Industrial Development and Japanese Industries*) (Tokyo: Shinhyoron, 1997); *Nihon Kigyo Chugoku Shinshutsu no Shin Jidai: Dairen no Junen no Keiken to Shorai* (*New Age for Japanese Industries to Invest in China: A Decade of Experience in Dalian and Their Future*) (Tokyo: Shinhyoron, 2000); *Chosen suru Chugoku Nairiku no Sangyo: Shisen, Jukei no Kaihatsu Senryaku* (*Challenges of Industries in Interior China: Development Strategies of Sichuan and Chongqing*) with Masaki Nishizawa (Tokyo: Shinhyoron, 2000), *Sekai no Kojo: Chugoku Kanan to Nihon Kigyo* (*Factory of the World: South China and Japanese Industries*) (Tokyo: Shinhyoron, 2002); and *Hokuto Ajia no Sangyo Renkei: Chugoku Hoppo to Nikkan no Kigyo* (*Industrial Cooperation in Northeast Asia: Japanese and Korean Industries in North China*) (Tokyo: Shinhyoron, 2003). The books edited by Seki and his colleagues are as follows; Mitsuhiro Seki and Kaichi Ikegaya (eds), *Chugoku Jidosha Sangyo to Nihon Kigyo* (*China's Automobile Industry and Japanese Industries*) (Tokyo: Shinhyoron, 1997); Mitsuhiro Seki and Fan Jianting (eds), *Genchika suru Chugoku Shinshutsu Nihon Kigyo* (*Localization of Japanese Industries in China*) (Tokyo: Shinhyoron, 2003); and Mitsuhiro Seki (ed.), *Taiwan IT Sangyo no Chugoku Choko Deruta Shuseki* (*Agglomeration of Taiwan IT Industries in the Yangze River Delta*) (Tokyo: Shinhyoron, 2005).

42 There are a number of studies of this kind published in the Japanese leading journals of Asian studies; *Ajia Kenkyu* and *Asia Keizai*. Full texts of both journals can be viewed. Visit the following websites, http://www.jaas.or.jp/pages/publications/asia-studies. htm for *Ajia Kenkyu* and http://www.ide.go.jp/Japanese/Publish/Asia/back_no.html for *Ajia Keizai*.

43 Hiroshi Sato, Kazutsugu Oshima and Hiroyuki Kato, "Kanan Chiiki ni okeru Dekasegi Rodosha no Jittai: Kantonsho Hoanken M Denshisho no Baai" ("Migrant Workers in South China: A Case of M Electronics Factory in Bao'an County, Guangdong"), *Ajia Kenkyu*, Vol. 40, No. 1, 1993.

44 Satoshi Amako, Kyoichi Ishihara, Zhu Jianrong, Kogo Tsuji, Masaharu Hishida and Yujiro Murata (eds), *Gendai Chugoku Jiten* (*Encyclopedia of Contemporary China*) (Tokyo: Iwanami Shoten, 1999).

45 Kazuo Yamanouchi (ed.), *Iwanami Koza Gendai Chugoku 2: Chugoku Keizai no Tenkan* (*Iwanami Series Contemporary China 2: Shift of China's Economy*) (Tokyo: Iwanami Shoten, 1989).

46 Katsuji Nakagane (ed.), *Volume 2: Keizai – Kozo Hendo to Shijoka.*

47 Katsuji Nakagane, *Volume 1: Keizai Hatten to Taisei Iko* (*Economic Development and System Transition*), 2002, Yan Shanpin, *Volume 2: Nomin Kokka no Kadai* (*Challenge to the Peasant State*), 2002, Tomoo Marukawa, *Volume 3: Rodo Shijo no Chikaku Hendo* (*Crustal Change of Labor Market*), 2002, Kenichi Imai and Mariko Watanabe, *Volume 4: Kigyo no Seicho to Kinyu Seido* (*Growth of Enterprise and Financial System*), forthcoming, Hideo Ohashi, *Volume 5: Keizai no Kokusaika* (*Globalization of Economy*), 2003, Hiroyuki Kato, *Volume 6: Chiiki no Hatten* (*Regional Development*), 2003, Hiroshi Sato, *Volume 7: Shotoku Kakusa to Hinkon* (*Income Disparity and Poverty*), 2003, and Masaharu Hishida and Shigeto Sonoda, *Volume 8: Keizai Hatten to Shakai Hendo* (*Economic Development and Social Change*), 2005.

48 Tomoo Marukawa (ed.), *Ikoki Chugoku no Sangyo Seisaku* (*Industrial Policy in Transitional China*) (Chiba: IDE, 2000); and *Chugoku Sangyo Handobukku* (*China Industrial Handbook*) (Tokyo: Sososha, 2003).

49 See the following textbooks. Katsuji Nakagane, *Chugoku Keizai Hattenron* (*Economic Development and Transition in China*) (Tokyo: Yuhikaku, 1999); Hiroyuki Kato and Kazuyoshi Uehara (eds), *Chugoku Keizairon* (*China's Economy*) (Kyoto: Minerva Shobo, 2004); Ryoshin Minami and Fumio Makino (eds), *Chugoku Keizai Nyumon, Dainihan* (*Economic Development in China, 2nd Edition*) (Tokyo: Nihon Hyoronsha, 2005); Hideo Ohashi, *Gendai Chugoku Keizairon* (*Contemporary China's Economy*) (Tokyo: Iwanami Shoten, 2005); and C.H. Kwan, *Chugoku Keizai no Jirenma* (*China's Economic Dilemma*) (Tokyo: Chikuma Shobo, 2005).

50 Ryoshin Minami, *Chugoku no Keizai Hatten...*, Toshio Watanabe (ed.), *Chugoku no Keizai Kaikaku to Shin Hatten Mekanizumu* (*China's Economic Reform and New Development Mechanism*) (Tokyo: Toyokeizai Shinposha, 1991); Kenji Furusawa, *Chugoku Keizai no Rekishiteki Tenkai* (*Historical Development of China's Economy*) (Kyoto: Minerva Shobo, 1993).

51 Katsuji Nakagane, *Chugoku Keizairon: Nokokan no Seiji Keizaigaku* (*China's Economy: Political Economic Analysis on the Relations between Agricultural and Industrial Sectors*) (Tokyo: University of Tokyo Press, 1992).

52 Ryoshin Minami and Fumio Makino (eds), *Nagare Yuku Taiga: Chugoku Noson Rodoryoku no Ido* (*A Great River Flows: Migration of Rural Labor in China*) (Tokyo: Nihon Hyoronsha, 1999).

53 Kazutsugu Oshima, *Chugoku no Dekasegi Rodosha* (*Migrant Workers in China*) (Tokyo: Ashi Shobo, 1996).

54 Yan Shanping, *Chugoku no Jinko Ido to Minko: Makuro/Mikuro Deta ni motozuku Keiryo Bunseki* (*Population Migration and Migrant Workers in China: Quantitative Analysis Based on Macro and Micro Data*) (Tokyo: Keiso Shobo, 2005).

55   Hiroshi Sato, *Volume 7: Shotoku Kakusa to Hinkon* ...; See also Hiroshi Sato, *Growth of Market Relations in Post-Reform Rural China: A Micro-Analysis of Peasants, Migrants and Peasant Entrepreneurs*) (London, RoutledgeCurzon, 2003).
56   Hideo Ohashi, *Gendai Chugoku Keizairon.*
57   Shigeru Ishikawa, *Kaihatsu Keizaigaku no Kihon Mondai.*
58   Hiroyuki Kato, *Chugoku no Keizai Hatten to Shijoka* (*Economic Development and Market Economy in China*) (Nagoya: University of Nagoya Press, 1997).
59   Wang Baolin, *Chugoku ni Okeru Shijo Bundan* (*Divided Markets in China*) (Tokyo: Nihon Keizai Hyoronsha, 2001).
60   Zhang, Zhongren (2002), *Gendai Chugoku no Seifukan Zaisei Kankei* (*Intergovernmental Fiscal Relations in Contemporary China*) (Tokyo: Ochanomizu Shobo, 2002); Jiro Naito, *Chugoku no Seifukan Zaisei Kankei no Jittai to Taio* (*Actual Conditions and Measures of Intergovernmental Fiscal Relations in China*) (Tokyo: Nihon Tosho Senta, 2004); and Kai Kajitani, "Zaisei Kinyu Kara Mita Chuo to Chiho" ("Central-Local Relations from the Fiscal and Financial Viewpoints"), in Kato and Uehara (eds), *Chugoku Keizairon.*
61   Hideo Ohashi, "Chuo Chiho Kankei no Keizaiteki Sokumen ("Economic Aspects of Central-Local Relations")," in Amako (ed.), *Volume 4: Seiji – Chuo to Chiho no Kozu.*
62   Haruhiko Kuroda and Masahiro Kawai, "Time for Switch to Global Reflation," *Financial Times*, December 2, 2002.
63   Yoshikazu Kano (ed.), *Sangyo Kudoka wa Dokomade Susumunoka* (*How Far Will Hollowing Out Proceed?*) (Tokyo: Nihon Hyoronsha, 2003).
64   Sadao Nagaoka, "Chugoku Keizai tono Kyoso to Nihon Sangyo Kudoka no Kyojitsu" ("Truthfulness or Falsehood: Competition with China's Economy and the Hollowing Out of the Japanese Industries"), in Motoshige Ito (ed.), *Nicchu Kankei no Keizai Bunseki.*
65   Kyoji Fukao and Tomofumi Amano, "Taigai Chokusetsu Toshi to Seizogyo no 'Kudoka'" (Japan's Overseas Direct Investment and 'Hollowing Out' of Manufacturing Industries"), *Keizai Kenkyu*, Vol. 49, No. 3, 1998.
66   Kyoji Fukao and Yuan Tangjun, "Nihon no Taigai Chokusetu Toshi to Kudoka (Japan's Overseas Direct Investment and Hollowing Out of Industries)," *RIETI Discussion Paper Series*, 01-J-003, 2001.
67   For example, Mineo Nakajima and Yoshihisa Komori, the Japanese leading opinion leaders, are very critical of China. Their books include *Chugoku wa Kyoi ka* (*Is China a Threat?*) (Kyoto: PHP Kenkyusho, 2000); *Haken ka Hokai ka* (*Hegemony or Collapse*) (Tokyo: Bijinesusha, 2002); and *Chugoku Bohatsu* (*Accidental Discharge of China*) (Tokyo: Bijinesusha, 2004).
68   See Koichi Hamada (ed.), *Sekai Keizai no Naka no Chugoku*; and Motoshige Ito (ed.), *Nicchu Kankei no Keizai Bunseki.*
69   A series of books on China written by Kenichi Omae include *Chaina Inpakuto* (*China Impact*) (Tokyo: Kodansha, 2002), *Chaina Shifuto* (*China Shift*) (Tokyo: Shogakkan, 2002); and *Chuka Renpo* (*The Emergence of the United States of Chunghwa*) (Kyoto: PHP Kenkyusho, 2002).
70   Hideo Ohashi, *Volume 5: Keizai no Kokusaika.*
71   Kyoji Fukao, "Chugoku no Sangyo Boeki Kozo to Chokusetsu Toshi: Chugoku Keizai wa Nihon no Kyoi ka" ("China's Industry and Trade Structure and FDI: Is the China's economy a Threat to Japan?"), in Motoshige Ito (ed.), *Nicchu Kankei no Keizai Bunseki.*
72   C.H. Kwan, *Kyozon Kyoei no Nicchu Keizai* (*Japan-China Economy: Coexistence and Co-prosperity*) (Tokyo: Toyokeizai Shinposha, 2005).
73   Fukunari Kimura, "Kokusai Boeki Riron no Aratana Choryu to Higashi Ajia (New Analytical Approaches in International Trade Theory and East Asia)," *Kaihatsu Kinyu Kenkyushoho*, No. 14, 2003. See also Mitsuyo Ando and Fukunari Kimura,

"The Formation of International Production and Distribution Network in Asia," *NBER Working Paper*, No. 10167, 2003.

74 Hideo Ohashi, "Higashi Ajia Keizai no Saihen ni okeru Nicchu no Yakuwari" ("Roles of Japan and China in the Economic Realignment in East Asia"), *Toa*, No. 427, 2003; and "Chugoku no Taigai Keizai Seisaku no Tenkai (Development of China's Foreign Economic Policy)," *Kokusai Mondai*, No. 514, 2003.

75 Toshio Watanabe (ed.), *Higashi Ajia Shijo Togo eno Michi* (*A Road to Market Integration in East Asia*) (Tokyo: Keiso Shobo, 2004).

76 Shujiro Urata (ed.), *Nihon no FTA Senryaku* (*Japan's FTA Strategy*) (Tokyo: Nihonkeizai Shinbunsha, 2002).

77 Nihon Boeki Shinko Kiko, *Chugoku Chusho Kigyo Hatten Seisaku Kenkyu* (*The Study on the Development Policies of the Small and Medium-Sized Enterprises in China*) (Tokyo: Overseas Research Department, Japan External Trade Organization, 2004).

78 Tetsuya Komagata, *Ikoki Chugoku no Chusho Kigyoron* (*Small and Medium-Sized Enterprises in Transitional China*) (Tokyo: Zeimu Keiri Kyokai, 2005).

79 Tetsushi Sonobe and Kenjiro Otsuka, *Sangyo Hatten no Rutsu to Senryaku: Nichi Chu Tai no Keiken ni Manabu* (*Roots and Strategies of Industrial Development: Lessons from the East Asian Experience*) (Tokyo: Chisen Shokan, 2004).

80 Masahisa Fujita, Paul Krugman, and Anthony J. Venables, *The Spatial Economy: Cities, Regions, and International Trade* (Cambridge: MIT Press, 2001).

81 Takahiro Fujimoto and Junjiro Shintaku (eds), *Chugoku Seizogyo no Akitekucha* (*Architecture Analysis on China's Manufacturing Industries*) (Tokyo: Toyokeizai Shinposha, 2005).

82 Kenichi Yasumuro, *Chugoku Kigyo no Kyosoryoku* (*Competitiveness of Chinese Enterprises*) (Tokyo: Nihonkeizai Shinbunsha, 2003).

83 Masanori Moritani, *Chugoku Keizai: Shin no Jitsuryoku* (*Real Competence of China's Economy*) (Tokyo: Bungei Shunju, 2003).

84 C.H. Kwan (ed.), *Jinmingen Kiriage Ronso*.

85 Haruhiko Kuroda, *Gen Kiriage* (*Revaluation of Renminbi*) (Tokyo: Nikkei BP Sha, 2004), and Noriki Hirose and Taku Morifuji, "Yushutsu Shudo kara Naiju Shudo eno Kawase Seisaku no Yakuwari" ("The Role of Exchange Rate Policy in the Process from Export- to Domestic Demand-led Growth"), in Koichi Hamada (ed.), *Sekai Keizai no Naka no Chugoku*.

86 Yoshihisa Onishi, *En to Jinmingen*; and Masaru Yoshitomi, *Ajia Keizai no Shinjitsu* (*Reality of Asian Economy*) (Tokyo: Toyokeizai Shinposha, 2003).

87 Sayuri Shirai, *Jinmingen to Chugoku Keizai* (*Renminbi and China's Economy*) (Tokyo: Nihonkeizai Shinbunsha, 2004).

88 NAM, *The NAM 2003 Annual Labor Day Report* (Washington, D.C.: National Association of Manufacturers, 2003).

89 IMF, "People's Republic of China: 2004 Article IV Consultation," *IMF Country Report*, No. 04/351, 2004.

90 Katsuji Nakagane, "Chugoku no Keizai Hatten Patan" ("Economic Development Patterns of China"), in Koichi Hamada (ed.), *Sekai Keizai no Naka no Chugoku*.

91 Yoichi Yokoi, *Chugoku no Sekiyu Senryaku* (*China's Petroleum Strategy*) (Tokyo: Kagaku Kogyo Nipposha, 2005), and Chugoku Kankyo Mondai Kenkyukai (ed.), *Chugoku Kankyo Handobukku* (*China Environment Handbook*) (Tokyo: Sososha, 2004).

4 Studies of China's Economy in the United States

Penelope B. Prime

With China's rapid change and growing importance in the international arena, scholars from around the world have increasingly focused on studying China's economy. Scholars with no previous training in Chinese or the case of China have propelled this trend. In a previous review of the literature on China's economy, the majority of authors were China experts, with deep knowledge of history and culture, as well as the economy, and with the ability to read and speak the language.[1]

Two new developments have allowed the generalist to study China. First, collaboration with scholars from China, either those studying or working outside of China, or those based in China, has become standard practice. Institutions that award research grants have encouraged collaboration, and often require it. Opportunities to meet a compatible collaborator have also increased as universities in China have developed exchange programs and joint degrees with foreign counterparts, and many Chinese students have gone abroad for university and graduate studies.

Second, China's State Statistical Bureau and other agencies in the government have made data available in both Chinese and English. In addition to the annual statistical yearbooks with macro data, a plethora of sector-based, enterprise-based, trade-related and local-level yearbooks are also published on a regular basis. Monthly and daily data are also collected. Both for-profit and non-profit organizations have been created to help collect and disseminate this large amount of information. One example is the China Data Center based at the University of Michigan.

In addition to the generalists working on China, many Chinese students who have studied economics in the U.S. and elsewhere have added to the volume of research papers on the Chinese economy. Many of these academics work on China related topics in addition to the main fields in which they earned their Ph.Ds.

To accommodate the rising interest in research on China's economy, new journals have also been established. The *China Economic Review*, for example, is the official journal of the Chinese Economists Society (CES), which began as an association for Chinese students studying economics in the U.S. in the 1980s. CES has since broadened its membership beyond the U.S., and has always welcomed non-Chinese members. The vast majority of articles published in the *China*

Economic Review deal with China's economy. Other new China-focused journals include *Chinese Economy,*[2] *China Review*, the *Journal of Chinese Economics and Business Studies*, and *The Journal of Contemporary China.*

The study of China, along with the field of economics, has increasingly become an international scholar community, both in the sense of geographical distribution of research and interconnections between centers of research. Despite fiscal constraints on international travel at some universities, international conferences and collaboration across continents have noticeably increased.

Non-economists have also made significant contributions to the study of China's economy. These scholars have focused on issues concerning centralized versus decentralized political and financial power, the political implications of economic reform, the reasons why reform began and the nature of its progression, and the role of the state in economic development, the role of geographic and demographic factors, among others. Work by Elizabeth Economy, Jean Oi, Clifton Pannell, Margaret Pearson, Susan Shirk, Vivian Shu, Dorothy Solinger, Kellee Tsai, Susan Walcott, Andrew Walder, Fei-ling Wang, Dali Yang and David Zweig, to name a few, would be included in this category of research.

Against this background, the purpose of this chapter is to review recent trends in research on China's economy from the perspective of U.S.-based scholars trained in economics.[3] Therefore this chapter represents a review of only a small part of the relevant scholarly activity. The primary research covered here are those articles that have been published in professionally refereed economics journals, as these publications are the key determinants of the intellectual trends in the field as well as the careers of the scholars doing research. Defining the scope of this chapter primarily with the authors and topics covered in journal articles helps to manage the enormity of the survey task. This approach is not meant to ignore the important contributions that have been made available via books, government reports, and think-tank publications. These outlets, however, are too vast to be covered here, and one could argue, mirror the issues and debates found in the journals.

In fact, a comprehensive coverage of the research published in refereed journal articles on China in recent years is also a near impossibility. A search in EconLit, one of the main catalogs for economic journals, found 3,318 references with "China" or "Chinese" in the title between January 1995 and October 2005, and almost two-thirds of these were published in the last five years.[4] This compares with 873 found in the previous decade and only 351 between January 1965 and December 1984.

To give coherence to this impressive explosion of work on China's economy, this review will focus on several key theoretical economic questions that have benefited from research on China, and several puzzles that the case of China itself has raised for scholars. The core of research covered centers on the fundamentals of long-run economic growth in terms of the resources and capabilities available and the question of convergence, and the institutional context within which the growth process takes place. As argued next, these questions have come to the forefront of economic inquiry with the end of the Cold War and the rise of globalization.

China and Economic Theory

The field of economics used to be very divided – between those who studied "markets" and those who took a more system and policy approach because markets were undeveloped. Studies of centrally planned economies and very poor countries with immature institutions are examples of the latter. After the fall of the Berlin Wall in 1989, economic research turned a corner along with economic history. The independent fields of economic development and comparative economic systems (not to mention economic history and history of economic thought) have all but disappeared in Ph.D. programs.[5]

Ironically, however, serious research on Eastern Europe and the former Soviet Union, as well as China, and topics relating to economic transition and the elimination of poverty, has taken off. The field journals, such as the *Journal of Comparative Economics*, *Economics of Transition*, *Economic Development and Cultural Change* and the *Journal of Economic Development* have also prospered, despite the devaluation of these topics as independent fields.

One can speculate on the reasons for these contradictory trends. First, policy makers in the "economies in transition" from planning to markets have been struggling with building effective market institutions from scratch. The challenge of this task alone has attracted the interest of many scholars. Second, for the first time data on these economies began to be available, via international organizations such as the World Bank as well as opportunities to conduct independent surveys. As economists have a difficult time being taken seriously by their peers unless "good" data exists, this development is critical. Third, Amartya Sen won the Nobel Prize in economics in 1998 for his contribution to welfare economics, lending panache to the study of poor countries and the role of policy in economic performance.

The fourth reason for rising mainstream attention to transition and development is an increasing sophistication in modeling institutional behavior, estimating thresholds such as minimum levels of human capital, and incorporating geographical information. This sophistication, combined with economic behavior in poor and transition economies that increasingly resemble markets, allows application of standard economic theory to the new emerging economies. The more that standard theory explains phenomena in developing economies, the less there is a need for specialized fields.[6]

The study of China has played a major part in this process. China began its economic reforms earlier than the Soviet Bloc, and earlier than India, which brought it special attention. Probably more significantly, however, China's economic reforms are perceived to be quite successful. The rest of the chapter will discuss specific work on China surrounding two aspects of debate: measurement and reasons for growth, and various aspects of institutional change during China's period of transition.

Measuring and Understanding Growth

Aggregate Growth

A basic aspect of economic theory focuses on why economies grow. Growth models have evolved from very simple capital-output models such as the Harrod–Domar model to today's endogenous growth approaches. Nonetheless, the fundamental questions center around the relative importance of increasing inputs versus improvements in the efficiency of those inputs. Paul Krugman's and Alwyn Young's work critiquing growth in the East Asian countries as being driven by investment rather than technology or efficiency improvements brought this question to the forefront of debate.[7] These are also very important questions for China, especially as it relates to the sustainability of growth, and hence much research has focused in this area.

The first question is how fast has China really grown? This debate focuses on the quality of data generated by the Chinese statistical system.[8] Official figures are impressive – averaging above 10 percent in some years. The World Bank, in contrast, consistently reports substantially lower growth rates in its indicators, which have been adjusted to match methodology allowing for cross-country comparisons. Another reevaluation of growth rates for the reform period by Chinese scholars resulted in a reduction of average official figures from 9.8 to 7.9 percent.[9]

Problems with China's statistical system are legendary. Thomas Rawski renewed the attention to the quality of China's data with his observations on inconsistencies in reported growth across sectors and for key inputs after 1997 and the Asian crisis.[10] *China Economic Review* published a symposium on data issues that included one of Rawski's pieces.[11] Others are less skeptical of the official data. For example, using a principal components analysis, Klein and Ozmucur concluded that China's GDP estimates match the expected trends of monthly, quarterly, and annual key indicators.[12] Gregory Chow also concluded that official data can be used cautiously, especially for trends over time.[13]

Most recently, results from an extensive economic census conducted by China's National Bureau of Statistics suggest that the absolute size of China's economy has been seriously underestimated. Largely due to recalculations of the service sector – telecom, real estate, and retail in particular – China's official GDP numbers have been increased by over 16 percent. This increase has led to preliminary revised official growth rates between 1979 and 2004 of approximately 0.2 percentage points higher per year.[14]

Therefore, while debate continues about how much growth has occurred, few would dispute the positive trend. The next relevant question, then, is what is causing growth. How much is due to increased inputs, and how much is due to more efficient use of inputs and better technology? The different perspectives in this debate are also primarily due to what data is used, how the variables are measured, how they are adjusted, and what deflators are used, as well as what sectors are investigated. Using official data, Gregory Chow's study of China's aggregate economy concluded that before reform, China's economy grew an average of 6 percent per year, but with no improvements in productivity, while the reform period benefited from higher capital growth and increasing productivity of an average of 3 percent per year, leading to an average annual growth of 9.7 percent.[15]

Focusing on the non-agricultural sector, Alwyn Young calculated productivity estimates for the reform period 1978–1998 using official data but making adjustments for rising labor force participation, human capital and deflators.[16] His results show improvements similar to other fast-growing economies but substantially less than the unadjusted official numbers. For the aggregate economy, he finds that output per worker increased 5.2 percent per year instead of the official 6.9 percent between 1978 and 1998. For the non-agricultural sector, he finds that labor productivity increased 3.6 percent rather than the official 6.1 percent, and that total productivity improved by 1.4 percent per year as opposed to the 3 percent implied by the official unadjusted data.

A paper by Wang and Yao of the World Bank also take human capital improvements into account to allow for estimates that more strictly measure total factor productivity.[17] Their results suggest that productivity did increase during the reform period (1978–1999) somewhere between 1.75 and 3.06 percent per year depending on what input shares are used. However, they also report that growth in human capital slowed in the reform period as compared with the pre-reform years. They argue that this trend, if accurate, does not bode well for sustainable growth as China will have to rely increasingly on productivity improvements via efficiency improvements from continued reforms or innovation driven growth. Human capital would be critical to both of these factors.

Regional Growth Studies

Analysis of regional trends is another way to approach the basic questions of growth. In China's case, it is also a way around the paucity of data points, especially annual data. Because China is divided into provinces, autonomous regions, and municipalities that are treated as provinces for policy and data collection purposes, it is possible to build cross-sectional and pooled cross-section, time series data, greatly adding to the number of observations for use in statistical estimation.

The approaches used for China tend to mirror those applied in cross-country growth regressions. The typical model will start with a standard production function with capital and labor, and then refine the relationship in a variety of ways, such as to separate foreign and domestic capital, measure the effects of labor supply versus human capital, divide the data into state and non-state ownership in some way, and add at least one variable, such as exports, to capture the effect of the opening policies. Other models also attempt to control for geographic factors such as distance to ports and quality of transportation in order to make stronger cases that certain characteristics are effecting growth across regions. In addition to finding factors affecting growth, these models often have implications for whether growth and living standards are converging across countries or other regional units.

Numerous cross-provincial studies have been done for China, so just a few examples will be mentioned here. An early study by Park and Prime showed a positive effect on growth from exports in the 1985 to 1993 period, although the results varied by inland and coastal provinces.[18] Many studies done since have found similar results with respect to exports and regional variations.

Two studies published in 2000 for the 1980s supported the idea that growth rates were converging across regions within China. Chen and Feng found that the presence of a non-state sector and higher education, in addition to international trade (exports plus imports), explain growth between 1978–1989, while the state sector, high fertility, and inflation reduced growth, using real provincial income per capita as the dependent variable.[19]

Liu and Yoon performed their estimates for manufacturing rather than overall output from 1986 to 1991.[20] The authors hypothesized that urban reforms, which largely affected the industrial sector and had been implemented by 1986, affected growth and productivity. They found that coastal areas exhibited higher industrial productivity, but that over time this region's productivity fell somewhat. For a variety of reasons, the authors expect that the coastal advantages will decrease over time, reinforcing convergence of growth across China.

One recent study focused on the contribution of the state sector to growth.[21] Their theoretical model implied a negative contribution of the state sector to regional growth. Consistent with their hypothesis, the empirical regressions showed a significant impact on growth and employment when the state sector was reduced.

Another cross-provincial study focused on the role of foreign investment in the regional growth convergence process in China for 1978–1997.[22] This study found some convergence between regions but that different regions were converging towards different levels of income per capita. These authors also emphasized that their results may be valid in the short run, but that in the long run more commercialization of the economy should help promote convergence.

In contrast, geographic factors are found to matter a great deal in the study by Bao *et al.* In this study having a coastline explained 60 percent of the variation in growth across regions.[23] While the conditions for foreign investment and other aspects of China's economy may change over time, the importance of having a coastline may not necessarily be overcome by inland areas. Similar results were found by Chen and Fleisher.[24]

A study by Kanbur and Zhang looked at regional growth from 1983 to 1995 with the goal of separating urban–rural from inland–coastal inequality in China.[25] They found that the urban–rural differences were about the same as the inland–coastal differences, but that the inland–coastal inequalities have increased much faster. A study by Lu and Wang found changes in both urban–rural and inter-provincial inequalities fluctuated over time, largely attributable to government policies.[26] Dennis Yang hypothesized that policies and institutions may be hindering the decrease in inequalities normally expected from market allocation of resources.[27] Gene Chang also argued that income inequalities will not decrease soon, largely because China is still more of a dual economy rather than one national market.[28]

In a piece that considers the evidence on cross-provincial convergence, Barry Naughton argued that the early studies showing convergence are perhaps misleading for future trends.[29] The evidence is growing that divergence may be dominant in the next stage. Naughton suggested that the end of the price system that played a redistribution role, and an erosion of government-directed investment that created artificial pockets of economic strength, have ended. Increasingly growth will depend on resource flows driven by relatively higher market returns. If the poorer areas of China can attract these resources, then convergence will be possible. Well-functioning national resource markets will be a key determinant in this process, as will be addressed below in the section on institutions.

Looking across sectors, a study by Gao analyzed regional growth across provinces for 1985–1993 using 32 industrial categories at the two-digit classification level.[30] Gao's innovation in the Chinese case was to include local specialization, local competition, and local industrial diversity to capture technological spillovers as indicated by the endogenous growth literature. The study also used standard variables such as the share of state activity, foreign investment, exports, human capital and various regional characteristics. Of the externality measures, only local competition had a significant influence on growth in these results, and the author acknowledged that the measure used may be picking up a firm size effect instead of true competition. On the other hand, the standard variables of exports, foreign investment and a viable non-state sector did help explain growth, which is consistent with numerous other studies.

A study by Hare and West comparing rural manufacturing between 1986 and 1994 in coastal and inland areas did not find evidence that inland growth was being supported by expected economic strengths such as low-cost labor.[31] In addition, coastal advantages appeared to persist. These results suggest that regional income inequalities will not disappear in the near future.

In summary, while many researchers expect to find increased resource flows in the case of China as reforms progress, and for this eventually to help reduce income differences as theory would predict, much evidence so far contradicts these expectations. Nonetheless, despite regional variations, research results concerning growth in China have generally been impressive. There are many holes, however, in the understanding of the factors behind growth.

Assessing Institutional Change

Underlying the fundamentals of resources and efficiency are substantial institutional changes as China moves from planning to a market-oriented economic system. Many of the studies mentioned in the previous section tested the role of the state versus non-state sector in determining growth. Most found that the non-state sector was positively related to growth while the state sector often was not. This section on institutions will cover ownership issues, the question of national market development, the significance of fiscal decentralization and issues created by the changing financial system.

Ownership

Research approaches to the role of the private sector in China's transition have varied. Influenced by the experience of transition economies generally, one approach has hypothesized that broad privatization early in the transition process would be necessary for success.[32] This argument rests on the expectation that state-owned enterprises (SOE), especially those that functioned for years under a planned system, would not have the incentives or skills to make efficient resource allocation decisions or to be innovative regardless of the reforms imposed on them. A range of theoretical propositions within theory leads to this conclusion, including difficulties in making contracts, the ease with which government can intervene in SOEs, and the likelihood of government bailouts for less successful firms.[33] Empirical work in a variety of countries also tends to support the tendency for private firms to exhibit better performance based on a number of measures.[34]

In the specific case of China, a second approach to privatization argues that a gradual introduction of private firms will be sufficient for transition to succeed, and some argue that this might be superior to rapid, early privatization.[35] In this case the share of state-owned enterprise activity in the economy decreases over time but would not necessarily disappear.[36] In the case of China, many studies suggest it is likely that the non-state sector will continue to outpace the state sector, and therefore market transition could progress.

A second angle on this gradual approach is that a number of studies have found that state enterprise performance itself has improved with reforms.[37] In the cross-country studies reported by Dewenter and Malatesta, China was sometimes an outlier because of improvements in the state sector, which has not usually been found in other settings.[38] Numerous studies focusing on the state sector in China have found positive changes,[39] although, in general, state sector performance has been found to be poor relative to the non-state sector.[40]

A third approach to this issue is that a gradual and partial move to privatization can work for some time, but that eventually the costs of state enterprise inefficiencies would become too large to allow economic progress to continue.[41] While theoretically plausible, few have found empirical support for this result in China because China's economy has continued to grow at very reasonable, and sometimes impressive, annual rates. For example, a number of studies have estimated the size of China's debt and bad loans, which are a direct result of financial support for SOEs, and have concluded that these are serious problems that should be dealt with, but that they are not likely to lead to a financial crisis.[42] Nonetheless, debate within China has begun to seriously consider the role of the private sector in sustainable growth and policy has moved toward sanctioning private ownership as seen in the Sixteenth Party Congress decisions to change the constitution to include private property and expand the categories of people who can belong to the party.

From the beginning of reforms, however, the private sector has systematically been discriminated against in terms of what activities these firms were allowed to participate in, their access to capital, their expansion options, and the risks they faced even if they did well – and especially if they competed favorably with state-owned firms.[43] Yasheng Huang argues that private Chinese firms generally have been at a disadvantage relative to Chinese state firms in terms of access to resources and markets, resulting in both types of firms being non-competitive.[44] These conditions, he argues, combined with restrictions on foreign debt and imports, created a vacuum that allowed foreign firms to make unusual inroads into China's economy.

The most consistent result across this body of research, however, is that the non-state sector, defined in numerous ways, outperforms the state sector. This is a very important result but somewhat surprising given all of the documented disadvantages under which the non-state, and especially private, sector has functioned.

Market Integration

A second line of inquiry relating to institutions has been to what extent national markets have developed in China's continental economy. Internal specialization, economies of scale, and healthy domestic demand have benefited large economies such as the U.S., and China has the opportunity to capture these gains as well. However, under the Maoist planned system, local self-sufficiency was pursued to extremes, distorting horizontal resource and product flows even beyond what underdeveloped markets might normally entail.

With reforms, the breakdown of these barriers became possible, but not guaranteed. Most research on this issue still finds serious fragmentation within China's economy, and in some cases even growing fragmentation, partly explained by local officials protecting their own markets and firms.[45] A study by Sandra Poncet concluded that even while provinces were becoming more integrated into the global economy via international trade, inter-provincial trade intensity declined between 1987 and 1997.[46]

In contrast to these studies, some recent work suggests that progress with national market integration has occurred.[47] For example, Li Qi's study isolated government directed loans, foreign funds and official bank loans to show that private commercial capital has become more mobile across China's domestic economy. This result is more consistent with rapid growth than a view that finds a weak financial system underwriting economic progress. Nonetheless, the expected outcome that market development with increased domestic market integration would occur with reforms has been difficult to document in either capital or output markets.

With respect to labor, the picture is somewhat different. A series of household surveys, along with the national census data, have provided a window into migration decisions. Despite institutional constraints such as the household registration system, labor migration has been a rising phenomenon in China's reform process. Evidence suggests that migrants are making expected choices based on income differentials and job opportunities, which is consistent with growing market integration.[48] Some suggest, however, that labor mobility is primarily an urban-rural phenomenon within provinces, rather than representing a national labor market.[49]

Fiscal Decentralization

A key factor in the discussions of incentives for local protectionism that can hinder national market integration is reforms in China's fiscal system. These institutional changes, however, have also been given credit for creating incentives for local officials to push development and create jobs, underpinning China's rapid growth generally. Much work has been done by economists such as Christine Wong and Roy Bahl sorting out the effect of fiscal reforms on local budgets and extra-budgetary funds, and the underlying incentive changes they created.[50] Although many challenges remain, Chinese policy makers have attempted to reform the tax system to both fund appropriate local government responsibilities, and to maintain reasonable central government resources.

The idea that China's form of fiscal decentralization imbedded growth promoting incentives that were able to counter balance political resistance to reform was put forward by Yingyi Qian and Barry Weingast.[51] They argue that China's form of decentralization led to competition among local governments, diluting monopoly power and rent-seeking ability, in addition to economic competition among firms consistent with market development. Others, such as Alywn Young's work mentioned in the section on regional integration, find just the opposite with local rent-seeking disrupting market development.[52] A paper by Zhang and Zou also found a negative relationship between fiscal decentralization and provincial growth in China between 1987 and 1993, where as they found a positive association in the case of India where markets were never as severely dismantled as in China.[53]

Another study by Feltenstein and Iwata looks at decentralization and macro performance and finds that economic decentralization (i.e. more resources flowing to the non-state sector) has promoted growth in China since the 1950s, while fiscal decentralization (i.e. the increased fiscal role of local governments instead of the central government) is associated with macro instability, and inflation in particular.[54] The first result is hypothesized to result from better efficiency in the non-state sector, while the second is due to increased state sector access to local bank loans, which is not based on economic rationality. In terms of the overall effect on China's long run growth, these effects, of course, work at cross purposes. In addition, Eckaus argued that part of the fiscal decentralization has involved the increasing importance of funds outside of the normal budget process, creating perverse incentives and lack of oversight and normal fiscal planning.[55] A related phenomenon with negative consequences, that is, growing local fees to supplement the normal array of taxes, is explored by Shuanglin Lin.[56]

The Financial System

A fourth key area for research on institutions, with specific implications for long-run growth, has been the financial system. China's banking system is by all accounts technically bankrupt, but continues to attract household savings that have kept it running.

Nicholas Lardy's early study on this phenomenon laid out the institutional history and dynamics behind this challenge.[57] One of the main stresses on the system, which also serves as a constraint on reform, is the mixed or poor (depending on the study) performance of state enterprises but the political necessity to keep them afloat.

Further, it is increasingly accepted that state firms cannot both behave in profit-maximizing ways and be the main source of social security and government revenues.[58] While the state sector has had access to virtually all of the formal financial system's resources, the state sector's social security and tax roles have kept it from being able to compete with firms without these burdens. In hindsight, developing social safety nets before attempting enterprise reforms might have been more successful in achieving a viable and sustainable state sector.[59] At this stage in China's transition, however, it may be simply too late for this option.

In light of this situation, research in this area has focused on if, and how, efficiencies have improved, and if reforms will be sufficient and timely to avoid a financial crisis. For example, Park and Sehrt look at the 1991 to 1997 period and find that not much progress was made with commercial financial intermediation, and that politically motivated policy lending did not diminish.[60] Others find progress, but anomalies, such as serious constraints in investment banking,[61] or a tendency for governments to try to reform state-sector institutions rather than encourage new entry, especially from the private sector.[62]

The fundamental puzzle raised in this line of inquiry is why China's economy has been able to grow so quickly despite the lack of a sound banking system and clear and enforceable financial laws and regulations. One response is that the economy would have grown even faster if better institutions were in place, and that more progress with financial reform will be required for growth to continue.[63] Another is that we really do not understand how economic incentives and transactions work in an economy based primarily on personal relationships. That success is possible with alternate institutions that seem to defy the necessary pieces of a well-functioning market economy is a new line of research. For example, Allen *et al.* explore alternative forms of financing and governance as an explanation for private sector growth.[64]

In sum, based on theory, all four institutional aspects – privatization, market integration, fiscal decentralization and reforms in the financial and banking system – should lead to positive growth and more efficiency. The empirical research results investigating these propositions, both in terms of how much reform has taken hold and what the results have been, however, are mixed and often contradictory. Clearly there continue to be many unresolved questions about how well China's economy has actually performed.

China Economic Research: Trends, Puzzles and Challenges

In previous decades, the main theoretical issues from an economic perspective addressed in the case of China were the feasibility and process of transforming a planned economy into a market-oriented one. Barry Naughton's work explaining how China "grew out of the plan" is one example of this line of inquiry.[65] Today the theoretical concerns have shifted to focus more on the fundamentals of long-run, sustainable growth.

Nonetheless, institutional change continues to be central to China, and will, in part, determine how long-run growth occurs. When there is rapid and substantial institutional change, economic theory implies that parameters are changing along with the key variables. This makes estimation, and analysis, much more difficult in the short and medium-run.

Major and rapid institutional change may also be why China at this stage often seems to represent a special case. The "special case" phenomenon challenges researchers to identify initial or specific conditions in order to understand the process taking place in China and to know what is replicable elsewhere. In this regard comparative work, with India for example, could be insightful.

Change in China today is also embedded in shifting global resource flows. To try to understand certain changes within the domestic economy without taking the global economy into consideration could be quite misleading. For example, Edward Steinfeld proposes important hypotheses about the process of industrial development in the context of the evolving global supply chain using the case of China.[66] Based on enterprise case studies and other survey data, he postulates a series of new challenges for countries to catch-up in terms of industrial capacity, even when large domestic markets and basic capabilities are available. Inquiry into the nature and extent of foreign investment and trade spillovers will be important to answer these types of questions. Understanding domestic development within the global context may well lead to re-evaluations of the implications of standard growth theory that emphasize technological change and human capital as the guarantors of sustainable growth. Hence, research on China could lead the way to advancements in long-run growth theory.

Finally, the greatest challenge for economic research on China is the limited coverage and dubious quality of the data available. On the surface there seems to be lots of data with every government agency and geographic region producing yearbooks and other information tools. Look slightly deeper, however, and the actual use of this information is limited if the goal is to apply an economic model and test it with econometric analysis. Many researchers, therefore, are resorting to government survey data or are building their own survey instruments. This certainly is one solution, although survey research carries its own limitations.

In conclusion, in general economists' view of market development and growth potential in China is optimistic despite problems such as rising inequality, poor financial health, and conflicting local government incentives. These problems are mostly seen as short-run issues for China, with the long run expected to be dominated by further market development leading to more efficient use of resources. Typically when studies warn of impending or future crises in China, there is a significant political component to the argument. The significance of unequal change in economic and political systems remains to be better understood.

Notes

1   Penelope B. Prime, "The Study of the Chinese Economy," in David Shambaugh (ed.), *The American Study of Contemporary China* (Armonk, NY: M.E. Sharpe, 1993), pp. 82–119.

2   *Chinese Economy*, published by M.E. Sharpe, publishes both translated articles from sources within China as well as original articles from China and elsewhere.

3   Scholars' affiliation at the time of publication was the criterion used in this paper. When necessary to make a point or round out a debate, work by authors not based in the U.S., as well as chapters and books, are cited.

4   The search was conducted on October 19, 2005, and was restricted to journal articles.

5   See Krugman's thoughts on this division for earlier years: Paul Krugman, "The Fall and Rise of Development Economics," available at http://www.wws.princeton.edu/pkrugman/dishpan.html.

6   One example of a study that reflects all four of these trends is Modigliani's work on savings in China. Franco Modigliani and Shi Larry Cao, "The Chinese Saving Puzzle and the Life-Cycle Hypothesis," *Journal of Economic Literature* Vol. XLII (March 2004), pp. 145–70.

7   Paul Krugman, "The Myth of Asia's Miracle," *Foreign Affairs* Vol. 73 (1994), pp. 62–78, and Alwyn Young, "The Tyranny of Numbers: Confronting the Statistical Realities of the East Asian Growth Experience," *Quarterly Journal of Economics* (1995), pp. 641–80, and "Lessons from the East Asian NICs: A Contrarian View," *European Economic Review* Vol. 38 (1994), pp. 964–73.

8   See, for example, Carsten A. Holz, "Deconstructing China's GDP statistics," *China Economic Review* Vol. 15, No. 2 (2004), pp. 164–202, followed by a response from the State Statistical Bureau in China, Xianchun Xu, "China's Gross Domestic Product Estimation," *China Economic Review* Vol. 15, No. 3 (2004), pp. 302–22.

9   Xiaolu Wang and Lian Meng, "A Reevaluation of China's Economic Growth," *China Economic Review* Vol. 12, No. 4 (2001), pp. 338–46. Both authors are affiliated with institutions in China, and Wang is also affiliated with Australian National University.

10 Thomas G. Rawski, "What is Happening to China's GDP Statistics?," *China Economic Review* Vol. 12, No. 4 (2001), pp. 347–54.

11 *China Economic Review* Vol. 12, No. 4 (2001).

12 Lawrence R. Klein and Suleyman Ozmucur, "The Estimation of China's Economic Growth Rate," *Journal of Economic and Social Measurement* Vol. 28 (2002/2003), pp. 187–202.

13 Gregory Chow, "China's Economic Growth: 1952–2010," *Economic Development and Cultural Change* Vol. 51, No. 1 (2002), pp. 247–56.

14 Antoaneta Bezlova, "China's Economists Grapple with Higher GDP," *Asia Times*, 13 January 2006, www.atimes.com.

15 Gregory Chow, "China's Economic Growth: 1952–2010," *Economic Development and Cultural Change* Vol. 51, No. 1 (2002), pp. 247–56.

16 Alwyn Young, "Gold into Base Metals: Productivity Growth in the People's Republic of China during the Reform Period," *Journal of Political Economy* Vol. 111, No. 6 (2003), pp. 1220–61.

17 Yan Wang and Yudong Yao, "Sources of China's Economic Growth 1952–1999: Incorporating Human Capital Accumulation," *China Economic Review* Vol. 14, No. 1 (2003), pp. 32–52.

18 Jong H. Park and Penelope B. Prime, "Export Performance and Economic Growth in China: Evidence from Cross-Provincial Analysis," *Applied Economics* Vol. 29 (1997), pp. 1353–63.

19 Baizhu Chen and Yi Feng, "Determinants of Economic Growth in China: Private Enterprise, Education, and Openness," *China Economic Review* Vol. 11, No. 1 (2000), pp. 1–15.

20 Bai-Yang Liu and Bong Joon Yoon, "China's Economic Reform and Regional Productivity Differentials," *Journal of Economic Development* Vol. 25, No. 5 (2000), pp. 23–41.

21 Kerk L. Phillips and Kunrong Shen, "What Effect Does the Size of the State-Owned Sector Have on Regional Growth in China?," *Journal of Asian Economics* Vol. 15, No. 6 (2005), pp. 1079–102.

22 Anuradha Dayal-Gulati and Aasim M. Husain, "Centripetal Forces in China's Economic Takeoff," *IMF Staff Papers* Vol. 49, No. 3 (2002).

23 Shuming Bao, Gene Hsin Chang, Jeffrey D. Sachs and Wing Yhye Woo, "Geographic Factors and China's Regional Development under Market Reforms, 1978–1998," *China Economic Review* Vol. 13, No. 1 (2002), pp. 89–111.

24 Jian Chen and Belton M. Fleisher, "Regional Income Inequality and Economic Growth in China," *Journal of Comparative Economics* Vol. 22, No. 2 (1996), pp. 141–64.

25 Ravi Kanbur and Xiaobo Zhang, "Which Regional Inequality? The Evolution of Rural-Urban and Inland-Coastal Inequality in China from 1983 to 1995," *Journal of Comparative Economics* Vol. 27, No. 4 (1999), pp. 686–701.

26 Max Lu and Enru Wang, "Forging Ahead and Falling Behind: Changing Regional Inequalities in Post-reform China," *Growth and Change* vol. 33, No. 1 (2002), pp. 42–71.

27 Dennis Tao Yang, "What Has Caused Regional Inequality in China?," *China Economic Review* Vol. 13, No. 4 (2002), pp. 331–334.

28 Gene H. Chang, "The Cause and Cure of China's Widening Income Disparity," *China Economic Review* Vol. 13, No. 4 (2002), pp. 335–40.

29 Barry Naughton, "Provincial Economic Growth in China" Causes and Consequences of Regional Differentiation," pp. 57–86 in *China and Its Regions: Economic Growth and Reform in Chinese Provinces* (Northampton, MA: Elgar, 2002).

30 Ting Gao, "Regional Industrial Growth: Evidence from Chinese Industries," *Regional Science and Urban Economics* Vol. 34 (2004), pp. 101–24.

31 Denise Hare and Lorraine A. West, "Spatial Patterns in China's Rural Industrial Growth and Prospects for the Alleviation of Regional Income Inequality," *Journal of Comparative Economics* Vol. 27, No. 3 (1999), pp. 475–97.

32 Jeffrey Sachs, Wing Thye Woo, Gordon Hughes and Stanley Fischer, "Structural Factors in the Economic Reforms of China, Eastern Europe, and the former Soviet Union," *Economic Policy* (April 1994), pp. 101–46; Wing Thye Woo, "Recent Claims of China's Economic Exceptionalism: Reflections Inspired by WTO Accession," Center for International Development Working Paper No. 70, Harvard University (2001), http://www.cid.harvard.edu/cidwp/070.htm.

33 William L. Megginson and Jeffry M. Netter, "From State to Market: A Survey of Empirical Studies on Privatization," *Journal of Economic Literature* Vol. XXXIX (2001), pp. 321–89.

34 Kathryn L. Dewenter and Paul H. Malatesta , "State-Owned and Privately Owned Firms: An Empirical Analysis of Profitability, Leverage, and Labor Intensity," *American Economic Review* Vol. 91, No. 1 (2001), pp. 320–34.

35 Putterman, Louis, "The Role of Ownership and Property Rights in China's Economic Transition," *The China Quarterly*, No. 144 (1995), pp. 1065–82; Jean C. Oi, *Rural*

China Takes Off: Institutional Foundations of Economic Reform (Berkeley, CA: University of California Press, 1999).

36 Barry Naughton, *Growing Out of the Plan: Chinese Economic Reform 1978–1993* (Cambridge: Cambridge University Press, 1996).

37 William L. Megginson and Jeffry M. Netter, "From State to Market: A Survey of Empirical Studies on Privatization," *Journal of Economic Literature* Vol. XXXIX (2001), pp. 321–89.

38 Kathryn L. Dewenter and Paul H. Malatesta , "State-Owned and Privately Owned Firms: An Empirical Analysis of Profitability, Leverage, and Labor Intensity," *American Economic Review* Vol. 91, No. 1 (2001), pp. 320–34.

39 Wei Li, "The Impact of Economic Reform on the Performance of Chinese State Enterprises, 1980–1989," *Journal of Political Economy* Vol. 105, No. 5 (1997), pp. 1080–106; Theodore Groves, Yongmiao Hong, John McMillan and Barry Naughton, "China's Evolving Managerial Labor Market," *Journal of Political Economy* Vol. 103, No. 4 (1995), pp. 873–92; Peter Nolan and Wang Xiaoqiang, "Beyond Privatization: Institutional Innovation and Growth in China's Large State-Owned Enterprises," *World Development* Vol. 27, No. 1 (1999), pp. 169–200; Lawrence J. Lau, Yingyi Qian, and Gerard Roland, "Reform without losers: An Interpretation of China's Dual-Track Approach to Transition," *Journal of Political Economy* Vol. 108, No. 11 (2000), pp. 120–43; Gary Jefferson, Thomas G. Rawski, and Y. Zheng, "Growth, Efficiency and Convergence in China's State and Collective Sector," *Economic Development and Cultural Change* Vol. 40, No. 2 (1992), pp. 239–66.

40 See a summary of the literature in Anming Zhang, Yimin Zhang, and Ronald Zhao, "Profitability and Productivity of Chinese Industrial Firms Measurement and Ownership Implications," *China Economic Review* Vol. 13, No. 1 (2002), pp. 65–88. They also find SOE financial performance to be poor. See also a summary by Yasheng Huang, *Selling China: Foreign Direct Investment During the Reform Era* (Cambridge: Cambridge University Press, 2003), pp. 103–5.

41 George Yarrow, "A Theory of Privatization, or Why Bureaucrats are Still in Business," *World Development* Vol. 27, No. 1 (1999), pp. 157–68; Penelope B. Prime, "Funding Economic Transition in China: The Privatization Option," *Eurasian Geography and Economics* Vol. 45, No. 5 (2004), pp. 382–94.

42 Shuanglin Lin, "China's Government Debt: How Serious?," *China: An International Journal* Vol. 1, No. 1 (2003), pp. 73–98; M.J. Gordon, "Is China's Financial System Threatened by its Policy Loans Debt?," *Journal of Asian Economics* Vol. 14, No. 2 (2003), pp. 181–88.

43 Jahangir Aziz and Christoph K. Duenwald, Asia and Pacific Department, "Growth-Financial Intermediation Nexus in China," International Monetary Fund, Working Paper No. 02/194 (Washington, D.C.: IMF, 2002); Gordon Chang has numerous examples of successful private firms being taken over by or closed down for being too successful or competitive with the state sector, in *The Coming Collapse of China* (New York: Random House, 2001).

44 Yasheng Huang, *Selling China: Foreign Direct Investment During the Reform Era* (Cambridge: Cambridge University Press, 2003).

45 Alwyn Young, "The Razor's Edge: Distortions and Incremental Reform in the People's Republic of China," *The Quarterly Journal of Economics* Vol. CXV, No.4 (2000), pp. 1091–135; Genevieve Boyreau-Debray and Shang-jin Wei, "Can China Grow Faster? A Diagnosis of the Fragmentation of Its Domestic Capital Market," IMF Working Paper No. 04/76 (Washington, D.C.: IMF, 2002); Yasheng Huang, *Selling China: Foreign Direct Investment During the Reform Era* (Cambridge: Cambridge University Press, 2003), Chapter 6; Anuradha Dayal-Gulati and Assim M. Husain, "Centripetal Forces in China's Economic Takeoff," *IMF Staff Papers* Vol. 49, No. 3 (2002), p. 392.

46 Sandra Poncet, "Measuring Chinese Domestic and International Integration," *China Economic Review* Vol. 14, No. 1 (2003), pp. 1–23. Poncet is based in France.

47 Barry Naughton, "How Much Can Regional Integration Do to Unify China's Markets,?" pp. 204–32 in Nicholas Hope, Dennis Yang and Mu Yang Li (eds), *How Far Across the River? Chinese Policy Reform at the Millennium* (Stanford, CA: Stanford University Press, 2003); Li Qi, "Capital Flows and Domestic Market Integration in China," working paper Department of Economics, Agnes Scott College, Atlanta, GA (2004).

48 See, for example, Kevin Honglin Zhang and Shunfeng Song, "Rural-urban Migration and Urbanization in China: Evidence from Time-series and Cross-section Analyses," *China Economic Review* Vol. 14, No. 4 (2003), pp. 386–400. For an analysis of the *hukou* system on urban–rural inequality and migration decisions, see Zhiqiang Liu, "Institution and Inequality: the *Hukou* System in China," *Journal of Comparative Economics* Vol. 33 (2005), pp. 133–57; Cindy C. Fan, "Modeling Inter-provincial Migration in China, 1985–2000," *Eurasian Geography and Economics* Vol. 46, No. 3 (2005), pp. 165–84.

49 Anuradha Dayal-Gulati and Assim M. Husain, "Centripetal Forces in China's Economic Takeoff," *IMF Staff Papers* Vol. 49, No. 3 (2002), p. 391.

50 Roy Bahl, *Fiscal Policy in China: Taxation and Intergovernmental Fiscal Relations* (San Francisco, CA: 1990 Institute, 1999); Christine W.P. Wong, *Financing Local Government in the People's Republic of China* (New York: Oxford University Press, 1997). Political scientists have also done a great deal of research in this area.

51 Yingyi Qian and Barry R. Weingast, "China's Transition to Markets: Market-Preserving Federalism, Chinese Style," *Policy Reform* Vol. 1 (1996), pp. 149–85. "Market preserving federalism" and related concepts have been developed within the political literature. See, for example, Eric Thun, "Keeping Up with the Jones': Decentralization, Policy Imitation, and Industrial Development in China," *World Development* Vol. 32, No. 8 (2004), pp. 1289–308.

52 Alwyn Young, "The Razor's Edge: Distortions and Incremental Reform in the People's Republic of China," *The Quarterly Journal of Economics* Vol. CXV, No. 4 (2000), pp. 1091–135.

53 T. Zhang and H-F. Zou, "The Growth Impact of Intersectoral and Intergovernmental Allocation of Public Expenditure: With Applications to China and India," *China Economic Review* Vol. 12, No. 1 (2001), pp. 58–81.

54 Andrew Feltenstein and Shigeru Iwata, "Decentralization and Macroeconomic Performance in China: Regional Autonomy Has Its Costs," *Journal of Development Economics* Vol. 76 (2005), pp. 481–501.

55 R.S. Eckaus, "Some Consequences of Fiscal Reliance on Extra-budetary Revenues in China," *China Economic Review* Vol. 14, No. 1 (2003), pp. 72–88.

56 Shuanglin Lin, "Excessive Government Fee Collection in China," *Contemporary Economic Policy* Vol. 23, No. 1 (2005), pp. 91–106.

57 Nicholas R. Lardy, *China's Unfinished Economic Revolution* (Washington, D.C.: Brookings Institution, 1998).

58 Xiao-Yuan Dong and Louis Putterman, "Soft Budget Constraints, Social Burdens, and Labor Redundancy in China's State Industry," *Journal of Comparative Economics* Vol. 31 (2003), pp. 110–33.

59 Pieter Bottelier, "Where is Pension Reform Going in China? Issues and Options," *Perspectives* 3.5 (2002), available at http://www.ogcf.org?Perspectives/17_063002/Pension_China.htm.

60 Albert Park and Kaja Sehrt, "Tests of Financial Intermediation and Banking Reform in China," *Journal of Comparative Economics* Vol. 29, No. 4 (December 2001), pp. 608–44.

61 Alan Guoming Huang and Hung-Gay Fung, "Stock Ownership Segmentation, Floatability, and Constraints on Investment Banking in China," *China and the World Economy* Vol. 12, No. 2 (March–April 2004), pp. 66–78.
62 Lawrence Saez, "Banking Reform in India and China," *International Journal of Finance and Economics* Vol. 6, No. 3 (July 2001), pp. 235–44.
63 Joanne Li and Jot Yau, "China's Banking Reform: A Single Step in a Thousand-Mile Journey," *International Journal of Business* Vol. 6, No. 2 (2001), pp. 87–110.
64 Franklin Allen, Jun Qian and Meijun Qian, "Law, Finance, and Economic Growth in China," *Journal of Financial Economics* Vol. 77, No. 1 (July 2005), pp. 57–116.
65 Barry Naughton, *Growing Out of the Plan: Chinese Economic Reform 1978–1993* (Cambridge: Cambridge University Press, 1996).
66 Edward S. Steinfeld, "China's Shallow Integration: Networked Production and the New Challenges for Late Industrialization," *World Development* Vol. 32, No. 11 (2004), pp. 1971–87.

II. Studies of Chinese Politics

5 Studies of Chinese Politics in Europe

Jean-Pierre Cabestan

This chapter offers a review of the state of European studies of contemporary Chinese politics in recent years. European scholars have shown a keen interest in Chinese politics for a long time. In the late 1960s and early 1970s, this interest was partly driven by the growing influence of Maoist and more generally leftist ideas among intellectuals and elites. But the dramatic political changes that occurred in China after Mao Zedong's death and the renewed attraction in Europe for liberal democracy and human rights have restored more traditional factors of interests: China's economic development, ideological opening, growing diplomatic and strategic power as well as social stability and political future have become again the main drivers of European studies of Chinese politics.

For these reasons, Europe's interest in Chinese domestic politics has increased strongly since China began implementing its reforms in 1978. Yet, despite the growing interest, European studies of Chinese politics have always been concentrated in a few large Western European nations, primarily France, Germany, and the United Kingdom, with a few additional researchers in the Netherlands and Scandinavia.[1] In other parts of Europe, it is harder to identify individuals specializing in and publishing on Chinese politics, as most of the scholars from these countries adopt a more generalist approach, conducting research into both Chinese politics and contemporary history, or into both China and other East Asian countries.

While over-specialization is often considered to be a distinguishing feature of American scholarship on contemporary China, conversely, the lack of specialization appears as an important characteristic of European studies of Chinese politics. Several reasons explain this relative weakness and under-specialization:

- the narrowness of the national market, in particular in small European countries and/or countries using a non-international language, as is the case in most European Union (EU) member states apart from the U.K.;
- the lingering weight of European studies of classical China or Sinology;
- the lack of European security responsibilities in the Asia-Pacific region and, in particular, around China;
- the very uneven level of governmental demand and support for studies of contemporary Chinese politics;

- the lack of private resources able to complement any governmental support;
- the concentration of European public and private funding of research into contemporary China in the economic, and to some extent, legal fields (owing to the growing importance of EU–China economic and trade relations).

Despite these factors, two major factors have contributed to the rapid development and qualitative improvement of European studies of Chinese politics. On the one hand, EU-level financial support for research into Chinese politics and the legal system has steadily increased in the last two decades. On the other, European China scholars have become more and more integrated in the world community of researchers studying contemporary China – whether they are from North America, East Asia, or Australia. While European studies of Chinese politics have continued to develop at a national level, the multiplication of cross-border communications, in particular within the EU, has played a part in creating a European community of China scholars gradually more integrated in the world community of scholars studying contemporary Chinese politics. True, this trend has not affected every European specialist of contemporary China. Nevertheless, a larger proportion of European scholars have benefited both financially and intellectually from these growing contacts and cooperation, publishing more specialized studies more often in English that can be included in American or international journals or edited volumes. An indicator of these changes is the existence today of three journals specializing in contemporary China in English published in Europe or funded by EU member-states (*China Information, China Perspectives* and *The China Quarterly*) compared with just one 20 years ago (*The China Quarterly*).

While these features and new trends can also apply to European studies of China's economy or international relations, they have on the whole contributed to strengthening European research into Chinese politics and making this field better understood on the Old Continent. On the whole, the picture has changed substantially and improved since the mid-1990s, when *The China Quarterly* published a very useful and welcome series of articles on contemporary China studies in particular in France and in Scandinavia.[2]

Chinese Political Studies in France, Germany, and the United Kingdom

France

As France is both an administratively and intellectually centralized country, most of the scholars studying Chinese politics are concentrated in Paris. However, Lyons and Marseilles, the second and the third largest French cities, have centers that are home to a few researchers in this field. France has also run a Centre for Research on Contemporary China (Centre d'Études Français sur la Chine Contemporaine, or CEFC) in Hong Kong, with a branch in Taipei, since 1991.

In Paris, the major research locus for Chinese politics is the Center for International Studies and Research (Centre d'Études et de Recherches Internationales) of the French National Foundation for Political Sciences (Fondation Nationale des Sciences Politiques). This center has five researchers specializing in this field. They are, by order of seniority, Jean-Luc Domenach, Jean-Philippe Béja, Françoise Mengin, Jean-Louis Rocca and Stéphanie Balme. Béja is on the payroll of the French National Center for Scientific Research (Centre National de la Recherche Scientifique, or CNRS) while the four others are paid by the Foundation. Claude Cadart and his wife Cheng Ying-hsiang, both CNRS researchers, were also attached to this center until they retired in 2000.[3] While Domenach and Mengin have also conducted research into China's (and, in Mengin's case, Taiwan's) foreign relations and security, they all devote most of their time to the study of domestic Chinese politics.

Since making a name for himself in the English-speaking community with his path-breaking monograph on the origins of the Great Leap Forward in Henan province,[4] Domenach has published widely on contemporary China and on Asian politics in French. His doctoral dissertation dealt with the Chinese *Laogai* (gulag): *Chine, l'archipel oublié* (*China, the Forgotten Archipelago*) was published in French in 1992 and later in German.[5] His most recently published book, *Où va la Chine?* (*Where is China Headed?*), is an overview of Jiang Zemin's China at the time power was gradually transferred to Hu Jintao.[6] His previous overview, *Chine* (Volume 1: 1949–1971, Volume 2: 1971–), has been a principal textbook in French universities since it was first published in 1987.[7]

Jean-Philippe Béja is also a prolific author, both in French and in English. He initially conducted research into and published on the Chinese democratic movement of 1979 and intellectuals. He participated in the group of (then) young French Sinologists (including Michel Bonnin and Jacques Andrieu) who, just returned from China where they had received language training in the early 1970s, translated into French and published many documents related to this movement.[8] In the same period of time, he translated into French and presented Liu Binyan's most famous reports (*baogao wenxue*).[9] Béja has maintained a strong interest in democratic ideas in China ever since. After the Tiananmen massacre, in collaboration with Michel Bonnin and Alain Peyraube, he translated into French and presented many documents written by the main players of the 1989 Beijing Spring.[10] More recently, he has published an essay on the democratic movement in China since 1919[11] and edited the French translation of Zhang Liang's *Tiananmen Papers*.[12] Béja spent four years (1993–1997) in Hong Kong as scientific director of the CEFC, and he has also developed an interest and studied the territory's political life and transition from British rule to Chinese sovereignty[13] as well as problems of migrant workers and social re-stratification in mainland China.[14] Béja is, moreover, a regular contributor on Chinese politics to the well-known French journal *Esprit* (created by the existential philosopher Emmanuel Mounier in 1932).

Françoise Mengin wrote her Ph.D. dissertation on France's relations with Taiwan, developing from that a strong interest in Taiwan's democratization, identity, nation-building and changing relations with mainland China. Focusing on the re-mapping of the Greater China area, in 1998 she published *Trajectoires chinoises: Taiwan, Hong Kong et Pékin (Chinese Trajectories: Taiwan, Hong Kong and Beijing).*[15] She has also conducted research into the linkage between Taiwanese politics and the China market and its impact on the moving "frontiers" between China and Taiwan.[16] In more recent years, she has extended her field of interest to the Internet and its impact in Greater China.[17] In addition, Mengin has maintained an interest in China's foreign policy, in particular France's China policy.[18]

Jean-Louis Rocca joined CERI in the mid-1990s, around the same time as Françoise Mengin. Before that, as a native of Lyons, he taught at the Catholic University of Lyons and was associated with the Institute for East Asian Studies (Institut d'Asie Orientale) of the CNRS and the University of Lyons II, headed at the time by the China historian Christian Henriot. Rocca's Ph.D. dissertation, a political analysis of criminality in post-Mao China, was published in 1991 under the title *L'Empire et son milieu: La criminalité en Chine populaire (The Empire and its Criminals).*[19] He later studied corruption in China from a comparative approach.[20] Since joining the CERI, Rocca has conducted research into labor issues and welfare policies in China, in particular in Manchuria, Sichuan, and Shanghai.[21] As a visiting professor at the Renmin (People's) University in Beijing and attached to the CEFC in Hong Kong from 2000 to 2003, Rocca has published many articles in academic journals as well as contributions to edited volumes comparing unemployment and employment policies in China and in some European countries.

Stéphanie Balme (née Lautard) joined the CERI in 2001. In 2004, she published a revised version of her Ph.D. dissertation under the title: *Entre soi: L'élite du pouvoir dans la Chine contemporaine (Among One Another: The Elite in Power in Contemporary China).*[22] Since 2002, rather than pursuing research into China's political elite, Balme has focused on the relationship between law and politics in China. In late 2003, she moved to Hong Kong and since then has been an honorary research associate at the Chinese University of Hong Kong.

The second most important locus of Chinese political studies is the Research Center on Modern and Contemporary China (Centre sur la Chine Moderne et Contemporaine) of the Higher School in Social Sciences (École des Hautes Études en Sciences Sociales or EHESS).[23] Created by former military attaché in Beijing, General Jacques Guillermaz in the late 1960s, it has been led by such well-known historians of contemporary China as Marie-Claire Bergère and Lucien Bianco. Co-directed by Christian Lamouroux, a historian specializing in the Song Dynasty, and Isabelle Thireau, a sociologist of contemporary China, this center has only three political scientists: Jacques Andrieu, Michel Bonnin, and Yves Chevrier, a former director. However, the "Centre Chine," as it is commonly called, holds regular public seminars (and supervises Ph.D. students) and is considered a meeting point for all scholars interested in contemporary China. Some of its members are CNRS researchers (such as Thireau, Andrieu and economist François Gipoloux), while most are EHESS "directeurs d'études" (study directors), such as former director

Joël Thoraval, a specialist in Chinese contemporary philosophy. The center also hosts a few associate researchers involved in political studies, though with another main affiliation, such as Samia Ferhat-Dana and Guilhem Fabre (see below).

Andrieu, previously known under his penname Zafanolli, published a few books and book chapters in the 1980s and 1990s on intra-Communist Party struggles, intellectuals, dissidents and the revival of literature in post-Mao China.[24] He has also worked on corruption. More recently, he has focused his research on a political biography of Mao Zedong.[25]

Based in Hong Kong in the 1970s, Michel Bonnin originally conducted in-depth research into and wrote his Ph.D. thesis on the *zhiqing*, the educated youth sent to the countryside by Mao during the Cultural Revolution. However, after much updating and taking advantage of the publication of many new materials and memoirs, this research was developed into a very comprehensive book on the subject in 2004.[26] When he was in Hong Kong, Bonnin interviewed a number of refugees from China and published these interviews in a book that, for the first time since 1949, gave the French public direct and disillusioned access to China's rural society.[27] Upon his return to France, Bonnin became very interested in the democratic movement of 1978–1979 in China, translating into French and presenting several important documents on this theme.[28] While he also studied the changing life and status of intellectuals in post-Mao China (with Yves Chevrier),[29] he continued to focus on democratic ideas and movements in China.[30] Bonnin was the first director of the CEFC from 1991 to 1998 and it was there that he started to study and publish on Hong Kong politics in particular in the journal launched by the center in 1992, *Perspectives chinoises*. His research became known by a wider audience after he started in 1995 an English edition of *Perspectives chinoises – China Perspectives*.[31] Bonnin's research subjects have also included migrant workers moving to the cities (with Béja) and the question of social stability in China.[32]

Yves Chevrier has studied China's transition towards modernity, both from the view point of a historian and that of a political scientist.[33] Alongside his seminal handbook on *Modern China*,[34] Chevrier has published studies on Mao Zedong and the Chinese revolution career as well as the "temps long" or "longue durée" (long-period approach favored by French historian Fernand Braudel) of Chinese politics.[35] Chevrier has also developed (together with Bonnin) an interest in the changing life and status of intellectuals in post-Mao China.[36]

Although Thireau is a sociologist, some of her research work has a genuine political science dimension, such as her edited volume based on fieldwork on the resolution of disputes in Chinese villages[37] or her study (with her husband Hua Linshan) of appeals by Chinese workers to the recently revived letter and visit offices.[38] Hua Linshan himself wrote a very poignant account of his years as a Red Guard in Guangxi, also a very useful testimony of the Cultural Revolution in a rather understudied region of China.[39] Thireau has published contributions on the new peasant movements with her husband.[40]

In Paris, outside of these two centers, there are a few students of Chinese politics who are either attached to an institute focusing on a different discipline, such as the author of this paper, Jean-Pierre Cabestan, who, although a CNRS researcher, is part of the Institute of Comparative Law of the University of Paris I, or to another university, such as Samia Ferhat-Dana, who specializes in Taiwan, at the University of Paris X, Nanterre (she is also associated with the Centre Chine).[41] There are also independent China researchers, such as General Henri Eyraud (now retired),[42] Marie Holzman, a specialist on Chinese dissidents (in particular Wei Jingsheng) and democratic ideas in China,[43] or researchers with non-scholarly affiliations, such as Chen Yan, a Radio France International journalist who has studied new intellectual and political debates in China.[44]

The author of this chapter joined the CNRS in 1983. Previously, for a decade I was attached to the Institute of Comparative Law and Institutions under the CNRS, located in Ivry-sur-Seine just outside Paris. I was also a consultant at the Foundation for National Defense Studies from 1981 to 1988. I then developed research first into the administrative, political, and legal reforms of the post-Mao era and then into China's foreign and security policy.[45] In late 1993, I moved to Taiwan, where in July 1994 I opened the Taipei office of the Hong Kong-based CEFC. After four years in this post, I moved to Hong Kong in 1998 and became director of the CEFC until 2003. Since 1993, I have published several books in French,[46] and a few book chapters and articles in English on Taiwan and relations across the Taiwan Strait, in particular in *China Perspectives*.[47] However, I have maintained an interest in China's foreign policy and political and legal developments that has become stronger since I moved back to France and took up my current affiliation in September 2003.[48]

Outside of Paris, the picture is more fragmented and complex. Most of the research conducted on contemporary Chinese politics is concentrated in Lyons and Aix-en-Provence-Marseilles with a pronounced penchant for Taiwanese politics. In Lyons, the East Asia Institute, a rather large entity headed by Japanologist Eric Seizelet, today includes just one political scientist specializing in China: Stéphane Corcuff, who has been a lecturer at the Lyons Institute for Political Studies since 2004 and whose research has concentrated on Taiwan.[49] At the Aix-Marseilles University, the Institute for South East Asian Studies includes two anthropologists who have occasionally published on Taiwanese politics: Fiorella Allio and Chantal Zheng; the law faculty of Aix-Marseilles University also includes a jurist specializing in China international law and Taiwan, Christine Chaigne.[50]

A few other provincial universities also have contemporary China specialists who have published on political subjects, such as Guilhem Fabre, a professor at Le Havre University, who is also associated with the Paris-based Centre Chine and who has published on the history of the Chinese Communist Party, on the connections between economic, social, and institutional reforms in post-Mao China as well as on corruption, drug-trafficking, and money laundering from a comparative perspective.[51]

Finally, as already indicated, the French academic community studying contemporary China includes a center based in Hong Kong with an office in Taipei and a few researchers on the mainland, the CEFC.[52] Directed since 2003 by Gilles Guiheux, an economic sociologist who has specialized in private businesspeople in China, the CEFC is part of a network of 27 research centers administered by the French Foreign Ministry. It may in the near future move its headquarters to Beijing and merge with the structure created by Jean-Luc Domenach in 2001, the French-Chinese Seminar in Social Sciences based at Tsinghua University, after Domenach moves back to France. The CEFC has a few political scientists, including two researchers (Patricia Batto, the editor of *Perspectives chinoises* and its English translation, *China Perspectives*, who specializes in China and Taiwan's written media, and Frank Muyard, the director of the CEFC Taipei Office, who has mainly conducted research into and published on Taiwan's nationalism and elections). The CEFC also trains Ph.D. candidates in political science, who currently include Rémi Castets, who is preparing a dissertation on Uighur nationalism in Xinjiang; Chloé Froissart, who is writing a dissertation on public policies for migrant workers in the municipality of Chengdu; Vincent Rollet, who is conducting research in Taiwan on sanitary security and cross-Strait relations; and Emilie Tran, who is completing a thesis on the Communist Party Schools and the new forms of cadre training in China. All of these candidates have published articles in *China Perspectives*.

Germany

Typically, the German organization of research on Chinese and Taiwanese politics is more decentralized. There are two main research centers focusing on Asia which are home to political scientists specializing in such areas: The Institute for Asian Affairs (Institut für Asienkunde) in Hamburg and the Institute of East Asian Studies (Institut für Ostasienwissenschaften) at the Gerhard Mercator University in Duisburg, near Essen. Major universities, such as those in Berlin, Cologne, Heidelberg, Munich, and Tübingen, have specialists in Chinese politics, but they are usually individual scholars who belong to political science and comparative politics departments, or are adjunct faculty.

Subsidized by the federal government and part of the German Overseas Institute (Deusches Übersee-Institut), the Hamburg Institute for Asian Affairs offers the largest concentration of China specialists in Germany.[53] Directed by Günter Schucher, it hosts several political scientists specializing in Chinese studies, such as Schucher himself, Margot Schüller and Hans-Wilm Schütte. Schucher and Schüller have in particular conducted research into social integration and economic interaction across the Taiwan Strait. The Institute for Asian Affairs publishes the monthly journal *China Aktuell* in German with an extremely useful English supplement chronicling monthly leadership and institutional changes, as well as bibliography. Its articles provide thorough and detailed analyses of major political, institutional, legal, economic and social developments not only in the People's Republic of China (PRC) but also in Taiwan, Hong Kong, and Macau. The *China Aktuell* editors are Karsten Giese, a political scientist who has conducted research into the Internet in and emigration from China, and Heike Holbig, another political scientist who has already published a great deal on ideology, the media, and the Chinese political system.[54] The Institute of Asian

Affairs also publishes books on similar topics, mainly in German, with a few titles in English.[55] China specialists based at other institutions have also taken advantage of the institute's collection (MIA or Mitteilungen des Instituts für Asienkunde) to publish their own research work.[56]

Created in 1994 and today headed by Markus Taube, an economist specializing in China, the East Asian Institute of the University of Duisburg-Essen studies the whole Asian continent east of Afghanistan, including Japan, China, Korea, Southeast Asia and South Asia.[57] Around 30 specialists, among them half a dozen China scholars, are attached to it. It produces several publications: monographs (*Monographien*), often published by the Institut für Asienkunde in Hamburg, and four working paper series, including a green one (*Grüne Reihe*) for in-house papers, a blue one (*Blaue Reihe*) and a black one (*Schwarze Reihe*) for papers on economic development in the Pacific Rim, and an orange one (*Orangen Reihe*) for papers related to the program on the "discourses on political reform and democratization in East and Southeast Asia in the Light of New Processes of Regional Community-Building."[58]

As this latest program indicates, a few of its members conduct research into Chinese politics, for example political science professors Thomas Heberer, Claudia Derichts, Christian Göbel, Anka-Désirée Senz and, until early 2005, Nora Sausmikat.[59] A former director of the institute, Heberer has himself published extensively in this field (in German, English, French and Chinese) – in particular on private entrepreneurs, local elections, civil society and the political system in China.[60] While Derichts specializes more in Malaysia, Göbel has worked both on civil society in China and Taiwan as well as on political corruption and organized crime in Taiwan.[61] Senz has conducted research into national minorities and local political participation in China,[62] while Sausmikat has published several articles on intellectuals and the state as well as women NGOs in China.[63]

The Free University of Berlin (Freie Universität) has had a long and strong Sinological tradition, including a chaired professorship in Chinese Politics. The current holder is Eberhard Sandschneider, a former student of the late Professor Jürgen Domes of the University of Saarbrücken (1932–2001), a leading international authority on Chinese politics. Sandschneider has published extensively on various aspects of Chinese politics and foreign relations.[64] Although he took leave from FUB to become Director of the DGAP (Deutsche Gesellschaft für Auswärtige Politik, or German Council on Foreign Affairs) in 2003, he has managed to continue his publishing and public speaking on China. During his absence from the Free University, Sandschneider has been replaced on the faculty by Bettina Gransow van Treeck, who has published extensively on rural politics and migrants in China. The Free University has concentrated its study of contemporary China in two institutions. The first is the Center for Chinese and East Asian Politics under the Otto Suhr Institute of Political Science,[65] which includes Professor Werner Pfennig – who has published widely on East Asian comparative politics, including judicial and political reform in China and cross-strait relations. The second is the Sinology Institute of the Seminar on East Asian Studies.[66] Researchers there include Gransow van Treeck (noted above), Republican era historian Mechthild

Leutner, Martina Wobst (Chinese foreign policy), and Jens Damm (contemporary Chinese and Taiwanese politics).

Berlin also hosts a major institution with a strong interest in contemporary China: the Stiftung Wissenschaft und Politik (German Institute for International and Security Affairs), Europe's largest research institute of its kind. Although most of its researchers focus on foreign and security questions, a few of them, among them Gudrun Wacker (the Head of the Asia Research Unit), have published on China's domestic political problems. Having a Ph.D. in Sinology from the University of Tübingen with a dissertation on advertising in China (1991), Wacker has more recently researched on the Internet and generational changes in domestic Chinese politics.[67] Kay Möller, who also works in the Asia Research Unit, concentrates on China's foreign and security policy, although some of his writings deal with domestic politics. Möller has recently published a major study of China's domestic politics and foreign policy.[68]

Another important university is Cologne, where Professor Thomas Scharping and Professor Herman Halbeisen both teach. The former has published a large number of books and articles since the 1970s on various subjects, including KMT-CCP relations and Mao Zedong, but since the mid-1990s he has specialized in the study of migration and birth control policies in China.[69] The latter, attached to the Research Institute for Political Science and European Affairs, has conducted research into Taiwanese politics for more than 20 years. Professor Robert Heuser, one of Germany's best specialists in contemporary Chinese law, also teaches at this university.

The University of Munich has four scholars (two retired, two active) working on China's foreign and security policies – although all four have published on aspects of domestic politics as well. These include retired Professors Peter Opitz and Karl Gottfried Kindermann, and younger scholars Franco Algieri and Saskia Hieber. Algieri has developed a strong expertise in China–Europe relations, while Hieber concentrates on the Chinese military, security, and energy policies.

At the University of Tübingen, Gunter Schubert has held the Chair in Chinese Politics since 2003. Although still rather young, he has published extensively on Taiwanese politics and identity, as well as Chinese nationalism, local elections, and democratization, both in German and in English. He is one of the editors of *Asien*, one of the major German journals on Asia (that often includes articles both in German and English on Chinese politics).[70]

Other German universities have specialists in Chinese politics, such as the University of Heidelberg with its famous Sinological Institute (Sinologisches Seminar) directed by Rudolph Wagner, a scholar of traditional China. At this institute, since the departure of Professor Susanne Weigelin-Schwiedrzik (a specialist in Chinese Communist Party history) for the University of Vienna in the late-1990s, Thomas Kampen has taken over the teaching of, and research on, Chinese politics.[71] Other political scientists, such as Gunter Schubert, are also associated with this institute.

In Germany, as elsewhere in Europe, Taiwan politics have attracted fresh and vigorous interest since the democratization of the island-state in the late 1980s.

In addition to Halbeisen, Schubert, Göbel, and Damm, China scholars at the Ruhr University of Bochum, such as Henning Klöter of the Department of Chinese Language and Literature, although more specialized in literature or history, have also published on topics with a political dimension.[72]

The United Kingdom

Great Britain has always enjoyed a strong tradition of political study of contemporary China. Although a large number of scholars in this field are concentrated in London and at traditional universities such as Oxford and Cambridge, in the last decade or so, they have developed structures that have allowed them to conduct in-depth research into Chinese politics and attract world-class specialists in Chinese politics. Recent arrivals include, for example, Vivienne Shue in Oxford, Flemming Christiansen in Leeds, and Zheng Yongnian at Nottingham. It is interesting to note that none of these individuals are British-trained and are not British citizens – bespeaking a weakness in domestic higher education for the training of specialists in Chinese politics. Since the departure of Stuart Schram and David Shambaugh from SOAS in the early and late 1990s respectively, few Ph.D.s in Chinese politics have been trained in British universities. Nonetheless, the arrival of Shue, Christensen, and Zheng has begun to reverse the steady attrition and negative trend of departures dating back to the 1980s, after which a number of leading China specialists left the U.K. for positions in America and Australia – including political scientists David Goodman, Roderick MacFarquhar, Tony Saich, David Shambaugh, Stuart Schram, and Michael Yahuda; economists Y.Y. Kueh, Qi Luo, Elspeth Thomson; and historians Mark Elvin and W.J.F. Jenner.

In London, the main institution is the School of Oriental and African Studies (SOAS) of the University of London,[73] but the London School of Economics and Political Science (LSE) has also long attracted high-level scholars of Chinese politics.[74] Since the departure of David Shambaugh, SOAS has been home to three political scientists specializing in China: Julia Strauss, Phil Deans, and Dafydd Fell. Strauss, the current Editor of *The China Quarterly,* primarily works on Republican-era Chinese politics,[75] although her research interests in recent years have moved into the evolution of the communist state apparatus during the 1950s and the area of forestry policy. Deans and Fell have both mainly conducted research on Taiwan, the former into foreign policy and Taiwan–Japan relations,[76] the latter into party politics.[77] Joji Kijima, of the Department of Political Studies also conducted research on Japan-Taiwan relations. This renewed interest in Taiwan at SOAS has benefited from the support of the Chiang Ching-kuo Foundation which has financed a chair in Taiwan studies, first occupied by Professor Robert Ash, and the creation of a multidisciplinary Master's Degree in this specialty with a strong political science dimension.

At the London School of Economics (LSE), since the early retirement and departure for the United States of Michael Yahuda in 2004, an internationally respected specialist of China's foreign policy and Hong Kong politics, two scholars teach Chinese politics at the LSE: Christopher Hughes, who has made himself known for his writings on Chinese and Taiwanese nationalism, as well as on Taiwanese politics, and Jude Howell – a specialist on Chinese governance. Odd Arne Westad also works on China's foreign relations in the context of Cold War history.[78]

In the late 1990s, the University of Westminster in London (formerly Central London Polytechnic) established a Centre for the Study of Democracy, which has developed a strong interest in the changes of the Chinese political system and the prospects of democratization. Harriet Evans is the main figure in Chinese Studies at the center. A Council Member of the British Association for Chinese Studies, Evans has published on women and the Cultural Revolution in China,[79] and has also contributed many articles to journals and edited volumes. Her current research includes a project on mothers, daughters and gendered subjectivities, sexuality and reproductive health as well as political posters and visual culture in the People's Republic of China.

At Oxford University, contemporary China studies are spread across the university. At St Antony's College, Steve Tsang (a historian by training) has conducted research on China, Hong Kong, and Taiwan politics for many years. Although he has always exhibited a stronger interest in foreign policy, relations across the Taiwan Strait, and security issues, Tsang has also published extensively on Hong Kong and the political history in China.[80] He is currently preparing a political biography of Chiang Kai-shek. Rana Mitter, a young historian specializing in the Republican era (but holding a joint appointment in politics), also has a breadth of interests in post-1949 politics and has recently published an impressive study of Chinese nationalism that spans the twentieth century.[81] Other Oxford faculty active in researching aspects of Chinese politics include Rosemary Foot (foreign policy and human rights), Eric Thun (Chinese business), Frank Pieke (the Party School system of the Communist Party and ethnic issues), Daniel Buck (political economy around Shanghai), John Knight (an economist working on the labor market and politics), Tao Ran (political economy and local governance), and William Hurst (politics of labor reform).

In 2004, Oxford University invited Cornell University Professor of Government Vivienne Shue to take up the Leverhulme Chair of Contemporary Chinese Studies at St Antony's and the university's Institute for Chinese Studies.[82] The arrival of Shue has significantly strengthened British research in contemporary Chinese politics, which had been in decline for some time. Her research on the "reach of the state," the local state and its dynamic interaction with an ever changing society has already renewed the study of state–society relations on both sides of the Atlantic. Her more recent work on the patterns and processes of political legitimacy and on the relationship between the government and some new social organizations is also noteworthy.[83] Professor Shue has also been instrumental in rebuilding contemporary China studies at Oxford. She heads the Contemporary China Studies Program, established in 2002 with a grant from the Leverhulme Trust.[84] The program is explicitly interdisciplinary and exclusively concerns the social sciences. The program runs workshops and seminars, sponsors postdoctoral scholars in residence, and hosts distinguished visitors.

At Cambridge University, classical Sinology remains dominant, but there is also a growing interest in contemporary China, both in the economic field (for example Wei Zhang, a lecturer in the Chinese economy at the Faculty of Oriental Studies) and in the political field (Gerald Chan, a research fellow at the Centre of International Studies, who has worked on China's foreign policy).[85] Hans van de Ven, a historian specializing in the Republican era, also has strong interests in Chinese politics. Cambridge's best-known China specialist has long been economist Peter Nolan, a leading expert on China's economy at the Judge Institute of Management, also occasionally does work on Chinese politics.[86] In 2006 Sir Christopher Hum was appointed as Master of Gonville & Caius College, after retiring as British Ambassador to China and one of the Foreign Office's leading China hands. Hum joins Lord Wilson of Tillyorn, former Governor of Hong Kong, former Editor of *The China Quarterly*, and currently Master of Peterhouse at Cambridge. Both Hum and Wilson have an interest in improving contemporary China studies at Cambridge.

Aside from Oxford and Cambridge, the main center of research on Chinese politics outside of London is probably the new Institute of Contemporary Chinese Studies located in the China House of the University of Nottingham. Headed by Andrew Marton, a geographer, it is home to a few political scientists, in particular Jackie Sheehan, who has published on China's workers and enterprise management, and Sally Sargenson, who specializes in local governance and gender studies in China. Since 2003, the China House has also housed the China Policy Institute, the director of which is Richard Pascoe, a former head of Reuters Japan. In September 2005, Zheng Yongnian (on leave as senior research fellow at the East Asian Institute of the National University of Singapore), was appointed Head of Research and Director of the China Policy Institute.[87]

Zheng's arrival in Britain constitutes another sign of the revival of British research on contemporary China, as well as of the financial support Nottingham has received from the business community and other sources in the last few years. It is less common in European than in American universities to offer positions to Asians, and in particular scholars from China. Zheng's appointment should therefore be considered an asset that will help European, and especially British researchers on Chinese politics, to initiate more joint research programs as well as field studies with Chinese counterparts. The School of Politics and International Relations of the Faculty of Law and Social Sciences at the University of Nottingham has one other China specialist, Gary Rawnsney,[88] who focuses primarily on the Taiwanese media and communications.

The University of Leeds has been one of the major centers for Chinese language training in the UK for more than two decades. Its Department of Asian Studies has therefore attracted several teachers of Chinese politics, such as Christopher Dent, whose research interests concentrate on the political economy of East Asia, including South Korea, Singapore, and Taiwan.[89] More recently, the university has attracted the top-quality Sinologist, Flemming Christiansen from Denmark (although it was Leiden where he received his Ph.D. and taught for some years) to teach Chinese studies and take charge of the Institute for Research on Contemporary China. Christiansen is also deputy director of the Centre for Chinese Business and Development in the University of Leeds. In his research, Christiansen has directed particular attention to rural economic development and urbanization, the political system, identity in China and among Chinese as well as social stability in the context of economic globalization.[90]

The University of Durham in the north of England also has a long tradition of Asian and Chinese studies. Durham's School of Government and International Affairs hosts two scholars of China's foreign relations: David Kerr, who has published several articles on Sino–Russian economic and energy relations; Gordon Cheung, the editor of *East Asia: An International Quarterly*, which regularly includes articles on Chinese politics. [91]

At the University of Manchester, William Callahan has conducted research on China–East Asia relations as well as, more recently, Chinese nationalism.[92] He is also interested in comparative regionalism and the ASEM process between Europe and Asia.

Further north, in Scotland, the University of Glasgow's Department of Politics has Jane Duckett, a SOAS Ph.D., whose work on the "entrepreneurial state" and local governance has stimulated a vivid discussion on the state–enterprise relationship in China.[93] Duckett's research has, more recently, begun to work on the health care and pension systems.

The Department of Politics and International Studies at the University of Warwick includes Peter Ferdinand. A Soviet specialist by training and a student of comparative communist systems, Ferdinand has occasionally done work on China, Hong Kong, and Taiwan.[94] Warwick's faculty also includes Shaun Breslin, who has published a great deal on contemporary Chinese politics, in particular on central–provincial relations and Mao.[95]

After the death of Gordon White, an internationally-recognized specialist on Chinese politics, the University of Sussex is left with Professor Robert Benewick, who has published a few very useful handbooks in this field.[96]

Research on Taiwanese politics has also witnessed rapid growth in the U.K. over the last decade or so, spurred by the democratization of the island-state and funding from the Chiang Ching-kuo Foundation and Taiwan government sources. As noted above, SOAS is the primary British center for Taiwan studies, offering an M.A. degree in the subject.

Chinese Politics Studies in Other Parts of Europe

In other parts of Europe, the Netherlands and Scandinavia have a tradition of studying Chinese politics. Italy and, to lesser extents, Austria, Spain, and Switzerland, have a few political scientists interested in China but these countries have not invested many resources in a field which remains perceived as too specialized and loosely related to their main international interests and concerns.

The Netherlands

For well-known historical reasons (trade with East Asia and the colonization of Taiwan in the seventeenth century), the Netherlands has a long tradition of Chinese and Taiwanese studies. The Sinologische Instituut at Leiden University symbolizes this tradition. In 1969, the university founded its Documentation and Research Centre for Modern China at the same premises (Arsenaalstraat 1). This center has attracted several political scientists, including (in the 1980s) Tony Saich from England. Saich played a significant role in developing its activities, launching a new journal *China Information* in 1986, and published extensively on Chinese Communist Party history and other aspects of Chinese politics. Saich's departure to head the Ford Foundation's Beijing Office in the early 1990s (and subsequently to Harvard) was a real blow to European studies of contemporary China. Since then the center has continued to teach courses on government and politics in modern China and to improve the quality and distribution of *China Information*. Edited by Woei Lien Chong until the early 2000s and then by Tak-wing Ngo, this journal (three issues a year since 2004) is a good indicator of the new trends of European research on contemporary China.

There are a few political scientists researching China at Leiden University, including Tak-wing Ngo, Woei Lien Chong, Stefan Landsberger, Eduard Vermeer, and Benjamin van Rooij. Ngo, a native of Hong Kong who received his Ph.D. in Politics from SOAS, has published on the political systems of both Macau and Hong Kong and has more recently broadened his interests to political conflicts and state building in East Asia.[97] Chong has published many articles on Taiwanese and Chinese cinema, in particular in *China Information*. Vermeer, a historian by training, has for many years conducted research on China's economic history, environmental problems, and contemporary rural economy, in particular on rural cooperatives and income distribution through national and local surveys, as well as many topics of interest for political scientists.[98] Of the younger generation of Dutch Sinologists, it is also worth mentioning Benjamin Van Rooij, whose work on the implementation of environmental legislation has an obvious political dimension.[99]

Two other Dutch universities, Amsterdam and Groningen, have political scientists specializing in China. At the former, Leo Douw, a graduate from Leiden, conducts research on transnational Chinese networks, while at the latter, Peter Ho, also a graduate from Leiden, works on environmental issues and NGOs.

Finally, the Netherlands is the home of the International Institute for Asian Studies (IIAS), directed for a long time by Professor W.A.L. Stockhoff.[100] The IIAS subsidizes conferences and research projects on both ancient and contemporary Asia. For instance, it is supporting a research program on genomics and bio-ethnics in Asia, directed by Margaret Sleeboom, a social scientist who previously studied political control over the Chinese Academy of Social Sciences and other research institutes.[101]

The Nordic Countries

In Scandinavia, research on contemporary China is younger than in the rest of Western Europe, dating back just to the late 1960s and early 1970s. And political studies have only been very gradually and unevenly included in this new stream of research. All Nordic countries today have a few political scientists specializing in China, but Denmark and Sweden seem to have trained the ones who are best known outside of Scandinavia.

Denmark

There are four centers for Asian and Chinese studies in Denmark – three located in Copenhagen and one in at the University of Aarhus in northern Jutland. The three centers located in the Danish capital are the Department of Asian Studies and the Nordic Institute of Asian Studies, both at the University of Copenhagen, and the Asia Research Centre of the Copenhagen Business School. The location of the Department of Asian Studies, the NIAS, and the Asia Research Centre in the same city has turned Copenhagen into the major center for China studies in Scandinavia with about ten people engaged in studying Chinese politics.

Founded in 1960, the East Asian Institute of the University of Copenhagen became a proper department (Department of Asian Studies) in 1993. The first post in Modern East Asian history and society was held by Kjeld-Erik Brødsgaard in the 1990s.[102] Before that Brødsgaard had already become director of this university's Centre for East and South East Asian Studies (CESEAS) created in 1984. He contributed actively to the development of research on contemporary China and to the launch of a new publication, the *Copenhagen Journal of Asian Studies*. However, for "bureaucratic reasons," the CESEAS closed in 1994 and merged with the East Asian Department.

The Nordic Institute of Asian Studies (NIAS) was founded in 1967 with the support of the governments of Denmark, Norway, and Sweden and until the mid-1980s (when Finland joined the project) was named the Scandinavian Institute of Asian Studies (SIAS).[103] The NIAS is a good example of regional coordination, offering scholarships to Ph.D. and postdoctoral students with priority given to those coming from Nordic countries. Headed by Jorgen Delman, a China specialist, the NIAS nevertheless has only a few researchers studying China, and even fewer studying Chinese politics: Cecelia Milwertz researches on women in politics; Camilla Tenna Sorensen studies Taiwan's democratization and relations across the Taiwan Strait, and Wang Qi works on women's organizations and networks in politics.[104]

Kjeld-Erik Brødsgaard later moved to the Copenhagen Business School, where he is today both professor and director of its Asia Research Centre; at the same time, he remains a member of the NIAS Board. The Asia Research Centre has a focus on Chinese politics and Chinese business studies, while Brødsgaard himself has published extensively on Chinese politics, the Communist Party, the cadre system and the bureaucracy. The Asia Research Centre and Brødsgaard have taken over the responsibility of editing and publishing the *Copenhagen Journal of Asian Studies*, as well as a series of working papers "Copenhagen Discussion Papers."

The other main Danish center is the Institute of East Asian Studies of the University of Aarhus. Founded in 1973, this institute established a China Information Office in 1981 that since 1984 has published a newsletter called *Kina Information*. Today, there is one political scientist attached to this institute who is teaching at the Department of Political Science, Clemens Ostergaard, following the departure of his colleague Flemming Christiansen first to Leiden and then to Leeds University.[105] Although *Kina Information* has ceased publication, mention should be made of two other social scientists attached to the East Asian Institute in Aarhus, namely Søren Clausen and Stig Thøgersen. Søren Clausen is an authority on Chinese Marxism and social movements and Stig Thøgersen has published on education and educational movements in China. Liselotte Odgaard works on Chinese security and foreign policy in the Political Science Department at the University of Aarhus,.

Sweden

Research on Chinese politics in Sweden is very much centered around the universities of Stockholm and Lund, near Malmö. The University of Uppsala, however, has occasionally trained a few political scientists in Chinese studies.

In Stockholm, a Center for Pacific Asia Studies (CPAS) was set up in 1984 with the aim of stimulating academic research on political, economic, and social developments in the Asia-Pacific region. Among its activities, the CPAS publishes monographs, working papers, and a journal, *Stockholm Journal of East Asian Studies*.[106] Headed by Tom Hart for a long time, CPAS is now directed by Masako Ikegami, a specialist in security relations and confidence-building measures in East Asia. In the 1990s, Michael Schoenhals (see below) was associated with this center. Among the researchers there today, Oscar Almén has developed a project on the role of local governance in China's social transformation,[107] while another, Annette Son, has embarked on a comparative study of unemployment insurance policy in South Korea and Taiwan. Of CPAS' former projects, it is worth mentioning Haran Friberg's study of state formation in the Chinese Hinterland.

At Lund University, Chinese studies started in the 1970s but were boosted when a chair in modern Chinese history was created in 1989. Though focusing on language and literature, Lund University has more recently opened Ph.D. programs on politics, both in the Department of East Asian Studies and at the Political Science Institute. At one stage, in the late 1970s and the 1980s, when it was headed by Jon Sigurdson, the Research Policy Institute of Lund University was a dynamic research locus for contemporary China. But after Erik Baark and then Sigurdson, both specialists in science and technology in China, departed for positions overseas the center lost interest in China. At the Department of East Asian Languages of Lund University, the major specialist on China is Michael Schoenhals, whose publications on the Cultural Revolution and the politics of language are well known internationally.[108] Other China specialists include historian Roger Greatrex, the Director of the Centre of East and South-East Asian Studies, and Marina Svensson, who has published very thorough work on human rights in China.[109] A few Ph.D. students are preparing dissertations in political science in this department, among them Johan Lagerkvist.[110]

The Raoul Wallenberg Institute of Human Rights and Humanitarian Law is also located in Lund. In the last decade or so, this institute has developed both research on human rights and cooperation and training programs on human rights with Chinese jurists and judiciary personnel. Among this institute's researchers specializing in Chinese law and institutions is Jonas Grimheden, who has launched a project on judicial independence in the PRC under international human rights law after completing his Ph.D. in 2004.

Finally, Uppsala University has occasionally trained doctoral candidates on Chinese politics, including Mattias Burell, now an assistant professor in the Department of Government, who published his doctoral dissertation on labor-market policy in China.[111] One of his colleagues, Maria Edin, has specialized in the cadre system at the county level and has published some very interesting work on the subject.

Also in Sweden, mention must be made of the Stockholm International Peace Research Institute (SIPRI). World renowned for its research and publications on international security affairs, particularly its annual *SIPRI Yearbook*, the institute has long paid attention to Chinese military and defense issues. During the late 1980s–mid-1990s SIPRI staff included Bates Gill, an expatriate American who established SIPRI's East Asian security program (which seems to have lapsed since his departure). Along with Gill, Ravi Singh, Ian Anthony, and other SIPRI staff all published on Chinese security and defense matters during these years. Today, the China portfolio falls to Alyson J.K. Bailes.

Norway

In Norway, East Asian studies are also organized around two centers, the University of Oslo and the University of Bergen. Created in 1966, the East Asian Department of the University of Oslo was merged with the Department of East European Studies in 1991 – giving birth to the Department of East European and Oriental Studies. There, Professor Mette Halskov Hansen has developed research on ethnicity and minority areas in China.[112] Two other scholars who used to conduct research on Chinese politics at the University of Oslo must be noted: Børge Bakken, who was affiliated with the Department of Sociology and Kresten Nordhaug, of the Centre of Development and Environment, who has researched on Taiwan's democratization.[113] However, Bakken left Norway for the Australian National University in the 1990s, and then moved in 2005 to the University of Hong Kong, where he has continued his research on criminal justice and public security in China. Nordhaug now works at the Roskilde University Center in Denmark.

At the University of Bergen, Torstein Hjellum, senior lecturer at the Institute of Comparative Politics, is the senior political scientist specializing in contemporary

China. In 1995, he published a useful textbook on Chinese politics,[114] and two years later, with Jo Inge Bekkevold, edited a second volume of essays written by 16 Norwegian China scholars.[115] Sinologist Harald Bockman, who focuses on Chinese ethnic history and in particular the Naxi culture in Yunnan Province, is also attached to this university.

Finland

In Finland, two universities, Helsinki and Turku, also teach and conduct research on contemporary China. At the University of Helsinki, Asian studies are coordinated by Kauko Laitinen at the Renvall Institute for Area and Cultural Studies. Among the Asia-Pacific specialists of this institute, three conduct research on Chinese history, including Raisa Asikainen, who specializes in Chinese political history and is preparing a Ph.D. dissertation on "China's Involvement in the Politics of 'Democratic Kampuchea': Rhetoric, Revolution and Assistance." In this university's Department of Political Science, Mikael Mattlin is also preparing a doctoral dissertation on "The Post-Liberalization Period in Taiwanese Politics." He has already published several interesting articles on Taiwan's Democratic Progressive Party (DPP) and cross-strait relations.[116]

At the University of Turku (Abo), Marina Siika has conducted research and published on contemporary China for many years, in particular on its foreign policy and its relations with Nordic countries. Siika is also the coordinator of the Finnish National University Network for East and Southeast Asian Studies, which is located in the department of contemporary history where she teaches.[117]

Finally, the Finnish Institute of International Affairs in Helsinki has a China specialist on staff, Linda Jakobson, although she lives in Beijing. Jakobson has conducted a great deal of research on relations across the Taiwan Strait and the best way to find a peaceful solution to the conflict between Beijing and Taipei.[118]

Other European Countries

In other European countries research on China in general, and in contemporary Chinese politics in particular, is underdeveloped. Classical Sinology still dominates in Italy, which has a solid tradition in this area. Other than Marta Dassu, who directs the Aspen Institute office in Rome, it is hard to find Italian political scientists specializing in China. Maria Weber, a professor at the Bocconi University in Milan, is an exception.

In Switzerland, there are two China scholars. One is Harro von Senger. However, Senger is a jurist rather than a political scientist and his main teaching position is not in Lausanne, where he lives and conducts research with the Federal Institute for Comparative Law, but at the University of Freiburg in southern Germany. The other is Zhang Weiwei, a fellow of the School of Public Policy and Management in Tsinghua University in Beijing, and has been a research fellow at the Modern Asia Research Center in Geneva since the late-1990s. Zhang has researched and published on the political consequences of China's economic reforms.[119] Another Chinese émigré scholar at the Geneva-based Graduate Institute of International Studies Department of International History and Politics is Xiang Lanxin, whose work centers on China's foreign relations, but has also published on the history of the Chinese Communist Party.

In Austria, as in Spain, fresh interest in China and Taiwan has taken shape. Among the new scholars, one can cite Christian Ploberger, from the University of Salzburg, who is preparing a Ph.D. on Taiwanese politics and Mario Esteban Rodríguez, a research fellow at the Center of East Asian Studies of the Universidad Autónoma of Madrid, who is completing a doctoral dissertation on Taiwan's security and relations with the United States. Moreover, in the mid-1990s, the Complutense University in Madrid launched a journal on East Asia, *Revista de Estudios Asiaticos*, which includes some articles on Chinese politics. The senior Austrian specialist on Chinese politics is Professor Susanne Weigelin-Schwiedrzik, who specializes in Chinese Communist Party history and historiography.

In central and eastern Europe, one is hard-pressed to identify specialists on contemporary China, much less on Chinese politics. However, two Polish scholars at the Academy of Sciences, Michal Korzec and Karin Tomala, work on Chinese politics. Korzec's research is focused on the Chinese state and governance. In the Czech Republic, only one political scientist specializing in China can be identified, Rudolf Fürst of the Institute of International Relations (a government-affiliated research institute). Taiwan studies are also taking hold at the Charles University in Prague, with the assistance of generous grants from the Taiwan government. No political scientists working on China can be identified in Hungary or the Balkan countries. This is not the case of Russia, where the field is well-developed and would require a separate chapter.[120]

Finally, it is hard not to mention Portugal, because of its special relationship with Macau and its very old tradition of Asian studies. However, no university has a political scientist really specializing in China. The Foundation Oriente regularly organizes international conferences to which it invites foreign experts. This Foundation has also provided great support to the launching of a new journal in both Portuguese and English on East Asia: *Daxiyangguo – Revista Portuguesa de Estudos Asiaticos*. Published in coordination with the Institute of Social and Political Sciences of the Technical University of Lisbon, this journal is edited by Antonio de Saldanha, one of the few academics teaching Chinese history in Portugal.

The Main Features of European Studies of Chinese Politics

How are European studies in Chinese politics similar or different in their foci from those in the United States or Japan? It is difficult to give a clear-cut answer to this question, although the subsequent chapters by Professors Kojima and Baum provide good comparisons. To some extent the globalization of Chinese studies, in politics as in other fields, has contributed to a convergence between European and non-European studies of Chinese politics. The brief state of the field presented above tends to confirm this convergence.

As indicated in the introduction of this chapter, China's economic development and opening up, ideological relaxation, growing diplomatic interactions, rising strategic power, as well as social stability and questions about China's political future are probably the main drivers of European as well as American or Japanese studies of Chinese politics. More specifically, the subjects of democracy, human rights, good governance, nationalism, identity and nation-building are privileged topics of research in Europe. European specialists seem less focused on institutions, the policymaking process, or political economy – which characterize U.S. and Japanese studies. Social issues – such as migration, health and education policies, social conflicts and instability, and even gender studies – are subject matter for European as well as non-European scholars of Chinese politics.

Moreover, as in the U.S. or elsewhere, the organization of European research on Chinese politics has not overcome the persistent tension between area studies (East Asian institutes) and disciplinary structures (departments of political science), though the latter seem to have taken the lead in the last two decades. Finally, the rather recent development of the study of Taiwan politics is not very different either from what is happening on the other side of the Atlantic, spurred by an interest in this first case of the democratization of a Chinese society as well as funding by the Taiwan government and foundations.

Yet, it is still possible to identify at least four major differences between European and American studies of Chinese politics. First is the relatively small size and dispersal of the community: every European nation tends to rely on its own China experts before considering reading or consulting foreign scholars, forcing local specialists to meet the demand and publish in the first place in their own language, and in so doing preventing them from being too highly specialized.

The second difference, partly related to the first one, stems from the lingering gap between European and American field studies and data collections. A growing number of German, British, and to a lesser extent French, Dutch or Scandinavian scholars, are basing their research and publication on surveys, data collections, and field work. But these activities have on the whole remained, if not more superficial, at least more selective – less because of a dearth of financial resources than because of a lack of time and of a readiness to cooperate with Chinese co-researchers. Another impediment is the reluctance to embark on multinational research projects funded by the European Union, because application procedures are so cumbersome.

The selection of research topics made by European scholars of Chinese politics is probably a third difference between the U.S. and Japan. Three factors have however influenced their choices: resources, *Zeitgeist*, and job opportunities.

While election processes or any institution that would herald a possible democratization or liberalization of the Chinese political system has been a research priority in Europe, public policy and governance issues have received a relatively larger interest than in the United States. This interest is both reflected in, and stimulated by, the research priorities regarding China set by the European Commission and is indirectly the result of the EU political priorities towards China (sustainable development, transition towards a more open government and better governance, rule of law). Research agendas thus tend to follow available research monies and the priorities of the EU funding agencies. Hence, research on the legal and institutional reforms, local election processes, labor-conflict resolutions, education and environmental protection, are some of the key topics encouraged by the EU authorities.

Research on social policies and issues among European China scholars is also partly due to the strong and persisting influence of social-democratic ideas and ideals in the Old Continent. For the same reason, perhaps, minority and human rights issues appear well developed and even sometimes over-represented compared to other fields, in particular in Scandinavia. More recently, the questions of social inequalities and political stability have become a major theme, opposing, on the one hand, optimists who (like Rocca or Balme in France) estimate that continuous reforms and "modernization" will help the current political system to adapt itself and remain relatively stable, and, on the other hand, pessimists (like Béja) who think that the regime cannot change and will eventually collapse.[121]

Nevertheless, European political scientists' current *Zeitgeist* has also played its part. Two themes seem to dominate the research stage: democratization and social justice (and beyond the latter, the newer issue of social and political stability). As far as the former theme is concerned, Taiwan has gradually appeared, in the post-Tiananmen period, as a crucial research subject – both because of what it could reveal about China's political future, as well as what it can teach us about new nation-states, state-building, nationalism and separate identities in a Chinese cultural context. In other words, to many European scholars, Taiwan has become a microcosm helping to comprehend better many Chinese political issues. Beyond the financial support that the Taipei authorities can provide and the easy access every student can enjoy researching politics on Taiwan, the over-representation of the study of Taiwanese politics in Europe has been mainly driven by this set of questions.

Job opportunities have also determined the selection of research themes on Chinese politics in Europe. But in every European country, this driver seems to operate differently, being at the crossroad of the specific *Zeitgeist* that dominates at a particular time in the academic community and the methodological approaches that are privileged.

This brings us to the fourth difference between the European and American scholars of Chinese politics. There are obviously differences between European and American methodological and conceptual approaches to various political issues related to China and Taiwan. In Europe, as in the United States and Japan, every scholar of Chinese politics is influenced by the national political science traditions and debates of the country where he or she lives as well as his or her political leaning. Making the picture even more complex, over the last two decades there has been an intensified circulation of ideas across the Atlantic or the Pacific Oceans. For instance, thinkers like Foucault, Bourdieu, or Derrida are probably more influential today in the U.S. than in France, while Habermas is perhaps more widely read in the U.S. than in Germany. The United Kingdom is also a paradox by itself because of a shared language, deep influence by American political science (but also at the same time one of the fiercest critics of U.S. political "science"). In this respect, it would be interesting to assess the influence of Vivienne Shue or Zheng Yongnian's work, now that both have settled in Britain.

In the European study of contemporary Chinese politics, it can be generally said that the impact of domestic political science debates has been constantly influenced by the U.S. domination of the discipline, contributing to make American approaches better known among European political scientists as a whole.[122] Of course, these approaches have been digested, criticized, and sometimes ignored by European scholars. Marxist concepts and analyses are sometimes still privileged (e.g. Peter Nolan, Clemens Ostergaard). More importantly, the place occupied by historians in the study of contemporary China and its politics has also resulted in restraining the influence of American political science models (totalitarianism, behaviorism, elitism, etc.), favoring instead the popularization of historical concepts such as "revolution" (Bianco) or "modernization" (Chevrier). But on the whole, as in the U.S., the "democratic paradigm" is now prevailing.

Recognizing this basic feature only offers a vague and fragile framework that does not explain some specific interests. For instance, in the 1980s, French political scientists, including some China specialists such as Domenach and myself, rediscovered the "totalitarian model" ironically at a time when it had been abandoned for good in the U.S.[123] The growing awareness and criticism at the time of the lenient and sometimes compromising attitude of many both right-wing (neo-Gaullist and anti-US) and left-wing (intimidated by the then strong Communist Party) politicians and elites towards the Soviet Union as well as China are to be understood as the main cause of this short-lived revival. Similarly, as a reaction to the lingering strong influence of classical Sinology on French politicians and elites (represented today by François Jullien's work on China's "otherness" that is used by some to explain China's inability to democratize), the large majority of students of Chinese politics are keen to avoid any culturalist approaches to Chinese political phenomena. Even Balme, who in her book on the importance of *guanxi* in China, has tried to underscore the historical changes of these "special relationships" in the reform era.[124]

These methodological choices have had an impact on research. While field research *in situ* and good command of the Chinese language have become two basic requirements for good research (and later recruitment by universities or research centers), quantitative studies have not acquired the same status as in the U.S. universities' political science departments, where it is perceived as a "must" in order to obtain tenure. Instead, in most European universities, good theoretical background and capacity to undertake multinational comparative studies are still viewed as priorities for building an academic career. These requirements tend also to discourage over-specialization and too-detailed or specific field studies that may be regarded as not pertinent or useless for comparative work. However, the under-specialization of European students of Chinese politics is not necessarily a handicap to a better understanding of China. The late Michel Oksenberg, a well-known American China specialist, once said to me that he regretted that fewer and fewer American students of Chinese politics were looking at the "big picture," as he so successfully did.[125] His regret may be a source of inspiration for all and also allows us to cast a more positive eye on the achievements of European scholarship of Chinese politics. Despite the importance of field research in China, cross-fertilization among various theories and disciplines can actually help to a better understanding of China's political challenges and uncertain future.

Conclusion

European studies of Chinese politics have remained very unevenly distributed on the continent. In the last two decades, France, Germany, the United Kingdom, and to a lesser extent the Netherlands and the Nordic countries have both maintained and strengthened high-quality research on Chinese politics (increasingly based on fieldwork conducted in cooperation with Chinese colleagues). Nevertheless, other nations continue to rely on their diplomats, European or American secondary studies, and translated documents to understand Chinese politics. In other words, due to a dearth of expertise, resources, and interest, this second tier of European countries have not invested in autonomous research on China.

Yet, the balance sheet of European studies of Chinese politics is not a negative one. It is a positive and an improved one, the quality of which can be more readily compared today with Northern American, Japanese, or Australian research in the field. On the one hand, this is because European scholars of Chinese politics possess better Chinese language ability than in the past, and they more frequently have occasion to spend long periods of time and carry out in-depth surveys in China (or in Taiwan). European China scholars also know and interact with each other more frequently today than 20 years ago, in various forums – such as the European Association for Chinese Studies (EACS), European China Academic Network (ECAN), or the European Association for Taiwanese Studies (EATS). It should be noted that not only these two associations, but *every* European scholarly meeting on China operates in English. The International Institute of Asian Studies (IIAS) is also based in Europe, and has developed close working relations with its American counterpart the Association of Asian Studies.

Obviously, integration with North American and Asian scholars of Chinese politics is far from complete. Two kinds of European scholars seem to cohabit: the "globalized" ones that regularly publish in English and interact with non-European colleagues, and the "parochial" ones that still privilege, by necessity or by choice, the local audience and debates. In the China field, as in other fields, globalization is still perceived by some European scholars as an undesired "Americanization." However, this latter argument can and should be reversed: any isolation of European research on Chinese politics can only lead to a stronger American dominance of the field. Thus, exchanges and cooperation between European and American scholars and students of Chinese politics should continue to be actively encouraged. Compared to 20 years ago, a much larger number are involved today in transatlantic or international joint conferences and programs. This expanding communication within Europe and with specialists outside of Europe has been conducive to building up a stronger and more integrated community and to providing governments as well as the general public with a more diversified, pluralistic and, hopefully, better understanding of contemporary China.

Acknowledgements

I am particularly grateful to Kjeld-Erik Brødsgaard, David Shambaugh, and Vivienne Shue for their helpful suggestions and editing of previous drafts of this chapter.

Notes

1 This chapter does not do justice to Belgium's Simon Leys (Pierre Rickmans), who moved to Australia in the early 1970s. Although not a political scientist, his books on Chinese politics have had a large impact on both French- and non-French-speaking China specialists and public. See, for example, Simon Leys, *Ombres chinoises* (*Chinese Shadows*) (Paris: Union Générale d'Editions, 1974).

2 Lucien Bianco, "French Studies of Contemporary China," *The China Quarterly*, No. 142 (July 1995), pp. 509–20; Kjeld-Erik Brødsgaard, State of the Field, "Contemporary China Studies in Scandinavia," *The China Quarterly*, No. 147 (September 1996), pp. 938–61; Tony Saich, "Contemporary China Studies in Northern Europe," *Asian Research Trends*, No. 4 (1994), pp. 115–28.

3 The CNRS is France's largest publicly financed research institution; it is mainly devoted to natural and physical sciences but includes a Department of Human and Social Sciences. Around 1,000 full-time researchers are attached to this department and scattered in many different research institutes, some of them being associated with universities.

4 Jean-Luc Domenach, *The Origins of the Great Leap Forward: The Case of One Chinese Province* (Boulder, CO: Westview, 1995). The original French version was entitled *Aux origines du grand bond en avant, le cas d'une province chinoise* (Paris: Editions de l'EHESS, 1982).

5 Jean-Luc Domenach, *Chine, L'archipel oublié* (*China, the Forgotten Archipelago*) (Paris: Fayard, 1992).

6 Jean-Luc Domenach, *Où va la Chine?* (Paris: Fayard, 2002).

7 Jean-Luc Domenach and Philippe Richier, *Chine* (Volume 1: 1949–1971, Volume 2: 1971–) (Paris: Imprimerie nationale, 1987).

8 For instance, Liu Qing, *J'accuse devant le tribunal de la société* (*I Accuse before the Court of Society*) (Paris: Editions Robert Laffont, 1982).

9 Jean-Philippe Béja (with Wojtek Zafanolli, penname), *La face cachée de la Chine* (*The Hidden Face of China*) (Paris: Editions Pierre Emile, 1981).

10 Michel Bonnin, Alain Peyraube, and Jean-Philippe Béja (eds), *Le tremblement de terre de Pékin* (*Beijing's Earthquake*) (Paris: Gallimard, 1991).

11 Jean-Philippe Béja, *A la recherche d'une ombre chinoise. Le mouvement pour la démocratie en Chine (1919–2004)* (*In Search of a Chinese Shadow: The Movement in Favor of Democracy in China, 1919–2004*) (Paris: Editions du Seuil, 2004).

12 Zhang Liang, *Les archives de Tiananmen* (Paris: Editions Le Félin, 2004).

13 Jean-Philippe Béja and Michel Bonnin, *Hong Kong, 1997: fin d'un siècle, fin d'un monde?* (Brussels: Complexe, 1993).

14 Jean-Philippe Béja, Michel Bonnin, Feng Xiaoshuang and Tang Can, "How Social Strata Come to Be Formed. Social Differentiation among the Migrant Peasants of Henan Village in Peking," *China Perspectives*, No. 23 (May–June 1999), pp. 28–41 and No. 24 (July–August 1999), pp. 44–54.

15 Françoise Mengin, *Trajectoires chinoises: Taiwan, Hong Kong et Pékin* (*Chinese Trajectories: Taiwan, Hong Kong and Beijing*) (Paris: Karthala, 1998).

16 Françoise Mengin, "Taiwan Politics and the Chinese Market: Business's Part in the Formation of the State, or the Border as a Stake of Negotiations," in Françoise Mengin and Jean-Louis Rocca (eds), *Politics in China: Moving Frontiers* (London: Palgrave Macmillan 2002), pp. 232–57.

17 Françoise Mengin, "The Changing Role of the State in Greater China in the Age of Information," in Françoise Mengin (ed.), *Cyber China: Reshaping National Identities in the Age of Information* (London: Palgrave Macmillan, 2004), pp. 51–67.

18 Françoise Mengin, "France's China Policy: From the Myth of a Privileged Relationship to a Normalization Syndrome," in Jean-Pierre Cabestan and Werner Meissner (eds), "The Role of France and Germany in Sino-European Relations," *East West Dialogue*, special issue, Vol. VI, No. 2–Vol. VII, No. 1 (June 2002), pp. 99–125.

19 Jean-Louis Rocca, *L'Empire et son milieu: La criminalité en Chine populaire* (*The Empire and its Criminals*) (Paris: Plon, 1991). The title in French is an untranslatable joke since "milieu" in French can mean both middle, a reference to the Middle Kingdom, and organized crime.

20 Jean-Louis Rocca, "Corruption and Its Shadow: An Anthropological View of Corruption in China," *The China Quarterly*, No. 130 (June 1993), pp. 402–16.

21 Jean-Louis Rocca, "'Three at Once': The Multidimensional Scope of Labor Crisis in China," in Mengin and Rocca, *Politics in China*, op. cit., pp. 3–30.

22 Stephanie Balme, *Entre soi: L'élite du pouvoir dans la Chine contemporaine* (*Among One Another: The Elite in Power in Contemporary China*) (Paris: Fayard, 2004).

23 Its membership and publications can be found on its website at http://cecmc.ehess.fr/. Created by Fernand Braudel in the late 1960s, the EHESS is an unusual institution: it is outside of the university system but awards Ph.D.s, and is directly supervised by the Ministry of Education.

24 For instance, Wojtek Zafanolli, *Le Président clairvoyant contre la Veuve du Timonier* (*The Wise Chairman vs. the Helmsman's Widow*) (Paris: Payot, 1981); Wojtek Zafanolli and Jean-Philippe Béja, *La face cachée de la Chine*, op. cit.; Wojtek Zafanolli and Victor Sidane (penname of Michel Bonnin), *Procès politique à Pékin, Wei Jingsheng, Fu Yueha* (*Political Trial in Beijing*) (Paris: Editions Maspero, 1981); and Wojtek Zafanolli, "Le nouveau cours littéraire: Portrait d'une génération individualiste" ("New Trends in Literature: Portrait of an Individualistic Generation") in Claude Aubert, Yves Chevrier, Jean-Luc Domenach, Hua Chang-ming, Rolaw Lew and Wojtek Zafanolli, *La société chinoise après Mao. Entre autorité et modernité* (*Chinese Society after Mao: Between Authority and Modernity*) (Paris: Fayard, 1986). Zafanolli comes from the slogan of the Chinese radicals: *zaofan youli* (it is right to rebel).

25 Jacque Andrieu, *Psychologie de Mao Tsé-toung* (*The Psychology of Mao Zedong*) (Brussels: Editions Complexe, 2002). Part of his research was also published under the title "Mao Tsé-toung: ébauche d'un caractère" ("Mao Zedong: Character Sketch"), in a volume edited by Marie-Claire Bergère as a tribute to Lucien Bianco, *Aux origines de la Chine contemporaine* (*Origins of Contemporary China*) (Paris: L'Harmattan, 2002).

26 Michel Bonnin, *Génération perdue. Le mouvement d'envoi des jeunes instruits à la campagne en Chine, 1968–1980* (*Lost Generation: The Campaign to Send Educated Youths to the Countryside in China, 1968–1980*) (Paris: Éditions de l'École des Hautes Études en Sciences Sociales, 2004).

27 Jean-Jacques Michel and Huang He (pennames), *Avoir 20 ans en Chine... à la campagne* (*Being 20 Years Old in China ... in the Countryside*) (Paris: Le Seuil, 1978).

28 Bonnin was the main author, under the penname Victor Sinade, of *Le printemps de Pékin, novembre 1978–mars 1980* (*Beijing's Spring, November 1978–March 1980*) (Paris: Gallimard/Julliard, coll. Archives, 1980); later, a Spanish translation of this book was published: *La Primavera de Pekín* (Mexico: Folios Ediciones, 1982). He

then published with Andrieu-Zafanolli, *Procès politique à Pékin*, op. cit. Sidane obviously comes from the Xidan crossroad, a reference to the short-lived "Democracy Wall" of 1978–1979.

29   Michel Bonnin and Yves Chevrier, "The Intellectual and the State: Social Dynamics of Intellectual Autonomy during the Post-Mao Era," *The China Quarterly*, No. 127 (1991), pp. 569–93.

30   As we have seen, Bonnin is one of the authors of *Tremblement de terre à Pékin*, op. cit.

31   Bonnin's list of articles on Hong Kong politics and other themes can be consulted on the CEFC's website: www.cefc.com.hk.

32   Cf. note 11; Michel Bonnin, "Perspectives on Social Stability After the Fifteenth Congress," in Tien Hung-Mao and Chu Yun-han (eds), *China Under Jiang Zemin* (Boulder, CO and London: Lynne Rienner, 2000), pp. 153–61.

33   His contribution to *La société chinoise après Mao*, op. cit., is a good example of his approach: Yves, Chevrier, "Une société infirme: La société chinoise dans la transition 'modernisatrice'" ("A Disabled Society: Chinese Society in a 'Modernizing' Transition"), in *La société chinoise après Mao*, op. cit.

34   Yves Chevrier, *La Chine moderne* (Paris: PUF, 1983).

35   Yves Chevrier, *Mao Zedong et la Révolution chinoise* (Paris: Casterman, 1993), Yves Chevrier (ed.), *Mao Zedong and the Chinese Revolution* (Adlestrop: Arris Books, 2004); Yves Chevrier, "L'Empire distendu: esquisse du politique en Chine des Qing à Deng Xiaoping" "The Strained Empire: A Sketch of Chinese Politics from the Qing to Deng Xiaoping"), in Jean-François Bayard (ed.), *La greffe de l'état* (*The Graft Of The State*) (Paris: Karthala, 1996).

36   Cf. note 29.

37   Isabelle Thireau and Wang Hansheng (eds), *Disputes au village chinois: Formes du juste et recomposition locale des espaces normatifs* (Paris: Editions de la MSH, 2001).

38   Isabelle Thireau and Hua Linshan (penname), "The Moral Universe of Aggrieved Chinese Workers: Workers Appeals to Arbitration Committees and Letters and Visits Offices," *The China Journal*, No. 50 (July 2003), pp. 83–103.

39   Isabelle Thireau, *Les années rouges* (*The Red Years*) (Paris: Editions du Seuil, 1987).

40   Isabelle Thireau and Mak Gong, "Les nouveaux mouvements paysans," in Bergère, *Aux origines de la Chine contemporaine*, op. cit., pp. 229–49.

41   Samia Ferhat-Dana, *Le Dangwai et la démocratie à Taiwan: la lutte pour la reconnaissance de l'entité politique taiwanaise* (*The Dangwai Movement and Democracy in Taiwan: The Fight for the Recognition of the Taiwanese Political Entity*) (Paris: L'Harmattan, 1998).

42   Henri Eyraud, *Chine: la réforme autoritaire. Jiang Zemin et Zhu Rongji* (*China: The Authoritarian Reform of Jiang Zemin and Zhu Rongji*) (Paris: Bleu de Chine, 2001).

43   Marie Holzman and Noël Mamère, *Chine: on ne bâillonne pas la lumière* (*China: Light Cannot be Gagged*) (Paris: Ramsay, 1996); Marie Holzman and Bernard Debord, *Wei Jingsheng, un Chinois inflexible* (*Wei Jingsheng: An Unyielding Chinese*) (Paris: Bleu de Chine, 2005).

44   Chen Yan, *L'éveil de la Chine. Les bouleversements intellectuels après Mao, 1976–2002* (*China's Awakening. Intellectual Upheavals after Mao, 1976–2002*) (La Tour d'Aigues: Editions de l'Aube, 2002). Chen Yan and Marie Holzman (eds), *Ecrits édifiants et curieux sur la Chine du XXIème siècle. Voyage à travers la pensée chinoise contemporaine* (*Edifying and Curious Writings on 21st Century China: A Journey Through Contemporary Chinese Thought*) (La Tour d'Aigues: Editions de l'Aube, 2003).

45   Jean-Pierre Cabestan, *La politique asiatique de la Chine* (*China's Foreign Policy In Asia*) (co-author) (Paris: Fondation pour les Études de Défense Nationale, 1986);

Jean-Pierre Cabestan, *La Chine et le Pacifique* (*China And The Pacific Rim*) (co-author) (Paris: Fondation pour les Études de Défense Nationale, 1989); Jean-Pierre Cabestan, Lydie Koch-Miramond, Françoise Aubin and Yves Chevrier, *La Chine et les droits de l'homme* (*China and Human Rights*) (Paris: L'Harmattan, 1991); Jean-Pierre Cabestan, *L'administration chinoise après Mao, les réformes de Deng Xiaoping et leurs limites* (*China's Administration After Mao: Deng Xiaoping's Reforms and their Limits*) (Paris: Editions du CNRS, 1992); Jean-Pierre Cabestan, *Le système politique de la Chine populaire* (*The Political System of the People's Republic of China*) (Paris: PUF, coll. Thémis, 1994). My list of publications can be consulted at the following website: http://www.umrdc.fr.

46 Jean-Pierre Cabestan, *Taiwan – Chine populaire: l'impossible réunification* (*Taiwan – The People's Republic of China: The Impossible Reunification*) (Paris: Editions Ifri-Dunod, coll. Ramses, 1995); Jean-Pierre Cabestan, *Le système politique de Taiwan* (*The Taiwanese Political System*) (Paris: PUF, coll. Que sais-je?, 1999); Jean-Pierre Cabestan, *Chine – Taiwan: la guerre est-elle concevable?* (*China – Taiwan: Is a War Conceivable?*) (Paris: Economica, 2003); Jean-Pierre Cabestan and Benoît Vermander, *La Chine en quête de ses frontières: La confrontation Chine-Taiwan* (*China in Quest of its Frontiers: The Confrontation between China and Taiwan*) (Paris: Presses de Sciences po, 2005).

47 For example, Jean-Pierre Cabestan, "The Mainland China Factor in Taiwan's 1995 and 1996 Elections: A Secondary Role," in Greg Austin (ed.), *Missile Diplomacy and Taiwan's Future: Innovation in Politics and Military Power* (Canberra: Australian National University, Strategic and Defence Studies Centre, 1997), pp. 9–28; Jean-Pierre Cabestan, "Chen Shui-bian's Victory Rules out Détente in the Taiwan Strait," *China Perspectives*, No. 29 (May–June 2000), pp. 36–51; Jean-Pierre Cabestan, "Integration without Reunification," *The Cambridge Review of International Affairs*, Vol. 15, No. 1 (2002), pp. 95–103; Jean-Pierre Cabestan, "Marginalizing Taiwan Weakens Mainland Security," in Edward Friedman (ed.), *China's Rise, Taiwan's Dilemmas and International Peace* (London and New York: Routledge, 2006), pp. 227–45.

48 Jean-Pierre Cabestan, "Administrative Law-Making in the People's Republic of China," in Jan Michiel Otto and Yu Wenli (eds), *Law Making in the People's Republic of China* (Leiden: Van Vollenhoven Institute for Law, 2000); Jean-Pierre Cabestan, "The Relationship between the National People's Congress and the State Council in the People's Republic of China: A Few Checks but No Balances," *American Asian Review*, Vol. XIX, No. 3 (Fall 2001), pp. 35–73; Jean-Pierre Cabestan, "The Chinese Factor: China Between Multipolarity and Bipolarity," in Gilles Boquérat and Fredéric Grare (eds), *India, China, Russia: Intricacies of an Asian Triangle* (New Delhi: India Research Press, 2004), pp. 119–59; Jean-Pierre Cabestan, "Is China Moving Towards 'Enlightened' But Plutocratic Authoritarianism?" *China Perspectives*, No. 55 (September–October 2004), pp. 21–28; Jean-Pierre Cabestan, "The Political and Practical Obstacles to the Reform of the Judiciary and the Establishment of a Rule of Law in China," *Journal of Chinese Political Science*, Vol. 10, No. 1 (Spring 2005), pp. 43–64; Jean-Pierre Cabestan, "The Many Facets of Chinese Nationalism," *China Perspectives*, No. 59 (May–June 2005), pp. 26–40.

49 Stéphane Corcuff (ed.), *Memory of the Future: National Identity Issues and the Search for a New Taiwan* (Armonk, NY: M.E. Sharpe, 2002). His Ph.D. was entitled "Une identification nationale plurielle: les *waishengren* et la transition identitaire de Taiwan, 1988–1997" ("A Pluralistic National Identification: The *Waishengren* and the Identity Transition in Taiwan") (Paris: Institute of Political Studies, 2001). Though unpublished, this thesis has formed the basis of several articles published in French and in English.

50 Cf. for instance Allio's article on the Taiwanese Austronesians in *China Perspectives*, No. 21 (January–February 1999); Christine Chaigne, Catherine Paix and Chantal

Zheng (eds), *Taïwan: enquête sur une identité* (*Taiwan: Investigation into an Identity*) (Paris: Karthala, 2000).

51 Guilhem Fabre, *Genèse du pouvoir et de l'opposition: le printemps de Yanan, 1942* (*Genesis of Power and Opposition: The Yan'an Spring, 1942*) (Paris: L'Harmattan, 1990); *Chine: crises et mutation* (*China: Crises and Mutation*) (Paris: L'Harmattan, 2002); (co-author) *Criminal Prosperity: Drug Trafficking, Money Laundering and Financial Crisis after the Cold War* (London and New York: RoutledgeCurzon, 2003).

52 The CEFC's website can be found at www.cefc.com.hk.

53 http://www.duei.de.

54 Heike Holbig, "The Emergence of the Campaign to Open Up the West: Ideological Formation, Central Decision-making, and the Role of the Provinces," *The China Quarterly*, Special Issue, No. 178 (June 2004), pp. 335–57; Heike Holbig, "Hong Kong Press Freedom in Transition," in Robert Ash, Peter Ferdinand, Brian Hook and Robin Porter (eds), *Hong Kong in Transition. One Country, Two Systems* (London and New York: Routledge, 2003), pp. 195–209; Heike Holbig, "Gelingt die politische Steuerung der wirtschaftlichen Dynamik in China?" ("Assuming the Political Cost of the Economic Dynamic in China"), in Werner Draguhn (ed.), *Chinas und Japans Bedeutung für Ostasien und die Weltwirtschaft* (*The Significance of China and Japan for East Asia and the World Economy*) (Hamburg: Institut für Asienkunde, 2003), pp. 60–78.

55 Anja D. Senz, *Korruption in Hong Kong (Corruption in Hong Kong)* (Hamburg: MIA, 2003); Björn Alpermann, *Der Staat im Dorf: Dörfliche Selbstverwaltung in China* (*The State in the Village: Self-Administration in China*) (Hamburg: MIA, 2001); Günter Schucher, *Chinaforschung – Forschung in China* (*China Research, Research in China*) (Hamburg: MIA, 2001); Jörn-Carsten Gottwald, *Regionalpolitik in der chinesischen Provinz Hainan* (*Regional Politics in the Chinese Province of Hainan*) (Hamburg: MIA, 2002). Günter Schucher and Margot Schüller (eds), *Perspectives on Cross-Strait Relations: Views from Europe* (Hamburg: MIA, 2005).

56 Thomas Heberer, *Unternehmer als strategische Gruppen* (*Entrepreneurs as Strategic Groups*) (Hamburg: MIA, 2001). Robert Heuser, *Einführung in die chinesische Rechtkultur* (*Introduction to the Chinese Legal Culture*) (Hamburg: MIA, 2002).

57 http://www.uni-duisburg.de/Institute/OAWISS/ (unfortunately, this website is only in German).

58 Claudia Derichs, Thomas Heberer, Nora Sausmikat, *Why Ideas Matter: Ideen und Diskurse in der Politik Chinas, Japans und Malaysias* (Hamburg: Institut für Asienkunde, 2004).

59 Claudia Derichs, Thomas Heberer, *Einführung in die politischen Systeme Ostasiens: VR China, Hongkong, Japan, Nordkorea, Südkorea, Taiwan* (*Introduction to the Political Systems in East Asia: China, Hong Kong, Japan, North Korea, South Korea, Taiwan*) (Stuttgart: UTB, 2003).

60 Thomas Heberer, *Private Entrepreneurs in China and Vietnam. Social and Political Functioning of Strategic Groups* (Leiden: Brill, 2003). He has also contributed many entries to the large dictionary on China published in 2003 in Germany, Brunhild Staiger, Stefan Friedrich, Hans-Wilm Schütte (eds), *Das grosse China-Lexikon. Geschichte, Geographie, Gesellschaft, Politik, Wirtschaft, Bildung, Wissenschaft, Kultur* (Darmstadt: Wissenschaftliche Buchgesellschaft, 2003); Christian Göbel and Thomas Heberer (eds), *Task Force: Zivilgesellschaftliche Entwicklungen in China* (*Developments in Civil Society in China*) (Duisburg: Institut für Ostasienwissenschaften, 2005) (Grüne Reihe No. 64).

61 Cf. previous footnote and Thomas Heberer, "Beheading the Hydra: Combating Political Corruption and Organised Crime," *China Perspectives*, No. 56 (November–December 2004), pp. 14–25.

62 Anka-Desiree Senz (with Zhu Yi), "Von Ashima zu Yi-Rap: Die Darstellung nationaler Minderheiten in den Chinesischen Medien am Beispiel der Yi-Nationalität" ("From Ashima to Yi: The Representation of National Minorities in the Chinese Media, the Case of the Yi Nationality") (Duisburg: Duisburger Arbeitspapiere Ostasienwissenschaften, Nr. 39/2001); *Die Bedeutung lokaler Partizipationsformen für den Prozeß der Demokratisierung – eine vergleichende Analyse* (*The Significance of Local Forms of Participation for the Democratisation Process – A Comparative Analysis*) (Hamburg: Institut für Asienkunde, 2001. http://www.asienkunde.de/nachwuchs/index.html.

63 Nora Sausmikat, "China: Intellektuelle und der Staat: ein leidvolles Verhältnis. Neue Diskursstrategien in der VR China," *Kommune*, No. 10 (2001), pp. 45–50, 67–71; "NGO, Frauen und China," *ASIEN*, No. 80 (July 2001), pp. 81–92.

64 Sandschneider has published or edited ten books, including Eberhard Sandschneider, *The Study of Modern China* (London: Hurst, 1999) (dedicated to Jürgen Domes) and Eberhard Sandschneider, Jens Damm and Simona Thomas, *Chinese Cyberspaces: Technological Changes and Political Effects* (London: Routledge, 2006).

65 See http://web.fu-berlin.de/polchina/.

66 See http://web.fu-berlin.de/sinologie/.

67 Gudrun Wacker, "The Internet and Censorship in China," in Christopher R. Hughes and Gudrun Wacker (eds), *China and the Internet: Politics of the Digital Leap Forward* (London: RoutledgeCurzon, 2003), pp. 58–82; Gudrun Wacker, "Behind the Virtual Wall. China and the Internet," in P.W. Preston and Jürgen Haacke (eds), *Contemporary China: The Dynamics of Change at the Start of the New Millennium* (London: RoutledgeCurzon, 2003), pp. 127–56; Gudrun Wacker, *Führungswechsel in China. Herausforderungen und Spielräume der "vierten Generation"* (*Leadership Change in China: Challenges and Options for the "Fourth Generation"*) (Berlin: SWP, January 2003).

68 Kay Möller, *Die Außenpolitik der Volksrepublik China, 1949–2004: Eine Einführung* (Wiesbaden: Vs Verlag, 2005).

69 Thomas Scharping (ed.), *Floating Population and Migration in China, The Impact of Economic Reforms* (Hamburg: Institut für Asienkunde, 1997); Thomas Scharping (ed. and transl.), "The Evolution of Regional Birth Planning Norms 1954–97," Parts I–II, *Chinese Sociology and Anthropology*, Vol. 32, No. 3 and No. 4 (Armonk, NY: M. E. Sharpe 2000); Thomas Scharping, *Birth Control in China 1949–2000, Population Policy and Demographic Development* (London and New York: RoutledgeCurzon, 2003).

70 His impressive list of publications, including eight books (including five edited volumes) and 81 articles, can be found at: http://www.uni-tuebingen.de/sinologie/sino/personal/schubert/schriften_engl.pdf. One of his most recent and representative books is Gunter Schubert, *Der Kampf um die Nation. Dimensionen nationalistichen Denkens in der Volksrepublik China, Taiwan und Hong Kong an der Jahrtausendwende* (*China's Struggle for the Nation. Dimensions of Nationalist Thought in the People's Republic of China, Taiwan and Hong Kong*) (Hamburg: Institut für Asienkunde, 2002).

71 Thomas Kampen, *Die Führung des KP Chinas und der Aufstieg Mao Zedongs* (*The Leadership of the Chinese Communist Party and the Rise of Mao Zedong*) (Berlin: Verlag, 1998); Thomas Kampen, *Mao Zedong, Zhou Enlai and the Evolution of the Chinese Communist Party Leadership* (Copenhagen: Nordic Institute of Asian Studies, 1999).

72 Henning Klöter, "Language Policy in the KMT and DPP Eras," *China Perspectives*, No. 56 (November-December 2004), pp. 56–63. Klöter was the organizer of the 2nd Annual Meeting of the European Association of Taiwanese Studies, in Bochum (Ruhr University) in early April 2005.

73 SOAS's website is www.soas.ac.uk.

74 The Royal Institute of International Affairs (Chatham House) and the International Institute of Strategic Studies (IISS) are not included in this report, as the China specialists at these institutes usually focus on foreign policy and security.

75 Julia Strauss, *Strong Institutions in Weak Polities: State Building in Republican China, 1927–1940* (Oxford: Clarendon Press, 1998).

76 Philip Deans, "A Democracy Craving for Recognition: A Pessimistic View of the Impact of Democratisation on Taiwan's International Status," *China Perspectives*, No. 34 (March–April 2001), pp. 35–47; Philip Deans, "Taiwan and Japan's Foreign Relations: Virtual Diplomacy and Informal Politics," *Journal of Strategic Studies*, Vol. 24 (2001), pp. 151–78.

77 Dafydd Fell, "Inter-Party Competition in Taiwan since the 1990s," *China Perspectives*, No. 55 (November–December 2004), pp. 3–13; Dafydd Fell, *Party Politics in Taiwan: Party Change and the Democratic Evolution of Taiwan, 1991–2004* (London: Routledge, 2005).

78 Christopher Hughes, *Taiwan and Chinese Nationalism: National Identity and Status in International Society* (London: Routledge, 1997).

79 Harriet Evans, *Women and Sexuality in China: Discourses of Female Sexuality and Gender since 1949* (London: Continuum International Publishers Group, 1996), Harriet Evans and Stephanie Donald (eds), *Picturing Power in the People's Republic of China: Posters of the Cultural Revolution* (Lanham, MD: Rowman and Littlefield, 1999).

80 Steve Tsang, *Peace and Security Across the Taiwan Strait* (ed.) (Basingstoke: Palgrave, 2004); *A Modern History of Hong Kong* (London: I.B. Tauris, 2003); Steve Tsang (ed.), *Judicial Independence and the Rule of Law in Hong Kong* (Basingstoke: Palgrave, 2001); Taciana Fisac and Steve Tsang (ed.), *China en transicion: Sociedad, cultura, politica y economia* (Barcelona: Edicion Bellaterra, 2000); Hung-mao Tien and Steve Tsang (eds), *Democratization in Taiwan: Implications for China* (Basingstoke: Macmillan, 1999); *Hong Kong: An Appointment With China* (London: I.B. Tauris, 1997); Steve Tsang, *Government and Politics: A Documentary History of Hong Kong*, Volume I (Hong Kong: Hong Kong University Press, 1995); Steve Tsang (ed.), *In the Shadow of China: Political Developments in Taiwan since 1949* (London: C. Hurst and Company, 1993).

81 Rana Mitter, *A Bitter Revolution: China's Struggle with the Modern World* (Oxford: Oxford University Press, 2004).

82 Marc Blecher and Vivienne Shue, *Tethered Deer: Government and Economy in a Chinese County* (Stanford, CA: Stanford University Press, 1996); Joel S. Migdal, Atul Kohli, and Vivienne Shue (eds), *State Power and Social Forces: Domination and Transformation in the Third World* (New York: Cambridge University Press, 1994); Vivienne Shue, *The Reach of the State: Sketches of the Chinese Body Politic* (Stanford, CA: Stanford University Press, 1988); Vivienne Shue, *Peasant China in Transition: The Dynamics of Development toward Socialism, 1949–1956* (Berkeley, CA: University of California Press, 1980).

83 Vivienne Shue, "Global Imaginings, the State's Quest for Hegemony, and the Pursuit of Phantom Freedom in China: From Heshang to Falun Gong," in C. Kinnvall and J. Jonsson (eds), *Globalization and Democratization in Asia: The Construction of Identity* (London: Routledge, 2002); Marc Blecher and Vivienne Shue, "Into Leather: State-Led Development and the Private Sector in Xinji," *The China Quarterly*, No. 166 (2001), pp. 368–93; Vivienne Shue, "State Power and the Philanthropic Impulse in China Today," in Warren Ilchman, Stanley Katz, and Edward Queen (eds), *Philanthropy in the World's Traditions* (Bloomington, IN: Indiana University Press, 1998).

84 See http://www.leverhulme-chinese.ox.ac.uk/.

85 Zheng Yongnian, *China's Compliance in Global Affairs: Trade, Arms Control, Environmental Protection, Human Rights* (Singapore: World Scientific, 2006).

86 Peter Nolan, *China at the Crossroad* (Cambridge: Polity Press, 2003); Peter Nolan, *Transforming China. Globalization, Transition and Development* (London: Anthem Press, 2004).

87 Zheng has published extensively. His most significant opus in English is *Discovering Chinese Nationalism in China. Modernization, Identity, and International Relations* (Cambridge: Cambridge University Press, 1999). His list of publications can still be found on the EAI's website: www.nus.edu.sg/NUSinfo/EAI. He also co-edited several books: Wang Gungwu and Zheng Yongnian (eds), *Damage Control: The Chinese Communist Party in the Era of Reform* (Singapore: Eastern Universities Press, 2003); Kjeld-Erik Brødsgaard and Zheng Yongnian (eds), *Bringing the Party Back In: How China Is Governed* (Singapore: Eastern Universities Press, 2004); Kjeld-Erik Brødsgaard and Zheng Yongnian (eds), *The Chinese Communist Party in Reform* (London : Routledge, 2006).

88 Gary Rawnsney and Minh-yeh T. Rawnsley (eds), *Political Communications in Greater China* (London: RoutledgeCurzon, 2003); Gary Rawnsney, "Media Reform in Taiwan since 1987," *China Perspectives*, No. 56 (November–December 2004), pp. 46–55.

89 Gordon Cheung, *Foreign Economic Policies of Singapore, South Korea and Taiwan* (London: Edward Elgar, 2002); Gordon Cheung, "Taiwan and the New Regional Political Economy of East Asia," *The China Quarterly*, No. 182 (June 2005), pp. 385–406.

90 Flemming Christiansen and Ulf Hedetoft, *The Politics of Multiple Belonging: Ethnicity and Nationalism in Europe and East Asia* (London: Ashgate, 2004); Flemming Christiansen, *Chinatown, Europe: Identity of the European Chinese Towards the Beginning of the Twenty-First Century* (London: RoutledgeCurzon, 2003); Flemming Christiansen and Zhang Junzuo, *Village Inc.: Chinese Rural Society in the 1990s* (Richmond: Curzon Press, 1998); Flemming Christiansen and Shirin Rai, *Chinese Politics and Society* (Hemel Hempstead: Prentice Hall, 1996); Flemming Christiansen, "Will WTO Accession Threaten China's Social Stability?," in Heike Holbig and Robert Ash (eds), *China's Accession to the World Trade Organisation* (London: Routledge, 2002).

91 Gordon Cheung, *Market Liberalism: American Foreign Policy Towards China* (New Brunswick, NJ: Transaction Press, 1998).

92 William A. Callahan, *Contingent States: Greater China and Transnational Relations* (Minneapolis, MN: University of Minnesota Press, 2004).

93 Jane Duckett, *The Entrepreneurial State in China* (London and New York: Routledge, 1998); Jane Duckett, "State, Collectivism and Worker Privilege: A Study of Urban Health Insurance Reform," *The China Quarterly*, No. 177 (March 2004), pp. 155–73.

94 Peter Ferdinand and Martin Gainsborough (eds), *Enterprise and Welfare Reform in Communist Asia* (London: Frank Cass, 2003); Robert Ash, Brian Hook, Peter Ferdinand and Robin Porter, *Hong Kong in Transition: One Country, Two Systems* (London: RoutledgeCurzon, 2003); Peter Ferdinand (ed.), *Take-Off for Taiwan: A Profile of the 1980s and the 1990s* (London: Pinter for RIIA, 1996).

95 Shaun Breslin, *China in the 1980s: Centre-Province Relations in a Reforming Socialist State* (Basingstoke: Palgrave-Macmillan, 1996); *Mao* (Harlow: Longman, 2000).

96 Robert Benewick and Stephanie Donald, *The State of China Atlas: Mapping the World's Fastest Growing Economy* (Berkeley, CA: University of California Press, 2005); Robert Benewick and Paul Wingrove, *China in the 1990s* (Vancouver: University of British Columbia Press, 1995).

97 Richard Boyd, Benno Galjart, and Tak-Wing Ngo (eds), *Political Conflict and Development in East Asia and Latin America* (London: Routledge, 2006); Richard Boyd and Tak-Wing Ngo (eds), *State Making in Asia* (*Politics in Asia*) (London:

RoutledgeCurzon, 2006); Richard Boyd and Tak-Wing Ngo (eds), *Asian States: Beyond the Developmental Perspective* (London: RoutledgeCurzon, 2005); Hans Antlöv and Tak-Wing Ngo (eds), *The Cultural Construction of Politics in Asia* (Richmond: Curzon Press, 2000); Tak-Wing Ngo (ed.), *Hong Kong's History: State and Society under Colonial Rule* (London: Routledge, 1999); Herbert Yee, Liu Bolong, and Tak-Wing Ngo, *The Political Culture of the Macau Chinese* (Macau: Macau Foundation, 1993).

 98 Vermeer is the author or editor of a dozen books and many articles. At present, he is writing a book, *Chinese Colonization of the Agricultural Frontier in the Qing Dynasty, Family Fortunes in China 1930–1997: The Household Economy in Four Villages in Baoding*, and an article on China's "Development of the West" program, and co-editing a book on China's environmental policies. Cf. also one of his latest articles, Eduard Vermeer, "Egalitarianism and the Land Question in China," *China Information*, Vol. XVIII, No. 1 (March 2004), pp. 107–40.

 99 Benjamin van Rooij, "Organization and Procedure in Environmental Law Enforcement: Sichuan in Comparative Perspective," *China Information*, Vol. XVII, No. 2 (2003), pp. 36–64.

100 http://www.iias.nl.

101 Margaret Sleeboom (ed.), *Genomics in Asia: A Clash of Bioethical Interests?* (London: Kegan Paul, 2002).

102 Kjeld-Erik Brødsgaard and Susan Young (eds), *State Capacity in East Asia: Japan, Taiwan, China and Vietnam* (Oxford: Oxford University Press, 2001); Kjeld-Erik Brødsgaard and Bertel Heurlin (eds), *China's Place in Global Geopolitics: International, Regional and Domestic Challenges* (London: RoutledgeCurzon, 2002).

103 Brødsgaard, "Contemporary China Studies in Scandinavia," op. cit.

104 NIAS's website is www.nias.ku.dk.

105 Flemming Christiansen, Clemens Stubbe Ostergaard, and Jorgen Delman (eds), *Remaking Peasant China: Problems of Rural Development and Institutions at the Start of the 1990s* (Aarhus: Aarhus University Press, 1990).

106 See http://orient4.orient.su.se/cpas.

107 Oscar Almen's Ph.D. thesis is *Authoritarianism Constrained: The Role of Local People's Congresses in China* (Göteborg: Department of Peace and Development Research, Göteborg University, 2005).

108 Michael Schoenhals, *Doing Things with Words in Chinese Politics* (Berkeley, CA: Institute of East Asian Studies, 1992); Michael Schoenhals (ed.), *China's Cultural Revolution, 1966–1969; Not A Dinner Party* (Armonk, NY: M.E. Sharpe, 1996); Roderick MacFarquhar and Michael Schoenhals, *The Cultural Revolution* (Cambridge, MA: Harvard University Press, 2006, forthcoming).

109 Marina Svensson, *Debating Human Rights in China. A Conceptual and Political History* (Lanham, MD: Rowman & Littlefield, 2002).

110 Johan Lagerkvist, "The Techno-cadres' Dream: Administrative Reform by Electronic Governance in China Today?" *China Information*, Vol. XIX, No. 2 (July 2005), pp. 189–216.

111 Maria Edin, *The Rule-Governed State: China's Labor-Market Policy, 1978–1998* (Uppsala: Department of Government, Uppsala University, 2001).

112 Hansen has published *Lessons in Being Chinese: Minority Education and Ethnic Identity in Southwest China* (Seattle, WA: University of Washington Press, 1999), and *Frontier People: Han Settlers in Minority Areas in China* (Vancouver: University of British Columbia, 2005).

113 Borge Bakken, "Democracy and Development in Taiwan," in Kresten Nordhaug (ed.), *Democracy and Development in the Third World* (Oslo: University of Oslo Press, 1993).

114 Torstein Hjellum, *Kinesisk Politikk* (Oslo: Universitetsforlager, 1995).

115 Jo Inge Bekkevold, *The Chinese Challenge* (Bergen: Tano Aschehoug, 1997).

116 Mikhail Mattlin, "Same Content, Different Wrapping: Cross-Strait Policy Under DPP Rule," *China Perspectives*, No. 56 (November–December 2004), pp. 26–33.

117 Website: www.asianet.fi.

118 Cf. her contribution to the International Crisis Group, www.crisisweb.org; her publications can also be found on the institute's website: www.upi-fiia.fi.

119 Zhang Weiwei, *Transforming China. Economic Reform and its Political Implications* (Basingtoke: Macmillan Press, 1999).

120 In 2003, the Institute of East Asian Studies of the University of Duisburg published a Survey of East Asian Studies in Central and Eastern Europe (including country reports on Hungary, Poland, Russia and Ukraine), http://www.uni-duisburg.de/ Institute/OAWISS/download/doc/paper48.pdf.

121 I position myself in between, being pessimistic about the prospect for democracy in China but optimistic about the capacity of the government to address social inequalities.

122 On the impact in France of American research of contemporary Chinese politics, cf. Yves Viltard, *La Chine américaine. "Il faut étudier la Chine contemporaine"* (*American China: "One Must Study Contemporary China"*) (Paris: Belin, 2003), in particular, pp. 301–10.

123 Jean-Luc Domenach, "La Chine populaire ou les aléas du totalitarisme," in Guy Hermet (ed.), *Totalitarismes* (Paris: Economica, 1984); Jean-Pierre Cabestan, "La Chine: un totalitarisme oriental," in Léon Poliakov (ed.), *Les Totalitarismes du XXe siècle* (Paris: Fayard, 1987), pp. 321–57.

124 François Jullien, *La propension des choses. Pour une histoire de l'efficacité en Chine* (*Proclivity of Things: A History of Efficiency in China*) (Paris: Seuil, 1992). Stéphanie Balme, *Entre soi*, op. cit.

125 Interview with Michel Oksenberg, Stanford University, June 2000.

6 Studies of Chinese Politics in Japan

Tomoyuki Kojima

This chapter provides an overview of Japanese studies of domestic Chinese politics in recent years. This review will introduce four types of Japanese studies on China concerning the one-party system – including the relationship between the party and the state, the party's relationship with the People's Liberation Army and the National People's Congress, and the relationship between the party–state and society. After examining their general trends, I will also focus on the issues related to the one-party system and its sustainability. As a longtime observer of China and Chinese politics, and a person sharing such interests with other scholars, I have also recorded my observations of Chinese politics for 23 years in the monthly journal *The Toa (East Asia)*.[1]

China Studies Affected by Changes in Chinese Politics

Most Japanese scholars of contemporary China understand that domestic politics are important enough to make the study of China's politics indispensable in understanding the country itself. Frankly, however, it is difficult to conclude that Japanese studies on Chinese politics have achieved enough results to promote the understanding of China, and when compared with the state of research in Europe or the United States (see the accompanying chapters by Baum and Cabestan), Japanese studies of Chinese politics appear even more limited in scope. One of the significant explanatory factors seems to lie in the introspective nature of Japanese China studies.

Contemporary China is simultaneously a nation open to the world yet a nation inclined to enclose itself within Chinese traditions, setting its national goal as the "Great Revival of the Chinese Nation." Japanese studies on Chinese politics, which have been influenced by their object of study – China – appear, as a result, to enclose themselves within the world of China. With regard to many phenomena in Chinese politics, Japanese studies on Chinese politics have tended to seek factors only within the context of a political history or culture that is unique to China, rather than through an analytical framework and model of politics rooted in international political science.

Japanese studies on Chinese politics have, to a large extent, been influenced by the political stance one takes toward China. The various stances that China scholars adopt on Chinese affairs have frequently been the subject of disagreement and argument, and studies of Chinese politics in Japan have become so politicized that they restrained and inhibited empirical research. For example, on the one hand, the Gendai Chugoku Gakkai (Japanese Association of Contemporary China Studies) once proposed in 1951 the usage of the term "China" to refer only to the People's Republic of China, at a time when the Japanese government maintained diplomatic relations with the Republic of China (Taiwan). The Association adopted a resolution for rapprochement with the People's Republic of China, strongly reflecting its political stance. About the same time, the Ajia Seikei Gakkai (Japanese Association of Asian Political and Economic Studies) insisted on the terminology "certain independence from politics" in 1953. Since this association was a foundation under the jurisdiction of Japan's Ministry of Foreign Affairs, such insistence itself was criticized in Japanese China studies circles.

More recently, such politicized trends within Japanese studies on China have become less common. The question is whether this trend was a result of Chinese transformation or an independent decision by concerned scholars themselves. If the former is true, further changes in China, may again provoke politicization and ideological conflicts within China studies – this time in a different form.

For more than half a century, Chinese politics has experienced many turning points – including the "New Democracy," the transition to socialism, the Cultural Revolution, and the reforms and outward-looking policy. However, Japanese studies on China have not produced an independent and satisfactory summary and explanation of each of these turning points. It appears that Japanese studies of Chinese politics have been too deeply influenced by Chinese politics itself and the *explananda* offered by the Chinese government and scholars in China. Sometimes Japanese scholars became embroiled in the political wars taking place in China. For example, during the Cultural Revolution Japanese scholars engaged in "criticism and self-criticism." After the June 4 Incident in 1989, Japanese scholars also became trapped too quickly in the lexicon and explanations of the Chinese government.

Japanese scholars of China need greater detachment and analytical independence from their subject matter. In order to gain a better and clearer understanding of Chinese politics, Japanese studies must launch a comprehensive and sincere self-investigation, including making their methodology and research stances compatible with those found in Paul Cohen's *Discovering History in China* (Columbia University Press, 1984). Only with such self-reflection can the necessary independence of analysis emerge.

Changing Trends in Japanese Studies on Chinese Politics

In contrast to American studies of contemporary China, very little effort has been made to survey the field of contemporary Chinese studies in Japan. Professional introspection is not a norm in Japanese scholarship. One exception is the effort made by the Ajia Keizai Kenkyujo (the Institute of Developing Economies or IDE). Every decade since the 1970s, the IDE has repeatedly conducted a review of, and prospects for, the field of China studies. As early as the end of the 1970s, immediately before the reforms, an outward-looking policy was proclaimed: the "coming of a turning point in contemporary China studies" was identified in the first review conducted by the IDE. Tokuda Noriyuki criticized these studies at the time, stating that, "Few research products seem to bear a historical test." As its important factor, he "severely" criticized researchers' identity for being too closely affected by trends in China.[2] Tokuda further argued:

> China studies in Japan have seldom attempted any systemic argument on their research methodology. In response to unexpected situations in China, easy self-criticism was expressed, like the guilty confession by all of Japan's 100 million inhabitants after World War II, or factors of the difficulties to examine and assess them were made into the questions of the sentiment, consciousness, and posture of China scholars. As a result, the focal point has become obscure and self-criticism has not effectively been utilized in a fruitful direction.[3]

For his part, Tokuda had actively attempted to adopt political science models in his research on Chinese politics (however, he exhibited a rather stoic posture in this review article regarding correlations between theoretical models and studies on Chinese politics). He also proposed the full-fledged start of empirical studies on the politics in contemporary China:

> China studies on politics, even in the United States, seem to be one of the research fields with relatively lower levels of theorization. When we discuss any research methodology and viewpoint, we must in the first place recognize that few demonstrative case studies remain in China studies. Many of the important issues in the Chinese political process have not been addressed as subjects of academic studies [in Japan].[4]

Even as late as the 1980s, the issue of the political orientation and identity of China scholars continued to be questioned in Japanese scholarship. In his review article on Japanese studies on Chinese politics, Kagami Mitsuyuki stressed that "the tremendous changes in Chinese politics have had a great impact on China studies in Japan, and such impact has been related to the question of identity among scholars."[5] He polemically criticized the "poverty of academic research on Chinese politics."

According to his review article, many studies, including those conducted during the 1980s, have excluded from their research the periods of the Great Leap Forward and the Cultural Revolution. In spite of severe criticism by colleagues, Kagami argued for new approaches in Japanese studies of Chinese politics, especially the need for "achievements in demonstrative [read: empirical] studies on Chinese politics and political history and ... achievements by scholars consistent in their demonstrative analysis of political realities at the grassroots level so as to examine the real political process in China."[6]

It was in the 1990s that value-free research began to supersede the polemical studies previously dominant in Japanese China studies. At the outset of the 1990s, China encountered setbacks in her movement for democracy, such as the "June 4 Incident" in 1989, as well as remarkable economic development as a result of the progress of the reforms and outward-looking policy. Onishi Yasuo argued that, "Such a big change naturally also has a great impact and introduces new research topics to China studies on politics and political history."[7] According to Onishi, the changes in Japanese studies on Chinese politics in the 1990s reflected four principal characteristics: the first relates to "questioning the nature and character of Chinese socialism"; the second, "the objectivity of analyses has increased as a result of the disclosure of political information on the part of the Chinese"; the third is that "research methodologies, including field works, have been enriched"; and, fourth, "significant research achievements have been shown by Chinese scholars."[8]

A more noteworthy and important trend of the 1990s was the emergence of political science theory-conscious studies on Chinese politics. The first attempt is evident in the work of Kazuko Mori. She proposed a comprehensive hypothesis on Chinese politics by combining three models – a model of a socialist country, that of a developing country, and a model of traditional China.[9]

Amako Satoshi's works also attempt to present a model of Chinese politics. He introduced the hypothesis "Basic Structure and Systemic Transformation in Chinese Politics." Defining the "society difficult to change" as the "basic structure," he proposed the necessity of a theoretical framework to understand the Chinese political systems and their changes at various levels.[10]

Among other questions of concern to Japanese China watchers today is the widening gap between the rich and poor. This gap will imperil social stability without effective measures to narrow it. Certain effective political measures must be undertaken by the Chinese Communist Party to deal with this issue. Such academic concern reflects a longstanding fear among the Japanese public about the prospects for social and political instability in China.

On reflection, the implementation of the reforms and outward-looking policy, have brought to the fore many new issues to study in Chinese politics, although Japanese scholars – especially when contrasted with those in Europe and the United States – were relatively slow to investigate these new topics.

More recently, the most important issue facing China now is the contradiction between one-party rule and the changing political structure. The retreat of formally totalitarian one-party rule stemmed from factors such as the maturity of Chinese society, the development of the market economy, and globalization. In this situation, the question of how to reflect and absorb public interests must be addressed by the ruling party and government. The concept of "Three Representatives," proposed by Jiang Zemin, is one of the party's recent responses to this issue; Hu Jintao's "Harmonious Society" is another. Along with social stratification and widening inequality, workers and peasants – who had previously been the party's base of power – were now classified among the weaker group.

Furthermore, popular participation in the party's rule has become the important issue. While the party advocates "politics of the people first," recently popular revolts, protests, and objections have increased to a significant extent. The institutional immaturity of popular participation allowed not only long-established, but also newly-emerging, pockets of society to survive outside the rule of the party and the government. Here lies one issue of the relationship between the state and society in contemporary China.

The second important question for studies on Chinese politics is how to manage the complex "public goods" problems that China currently faces and those it will face in the future. Instead of Marxist-Leninist ideology, the party–state has used nationalism to maintain its national cohesiveness, and I anticipate it being used more often in near future. Moreover, China will confront political problems in the absence of democratization and liberalization. These real-world practical problems must be viewed as issues for study by China scholars, in order to create knowledge and advise on policies that will respond to the changing situation and needs in China.

Although Japanese studies are apt to follow developments in Chinese politics, they must maintain freedom of perspective and selection of topics. In order to do so, the field must establish a longer-term framework within which it would not be influenced by shorter-term political changes in China. During the 1950s, Japanese China scholars were inclined to discover something new without an adequate analysis of Chinese socialism. Again in the twenty-first century, some scholars seem to insist on the arrival of a new age of reforms without an adequate examination of the political impact of the Cultural Revolution, which was itself, at the time, regarded among China scholars as emphasizing a new kind of value. The precondition to recognize the newness of one age is to confirm the structural characteristics of the preceding age. In this context, Japanese studies of Chinese politics should be cognizant of the continuity as well as the changed aspects.

Japanese Institutions on Chinese Studies on Politics

Roughly speaking, a little more than 1,000 scholars in Japan concentrate on contemporary Chinese studies. Most of them belong either to the Ajia Seikei Gakkai (Japanese Association of Asian Political-Economic Studies) or the Gendai Chugoku Gakkai (Japanese Association of Contemporary China Studies). The former has 1,400 members, half of whom deal with Chinese issues. More than 700 members are registered members of the latter. As noted above, in the past, these two associations were distinguished by their respective political stances concerning diplomatic relations with China. Since normalization of relations commensurate with changes in China since the 1980s, the differences between associations have narrowed and today many China scholars participate in both of them.

Many universities and institutions are active in China studies and have faculty focusing on Chinese politics. Most notably, Tokyo University and Kyoto University have the longest history of China studies. Their full-fledged studies on

China started after the Boxer Rebellion in 1900. The Toyo Bunka Kennkyujo (the Institute of Oriental Cultural Studies) at Tokyo University and the Jinmon Kagaku Kenkyujo (the Institute of Humanities) at Kyoto University were established from financial reparations paid by the Qing Chinese government following China's defeat in the Sino-Japanese War of 1895 and subsequent Treaty of Shimonoseki. Inheriting a long tradition of China studies in these institutions, both of them continue to train and employ many fine and accomplished China scholars.

In the case of Tokyo University, Ishii Akira specializes in Chinese diplomacy and Japan–China relations. Takahara Akio is a leading specialist on Chinese domestic politics. Wakabayashi Masatake studies Taiwan politics and Hirano Kenichiro works on Chinese political culture (now at Waseda University). Most of them are students of Eto Shinkichi, one of the leading China scholars in Japan who played a leading role in contemporary China studies in the post-war period.

Kyoto University, too, has produced scholars on contemporary Chinese politics as well as those focusing on China's modern history. Thanks to the tradition of history-oriented studies in the Institute of Humanities, many of them chose research topics related to historical aspects of Chinese politics. Takeuchi Minoru, now over 80 years old, is still active in analyzing contemporary Chinese politics, and Kitamura Minoru of Ritsumeikan University is publishing a series of articles on Chinese socialism.

Keio University is another leading center of contemporary China studies in Japan. Many scholars of Chinese politics at Keio University are students of Ishikawa Tadao, its former university president, who assumed leadership of Japan's China studies along with Eto Shinkichi between the 1960s and 1980s. Among his students are Tokuda Noriyuki (Maoist era politics), Yamada Tatsuo (Kuomintang politics), Hiramatsu Shigeo (PLA studies), Kojima Tomoyuki of Chinese politics (party–state), Kokubun Ryosei (Chinese bureaucracy), Takahashi Nobuo (the Chinese Communist Party), Yasuda Jun (PLA studies), Kojima Katsuko (Chinese labor movement), Kamo Tomoki (National People's Congress), and Sasaki Tomohiro (Chinese domestic politics).

A new initiative for China studies has recently been instituted among several academic institutions: the program for "Centres of Excellence for the 21st Century (COE)," sponsored by Japan's Ministry of Education and Scientific Technology. This COE program started to cultivate a competitive academic environment among Japanese universities by giving targeted support to the creation of world-standard research and education bases in a range of disciplines. Waseda University, Aichi University, and Keio University were selected in the field of China studies. Waseda's program, whose leader is Mori Kazuko, one of leading scholars on Chinese politics, is to establish a new type of contemporary Asian studies, including Chinese studies. The main goal of Aichi's program, whose leader is Kagami Mitsuyuki, is to build an international center for Chinese studies. Keio's program attempts to create the research center of policy innovation focusing on Japan and the East Asian region. In this program, Kojima's group has been conducting a series of experiments on regional policy coordination between Japan and China.

In contrast to the United States, unfortunately, Japan does not have many think tanks and research institutes studying contemporary Chinese politics. The Ajia Keizai Kenkyujo (Institute of Developing Economies or IDE) is the institute where many researchers are concerned with regional studies on Asia, including China. Some of them study Chinese politics, although most of them are specialists on the economy. Among the former are Onishi Yasuo and Sasaki Tomoaki. Recently, however, this institute was absorbed by the Nihon Boeki Shinko Kiko (Japan External Trade Organization or JETRO), which is under the jurisdiction of the Ministry of Industry and Trade (MITI). JETRO has had a long and distinguished tradition of research on Chinese economy and trade matters, and the absorption of IDE will only serve to strengthen JETRO's competence and reputation. One potential danger, though, is that IDE's attention to Chinese politics will be lost and subsumed under JETRO's concentration on economic and policy-relevant issues.

China studies are occasionally undertaken at the Nihon Kokusai Mondai Kenkyujo (Japan Institute of International Affairs or JIIA), which is under the jurisdiction of the Ministry of Foreign Affairs. Over the years, JIIA has hosted a number of conferences and publications on China, and is a leading "window" through which foreign scholars interact with Japanese scholars. The Sekai Heiwa Kenkyujo (the Institute of World Peace) and the Nihon Kokusai Foramu (Japan's International Forum) and other institutes, including the Gaiko Forum, are also periodically active in the field (although they have few full-time specialists on Chinese politics). It must be recognized that the environment for China studies on politics in Japan has become rather poor and increasingly severe.

Research Trends in Japanese Studies on Chinese Politics

The Relationship Between the Party and the State in China

The relationship between the party–state and society in China is one of the most important subjects in studies of concern to Japanese scholars of Chinese politics. In order to elucidate this new relationship that resulted from the reforms and outward-looking policy, the actual condition of the power relationship between party and the state organs must be examined in detail.

This relationship between the leadership of the party (*lingdao*) and the subservient state organs (*bei lingdao*) has been extensively debated – sometimes in rather abstract terms such as the "party–state system" (*dangguo tizhi*), "substituting dictatorship by the party" (*daixing zhuanzhi*), and the "collusion system between the party and the state" (*dangguo hezuo*). However, few studies address the empirical aspects of these interrelationships.

With regard to this shortcoming, it is necessary to mention Mori Kazuko's first 1993 work.[11] Mori emphasized the importance of the state, the party, and the PLA as the main actors in China's political system, attempting to elucidate their structural characteristics and mutual relations through an examination of institutional backgrounds and their policy realities. In so doing, her work verified the role of party's counter organization (*duikoubu*) and party groups (*dangzu*) that control state organs, and the role played by central working conferences (*zhongyang gongzuo hui*) in the policy making process within the central party *apparat*. Her work should be regarded as one of the best products of Japanese studies on Chinese politics in the 1990s. She attempted to analyze the party's organizational structure, mechanism of political control, and process of decision making and implementation. Mori's work is the most comprehensive research on the power relationship between the party and the state.

Tang Liang's work should also be mentioned in this context.[12] With regard to the power relationship between the party and the state, although the National People's Congress is constitutionally assigned the position of the supreme legislative body and the supreme organ of state power, according to Tang, "its role is quite limited and [executive] organs actually execute the state power." According to his recognition, "the most important task to implement the party's guidance towards Chinese society as a whole is how the party leads and controls most of its executive organs." Based on this recognition, Tang focused on the power relationship between the party and the state's executive organs, attempting to analyze the institutional realities of this relationship. In his analysis, he demonstrated the party's control over the state's executive organs by examining the institutional background of the unification of the party and its administration: party groups (*dangzu*) function as the party's internal apparatus and united front organs (*duikoubu* or *tongzhan jiguan*) as its external apparatus to guarantee the party's guidance. Additionally, the party's monopoly of the power to appoint and dismiss high-ranking cadres in the state's executive organs, via the CCP Organization Department, is the key factor to ensure the party's control over these organs.

Kokubun Ryosei's work on China's bureaucracy addressed this issue by focusing on the State Planning Commission as the key institution for China's command economy.[13] Through detailed research on the activities of this commission as one of the core organs within the central power structure, his work succeeded in elucidating the structural problems in China's political system. According to his assessment, the SPC, which was regarded as the central organ to implement the economic construction of the command economy based on the Soviet model, failed to exercise its professional ability, which any bureaucratic organization could supposedly monopolize, as a result of the frequent intervention by China's leaders. However, Kokubun simultaneously indicated that this failure allowed the SPC to play a role in supporting the leaders' execution of power. He also impressively illustrated the decline and demise of this commission after the reform and outward-looking policy. Although this policy began in 1978 with an environment that was conducive to the activities of the SPC, the deepening of reforms progressively undermined the institution. Further, the word "plan" was erased from China's bureaucratic vocabulary when this commission was taken over by the State Commission for Development and Reform. Through this detailed examination, Kokubun defined Chinese bureaucracy as a type of "rule of man." According to his argument, this definition could be seen in the expanded power of the new State Commission of Economy and Trade, established in the institutional reform of the State Council in 1998. This new commission seemed to be a real power base. He concluded that the immature Chinese bureaucracy was still in the stage of "rule of man," whose root stemmed from the one-party system, and that its solution necessitated democratization.

The Comparative Study of the Relationship Between the Party and the State

Another contribution to Japanese studies on Chinese politics can be seen through a comparative study of the relationship between the party and the state. The studies included in this chapter are Professor Zhao Hengwei's work,[14] and that of Mori Kazuko.[15]

In his work, Zhao attempted to trace the origin of the current Chinese political system and its past transformations as well as predict its future direction and reveal its reality after the reform and outward-looking policy. He paid special attention to the strong relationship between the party's leadership and the state's subordination, apparent in the vertical relationship among the center, localities, and basic levels, and in the horizontal relationship among actors to assume responsibility for their respective policies at their respective levels. Zhao accordingly defined the Chinese political system as the "multi-strata system of centralization." He emphasized that this system differed from the Soviet type of centralized system, in which the power relationship was confined to the policy actors at local and basic levels, as well as from the centralized system under authoritarian states, in which the power relationship was confined to the policy actors at the same and different levels.

In the revised edition of *Contemporary Chinese Politics*, published in 2004, Mori added one chapter entitled "Chinese politics in comparison." In it, she attempted to analyze the current political system in China in terms of comparative politics. In addition to Chinese "cooperatism," she introduced the concept of the "governmental party system," which was proposed by Fujiwara Kiichi, a scholar of international politics. Professor Fujiwara compared the Chinese "governmental party" with some parties in Southeast Asian nations, which have established deep connections between government bureaucracy and business, or have enjoyed stable power by exclusively utilizing the resources of administrative institutions for their own organizations, officials, and financial expenditures. When such governmental parties seized the reins of government, the political system becomes excluded from competition among political parties, although nominally they operate in a competitive multiparty system. He defined this system as the "governmental party system."

Mori applied this definition to characterize the ideal type of "governmental party system" as the Chinese political system that gives the party the core position in the trinity of the party, state, and military, stating that "the unity between the government and the ruling party and the exclusive utilization of administrative resources by the ruling party fits exactly in the Chinese political system and party."

Another comparative viewpoint introduced by Mori was the "developmental system" proposed by Iwasaki Ikuo. Iwasaki defined this system as the state system in which "all the fields of politics, society, economy and administration are unified." In this system, "the army or one party occupies the core of power, bureaucrats support it, and the parliamentary system is introduced as a matter of form. The policy of inviting foreign capital plays an important role in its formation," and "it strengthens its power base through sustainable development and becomes a stable system for a long term." Mori emphasized the similarity between the Chinese political and developmental systems, stating that "the formation of capital and business by the party and its cadres in China is exactly the same as the developmental system in Southeast Asia." Further, she explained the possible reason for this application to China, by stating that "China may follow the road that ASEAN, South Korea, and Taiwan have taken in the past."

The Relationship Among the PLA, National People's Congress, and the CCP

When the actual relationship between the party and the state is examined, other relevant actors that must also be considered are the People's Liberation Army (PLA) and National People's Congress (NPC). Despite the pioneering works of Kawashima Kozo,[16] and Hiramatsu Shigeo,[17] Japanese studies on Chinese politics have not greatly contributed to scholarship on the relationship between the Chinese Communist Party and the PLA. With regard to studies on the NPC and people's congress system, several young scholars have developed an interest in the subject and carried out fieldwork in China, including Kawai Shinichi,[18] Nakaoka Mari,[19] Kamo Tomoki,[20] and others. The results of their research are anticipated in the near future.

The Relationship Between the State and Society

Political changes after the reform and opening policies can also be observed in the relationship between the state and society. According to Sonoda Shigeto, a leading sociologist of Chinese society, until recently Japanese studies on the changing structure of Chinese society have not been positively promoted as a "prerequisite" to studying the changed relationship between the state and the society. Sonoda is the front-runner in this subject. On the basis of comprehensive interviews conducted in the major cities in China, he has conducted a series of joint research projects with Chinese sociologists concerning the changed structure of Chinese society, as is seen in the diversified social strata.[21] Based on this investigation, he pointed out that,

> The reform and outward-looking policies have resulted in a great change in Chinese society and, as a result, have brought forth a new middle stratum, including self-employed individuals and white-collar employees working in foreign companies who are relatively independent from the state.

He proceeds to observe, "the situation does not look too simple, though the emergence of such a stratum and its expansion seem to suggest the birth of civil society in China." He evaluated the behavior of the middle stratum, particularly the self-employed individuals who "become rather inclined to build a new relationship of coexistence with the state instead of independence from the state." Within the bounds of the relationship between the newly-emerging stratum and the state, he confirmed the relationship of coexistence rather than the birth of civil society.

This trend can be confirmed by other Japanese sociologists on China. Hishida Masaharu,[22] and Amako Satoshi,[23] arrived at a similar conclusion through their works, which focus on rural society. Both these researchers emphasized the relationship of coexistence between the state and society in China. Hishida argued that,

> The society itself appears to develop through its coexistence with the state while the state exerting strong control appears dependent on society … This does not mean the direct confrontation of society against the state, though showing the rise of its independence from the state in a sense.

Hishida drew conclusions about the possible directions of Chinese society in the future. One direction follows the model of "counter-reform or defensive reform," in which the political party and the state attempt to contain from the above the initiative of civil society. Regarding the relevance of this model, Hishida stated the following:

> Among the power elite within the party–state system and the money elite as the newly-emerging social stratum, the latter has evidently become conservative due to its acquisition of something lost, and has become enthusiastic about building the personal network, like the exchanging network between money and power, due to its unstable self-recognition. In conclusion, the latter has offered a helping hand to the maintenance of the party–state system.[24]

Hishida describes the other direction as a model of "dual democratization." According to him, "the essence of this model lies in the duality that the democratization in the second society, including the social sphere and the informal sector outside the party's control, would penetrate deeply into the first society based on the party–state system as a whole and as a result would facilitate its democratization." However, his conclusion seems to be rather pessimistic with regard to this model of "dual democracy." He goes on to state that "the second society is not formulated as the public sphere independent from the party–state system, and its current characteristic may lie in the inclination for its symbiosis or coexistence with the first society controlled by the party–state system."

Another important work on the relationship between the state and society was conducted by Tang Liang.[25] He attempted to examine the change in Chinese political society from varied perspectives, including the transformation of the party, the development of democratization, the transformation of the state–society relationship accompanied by the progress of social independence, the transformation of mass media backed by the penetration of the market mechanism, and other perspectives. He defined these transformations collectively as "gradual democratization."

According to Tang's argument, although the reform of the political system initiated by the party has assumed a conservative character from its inception, its reform has expanded over time. Through various institutional reforms, the political management has steadily improved, the range of freedom widened, people's political consciousness has deepened, and their participation has broadened. These accumulated achievements of small reforms would affect the timing of future democratization. Supported by changes in domestic and foreign environments, the party itself has been inclined to make rather practical policy decisions. Although the party has been requested to be more flexible in its responses and exhibit more legitimacy, the people's consciousness of – and willingness to accept – democracy have grown steadily over time. Tang predicted a high possibility too that the CCP would institute democracy from above, as experienced in Taiwan and South Korea during the 1980s.

Concerning additional issues associated with the relationship between the state and society, Japanese studies on Chinese politics have addressed issues of rural and urban politics. In the case of rural politics, Professor Tahara Toshiki attempted to examine the power structure in the countryside. The formation of village committees is a topic that younger scholars, including Nakaoka Mari and Minami Yuko, have begun to pursue through detailed fieldwork and by residing in the countryside.[26]

In the case of the urban China, Kojima Katsuko focused on labor unions and district communities,[27] while Ako Tomoko and Okamura Mieko have researched social organizations such as labor unions, NGOs, and schools.[28]

Concluding Observations

Looking to the future of the field of Chinese politics in Japan, one must be optimistic about the new generation of scholars rising up through the ranks and wrestling with new data sources. In conjunction with China's rise since the 1980s, an increasing number of Japanese students have become interested in studying Chinese affairs in general.

While many of these young scholars have focused more and more on economic studies of China, studies on contemporary Chinese politics also seem to have increased to some extent. Unfortunately, however, the number of these scholars who have recently begun to study Chinese politics while focusing on the party does not seem to have increased substantially, even after the 1990s. The popular subjects among young scholars are related to recent events and social trends. In their minds, these are the subjects that can produce good research results because the availability of sources pertaining to these subjects. By comparison, studies on Chinese politics related to the party–state still involve certain obstacles to in-depth research, owing to the secrecy of the institution.

To a large extent, however, political studies have become more open and transparent. Some younger scholars have launched their challenging research on subjects with which Chinese scholars have not dared to deal, due to their self-censorship. For instance, they have begun to study the Cultural Revolution with some success, which is one of the main subjects in Chinese politics.[29] Sasaki Tomohiro at the the IDE has just completed a book on political changes in contemporary China focusing on structural changes and diversification of actors in Chinese political society.[30] Seven younger scholars between 30 and 40 years old, who have conducted fieldwork at various places in China for many years, have contributed to this book. All of the chapters in this book are case studies paying attention to changes at micro aspects of Chinese politics. Under the relative stability of the political system stemming from social diversification accompanied by the introduction of market mechanisms, what kinds of political activities have been undertaken by various actors including politicians, political parties, bureaucrats, interest groups, citizens and minorities for their own interests? The analysis of dynamism in such political process is common in these chapters. Examining actors on the urban side, Tang Liang points out that non-elite groups of workers who have lost chances for social promotion are strengthening their self-assertiveness through a variety of either institutional or non-institutional measures though the deepened collusion between private-sector entrepreneurs and local political elites stabilizes the existing political system. Hoshino Masahiro's research is quite successful in elaborating the independent movement of Uighurs for obtaining international support. Examining the political process in the field of telecommunication, Sasaki points out that its government agency whose control has become weakened as a result of the intensified competition among enterprise are merely playing a role of balancer.

Japanese scholars on Chinese politics still feel limited due to the restriction in the access to original resources. But their research will make more achievements in the future. The field of Chinese politics in Japan has come a long way, but it has even further to go. This is particularly evident when contrasted with our counterparts in Europe and the United States – but, hopefully, increased interaction with these colleagues will help the field develop further and catch up to the West. Japanese scholars of China must break out of their relative insularity and join the mainstream of contemporary China studies in the world!

Notes

1 Kojima Tomoyuki, "Chugoku no Doko" ("Trends in China"), *Toa* (March 1983–). Also see Tomoyuki Kojima, *Hukyo Taikoku no Chugoku* (*China Rising as a Major Power with Prosperity and Strength*) (Tokyo: Ashi Shobo, 2003); and Tomoyuki Kojima, *Kukkisuru Chugoku* (*The Rise of China*) (Tokyo: Ashi Shobo, 2005).
2 Tokuda Noriyuki, "70 nendai Nihon niokeru Hattentojokoku Chiki Kenkyu: Chugoku-Seiji" ("Japan's Studies on Developing Regions during the 1970s: Politics in China"), *Ajia Keizai*, Nos. 1–2 (1978).
3 Ibid.
4 Ibid.

5 Kagami Mitsuyuki, "Nihon niokeru Hattentojokoku Chiki Kenkyu,1978–85: Chugoku-Seiji" ("Japan's Studies on Developing Regions, 1978–85: Politics in China"), *Ajia Keizai,* Nos. 9–10 (1986).

6 Ibid.

7 Onishi Yasuo, "Nihon niokeru Hattentojokoku Chiki Kenkyu, 1986–1994" ("Japan's Studies of Developing Regions, 1986–1994"), *Ajia Keizai*, Nos. 6–7 (1995).

8 Ibid.

9 Mori Kazuko, *Gendai Chugoku Seiji (Contemporary Chinese Politics)*, (Nagoya: Nagoya University Press, 1993).

10 Amako Satoshi, *Gendai Chugoku: Ikoki no Seiji Shakai* (*Contemporary China: The Political Society in Transition*), (Tokyo: Tokyo University Press, 1998).

11 Cf. 9.

12 Tang Liang, *Chugoku Seiji to Tosei Kankei* (*Chinese Politics and the Party–State Relationship*), (Tokyo: Keio University Press, 1997).

13 Kokubun Ryosei, *Gendai Chugoku to Kanryosei* (*Contemporary Chinese Politics and Bureaucracy*), (Tokyo: Keio University Press, 2004).

14 Zhan Hengwei, *Chugoku no Jusoshuken Taisei to Keizai Hatten* (*Chinese Multi-Strata System of Centralization and Economic Development*), (Tokyo: Tokyo University Press, 1998).

15 Mori Kazuko, *Gendai Chugoku Seiji Kaiteiban* (*Contemporary Chinese Politics*, revised edn), (Nagoya: Nagoya University Press, 2004). Subsequent quotations are drawn from this edition.

16 Kawashima Kozo, *Chugoku Togun Kankei no Kenkyu* (3 volumes) (*The Study on the Relationship between the Party and the Army in China*), (Tokyo: Keio University Press, 1989).

17 Hiramatsu Shigeo, *Ko Takumin to Chugoku Gun* (*Jiang Zemin and Chinese Army*), (Tokyo: Keio Press, 1999).

18 Kawai Shinichi, "Chugoku Jinmin Daihyo Taikai Daihyo Chokusetu Senkyo nimirareru Seiji Sanka" ("China's Political Participation as Seen in the Direct Election of Representatives in People's Congresses"), *Ajia Keizai*, Vol. 34, No. 8 (1993).

19 Nakaoka Mari, "Chugoku Kyosanto Seiken no Seitosei no Kyoka" ("The Re-strengthened Legitimacy of the Chinese Communist Party"), *Housei Kenkyu*, Vol. 51 (Dec. 2001).

20 Kamo Tomoki, *Chugoku Seiji to Jinmin Daihyo Taikai* (*Chinese Politics and the People's Congress*) (Tokyo: Keio University Press, 2006).

21 Sonoda Shigeto, *Gendai Chugoku no Kaiso Hendo* (*The Strata Changes in Contemporary China*), (Tokyo: Chuo University Press, 2001). The following quotations are drawn from this text.

22 Hishida Masaharu (ed.), *Gendai Chugoku no Kozo Hendo* (*The Relationship of Coexistence Between the Society and the State*), (Tokyo: Tokyo University Press, 2000).

23 Amako Satoru and Hishida Masaharu (ed.), *Shinso no Chugoku Shakai* (*The Deep Structure of Chinese Society*), (Tokyo: Keiso Shobo, 2000). The following quotations are drawn from the text of these works.

24 Ibid.

25 Tang Liang, *Henbosuru Chugoku Seiji: Zenshin Rosen to Minshuka* (*Chinese Politics in Transition: The Steady Line and Democratization*), (Tokyo: Tokyo University Press, 2001).

26 Nakaoka Mari, "Noson niokeru Minshu Hosei Kensesu" ("The democratic legalization in the Chinese countryside: on the village committees") in *The Deep Structure of Chinese Society*, op cit. Minami Yuko, "Chugoku Noson niokeru 'Nonmin Daihyou Kaigi no Setsuritu to Mura no Ishi Kettei Katei'" ("The Study on the Rural Society: 'The Establishment of the Village Representative Congresses in the Chinese Countryside'"), No. 6 (Sept. 1999).

27 Kojima Katsuko, "'Shadan' karamita Chugoku no Seiji Shakai" ("Chinese Political Society Watching from the Social Community") in *Hikaku nonakano Chugoku Seiji* (*Chinese Politics in Comparison*), (Tokyo: Waseda University Press, 2004).

28 Ako Tomoko, "Gakko Soshiki wo toshitemiru Gendai Chugoku niokeru Kokka to Shakai no Kankei" ("The Relationship Between the State and the Society Seen in the Case Study on Public and Private Schools in Shanghai"), *Ajia Kenkyu*, Vol. 48, No. 2 (May 2002); Okamura Mieko and others, *Chugoku no NPO* (*NGOs in China*), (Tokyo: Daiichi Shoten, 2003).

29 Kokubun Rosei (ed.), *Chugoku Bunka Daikakumei Saihen* (*Retrospect on China's Great Cultural Revolution*), (Tokyo: Keio University Press, 2003).

30 Sasaki Tomohiro (ed.), *Gendai Chugoku no Seiji Hendo* (*Political Changes in Contemporary China*), (Tokyo: Ajia Keizai Kenkyujo, 2006).

7 Studies of Chinese Politics in the United States

Richard Baum

The Birth of the Field

In the United States, the study of Chinese politics has undergone a number of conceptual and methodological shifts since splitting off from the field of modern Chinese history in the late 1950s.[1] Initially stimulated by Cold War political dynamics, the field of contemporary Chinese politics was first developed by a small group of distinguished Asianists, including John K. Fairbank (Harvard); Lucian Pye (MIT), Robert A. Scalapino (U.C. Berkeley), Alexander Eckstein (Michigan), A. Doak Barnett (Columbia, Brookings, and later SAIS), George E. Taylor (Washington), John M. Lindbeck (Columbia); and Tang Tsou (Chicago).

Coming from a variety of diverse intellectual backgrounds and traditions,[2] these academic pioneers are credited with training the first generation of social science-oriented Chinese politics specialists. Together, they and their students published many of the seminal works on Chinese politics of the 1960s, with their research often focusing on decision-making elites and institutions at the upper end of the Chinese political hierarchy. Key works in this period included Barnett's *Cadres, Bureaucracy, and Political Power in Communist China*; Pye's *The Spirit of Chinese Politics*; James Townsend's *Political Participation in Communist China*; Ezra Vogel's *Canton under Communism;* John Lewis's *Leadership in Communist China;* and Chalmers Johnson's *Peasant Nationalism and Communist Power.*[3]

Many of the key first-generation studies of Chinese politics were funded through a new non-governmental agency, the Joint Committee on Contemporary China (JCCC) of the Social Science Research Council and the American Council of Learned Societies. Founded in 1959, the JCCC brought together the resources of the U.S. government and the Ford and Carnegie Foundations to promote the study of contemporary China. Its research and training grants were initially concentrated on a small number of elite academic institutions, including Harvard, Columbia, Michigan, California-Berkeley, Stanford, and Washington. Chinese Language and area studies were also underwritten by the U.S. government under the National Defense Education Act of 1958. Later, allegations would arise that a hidden governmental agenda of Cold War "enemy studies" underpinned the allocation of funds for academic research and graduate student training in this period.[4]

Barred from traveling to mainland China as a result of diplomatic non-recognition, the first generation of U.S. China specialists sharpened their Sinological skills by studying Chinese language in Taiwan and Chinese society and politics in Hong Kong. Their research was marked by broad inquiry into the institutional and societal dynamics of the communist system in China; and their methods included systematic exploitation of official CCP documentary sources, often supplemented with Taiwanese intelligence reports, Japanese archival materials, and a scattering of intensive interviews with mainland Chinese *émigrés*. When comparative studies involving China were undertaken, these tended to focus almost exclusively on other Marxist-Leninist systems, principally the Soviet Union and Eastern Europe;[5] non-Communist systems were rarely used as reference points for the analysis of Chinese politics in this period.[6] Also with few exceptions, China's pre-communist society and culture were excluded from the research agenda, with the result that "Communist China" tended to be treated as a new and distinct object of study in the 1960s, walled off in relative isolation from the study of China's pre-modern and Republican culture, society, and politics.

The Rise of the Second Generation

A major watershed in American studies of post-1949 Chinese politics was reached during – and largely in reaction to – China's Great Proletarian Cultural Revolution. For over a decade, from the late 1960s until the end of the 1970s, U.S. China scholarship was focused centrally on this unprecedented political upheaval. Many young Ph.D. students in this period (including the present author) were drawn to the Cultural Revolution (CR) as a research topic by the availability of substantial new sources of information on the origins and development of the CR, including large quantities of Red Guard documents that purportedly laid bare the inner workings of the Chinese political system and its Communist Party leadership. As Harry Harding put it in his incisive study of this second generation of U.S. China scholars:

> Where the first generation had been based largely on the official press, supplemented by interviews with refugees, the second relied principally on Red Guard materials ... Red Guard newspapers and periodicals offered the first clear evidence that policy was made at central work conferences rather than at formal Central Committee plenums. They provided intriguing arguments from classified speeches and reports, and extensive collections of previously unpublished writings by Mao Zedong. They contained the raw materials for histories of the evolution of socioeconomic programs across a wide range of policy areas. And they offered tantalizing glimpses of life among the Chinese elite: the factional connections between central and local leaders; the maneuvers for power and influence ...; and the relations between Mao and his lieutenants ... All this new information made it possible to move the study of Chinese politics from the general to the specific, and from the formal to the informal.["7]

A brief listing of some of the monographic studies authored by second-generation political scientists and political sociologists in this period will suffice to give a sense both of the extraordinary influence exerted by a half-dozen major research universities on the training of Chinese politics specialists in the 1960s and 1970s and of the breadth of research opportunities and possibilities that opened up for research scholars during the Cultural Revolution. Key studies in this period (with their authors' academic mentors in parentheses) included Richard Solomon (Lucian Pye), *Mao's Revolution and the Chinese Political Culture*; Lowell Dittmer (Tang Tsou), *Liu Shao-ch'i and the Chinese Cultural Revolution*; Frederick C. Teiwes (Doak Barnett), *Politics and Purges in China*; Thomas P. Bernstein (Doak Barnett), *Up to the Mountains and Down to the Village: The Transfer of Youth from Urban to Rural China*; Harry Harding (John Lewis), *Organizing China: The Problem of Bureaucracy, 1949–76*; Hong-Yung Lee (Tang Tsou), *The Politics of the Chinese Cultural Revolution*; Martin K. Whyte (Ezra Vogel), *Small Groups and Political Rituals in China*; Susan Shirk (Lucian Pye), *Competitive Comrades: Career Incentives and Student Strategies in China*; Parris Chang (Doak Barnett), *Power and Policy in China*; David M. Lampton (John Lewis), *The Politics of Medicine in China*; Richard Baum (Robert Scalapino), *Prelude to Revolution: Mao, the Party, and the Peasant Question, 1962–66*; and Gordon Bennett and Ronald Montaperto, *Red Guard: The Autobiography of Dai Siao-ai.*

Alongside these monographic studies, a number of research guides to documentary sources on contemporary Chinese politics were published in the 1970s. Prominent examples included Michel Oksenberg and Gail Henderson, (eds), *Research Guide to People's Daily Editorials, 1949–75*; and Kenneth Lieberthal, (ed.), *A Research Guide to Central Party and Government Meetings in China.*

Funded by the JCCC, a number of specialized, topically-focused China conferences were organized in the late 1960s and early 1970s. Chaired by senior first-generation scholars, these conferences provided a forum for presenting the research of the younger generation of China politics specialists. The edited volumes that emerged from these important conferences included Doak Barnett, (ed.), *Chinese Communist Politics in Action*; Robert Scalapino, (ed.), *Elites in the People's Republic of China*; John Lindbeck, (ed.), *China: Management of a Revolutionary Society*; and Chalmers Johnson, (ed.), *Ideology in Communist China.*

Mention should also be made of a number of important studies of regional political development in China written in the 1970s by members of the second generation. These included Kenneth Lieberthal's *Revolution and Tradition in Tientsin, 1949–52;* Dorothy Solinger's *Regional Government and Political Integration in Southwest China, 1949–54;* June Dreyer's *China's Forty Millions: Minority Nationalities and National Integration in the People's Republic of China*; and Lynn T. White III's *Careers in Shanghai.*

In addition to the works cited above, a number of important insights into Chinese politics were recorded by second- (and some first-) generation scholars writing in academic journals in this period. Key contributions included, *inter alia*, Michel

Oksenberg, "The Institutionalization of the Chinese Communist Revolution: The Ladder of Success on the Eve of the Cultural Revolution" (1968); Edwin Winckler (with G. William Skinner), "Compliance Succession in Rural Communist China: A Cyclical Theory" (1969); Andrew Nathan, "A Factionalism Model for CCP Politics" (1973); Tang Tsou, "Prolegomenon to the Study of Informal Groups in CCP Politics" (1976); and Anita Chan, Stanley Rosen, and Jonathan Unger, "Students and Class Warfare: The Social Roots of the Red Guard Conflict in Canton" (1980).

Research Opportunities and Obstacles in the 1970s

Despite important advances made by the second generation in terms of the depth and sophistication of scholarly research on Chinese politics, a key limitation facing U.S. China scholars throughout the 1970s was the lack of direct access to China itself. Advanced language training for American scholars was centered at the Inter-University Program for Chinese Language Studies in Taipei (the IUP, known generically as the Stanford Center, which relocated in 1997 to the campus of Tsinghua University in Beijing), and dissertation field research was most often conducted in Hong Kong, utilizing the extensive newspaper and documentary files of the Universities Service Centre, where young scholars also benefited from the availability of a small but growing stream of émigré Chinese informants.

A word should be said about the important role played by the Universities Service Centre in the development of contemporary Chinese political studies. From its birth in Kowloon in 1963 through its transfer to the Chinese University of Hong Kong in the late 1980s, the USC was perhaps the single most important institutional locus of research on contemporary China anywhere in the world. Recently, Lucian Pye, one of the founders of the USC, reminisced about the early years of the Centre:

> What made the USC distinctive was not just the services it provided scholars, but the fact that it brought together scholars, journalists and Foreign Service officers. Jerry [Jerome Cohen, the first USC director] set up lunch talks to which he brought in people from the American Consulate General. Indeed, a veritable who's who of soon-to-be distinguished diplomats on Chinese affairs turned up ... The visitors also included some outstanding Hong Kong based journalists ... Jerry also caught anyone knowledgeable about China who might be passing through Hong Kong ...
>
> The Centre also had close contacts with the Union Research Institute (URI) ..., who for a fee loaned us materials from its extensive clipping files of Chinese newspapers and journals ... Gradually the USC built up its own collection of books and Chinese newspaper files to the point that it had one of the best collections of Chinese materials in the world ... We were a real community of China watchers who shared with each other whatever we had been able to learn about developments in the still closed-off China. Many of us were engaged in interviewing refugees from the

Mainland. Different informants were more knowledgeable about different matters, and we would therefore pass them on to the scholars who were working on the appropriate subjects.[8]

With respect to mainland Chinese informants, it has been noted that many (if not most) of the academic studies of contemporary China written from the mid-1960s to the late 1970s by American scholars based in Hong Kong drew on interviews conducted with a small handful of recent Chinese emigrants who were plugged into the *guanxiwang* of the USC and were (as Pye noted) "passed around" from scholar to scholar. Indeed, two young PRC expatriates in particular, given the sobriquets "Xiao Yang" and "Lao Yang" to protect their identities, featured prominently in as many as a dozen Ph.D. dissertations and scholarly monographs written during the Cultural Revolution decade.

Although opportunities for research and travel in the PRC were virtually nonexistent for most American China scholars throughout the 1960s and early 1970s, the research produced in this period was nonetheless of generally high quality; and much of it has endured over time. As Elizabeth Perry noted in 1999,

> Under the circumstances, the quality of work produced by this newly-trained generation of American social scientists – with no first-hand knowledge of China – was actually quite remarkable. Relying almost exclusively upon official documents from the PRC (subsequently supplemented by Hong Kong interviews and the Red Guard press), their analyses of bureaucratic behavior and political mobilization have withstood the test of time surprisingly well.[9]

Throughout the 1960s and 1970s (and well into the 1980s), the "bible" of contemporary China studies in the West was *The China Quarterly*, published at SOAS in London. Founded in 1960 with a covert financial boost from the U.S. intelligence community, *CQ* was by far the most influential journal among scholars specializing in the Chinese revolution and post-1949 Chinese society and politics. Virtually everyone in the field aspired to publish in *CQ*, and over the years many of the most intense debates in the profession were played out in its pages. The *CQ*'s virtual publishing monopoly on article-length research on contemporary China was broken only in the mid-1980s when the *Australian Journal of Chinese Affairs* made its appearance, followed a few years later by a number of other specialized journals, including *Journal of Contemporary China*, *China Information*, *China Perspectives*, *and China Review.*

The Impact of the Vietnam War

The close connection between the U.S. government and academic China scholarship that had been established in the early 1960s proved highly controversial during the Vietnam War decade, 1965–1975. The War itself was immensely divisive in the United States, both within the general public and among American China scholars.

At issue, among other things, was the putative linkage between American military involvement in Vietnam and U.S. government sponsorship of academic research on contemporary China.[10] A second, related issue centered on the potential value of the "Maoist model" of radical socialism as a viable developmental path for Third World countries seeking to escape the suffocating embrace of "U.S. Imperialism." As one young scholar put it,

> The United States participation in the Vietnam War made Western scholarship on China conspicuously political. ... China, in the minds of many, offered insight into the confusion of the Vietnam War because China was an Asian, peasant-based, communist country, and because it aspired to lead the rest of the "Third World" to achieve a communist revolution ... The war in Vietnam required China scholars to reevaluate the political implications of the topics they chose to study as well as their approaches to them. China scholars found particular significance in the Cultural Revolution, distinctions between Chinese and Soviet communism, and the Communist Revolution of 1949. The concomitant rise of the chaos of the Cultural Revolution in China injected this domestic movement with international import. Maoism offered concerned scholars a means of countering the scare that the world was sinking under a sprawling monolithic communist entity.[11]

In response to deepening U.S. involvement in the Vietnam War, a schism emerged at the end of the 1960s between a younger generation of left-wing U.S. and European Asia scholars and their more mainstream academic counterparts. The "rebel" faction created their own professional association – the Committee of Concerned Asian Scholars (CCAS) – as a rival to the more establishment-oriented Association for Asian Studies, as well as their own journal for the promulgation of "progressive" views and research on Asia, the *Bulletin of Concerned Asian Scholars.*

Influenced by the worldwide student revolution of 1968, in the early 1970s the schism in Asian studies resulted in an intense polarization of a good deal of China scholarship in the West. For their part younger, more radical anti-war scholars frequently embraced the visionary ideals of Maoism (though not necessarily its methods or results) while remaining generally uncritical of Maoist and Red Guard excesses; more "established" scholars, on the other hand, while often skeptical of the propriety of American involvement in Vietnam, were less inclined to suspend critical judgment about the nature and consequences of the Maoist program for "revolutionizing" China.[12]

This schism persisted throughout the 1970s, until the death of Mao and the advent of China's economic reforms and "opening up" under Deng Xiaoping necessitated a fundamental reassessment of Mao Zedong's historical legacy both within China and abroad. At that point, many erstwhile admirers of the "Chinese model of development" began to acknowledge – sometimes grudgingly – the shortcomings of the Maoist project.[13]

"Normalization" of Relations and the Maturation of U.S. Scholarship on Chinese Politics

Following President Richard Nixon's pathbreaking visit to China in 1972, direct contact between scholars of the two countries increased noticeably. Although visas remained difficult to obtain for U.S. citizens until the normalization process was completed in December 1978, dozens of American China specialists gained their first opportunity to travel to mainland China in the 1970s as members of a widening stream of educational and cultural delegations, "friendship" groups, and scientific and technological exchanges.[14]

As American scholars began to experience Chinese society and culture at first-hand, some of the old stereotypes about the nature of Chinese "totalitarianism" were subject to revision. For example, an important meeting sponsored by the Social Science Research Council (SSRC) in 1977 addressed the question of how different groups and strata in China, both within and outside the Chinese government, manage to pursue their particular political interests within a Leninist institutional framework.[15] The study of bureaucratic politics and interest groups in communist systems, initially adapted from the field of Soviet Studies in the post-Stalin era, also began to make its appearance in scholarship on contemporary China in the post-normalization period.[16]

The final, full normalization of U.S.–China relations in the winter of 1978–1979 ushered in another significant shift in the study of Chinese politics. In the aftermath of normalization, American research scholars and graduate students were able, for the first time, to conduct field research in China proper. While such opportunities were at first limited and carefully controlled by the Chinese government, they served to open the door, however narrowly, for a new type of China scholarship, based on direct empirical observation, local archival research, in-depth interviews, and on-the-ground fieldwork. As a result of this initial opening, a number of important, often collaboratively-produced monographic studies were initiated in the 1980s, notably including the Michel Oksenberg–Kenneth Lieberthal study of bureaucratic politics in China's energy industry, *Policy Making in China* (1990); the Edward Friedman–Paul Pickowicz–Mark Selden–Kay Johnson collaborative study of agricultural collectivization in Raoyang county, Hebei, *Chinese Village, Socialist State* (1993); the Marc Blecher–Vivienne Shue investigation of county-level government in Shulu County, Hebei, *Tethered Deer: Government and Economy in a Chinese County* (1996); and the Andrew Walder-led project on a North China county, *Zouping in Transition* (1998).

The 1980s undoubtedly would have spawned an even larger number of micro-political case studies based on intensive fieldwork in China had it not been for the misadventures of one early anthropological researcher in China, Stanford University doctoral candidate Steven Mosher, who was expelled from the PRC in 1982 (and later from Stanford) for allegedly engaging in deceptive and dishonest fieldwork practices in a village in Guangdong province.[17] For the next several years, fieldwork opportunities for American social science researchers were narrowly limited in China.[18]

The Third Generation

In the first decade after normalization, a third and significantly larger (and better-trained) generation of political scientists and political sociologists came of age in U.S. research universities. With Michigan, Columbia, Harvard, Stanford and California-Berkeley continuing to lead the way, American universities expanded their course offerings in Chinese politics and foreign relations, often adding a second (and in a few cases, a third) China specialist to their political science faculties. With more faculty resources available, and with increased funding for graduate student research and training made possible by the U.S. economic boom of the mid-1980s, a substantial expansion of the Chinese politics field took place from 1983–1988.

In this new milieu of expanding China studies, one university stood above the rest as a training ground for specialists in Chinese politics – the University of Michigan. With an exceptionally strong core of political scientists – Richard Solomon, Michel Oksenberg, Allen S. Whiting, and later Kenneth Lieberthal – Michigan became the foremost institution for the advanced study of Chinese politics. From the late-1970s until the end of the millennium, no other university came close to the "Michigan mafia" for producing Ph.D.s in Chinese politics. The principal driving force behind this success was Michel Oksenberg, whose influence on the field continues to be felt long after his premature death in 2001.[19]

The academic preparation of graduate students in contemporary Chinese studies underwent significant change in the 1980s. For one thing, Chinese area studies – once virtually walled off from other subfields within parent departments and disciplines – now came to be increasingly integrated within the core social science disciplines. Political science was no exception, as the leading departments across the country began to impose more stringent social science requirements on their Chinese politics graduate students, including courses on statistical methods, survey research, comparative political economy, bureaucracy, and public choice theory, *inter alia*.

Not only were members of the third generation more rigorously trained in their own disciplines and associated methodologies, they also acquired superior language skills. Whereas many members of the second generation (including the present author) began their study of Chinese language only in graduate school, often supplemented with a year of intensive language training in Taiwan, the 1980s generation often had completed two or three years of Chinese before beginning their graduate training. Consequently, they were better able to take advantages of opportunities for conducting field research in China when entry barriers were eased later in the decade. Prominent members of this third generation, listed alphabetically with their first major book-length works, included David Bachman (*Chen Yun and the Chinese Political System*); Bruce Dickson (*Democratization in China and Taiwan*); Joseph Fewsmith (*Dilemmas of Reform in China*); William Joseph (*The Critique of Ultra-Leftism in China*); Melanie Manion (*Retirement of Revolutionaries in China*); Lyman Miller (*Science and Dissent in Post-Mao China*); Kevin O'Brien (*Reform without Liberalization*); Jean Oi (*State and*

Peasant in Contemporary China); Margaret Pearson (*Joint Ventures in the People's Republic of China*); Elizabeth Perry (*Rebels and Revolutionaries in North China*); David Shambaugh (*Beautiful Imperialist*); James Tong (*Disorder Under Heaven*); Andrew Walder (*Communist Neo-Traditionalism*); and David Zweig (*Agrarian Radicalism in China*). More than half of these younger scholars had trained under Oksenberg at Michigan.

In the mid-1980s, a small trickle of PRC-born Chinese graduate students began to enroll in U.S. doctoral programs in political science, bringing with them a deep knowledge of Chinese society and culture as well as native fluency in the Chinese language. By the end of the decade this small trickle had grown to a steady stream. Key members of the first cohort of PRC-born, U.S.-trained political scientists (listed alphabetically along with their major early works, mostly published in the 1990s) included Zhiyuan Cui (*Institutional Innovation and the Second 'Thought Revolution'*), Shiping Hua (*Chinese Political Culture*), Yasheng Huang (*Inflation and Investment Controls in China*), Cheng Li (*Rediscovering China: Dynamics and Dilemmas of Reform*), Xiaobo Lu (*Cadres and Corruption*), Minxin Pei (*From Reform to Revolution*), Tianjian Shi (*Political Participation in Beijing*), Wenfang Tang (*Chinese Urban Life Under Market Reform*), Shaoguang Wang (*Failure of Charisma: The Chinese Cultural Revolution in Wuhan*), Dali Yang (*Calamity and Reform in China*), Suisheng Zhao (*China and Democracy*), and Shiping Zheng (*Party vs. State in Post-1949 China*).

A significant portion of field research conducted by the third generation of China politics scholars was funded by the Social Science Research Council and the Committee on Scholarly Communication with China (CSCC), successors to the JCCC and the CSCPRC, respectively. While the CSCC was initially dedicated to facilitating scientific and technical exchange with China, in the 1980s and 1990s the Committee also supported field research and traveling fellowships for scholars in the social sciences.

One final byproduct of the methodological revolution in social science research on China in the 1980s was that the dominant position previously occupied by "elite studies" in the first two generations of scholarship on Chinese politics was significantly attenuated. Although monographic works on key Chinese leaders and institutions continued to appear throughout the 1980s and 1990s, along with documentary studies of major central policies and political campaigns, such work no longer dominated the landscape of Chinese political studies.[20] In their stead micro-politics and the political economy of reform began to occupy center stage.

Chinese Politics in the Reform Era

In the 1980s, American social scientists began to focus their attention on the effects of China's post-Mao market reforms and "open [door] policy." Several scholarly conferences were convened under SSRC and CSCC auspices to examine the impact of post-Mao reforms in this period. Such gatherings (and the edited volumes they produced) summarized and disseminated the latest scholarly research on such subjects as the prospects for Chinese political reform;[21] the political economy of reform;[22] and post-Mao developments in Chinese science and technology.[23]

Three new intellectual trends gained considerable currency among Chinese politics analysts in the United States in the second half of the 1980s. First, China's accelerating market transition raised major new questions about the nature and structure of state-society relations in the reform era. Were China's market reforms and "opening up" serving to weaken the authority of the communist party-state or to strengthen it? And in what ways? Two important early contributions to this debate were Vivienne Shue's *The Reach of the State: Sketches of the Chinese Body Politic* and Dorothy Solinger's *China's Transition from Socialism: Statist Legacies and Market Reforms.*

A second focus of political research in the mid- and late 1980s was the evolving structure of administrative and fiscal relations between the central state and China's 31 provincial-level administrative units. The "unified command" model of the Maoist era was no longer adequate to account for the growing complexity of central–provincial relations. With the rise of fiscal and administrative decentralization in the 1980s, new incentive systems and policy making constraints were dramatically reshaping the Chinese political economy. Consequently, emergent phenomena of bureaucratic bargaining, "particularistic contracting," and "fragmented authoritarianism" increasingly captured the attention of American political scientists in their study of post-reform China. Susan Shirk's *The Political Logic of Economic Reform in China* and the David Lampton–Kenneth Lieberthal edited volume, *Bureaucracy, Politics and Decision-Making in Post-Mao China*, along with Lampton's companion volume, *Policy Implementation in Post-Mao China,* were three prominent contributions to the study of the evolution of central-local bargaining relationships and the nature of sub-national policy-making and administration in this period.

Alongside the new upsurge of research on the changing nature of state power and bureaucratic politics in the reform era, a third emergent trend in the late 1980s was the growing popularity of "civil society" models of Leninist transition. First popularized by the German philosopher Jürgen Habermas, in its original European setting "civil society" referred to the historical rise of autonomous, self-organizing *"pouvoirs intermédiares"* ("intermediate groups") that occupied an expanding "public sphere" between the state and its citizens in nineteenth-century Europe.[24] The concept of civil society enjoyed widespread intellectual currency in comparative communist studies in the late 1980s, when it was employed to analyze the emergence (or revival) of opposition groups within the Soviet bloc, such as the Catholic Church and Solidarity in Poland, and "Charter 77" in Czechoslovakia.[25] Imported into contemporary China studies by political sociologists such as Gordon White, Thomas Gold, and Martin K. Whyte at the end of the 1980s· the civil society model was adapted, with certain modifications, to study the progress and prospects of pluralistic group formation and intellectual/professional autonomy in the Chinese reform era.[26]

The new emphasis on the transformation of state-society relations in the 1980s also served to generate renewed research interest in Chinese political-institutional reform, and more specifically in the prospects for democratization. Books by Andrew Nathan, Benedict Stavis, and Barrett McCormick, among others, explored the historical precedents, structural requisites, recent trends, limiting factors, and possible future trajectories of democratic reform in China.[27]

The Impact of June 4

The events of April–June 1989 powerfully affected the intellectual and emotional climate of American research on contemporary Chinese politics. Where the mid-1980s had witnessed increased academic interest in (and enthusiasm for) the emergence of civil society and the prospects for political reform in China, the crackdown of June 1989 produced a veritable avalanche of articles, monographs, and edited volumes on the origins, development, and aftermath of the June 4 tragedy.[28] Emotions ran high on this sensitive subject, and the general tone of American China scholarship after June 4 was overwhelmingly sympathetic to the Chinese student movement and hostile to the Chinese government's harsh suppression of it. This initial wave of "revulsion scholarship" was followed in the mid- and late 1990s by a number of more detached and sober-minded, albeit still generally pessimistic, assessments of the prospects for a near-term Chinese breakthrough in systemic political reform.[29] Also in this period – in the aftermath of the Soviet Union's dramatic 1991 disintegration – several comparative studies of the reform process in China and the USSR were undertaken, as scholars probed the causes of the CPSU's collapse and the reasons for the CCP's survival.[30]

Closely related to the strong negative assessment of the Tiananmen crackdown and its aftermath, one of the more prominent intellectual trends in the 1990s was the rising use of "corporatist" models to describe emergent state-society relations in the reform era. Imported from the field of Latin American studies, the concept of corporatism focused attention on the cooptation and control of key functional and professional groups by state agencies. Three varieties of corporatism drew the attention of American China scholars in the post-Tiananmen period. One was the party-state's near-total ban on autonomous, interest-based associations and occupational groups, and its continued monopoly of leadership over nationwide mass organizations (or "peak associations") such as the All China Federation of Trade Unions, the All China Women's Federation and the All China Students' Federation.[31] The second was the Chinese government's concerted effort to control local associational life through requirement of state sponsorship, licensing, and other forms of "interpenetration" *vis-à-vis* newly-emerging local organizations such as trade associations, chambers of commerce, professional and occupational groups.[32] The third was the growing informal (and sometimes formal) bureaucratic partnership between market entrepreneurs and local state agents in the development of industry and commerce at the county, municipal, and township levels. The terms "local state corporatism" and "symbiotic clientelism," among others, were coined in this period to describe such arrangements.[33] To a significant extent, then, the 1990s witnessed the triumph of corporatist models (which generally emphasized the state's continuing domination of society) over earlier civil society and democratic transition models.[34]

Another focal point of research interest in the aftermath of June 4 was the phenomenon of burgeoning corruption in post-reform China. Half a dozen major scholarly inquiries into the nature, sources, and consequences of corruption were initiated by U.S. China scholars in the 1990s, most prominently by third-generation political scientists Xiaobo Lu, Melanie Manion, and Yan Sun.[35] By the late 1990s, research interest in corruption was being conjoined with a fresh wave of scholarly research on the growing fiscal burdens suffered by rural villagers, and the emergence of new forms of political participation and protest in the countryside – including village elections, "letters and visits", and a growing number of spontaneous – and sometimes violent – protest demonstrations.[36]

One additional byproduct of the post-Tiananmen politicization of Chinese studies in the United States was the heightened political pressure felt by young PRC-born scholars. Although several of them produced bold and innovative doctoral dissertations (and first books) in the years after the 1989 Tiananmen crisis, many of these young *Huaqiao* retained close ties of family, friendship, and employment in China, and hence experienced a certain amount of trepidation about conducting social science research in China. Such anxiety was heightened when, in a few highly publicized cases, overseas Chinese scholars were detained by security police when they went back to China to conduct research on politically sensitive topics such as the Cultural Revolution, China's entry into the Korean War, and China's nuclear weapons development.[37]

Nor were American-born scholars wholly immune from political pressures in the aftermath of Tiananmen. In the 1990s a number of eminent American academics and journalists – including Perry Link, Jonathan Mirsky, Andrew Nathan, Peter Perdue, Orville Schell, and Calla Wiemer – were denied visas to travel to China on the grounds of putative "anti-China" activities. Arguing that this has had a deterrent effect on other scholars, a few inveterate critics of China have expressed the view that American academics routinely "pull their punches" and avoid making strong criticisms of the Chinese government in order not to jeopardize their opportunity to travel and conduct research in the PRC.[38]

The Fourth Generation and the Triumph of Political Economy

The approach of the new millennium witnessed the coming of age of yet another new cohort of academically trained political scientists, comprising the first post-Tiananmen generation. Receiving their Ph.D. degrees in the 1990s, they generally had strong academic training in statistics, comparative political economy, and micro-political analysis. Some prominent members of this new generation, listed alphabetically along with their main topics of inquiry, included Elizabeth Economy (Chinese environmental issues), Mary Gallagher (labor relations), Peter Gries (Chinese nationalism), Daniel Kelliher (rural reform), Yawei Liu (local elections), Edward Steinfeld (SOE reform), Murray Scot Tanner (legislatures;

public security), Kellee Tsai (micro-finance), Fei-ling Wang (*hukou* system), Andrew Wedeman (political economy of local protectionism), and Susan Whiting (rural political economy).

By the late 1990s, considerable research attention was being focused on China's changing "state capacity" in the age of market transition. Earlier zero-sum debates over *state vs. society* and *center vs. province* now gave way to more highly nuanced assessments of the evolving *nature, shape,* and *configuration* of state power, and the *situational constraints* affecting the exercise of such power.[39] Among other things, the new discourse sought to specify the particular constellations of *interests and incentives* that affect key actors and "stakeholders" in specific policy arenas and sectors. While no broad consensus has emerged on "the state of the state" in post-reform China,[40] recent studies have yielded a more complex, multi-dimensional picture of the shifting political economy of state power and authority.[41]

Two other recent trends worthy of comment are, first, the rise of collaborative research between Chinese and American scholars; and second, the "rediscovery" by U.S. social scientists of major areas of continuity between China's pre-communist past and its post-reform present. Sino-American scholarly collaboration was slow to emerge in the 1980s and 1990s, due in large measure to continuing political sensitivities surrounding the conduct of in-country research, noted earlier. There have been some notable exceptions, however. These include the fruitful collaboration between Kevin O'Brien and Lianjiang Li on rural political reform and social protest; Wang Shaoguang and Hu Angang on uneven economic growth and rising income disparities; Tony Saich and Xuedong Yang on township elections; Elizabeth Perry and Li Xun on Shanghai in the Cultural Revolution; and Jean Oi and Zhao Shukai on the fiscal starvation of local governments in the reform era.[42] In addition to such paired collaborations, institutionalized Sino-American research ties have also been promoted and financially supported by NGOs such as the Committee on Scholarly Communication with China, the Henry Luce Foundation, the Chiang Ching-kuo Foundation, the Social Science Research Council, the American Council of Learned Societies, the Freeman Foundation, the Smith Richardson Foundation, and the Andrew W. Mellon Foundation.

The "rediscovery" of the relevance of China's pre-communist past to its post-reform present has been another significant trend of the past 15 years. Political scientists, political sociologists, and anthropologists such as Elizabeth Perry, Gregory Ruf, Douglas Guthrie, Yunxiang Yan and Mayfair Yang have written extensively about the resurgence of clans and clan feuds, *guanxi* networks, and various other traditional patterns of social structure and behavior in the reform era.[43] Moreover, the rediscovery of the relevance of the past has led social scientists increasingly to re-examine long-neglected aspects of pre-1949 Chinese society and politics. Noteworthy recent examples include books by Jeffrey Wasserstrom (on student protest in the May Fourth era), David Strand (on urban street life in the 1920s), Elizabeth Perry (on the Shanghai labor movement in the 1920s and 1930s) and Julia Strauss (on failed efforts at state-building in Republican China).[44]

Economic Models of Politics: Some Concerns About the Discipline

While growing interest in the field of comparative political economy has sensitized China scholars to the need to carefully examine (and compare) institutional structures, incentive systems, and systemic constraints, there is another aspect of the importation of economic models and methods into the field of Chinese politics that is perhaps more worrisome.

Much has been written in recent years about the decline of area studies in American universities.[45] Due in large measure to the dramatically increasing influence of (deductive) rational-choice and (quantitative) econometric models, imported wholesale into political science from economics starting in the 1970s,[46] graduate students studying comparative politics at the top U.S. research universities today appear to be investing less time and energy gaining deep cultural and linguistic knowledge of their country or region of interest, and proportionately more time studying formal modeling and statistical techniques. Most leading political science departments, for example, now require a rigorous sequence of quantitative and formal theory courses for their first-year graduate students. Many departments now also offer students the alternative of taking an advanced sequence of mathematics/statistics courses as a substitute for a foreign language requirement. Indeed, students in many graduate departments (including my own) may now choose "methodology" as a subfield of political science to replace one of the traditional, substantive fields. Increasingly, if almost imperceptibly, methodology has shifted from being a *set of tools,* i.e. means used to study politics, to being an *object of study*, namely an end in itself.

If I may be permitted a personal observation, in the field of Chinese politics I have noticed a significant shift in the research interests of my graduate students in recent years, away from consideration of *qualitative* research problems (driven by an interest in major theoretical/conceptual issues and guided by intensive exposure to the country, its institutions, culture and its language), toward *quantitative* research agendas, often driven by the availability of "large-N data sets" incorporating several standardized socio-economic variables which can be more-or-less mechanically regressed against one another to derive "statistically significant" tests of hypotheses (which were, in many cases, suggested in the first instance by the availability of the data sets themselves). Such research is reminiscent of the old anecdote about the drunk who looked for his lost car keys under a street lamp. When asked why he was concentrating his search under the lamp, he answered, "Because that's where the light is!"

The problem lies not with the techniques and methods of statistical and formal modeling themselves, but rather with their tendency, when used in isolation from other, more traditional research methods, to facilitate the displacement of *analytical thinking* by mere *technical procedure.*

Two anecdotes will serve to illustrate the dangers of such displacement. A few years ago I was asked to read a Master's thesis that employed multiple-regression analysis to explain Taiwan President Chen Shui-bian's unexpected victory over

Lian Chan and James Soong in the presidential election of March 2000. The student had set up a statistical model that included a rather large number of quantifiable socio-economic variables such as demographic factors (age, gender, education, location), economic factors (economic growth, household income, unemployment rates), political factors (strength of party identity and loyalty), and ethnic identity (mainlander vs. native Taiwanese), among others. The student's regressions "proved" that Chen Shui-bian's victory – and the size of his margin of victory – were explained primarily by the variables of ethnicity and unemployment. During the oral examination that followed the submission of the student's M.A. thesis, I asked her if there were any other factors she could think of that might have influenced the outcome of the March 2000 election. She thought for a bit and said, "No, I don't think so." I then asked her if she had considered the possibility that the growing escalation of cross-Strait military and political tensions between July 1999 (Lee Teng-hui's infamous "guo yu guo de tebie guanxi" remark) and February 2000 (Premier Zhu Rongji's warning to Taiwan voters not to elect a pro-independence candidate) might have influenced the election's outcome. (This seemed a distinct possibility insofar as public opinion polls had revealed that many Taiwanese voters were angry over mainland China's heavyhanded efforts to influence their votes on the eve of the election.) The student looked at me blankly for a moment and then responded, "I never thought of that." The point of this anecdote is that this particular student was so narrowly focused on her own quantifiable data that she hadn't taken the time to think about the "bigger picture."

The second example concerns a graduate student who wished to write a paper on the causes of corruption in post-reform China. He had just taken a course on formal modeling, and he enthusiastically set about trying to reveal the "hidden logic" underlying the spread of corruption in the reform period. He constructed an elaborate "two-level game" scenario involving a (hypothetical) local village cadre who had to decide whether or not to solicit a bribe from a villager who was applying for a license to run a TVE; the villager, in turn, had to decide whether or not to pay the bribe. The student first posited a set of parametric assumptions that simplified the game and reduced the number of variables that would have to be considered. He then formulated a set of "if … then" preliminary hypotheses governing all conceivable permutations of his chosen variables. He next drew up an elaborate "decision tree" posing a series of iterated binary "cooperate/defect" (or solicit/not solicit) choices at successive points in the game, covering every specific contingency facing the cadre and the villager at each point in the decision process. This required several pages of formal mathematical notation. At the end of his (largely unreadable) paper, the student reached the stunning conclusion that the cadre would solicit a bribe (and the villager would pay the bribe) if, and only if, the perceived risks of doing so were outweighed by the anticipated gains. Here was a case of a very sophisticated modeling technique being used to belabor a rather obvious, elemental point – akin to using an elephant gun to kill a flea.

The point of these illustrations is not to disparage either econometrics or formal modeling. Indeed, statistical methods and "rational choice" analysis have proved extremely valuable, for example, in laying bare hidden institutional constraints on behavior and in unraveling the logic of apparently counter-intuitive political outcomes. But this is most likely to occur when such analysis is used sensitively and in conjunction with more conventional, insight-oriented qualitative analysis (e.g. involving case studies, documentary research, personal interviews, impressionistic observations, and anecdotes), and when it is applied to problems of an appropriate scale and nature by analysts familiar with the historical, cultural, and institutional settings and nuances of their subject matter.[47]

The Future of Chinese Political Studies in the U.S.

Notwithstanding nagging questions about recent methodological trends within political science as a discipline, there is some reason for optimism about the future of the China politics field in the United States. For one thing, the overall quality of our graduate students appears to be improving steadily. Indeed, the ranks of the newly-emerging fifth generation of young Ph.D.s in Chinese politics include several first-rate young scholars possessing impressive language skills, superb training in social science and comparative political economy, and considerable field experience conducting research in China. Research projects undertaken by members of this post-2000 generation of China scholars include (in alphabetical order, along with their Ph.D.-granting institutions), Martin Dimitrov (Stanford, 2004), "Administrative Decentralization and the Rule of Law in Russia and China"; Kenneth Foster (U.C. Berkeley, 2003), "Associations and the State in Contemporary Mainland China"; William Hurst (U.C. Berkeley, 2005), "The Politics of Laid-Off Workers in China"; Scott Kennedy (George Washington, 2001), "The Business of Lobbying in China"; Jason Kindopp (George Washington, 2004), "The Politics of Religion in China"; Andrew Mertha (Michigan, 2001), "Intellectual Property in Contemporary China"; Benjamin Read (Harvard, 2003), "State, Social Networks, and Citizens in China's Urban Neighborhoods"; Alexei Shevchenko (UCLA, 2003), "The CCP as an Entrepreneurial Party"; Victor Shih (Harvard, 2003), "Factional Politics, Inflationary Cycles, and Non-Performing Loans in China"; Phillip Stalley (George Washington, 2006), "Foreign Firms and Environmental Governance in China"; and Lily Tsai (Harvard, 2004), "Informal State Governance and Public Goods Provision in Rural China."

At UCLA I am presently supervising 11 graduate students in the field of Chinese politics and foreign policy, including five PRC citizens, one Korean and one Japanese. Six of my students are currently writing doctoral dissertations. Their topics, which reflect the broad range of new research opportunities, interests, and methodologies that have emerged in the post-reform period, include: the political economy of banking reform; the determinants of political mobility for provincial leaders; the political economy of rural political participation and protest; the comparative effectiveness of environmental protection policies in China, Korea, and Taiwan; the political dynamics of periodic campaigns to reduce government bureaucracy and "simplify state administration"; the political economy of shifting fiscal relations between center and province; and the dynamics of U.S.–China relations in the 1960s. The outlook for this talented cohort of Ph.D. candidates is bright, limited mainly by a job market that appears rather sluggish and static at present.

Aside from a soft job market, two additional gray clouds loom on the horizon. First is the gradual shrinkage of funds available to support the training of graduate students in the social sciences generally, and area studies in particular. This problem appears to be particularly acute at public universities, many of which have suffered a decline in government financial support in recent years. With funding generally flat and educational costs continuing to rise, competition for graduate fellowships and assistantships has never been more intense. And since student tuition and incidental fees at most public universities are considerably higher for foreign students than for local residents, it has become increasingly less feasible to offer financial aid to foreign students.[48] At many universities this has resulted in a reduction, and in some cases a total suspension, in the recruitment of non self-supporting foreign graduate students. Since most PRC graduate students fall into this category, the number of Chinese students entering U.S. graduate programs in the social sciences has fallen off noticeably in recent years.

This trend, while alarming in itself, has been rendered even more worrisome by the imposition of new, post-9/11 U.S. immigration hurdles for Chinese graduate school applicants. With visa barriers raised to new levels of personal inconvenience, sometimes bordering on harassment, elite Chinese students are no longer flocking to American universities in the same numbers as before.[49] Increasingly, Japan, Western Europe, and Australia are successfully syphoning off graduate school applicants who had previously expected to complete their advanced studies in the United States. This is a disturbing trend that will need to be addressed seriously if America is to retain its competitive edge, not just in China studies but in the full range of academic, scientific, and technological fields and disciplines.

Acknowledgements

The author wishes to express his appreciation to Elizabeth Perry, Thomas Bernstein, and David Shambaugh for their helpful comments on an earlier draft.

Notes

1 For two excellent surveys of the development of the field of Chinese politics in American academia, see Harry Harding, "Chinese Politics: Toward a Third Generation of Scholarship," *World Politics* 36:2 (January 1984), pp. 284–307; and Elizabeth J; Perry, "Partners at 50: American China Studies and the PRC," in *Trends in China Watching: Observing the PRC at 50* (Washington, D.C.: The Sigur Center for Asian Studies, George Washington University, 1999), pp. 13–19. See also Harding's keynote address on "The Changing Roles of the Academic China Watcher," in ibid., pp. 65–73.

2 Fairbank was the dean of U.S. China historians; Barnett and Pye were raised in China by missionary parents. Barnett later worked as a journalist in Hong Kong, where he also represented the American Friends Service Committee; Pye was a pioneer in the field of comparative political culture. Eckstein was an economist; and Scalapino

studied Japanese history and politics under Fairbank at Harvard prior to enlisting in the U.S. Army in WWII.

3 Three other first-generation luminaries who contributed greatly to the genre of "elite studies" in Chinese politics in this period were Franz Shurmann (*Ideology and Organization in Communist China*); Stuart Schram (*Mao Tse-tung*); and Roderick MacFarquhar (*The Hundred Flowers Campaign and the Chinese Intellectuals*). Interestingly, none of the three were professionally trained as political scientists. Schurmann was a Harvard-trained sociologist/historian, while Schram, an American citizen, spent most of his research career working in England, and MacFarquhar, a British citizen (and former MP), moved to America in mid-career.

4 See Bruce Cumings, "Boundary Displacement: Area Studies and International Studies During and After the Cold War," *Bulletin of Concerned Asian Scholars*, available online at http://www.mtholyoke.edu/acad/intrel/cumings2.htm.

5 Key comparative studies in this genre were Donald Treadgold (ed.) *Soviet and Chinese Communism: Similarities and Difference* (Seattle, WA: University of Washington Press, 1967); Chalmers Johnson (ed.) *Change in Communist Systems* (Stanford, CA: Stanford University Press, 1970); and Thomas P. Bernstein, "Leadership and Mass Mobilization in the Soviet and Chinese Collectivisation Campaigns: A Comparison," *The China Quarterly* No. 31 (1967).

6 One prominent exception to this generalization was Lucian Pye, whose academic training in political psychology and Southeast Asian studies enabled him to bridge the academic divide between the study of Leninist and non-Leninist systems.

7 Harding, Cf. 1.

8 Lucian Pye, "Present at the Beginning," remarks delivered at the 40th anniversary celebration of the founding of the Universities Service Centre, January 2004. See also Ezra F. Vogel, "Foreword: The First 40 Years of the Universities Service Centre," *The China Journal* No. 53 (January 2005).

9 Perry, note 1 (above).

10 See Committee of Concerned Asian Scholars and Ezra Vogel, "The Funding of Chinese Studies," *Bulletin of Concerned Asian Scholars* No. 1 (July 1973).

11 E. Elena Songster, "China Scholars' Response to Vietnam," unpublished essay (2000), online at http://orpheus.ucsd.edu/chinesehistory/pgp/songster.htm.

12 Compare, for example, the enthusiasm of the authors of the CCAS volume, *China! Inside the People's Republic* (New York: Bantam Books, 1972) with the extended, deeply critical essay by Simon Leys, *Chinese Shadows* (New York: Viking Press, 1977). It should be noted that many – perhaps even most – American China scholars did not take sides in the ideological polarization of this period, remaining agnostic, on a case-by-case basis, about the more extreme claims of both sides.

13 In this connection, the present author recalls attending a conference at the end of the 1970s at a major university in the United Kingdom where a number of left-wing British and American China scholars painfully re-examined some of their own past perceptions and judgments about China in an effort to come to grips with newly-revealed flaws and flagrant shortcomings in the Maoist record.

14 The National Committee on U.S.–China Relations and the Committee on Scholarly Communication with the PRC of the National Academy of Sciences helped to organize and manage the American side of the non-governmental educational, scientific, and cultural exchanges initiated after the Nixon visit of 1972. Such exchanges provided expanded opportunities for U.S. China scholars to visit the PRC in the role of "academic escorts" in the 1970s. The present author visited China twice prior to the normalization of relations, first as deputy *chef de mission* of the U.S. AAU National Track and Field Team in May 1975, and then as academic escort to the Engineering Education Delegation from the National Academy of Engineering in September 1978.

15 Workshop on the "Pursuit of Political Interests in the PRC," Ann Arbor, Michigan, July 1977.

16 See Tang Tsou, "Prolegomenon to the Study of Informal Groups in CCP Politics", loc. cit.; and Victor Falkenheim (ed), *Citizens and Groups in Contemporary China* (Ann Arbor, MI: University of Michigan Press, 1987).

17 See "Steven Mosher and the Politics of Cultural Exchange," *The Nation* 237:6 (September 3, 1983); and D. Shapley, "Anthropologist Fired: Stanford Plays its China Card," *Nature*, March 24, 1983.

18 The travails of one U.S. China scholar who tried to conduct field research in the PRC in the 1980s are recounted in Eugene Cooper, *Adventures in Chinese Bureaucracy: A Meta-Anthropological Saga* (New York: Nova Science, 2000).

19 Among Oksenberg's many outstanding third- and fourth-generation Ph.D. students were Jae Ho Chung; Bruce Dickson, Elizabeth Economy, Nina Halpern, Melanie Manion, Jean Oi, Elizabeth Perry, Jonathan Pollack, David Shambaugh, Murray Scot Tanner, James Tong, Andrew Walder, Susan Whiting, and David Zweig.

20 Examples of elite-oriented research in this period include Roderick MacFarquhar's three-volume opus, *The Origins of the Cultural Revolution,* and his edited volume, *The Politics of China, 1949-89*; also Frederick C. Teiwes's *The Tragedy of Lin Biao* and *Politics at Mao's Court: Gao Gang and Party Factionalism in the early 1950s,* also Richard Baum, *Burying Mao: Chinese Politics in the Age of Deng Xiaoping;* Andrew Nathan and E. Perry Link (eds), *The Tiananmen Papers*; and Andrew Nathan and Bruce Gilley (eds), *China's New Rulers: The Secret Files.*

21 Conference on "To Reform the Chinese Political Order," Harwichport, Massachusetts, 1984.

22 Elizabeth Perry and Christine Wong (eds) *The Political Economy of Reform in Post-Mao China* (Cambridge, MA: Harvard University Press, 1985).

23 Denis Simon and Merle Goldman (eds), *Science and Technology in Post-Mao China* (Cambridge, MA: Harvard University Press, 1989).

24 See "Public Sphere/Civil Society in China? Paradigmatic Issues in Chinese Studies: A Symposium," *Modern China* 19:2 (April 1993).

25 See Robert F. Miller, (ed.), *The Development of Civil Society in Communist Systems* (Sydney: George Allen and Unwin, 1992); and Kazimierz Poznanski, *Constructing Capitalism: The Re-emergence of Civil Society and Liberal Economy in the Post-Communist World* (Boulder, CO: Westview Press, 1992).

26 See Timothy Brook and Michael Frolic (eds), *Civil Society in China* (Armonk, NY: M.E. Sharpe, 1997); Gordon White, "Prospects for Civil Society in China: A Case Study of Xiaoshan City," *Australian Journal of Chinese Affairs* 29 (January 1993); Thomas Gold, "The Resurgence of Civil Society in China," *Journal of Democracy* 1:1 (Winter 1990); and Martin K. Whyte, "Urban China: A Civil Society in the Making?" in Arthur Rosenbaum (ed.), *State and Society in China: The Consequences of Reform* (Boulder, CO: Westview, 1992). For an early insight into the incipient transformation of state-society relations in the reform era, see Tang Tsou, "Back from the Brink of Revolutionary-Feudal Totalitarianism," in Victor Nee and David Mozingo (eds), *State and Society in Contemporary China* (Itahca, NY: Cornell University Press, 1983).

27 Andrew Nathan, *Chinese Democracy* (Berkeley, CA: University of California Press, 1985); Benedict Stavis, *China's Political Reforms: An Interim Report* (New York: Praeger, 1988); and Barrett McCormick, *Political Reform in Post-Mao China* (Berkeley, CA: University of California Press, 1990).

28 See, inter alia, Timothy Brook, *Quelling the People*: *The Military Suppression of the Beijing Democracy Movement* (Berkeley, CA: Stanford University Press, 1992); Suzanne Ogden (ed.), *China's Search for Democracy: The Student and Mass Movement of 1989* (Armonk, NY: M.E. Sharpe, 1992); Lee Feigon, *China Rising: The Meaning of Tiananmen* (Chicago, IL: Ivan Dee, 1990); Craig Calhoun, *Neither Gods nor Emperors: Students and the Struggle for Democracy in China* (Berkeley,

CA: University of California Press, 1995); Tony Saich (ed.), *The Chinese People's Movement: Perspectives on Spring, 1989* (Armonk NY: M.E. Sharpe, 1990); Richard Baum (ed.), *Reform and Reaction in Post-Mao China: The Road to Tiananmen* (London: Routledge, 1991); and Andrew Nathan and Perry Link (eds), *The Tiananmen Papers* (New York: Public Affairs, 2001).

29   See, for example, the special issue, "Will China Democratize?", *Journal of Democracy* 9:1 (January 1998); Roderick MacFarquhar and Merle Goldman (eds), *The Paradox of Reform in Post-Mao China* (Cambridge, MA: Harvard University Press, 1999); Edward Friedman, *National Identity and Democratic Prospects in Socialist China* (Armonk, NY: M.E. Sharpe, 1995); Barrett McCormick and Edward Friedman (eds), *What if China Doesn't Democratize?* (Armonk, NY: M.E. Sharpe, 2000); David Shambaugh (ed.), *Is China Unstable? Assessing the Factors* (Armonk, NY: M.E. Sharpe, 2000); Lawrence Sullivan (ed.), *China Since Tiananmen* (Armonk, NY: M.E. Sharpe, 1995); and Joseph Fewsmith, *China Since Tiananmen: The Politics of Transition* (Cambridge: Cambridge University Press, 2001).

30   See, *inter alia*, Minxin Pei, *From Reform to Revolution: The Demise of Communism in China and the Soviet Union* (Cambridge, MA: Harvard University Press, 1994); Bruce Dickson, *Democratization in China and Taiwan: The Adaptability of Leninist Parties* (Oxford: Oxford University Press, 1997); and Lowell Dittmer, *Sino-Soviet Normalization and its International Implications, 1945–1990* (Seattle, WA: University of Washington Press, 1992).

31   See, for example, Anita Chan and Jonathan Unger, "Corporatism in China: A Developmental State in an East Asian Context," in Barrett L. McCormick and Jonathan Unger (eds), *China after Socialism: In the Footsteps of Eastern Europe or East Asia?* (Armonk, NY: M.E. Sharpe, 1996).

32   See, for example, Dorothy Solinger, "Urban Entrepreneurs and the State: The Merger of State and Society," in Rosenbaum (ed.), *State and Society in China;* and Margaret Pearson, "The Janus Face of Business Associations in China: Socialist Corporatism in Foreign Enterprises," *The Australian Journal of Chinese Affairs* 31 (January 1994).

33   See Jean Oi, "Fiscal Reform and the Economic Foundations of Local State Corporatism," *World Politics* 45:1 (October 1992); and David L. Wank, "Bureaucratic Patronage and Private Business: Changing Networks of Power in Urban China," in Andrew Walder (ed.), *The Waning of the Communist State* (Berkeley, CA: University of California Press, 1995).

34   These developments are documented in Richard Baum and Alexei Shevchenko, "The State of the State," in MacFarquhar and Goldman (eds), *The Paradox of Reform in Post-Mao China*, loc.cit.

35   Xiaobo Lu, *Cadres and Corruption: Organizational Involution of the Chinese Communist Party* (New York: Columbia University Press, 2000); Melanie Manion, *Corruption by Design: Building Clean Government in Mainland China and Hong Kong* (Cambridge, MA: Harvard University Press, 2004); and Yan Sun, *Corruption and Market in Contemporary China* (Ithaca, NY: Cornell University Press, 2004).

36   See, e.g. Kevin J. O'Brien, "Rightful Resistance," *World Politics* 49:1 (1996); Andrew Wedeman, "Stealing from the Farmers: Institutional Corruption and the 1992 IOU Crisis," *The China Quarterly* 152 (1997); and Thomas Bernstein and Xiaobo Lu, *Taxation without Representation in Contemporary Rural China* (Cambridge: Cambridge University Press, 2003).

37   Note, for example, the 1999 detention of Song Yongyi of Dickinson College, as detailed in *The Washington Post*, January 12, 2000; David Tsui's (Xu Zerong's) 2002 conviction for "leaking state secrets," in *Associated Press* (Beijing), February 2, 2002; Hua Di's 2000 arrest and conviction on similar charges, in *Hong Kong Standard*, April 3, 2000; and the 2004 detention of Wang Fei-ling, in "My Two-Week Ordeal in Shanghai" (unpublished manuscript, August 13, 2004).

38 See, for example, Steven Mosher, *China Misperceived: American Illusions and Chinese Reality* (New York: Basic Books, 1990). In the present author's personal view, there may be some – albeit limited – validity to this criticism, although the vast majority of American China scholarship remains essentially untainted by self-censorship.

39 See Vivienne Shue, "State Power and Social Organization in China," in Vivienne Shue and Joel Mygdal (eds), *State Power and Social Forces* (Cambridge: Cambridge University Press, 1994).

40 Cf., for example, the widely divergent assessments of state capacity made by Shaoguang Wang, Andrew Nathan, Bruce Dickson, Qinglian He, Bruce Gilley, Minxin Pei, and Dali Yang in *Journal of Democracy* 14:1 (January 2003).

41 See, for example, Bruce Dickson, *Red Capitalists in China: The Party, Private Entrepreneurs, and Prospects for Political Change* (Cambridge: Cambridge University Press, 2003); Richard L. Edmonds (ed.), *Managing the Chinese Environment* (Oxford: Oxford University Press, 1998); Mary Gallagher, *Contagious Capitalism: Globalization and the Politics of Labor in China* (Princeton, NJ: Princeton University Press, 2005); Scott Kennedy, *The Business of Lobbying in China* (Cambridge, MA: Harvard University Press, 2005); Barry Naughton and Dali Yang (eds), *Holding China Together: Diversity and National Integration in the Post-Deng Era* (Cambridge: Cambridge University Press, 2004); Jean Oi, *Rural China Takes Off* (Berkeley, CA: University of California Press, 1999); Minxin Pei, *China's Trapped Transition* (Cambridge, MA: Harvard University Press, 2006); Dorothy Solinger, *Contesting Citizenship in Urban China: Peasants, Migrants, the State, and the Logic of the Market* (Berkeley, CA: University of California Press, 1999); Edward Steinfeld, *Forging Reform in China: The Fate of State-Owned Industry* (Cambridge: Cambridge University Press, 1998); Kellee Tsai, *Back-Alley Banking: Private Entrepreneurs in China* (Ithaca, NY: Cornell University Press, 2002); Andrew Wedeman, *From Mao to Market: Local Protectionism, Rent-Seeking, and the Marketization of China, 1984–1992* (Cambridge: Cambridge University Press, 2003); Lynn T. White III, *Unstately Power* (2 Vols.) (Armonk, NY: M.E. Sharpe, 1998); Susan Whiting, *Power and Wealth in Rural China: The Political Economy of Institutional Change* (Cambridge: Cambridge University Press, 2001); Dali Yang, *Remaking the Chinese Leviathan: Market Transition and the Politics of Governance in China* (Stanford, CA: Stanford University Press, 2004); and David Zweig, *Internationalizing China: Domestic Interests and Global Linkages* (Ithaca, NY: Cornell University Press, 2002).

42 See Kevin O'Brien and Lianjiang Li, *Rightful Resistance in Rural China* (Cambridge: Cambridge University Press 2006); Wang Shaoguang and Hu Angang, *The Political Economy of Uneven Development: The Case of China* (Armonk, NY: M.E. Sharpe, 1999); Tony Saich and Xuedong Yang, "Township Elections in China: Extending Democracy or Institutional Innovation?" *China Report* 39:3 (2003); Elizabeth Perry and Li Xin, *Proletarian Power: Shanghai in the Cultural Revolution* (Boulder, CO: Westview, 1997); and Jean Oi and Zhao Shukai, "Fiscal Crisis in China's Townships: Causes. and Consequences" (presented at the Harvard conference on "Grassroots Political Reform" (2005).

43 See Elizabeth Perry, "Rural Collective Violence: The Fruits of Recent Reforms," in Perry and Wong (eds), *The Political Economy of Reform in China,* loc. cit.; Douglas Guthrie, *Social Connections in China: Institutions, Culture, and the Changing Nature of Guanxi* (Cambridge: Cambridge University Press, 2002); Gregory Ruf, *Cadres and Kin: Making a Socialist Village in West China, 1921–1991* (Stanford, CA: Stanford University Press, 1998); Mayfair Yang, *Gifts, Favors, and Banquets* (Ithaca, NY: Cornell University Press, 1994); and Yunxiang Yan, *Private Life under Socialism: Love, Intimacy, and Family Change in a Chinese Village, 1949–1999* (Stanford, CA: Stanford University Press, 2003).

44 See Jeffrey Wasserstrom, *Student Protest in 20th Century China: The View from Shanghai* (Stanford, CA: Stanford University Press, 1991); David Strand, *Rickshaw Boy: City People and Politics in the 1920s* (Berkeley, CA: University of California Press, 1999); Elizabeth Perry, *Shanghai on Strike: The Politics of Chinese Labor* (Stanford, CA: Stanford University Press, 1993); and Julia Strauss, *Strong Institutions in Weak Polities: State Building in Republican China, 1927–1940* (Oxford: Oxford University Press, 1998).

45 See, for example, the debate among leading Asian scholars in "Viewpoints: The Futures of Area Studies," Association for Asian Studies, July 1997, available at: http://www.aasianst.org/Viewpoints/futures.htm.

46 The rational choice approach began to be widely accepted in political science following publication of Mancur Olson's pioneering book, *The Logic of Collective Action: Public Goods and the Theory of Groups* (Cambridge, MA: Harvard University Press, 1965).

47 For an example of the sensitive application of formal modeling to the analysis of corruption in China, see Melanie Manion, "Corruption by Design," *Journal of Law, Economics and Organization* 12:1 (1996).

48 At UCLA, tuition and fees for foreign students are almost three times as high as for California residents – $15,000 compared to $5,500.

49 In 2003 there was a decline of 15 percent in the number of PRC citizens applying for student visas to the United States, followed by a further 17 percent decline in 2004. The decline in visa applications, however, was partially offset by an increase in the acceptance rate for Chinese applicants. As a result, the actual number of Chinese students studying in the United States dropped by only a few percentage points to around 60,000 in 2004. See Matt Williams and Jerome Cohen, in *The Christian Science Monitor*, September 30, 2005.

III. Studies of Chinese Foreign and Security Policies

8 Studies of China's Foreign and Security Policies in Europe

Kay Möller

Over time, those who have tried to deal with the Chinese developed three attitudes: the philosophers of enlightenment and the Maoists of our era projected their own illusions on the other about whom they were almost totally ignorant; disappointed, they directed their wrath at the fallen idol. The British traders and diplomats wanted to deal with the Chinese "on their own terms," thus causing many clashes and bad feelings. The Jesuits learned to know the other so as to identify common ground for understanding; their conversion effort was bound to fail, but their culture of dialogue remains a model.

(Alain Peyrefitte, French diplomat and politician, 1997)

When contrasted with the United States, China studies in Western Europe have been more traditionally dominated by Sinologists, who mainly concentrate on Chinese domestic developments, and by journalists – some of whom developed an interest in Beijing's foreign and security policies. Not only was there little in between, but both the Sinologists and the journalists emphasized China's exceptionalism in terms of internal developments, while viewing its foreign and security policies as little more than a reflex of Soviet strategy.[1] When the Sino–Soviet rupture became obvious in the early 1960s, rather than assuming a more regional perspective, West European experts extended the exceptionalist mantra to include foreign affairs forthwith. Even in France and the U.K., countries that prided themselves of uninterrupted historical links with the Far East, early protagonists with diplomatic, military, or intelligence backgrounds tended to underestimate China as a part of its own region.[2]

Interest in Chinese foreign and security policies was on the rise at the time of the Vietnam War when, due to the latter's coincidence with the Cultural Revolution, the discipline was once again caught in the ideological trap and split into romanticizing Maoist and hostile Cold warrior factions. Whereas the former was challenged from within European Sinology in the mid-1970s,[3] and soon afterwards fell apart together with its subject, Western Europe mostly viewed China as an inflexible pole in a global triangle,[4] and most of the time failed to understand the kind of regional and global dynamics that in the U.S. led to the emergence of "Pacific Rim" area studies. It was only ten years later that a distinct discipline of area studies developed in the U.K. and France with scholars such as Michael Yahuda and Jean-Luc Domenach taking the lead. In much of continental Europe, however, the influence of traditional Sinologists remained significant, the major difference with the previous decade consisting in a greater availability of public funding.

Subsequent limitations on government support were to some extent made up for by new programs launched by the European Commission after the signing of the Maastricht Treaty, among which a "Europe-China Academic Network" (ECAN) emerged.[5] More importantly, private companies with a stake in the PRC's expected "rise" to some extent discovered the field. The result was a certain commercialization of research and teaching at British universities as well as increased corporate sponsorship of selected think tank projects. However, this did not lead to a markedly greater interest in the study of Beijing's foreign and security policies, with the social sciences to some extent absorbing the subject as part of new globalization studies. What was left, was taken up by old and new journalists or journalist-turned-politicians who did their best to revive the former exceptionalism.[6]

It was mostly thanks to the efforts of expatriate North American scholars such as David Shambaugh, Gerald Segal, and Bates Gill, that the small and dispersed group of West European scholars of China's regional and international role started "networking" in the late 1980s.[7] At this point, governments in Europe and Asia had begun to close a perceived "Eurasian Gap" on the global map, thus inspiring new Europe–China and Europe–Asia dialogues some of which took the guise of "second tracks" to intergovernmental meetings. At the time of writing, one can discern contours of an emerging academic "strategic triangle," albeit a rather imbalanced and incoherent one.

This chapter undertakes a presentation and critical assessment of studies of China's foreign and security policies in Western Europe. It begins with an institutional survey, followed by an assessment of issues debated by European specialists.

The Network

Many of the following institutes are members of the European Alliance for Asian Studies at the International Institute for Asian Studies (IIAS) in Leiden,[8] the Netherlands. Established in 1997, the Alliance maintains a database on conferences and workshops and organizes an annual one day seminar called "Asia Update."

University Institutes

Whereas David Shambaugh is correct in stating that (particularly continental) "European universities have never done a good job of integrating area studies with the social sciences,"[9] one nevertheless finds a few departments that have been promoting the study and research of China's foreign and security policies. Among the latter figures Shambaugh's own former workplace at the University of London's School of Oriental and African Studies (SOAS), where he edited the prestigious *China Quarterly* from 1991–1996 and established the European Commission's "EU-China Academic Network." Established in 1992, the SOAS Centre of Chinese Studies has adopted an interdisciplinary approach, where Philip Deans presently conducts research on the PRC's international relations.[10]

Otherwise, and by no means exhaustive, the following specialists and institutions are involved in studying China's foreign and security policies:

United Kingdom

- The London School of Economics (LSE) Asia Research Centre, with Christopher R.H Hughes responsible for Asia-Pacific international relations with a focus on China.[11]
- Oxford University's St. Antony's College, with Rosemary Foot researching China in East Asian international relations and Steve Tsang focusing on Hong Kong and Taiwan.[12]
- Among the pioneers of British area studies outside London was Sheffield University's School of East Asian Studies, which began as a Centre for Japanese Studies in 1963.[13] Extended to Chinese and Korean studies in 1990, it has been conducting research on China's foreign policy under the direction of Robert Taylor.
- The University of Durham's School of Government and International Affairs established a Centre for Contemporary China Studies in 1999.[14] Research on China's international relations is being undertaken by David Kerr who, together with Gordon Cheung, also edits the international quarterly *East Asia*.
- Although not specializing in China, the University of Warwick's Centre for the Study of Globalization and Regionalization (CSGR) is co-directed by Asianist Richard Higgott and includes Christopher Hughes (no relation of Christopher Hughes at LSE), an expert on Japan's foreign and security policies.[15] Higgott edits *The Pacific Review*, one of Europe's foremost journals on international relations in the Asia-Pacific. Peter Ferdinand has also done considerable work on China's foreign relations and comparative communist foreign policies.

Outside the U.K., institutional traditions have been weaker with research often depending on individual intiative.[16] What follows is a list of university departments that have prepared the ground for a more long-term research.

Scandinavian Universities

- In 1984, Stockholm University established a multidisciplinary Centre for Pacific Asia Studies that publishes the *Stockholm Journal of East Asian Studies*.[17] China's foreign and security policies are presently covered by the Centre's director Masako Ikegami as well as senior researcher Ravinder Pal Singh.

- Since 2001, the European Institute of Japanese Studies at the Stockholm School of Economics has included a Stockholm School of Asian Studies directed by Tom Hart.[18]
- Helsinki University has an Asia-Pacific Studies Program,[19] where Kauko Laitinen is responsible for China and international relations. Currently based in the PRC, Linda Jakobson is Director of the China Program.
- At the University of Aarhus Department of Political Science,[20] Lisolette Odgaard and Clemens Stubbe Østergaard work on Chinese foreign and security policy. Although not conducting related research of its own, the Asia Research Centre at the Copenhagen Business School publishes the *Copenhagen Journal of Asian Studies*, which occasionally includes articles on foreign policy and security issues.[21]
- In 1968, the Nordic Council of Ministers founded the Nordic Institute of Asian Studies (NIAS),[22] which was taken over by a consortium comprising the Copenhagen Business School, the University of Copenhagen, and Lund University in January 2005. Although the institute's emphasis thus far has been mainly on domestic developments in Asian countries, it plans to broaden its agenda to include regional security issues.

Germany

- The Berlin Freie Universität's Otto Suhr Institut für Politikwissenschaften has a chair of Chinese politics that was founded by Jürgen Domes in 1967 and is currently held by Eberhard Sandschneider (on leave to DGAP, see below), one of Germany's leading experts on PRC foreign and security policies (see research institutes).[23]
- At Bochum University's Fakultät für Ostasienwissenschaften the subject is covered by Gu Xuewu in the Politics Department.[24]
- In 2003, the Institute of Chinese and Korean Studies at Tübingen University established a Chair for Greater Chinese Studies,[25] with Gunter Schubert as the first holder. One research focus is on mutual relations between the PRC, Taiwan, Hong Kong, Macau, Singapore, and the Chinese diaspora.
- The University of Munich includes Franco Algieri and Saskia Hieber, who both teach courses on and research Chinese foreign and security policies. Algieri is a specialist on EU–China relations, while Hieber (attached to the Political Academy in Tutzing) researches the Chinese military, Asian security, and particularly China's energy security.

The Netherlands

- The Sinological Institute at Leiden University,[26] although not itself specializing in China's foreign and security policies, houses a Documentation and Research Centre for Modern China that publishes the journal *China*

Information, which occasionally does publish articles on Chinese foreign policy.

Portugal

- Although not conducting research of its own either, the Instituto do Oriente at Lisbon Technical University's Instituto Superior de Ciências Sociais e Políticas,[27] does publish the biannual *Portuguese Review of Asian Studies*, that includes English-language articles on China's foreign and security policies.

European Research Institutes

Whereas David Shambaugh's review of Chinese studies in Europe viewed think tanks more kindly than European universities, he noted that as a consequence of the aforementioned deficit in university training, many researchers "do not speak Chinese or use primary Chinese sources in their research."[28] This remains true to a large extent – yet at the same time, Sinologists have always dominated research on the continent and have made a kind of a comeback following the early-1990s inconclusive experiments in trying to integrate better social sciences with area studies. Contrasted with the early 1990s, however, some of them have acquired a social sciences background.

Differing from the United States, most big European think tanks (research institutes) receive public funding and avoid partisanship.[29] Here one can distinguish beween Asian affairs institutes on the one hand and foreign policy think tanks with more or less substantial Asian departments on the other (a more recent trend towards privately-funded institutes and public–private partnerships has been most notable in countries with sizeable defence industries).

At the *international level*, the London-based International Institute for Strategic Studies (IISS) has been a leading center for the research of China's foreign and security policies,[30] with the late Gerald Segal and more recently Adam Ward working on China and Asian security. The institute is funded by a number of international corporations and foundations. Apart from the annual *Military Balance* and *Strategic Survey*, it publishes the "Adelphi Papers" monograph series, the international relations quarterly *Survival*, as well as the online briefings *Strategic Comments* and *Strategic Dossier*. *Survival* has become one of the world's two leading journals publishing articles on China external relations (*International Security* being the other). IISS also initiated and coordinates the Shangri-La Dialogue on Asian security, held annually in Singapore.

Based in Brussels, the International Crisis Group (ICG) is an independent, non-profit, non-governmental organization with over 100 staff members on five continents, working through field-based analysis and high-level advocacy to prevent and resolve conflict. ICG raises funds from governments, charitable foundations, companies, and individual donors.[31] It publishes special reports and briefings. ICG's Asia Program is directed by Robert Templer. The Group's

Northeast Asia office is based in Seoul and run by Peter Beck. Since 2002, the Seoul office has been monitoring tensions in the Taiwan Strait.

At the *European level*, the Brussels-based European Institute for Asian Studies (EIAS) has been conducting research on EU–China relations with funding from the EU Commission.[32] The Director is economist Willem van der Geest with Sebastian Bersick specializing in East Asian international relations. EIAS publishes a newsletter, regular briefing papers, and the *Eurasia Bulletin*.

Also in Brussels, is the European Policy Centre (EPC), an independent, non-profit think tank supported by Belgium's King Baudouin Foundation as well as international corporate sponsors, governmental, and non-governmental organizations.[33] EU–Asia relations and China are the responsibility of Axel Berkofsky.

The Centre for European Reform (CER), based in London, an independent think tank funded by European companies, has a EU–China program directed by Mark Leonard and including Katinka Barysch and Charles Grant.[34] Mainly concerned with EU–China relations, the Chinese economy, and transatlantic dialogue on China, the CER is beginning to establish a reputation for solid China work.[35]

United Kingdom

Also known as "Chatham House," the Royal Institute of International Affairs (RIIA) in London has an Asia Program,[36] with Yiyi Lu conducting research on China. To date, the program has focused on domestic developments, but has occasionally included foreign policy aspects.[37] Founded in 1920, the RIIA receives funding both from the British government and corporate sponsors. Chatham House publishes the journals *The World Today* and *International Affairs*, as well as working papers and books.

The Ministry of Defence's Royal United Services Institute (RUSI) in London was founded in 1831.[38] RUSI's Asia Programme is directed by Alexander Neill who edits the *Chinese Military Update*. Apart from the latter, the institute publishes the *RUSI Journal*, *RUSI Newsbrief*, *RUSI Defence Systems* and *Monitor*.

France

Launched by François Godement, the Centre Asie at the Institut Français des Relations Internationales (Ifri) in Paris,[39] has been the leading French center for research into China's foreign and security policies (the present head of the Centre is Valérie Niquet). Founded in 1979, Ifri is an independent research institute funded by the French government, French companies, and international foundations. Among the institute's publications are *Politique étrangère* and *Les Cahiers de l'Asie*.

The Paris-based Centre National de la Recherche Scientifique (CNRS)[40] is a national academy for natural and social sciences research. The contemporary China program is conducted by Jean-Pierre Cabestan, one of France's leading experts on the PRC's foreign and security policies, who enjoys a joint appointment with Université de Paris I. CNRS is in turn associated with the government-sponsored Centre Français d'Études sur la Chine Contemporaine (CFEC).[41] Founded in 1991 with headquarters in Hong Kong, CEMC in 1994 opened an office in Taipei. It is one of 27 French overseas research institutes run by the ministry of foreign affairs. CFEC has been publishing the journal *Perspectives Chinoises* (since 1995 also available in English as *China Perspectives*) that includes articles on China's foreign and security policies.

The Centre d'Études et de Recherches Internationales (CERI) is jointly run by CNRS and the Fondation Nationale des Sciences Politiques (FNSP),[42] by which the Centre was founded in 1952. Jean-Luc Domenach is director of research, and CERI's Asia program is headed by Françoise Mengin who has worked on China–Taiwan relations, among other things. The Centre's publications include reference papers and the journal *Critique Internationale*.

Also in Paris, the Fondation Pour la Recherche Stratégique (FRS) is a private foundation supported by the French government that conducts research on China from a global and international relations perspective.[43] Asian security issues are covered by a "Defence and Strategy Program" directed by Bruno Tertrais.

Funded mostly by French and European defense industries, the Institut de Relations Internationales et Stratégiques (IRIS) in Paris conducts research on China's foreign and security policies with Jean-Vincent Brisset senior researcher.[44] IRIS publishes *La Revue internationale et stratégique*, the *L'Année stratégique* yearbook, as well as reference papers.

Germany

The Institut für Asienkunde (IFA) in Hamburg was founded in 1956 on an initiative of the Bundestag and the Federal Foreign Office.[45] It is largely funded by the latter as well as the Hamburg state government. China's foreign and security policies come under the responsibility of Karsten Giese,[46] with Hans-Wilm Schütte conducting research on Taiwan. IFA publishes the internationally-renowned bimonthly *China Aktuell* as well as monographs on relevant issues.

Founded in 1962, Stiftung Wissenschaft und Politik (SWP) in Berlin is the German Institute for International and Security Affairs,[47] and is funded by the federal government. The Asia research section is headed by Gudrun Wacker who conducts research on China's foreign and security policies together with Kay Möller. The SWP organizes an annual (Transatlantic and Euro-Asian) conference series on Asia-Pacific security issues that frequently has a China angle (the Waldbröl Group now renamed the Berlin Group, see below). The institute edits two international relations series in cooperation with Nomos publishers. Its reference papers are available on demand.

The Deutsche Gesellschaft für Auswärtige Politik (DGAP) in Berlin was founded as a non-profit organization in 1955.[48] Its research programs are sponsored by private companies and non-governmental organizations. DGAP runs a China program led by the institute Director and respected Sinologist

Eberhard Sandschneider and an Asia-Pacific program directed by Frank Umbach. The institute publishes reference papers and books, including an annual *Jahrbuch für Internationale Politik*. Its journal *Internationale Politk* recently launched an English edition.

Scandinavia

At the Swedish Institute of International Affairs Utrikespolitiska Institutet (UI) in Stockholm,[49] Linus Hagström works on international relations in East Asia.

The Stockholm International Peace Research Institute (SIPRI)[50] has included China in serveral of its projects, particularly the Non-Proliferation and Export Control Program directed by Ian Anthony. SIPRI publishes research and policy papers as well as the renowned *SIPRI Yearbook*.

Linda Jakobson directs the China and Taiwan research programs at the Finnish Institute of International Affairs (FIIA) in Helsinki.[51] She is based in Beijing, but regularly commutes to Finland and meetings in Europe.

Switzerland

Founded in 1971 by the Graduate Institute of International Studies in Geneva, the Modern Asia Research Centre (MARC) focuses on the international relations of the Asia-Pacific.[52] Specializing in China's foreign and security policies are Harish Kapur and Xiang Lanxin.

Spain

Established in 2001, the Real Instituto Elcano (RIE) in Madrid is Spain's foreign affairs think tank.[53] Working on Chinese foreign and security policies in the Asia-Pacific section are Pablo Bustelo and Manuel Coma. RIE is funded from government and corporate sources. Among other things, the institute publishes the *Panorama estratégico* (*Strategic Yearbook*) and reference papers.

Portugal

The non-profit Instituto de Estudos Estratégicos e Internacionais (IEEI) was founded in Lisbon in 1980.[54] Its Asia-Pacific Department among other subjects researches European interests in Hong Kong and Macau. The department is headed by Miguel Nevel Santos. IEEI publishes the monthly *O Mundo em Português*, the English-language journal *Strategy*, as well as reference papers.

Italy

The Istituto per gli Studi di Politica Internazionale (ISPI) in Milan has a China program that includes research on foreign and security policies.[55] The program is conducted by Marco Rossi and Giacomo Boati. ISPI was founded in 1934.

The institute is a non-profit corporation funded and supervised by the Italian government. It publishes the journal *Relazioni internazionali* as well as policy briefing papers.

Intra-European Debates

"Multipolarity" (1985–1996)

Given the small size of the community and the continuing division between Sinologists on the one hand and political scientists on the other, it would be an exaggeration to claim that there has been a structured West European debate on contemporary Chinese foreign and security policies. However, when the old "strategic triangle" came apart in the 1980s, European scholars as much as their counterparts elsewhere, started discussing the implications. Early European attempts to view China's foreign and security policies independently of the East–West confrontation were inspired by Beijing's 1983 attempts to balance the "strategic triangle" through an "independent" foreign policy, signs of the impending end of world communism, and subsequent theorizing on the emergence/desirability of a "multipolar world."[56]

In this context, there were a few inconsequential attempts at regional specialization and, more importantly, at defining a framework for China–Europe relations that nevertheless appeared somewhat illusive. [57] In 1994, Michael Yahuda found that the emergence of "what many see as a more pluralistic or more multipolar pattern of international relations" had the effect of focusing the respective attentions of Europe and China on their own regions instead of on the others without even the 1990 Gulf crisis prompting a closer consultation.[58]

At this time, EU member states had started viewing the PRC market as an engine for growth at home while struggling with public opinion that was more interested in human rights violations and "China threat" theories.[59] In an attempt to reconcile commercial and normative interests, the European Commission in 1995 published a first China strategy paper emphasizing engagement and the necessity to reform the PRC's political system as well as the need to be represented on the world's most dynamic market.[60]

At the time, a considerable number of scholars characterized EU and national discourse as exercises in window-dressing, opportunism, and free-riding on U.S. policies,[61] a criticism that has since survived and distinguished the European discourse from others.[62] Underlying this criticism was the notion that EU governments and Brussels, albeit acknowledging China's internal deficits, failed to relate them to a foreign policy that tried to avoid regional and international integration, i.e. two of the mantras having grown out of of Europe's own experience.[63]

In response to this theme, much as in the U.S. and elsewhere, an "interdependence" school emerged that emphasized the constraints resulting from the internationalization of the Chinese economy and society. In such a setting, residual risks would be diffused by American, Russian, and Japanese power balancing as well as by regional efforts at multilateralism.[64] The EU Commission subsequently adopted the interdependence leitmotif as one side of a "peaceful evolution" model (the other side being Beijing's endorsement of market reform) and cited the PRC's "more responsible" foreign policy behavior as demonstrated in Cambodia, Korea, and Hong Kong as proof for the validity of this argument. At the same time, the Commission tried to play down the 1996 Taiwan Strait crisis while engaging China at the regional level through an Asia-Europe Meetings (ASEM) process launched in 1996.[65]

The majority of European scholars, however, were not prepared to close their eyes to persisting uncertainties and pointed to a latent Chinese nationalism that co-existed uneasily with the "new world" of interdependence.[66] At the same time, there was little enthusiasm for the kind of sanctions the first Clinton administration had considered in 1992/3. As a kind of compromise, Europeans positioned themselves in between Brussels technocracy and Washington conditionality,[67] an approach that appeared to be vindicated when Clinton himself abandoned his principled stance in 1994, opting instead for a "comprehensive engagement" framework.

On the eve of the 1997/98 Asian financial crisis, a Transatlantic consensus on China thus appeared to be in the making that European scholars had watched with sympathy, if not inspiration. What few of them realized at the time was that the 1996 Taiwan crisis, rather than representing a one time hiccup in Beijing's otherwise increasing acceptance of interdependence, was to increasingly dominate the Sino–American agenda, thus once again emphasizing balancing rather than integrational imperatives. In such an environment, however, Europe was condemned to passivity with subsequent attempts to turn the necessity into a virtue causing new divisions between policy makers and policy analysts.

"China's Rise" (1997–2005)

The small European community became both more interested in the wider Pacific region and more involved with the creation in 1995 of the European Council on Security Cooperation in the Asia-Pacific (ECSCAP) and in 1998 of the Waldbröl Group on the European and Euro-Atlantic Security Policies *vis-à-vis* the Asia-Pacific (after 2006 the Berlin Group).[68] It has since then engaged in a more or less continuous debate increasingly involving representatives of the foreign policy and defence bureaucracies.

At the same time, Maastricht euphoria, to the extent that it ever existed, had dampened in the Balkans, and the U.S. had revitalized their alliance with Japan while demonstrating a continued determination to defend Taiwan, three trends that inspired doubts about the emergence of a multipolar world. China, however, not only survived the Asian crisis on its own but resisted temptation to devalue the *renminbi*, an acceptance of regional responsibility for which the Clinton administration rewarded the PRC with the proclamation of a "strategic partnerhship." Amidst this backdrop, the multipolarity debate in Europe gradually gave way to a more spectacular discourse on China's supposed "rise" to an unspecified "global power" status with a few experts on U.S. policies picking up the theme. Perhaps because of the implicit demotion of their own continent, most European scholars hesitated, however, to embrace wholeheartedly the notion.

Whereas the European discourse has not differed from the American in substance (i.e. implications of China's "rise") it has been less polarized, less specialized, and slightly more relativist. Even in this respect, however, explicit attempts to organize research in a theoretical framework remain the exception and the domain of a new generation of scholars.

There is also little in terms of outright revisionism since the passing away of Gerald Segal in 1999.[69] Shortly before his death, Segal sent shockwaves all the way to Beijing by claiming that China was

> a small market that matters relatively little to the world … less a global rival like the Soviet Union than a regional threat like Iraq … a beacon to no one and an ally to no one … In sum, a merely middle power … that matters far less than it and most of the West think.[70]

To understand the underlying approach, it is useful to turn to an older text by the same author:

> The light of political reform (in the Soviet Union) has already had an impact on China, and the evolution in Eastern Europe may yet have an even greater one in the period of the Deng succession. Imagine if, when Deng dies, there is a resurgent Soviet economy and successful, stable political reform in Eastern Europe. This may be unlikely but if it happens, then China may feel added pressure to undertake genuine reform. Just as the Chinese economic reform helped to set the agenda in Eastern Europe in the 1980s, so the East Europeans may return the favor in the 1990s.[71]

The Neoliberal-Idealist School views the PRC as a regional security problem because of domestic structural deficits, while having shrunk amidst a backdrop of continued PRC economic growth and a higher PRC foreign policy profile, has not altogether disappeared. In 2003, Adam Ward, Segal's successor at the IISS, pointed to the "untransparent handling of the SARS epidemic by the new Chinese leadership, a continued temptation to respond to socioeconomic problems through nationalism, problems with the U.S. and an unresolved power struggle that risked exacerbating the former."[72] Others emphasized governance deficits and a lack of normative appeal as preventing Beijing from reshaping the international system.[73] Taiwan was correctly identified as a problem of legitimacy for the one party state that apart from nationalism had only consumerism to offer as a substitute for its former Marxist ideology.[74]

Compared with this "China Nuisance" approach, a small "China Threat School" has survived in Europe that alternatively draws mostly on internal or mostly external factors. Among the former, the current German Ambassador to China, Volker Stanzel notes a combination of regional divisions, environmental problems, and "totalitarian structures" with democratic movements, and scientific or technological progress, as limiting Peking's external margin of manoeuvre and foreign policy flexibility.[75] Among the latter, the DGAP's Frank Umbach in 2004 criticized the European debate for focusing "almost exclusively on human rights objectives" while neglecting the PRC's threat to Taiwan and related U.S. concerns.[76] Somewhere in between, Barry Buzan also in 2004 wrote about "regional hegemony coming steadily into (China's) grasp whether it liberalizes or not."[77]

There is also a Constructivist variation on the China threat (or rather an American threat, in this case) school. Writing in 1999, German political scientist Michael Minkenberg pointed to "the mixture of idealism and realism in Washington foreign policies ... rather than China's culture of realpolitik" as complicating the Sino-US relationship much in the example of the German Empire prior to World War I. At the same time, Minkenberg stressed that this situation needed not provoke a world war and that "much depends on the question as to whether the emperor will be on vacation again when a great crisis erupts."[78]

Contrasting with these views, a majority of European scholars can be described as belonging to a more optimistic "China Engagement School" that alternatively takes Beijing's relative weakness or relative strength as a point of departure. This approach, in turn, can be inspired alternatively by Neorealist power balancing theories or Neoliberal/Reflectivist regime theory. As a representative of the first school of thought, French scholar Valérie Niquet referred in 2001 to the post-September 11 regional environment with its strengthened U.S. military presence as playing "in the sense of a better equilibrium and thus lower(ing) the risk of regional confrontation."[79] Others pointed to a continued PRC emphasis on domestic stability and economic growth as contributing to more regional cooperation.[80] Lastly, at least one analyst pointed to a coexistence in China's foreign policy of regionalist rhetorics and "most classic state to state high level negotiations" while reserving his verdict on which of the two would eventually prevail.[81]

Cultural Relativists and Constructivists, while sharing the PRC's unhappiness with the unipolar world, nevertheless had to come to terms with China's variety of Wild West capitalism and lack of sensitivity *vis-à-vis* smaller neighbors, not to mention Taiwan. Their most recent escape route, and one for many Chinese scholars as well, have been Beijing'ssupposed "soft power" and "new multilateralism:" Here again, September 11, 2001 was being viewed as a kind of turning point with the terrorist attacks in New York and Washington bringing Beijing into a global coalition for the defence of (unspecified) common values. For this to happen, German international relations expert Karl Kaiser in 2002 even made allowances for "differing interpretations of democracy and human rights" in the PRC and the West. Over optimistically, the same author mentioned two levels of cooperation, namely, a "hopefully quickly reformed UN with a Security Council enlarged to comprise Germany, Japan, and other countries, as well as a G8 extended to include China."[82] As neither expectation has since materialized, one is inclined to question the underlying "joint values" supposition, however.

Given Europe's limited strategic role in the Asia-Pacific, the international level would nevertheless appear to be appropriate as a focus for a future debate (and so much the more so that an eventual lifting of the EU arms embargo is going to require a significant strenghtening of a 1998 Code of Conduct on *all* European weapons exports). The most recent EU strategy paper on China (albeit much as Kaiser overemphasizing supposed common world order interests) makes the same point,[83] and the PRC's new "resource diplomacy" in Africa and Latin America has made an impact on European as much as on American scholarship. Taking the previous debates as an orientation, one may thus expect the emergence of a third one between transatlantic protagonists of "roll back" on the one hand and old/new multipolarists/engagers on the other that increasingly takes risks to succumb to the general "China hype," thus to some extent vindicating the small Constructivist faction. Arguably, Europe much more than the U.S. (or Japan, for that matters) risks losing sight of itself in such a setting, which is why, in conclusion, I shall suggest a somewhat different approach that draws its inspiration from the "China nuisance" rather than "threat" or "strategic partnership" schools.

Beyond Containment and Engagement

The evolution of the European debate over two decades points to an early dominance of Sinological exceptionalists, followed by a challenge by "internationalists" that pulled the Sinologists back in conceptional terms, followed in turn by the emergence of constructivism that provided the Sinologists with an excuse to once again turn exceptionalist. Perhaps due to the moderating influence of the "English School" of international relations and a longer tradition in area studies, this continental dialectic was less pronounced in the U.K.

It is probably no coincidence if this "waxing and waning" of relativism echoes a a similar debate in China itself, evolving from Maoist (rhetorical) revisionism to Dengist "normality" to "Zheng Bijian exceptionalism" (i.e. "peaceful rise"). At the same time, it would be more difficult to find the kind of specialization and policy-orientation prevalent in (non-partisan) U.S. think tanks. This is due to empirical problems (European scholars usually do not have the same access to government sources) as well as a more recent and more limited role of social-sciences based political consultancy.

If the discipline is to break out of its empirical and ideological constraints, however, "going American" would be one of two possible approaches. This would suppose constant government sponsorship (which is *not* the case in the United States), something that cannot be taken for granted in most EU member states any more, and the emergence of a dialogue culture that has recently made some headway. Yet even if researchers should always be thinking two steps ahead, the quality of their research cannot be much better than the quality of policymaking. Faced with official policies that can hardly disguise a commercial imperative, European scholars, rather than developing a distinctly European research agenda, have frequently let theirs be dictated by the U.S. and China with the result of inconclusive "China threat," "rise," or "non-rise" debates on the one hand and meticulous analyses of EU arms export procedures on the other. Almost entirely absent from this hyped Eurasian–Transatlantic nonlinkage have been attempts at defining Europe's place in the world and addressing the region from a global perspective.

If one wanted to do that, a second approach could turn out to be crucial. This would consist in the anchoring the subject in political science, namely the studies of international relations and political economy, something that has been successfully undertaken at U.S. universities for quite some time. It is only here that the exceptionalist placebo can be overcome. And it should be overcome, to use more normative terms, as Europeans need not be defensive about Athens, Runnymede, the Bastille, Rome or Maastricht and should, to use Peyrefitte's terms, be inspired by their own origins in (unemotional) enlightenment rather than missionizing of one kind or the other. If the Bush and Hu administrations, for example, seem to be in perfect agreement as far as the relative importance of power politics and the relative unimportance of social justice and protection of the global environment are concerned, there is no reason why Europe should align itself with such a world order by entering into "strategic partnerships" with anyone and sundry.

Neither is there a reason why Europe should not drop its inefficient arms embargo on China if it can be replaced with an efficient global code of conduct. Neither is there a reason why Europe should subscribe to the hollowing-out of global regimes because of commercial, anti-terrorist, or other imperatives. On the other hand, there are many good reasons for Europe to improve its policymaking tools for putting many an excellent strategy paper into practice. All this would require far more than Sinology or area studies, and I shall just outline one possible "European" approach:

As a point of departure, I suggest that contemporary studies of China's foreign and security policies cannot avoid looking at the inside, i.e. at the socio-economic and politico-systemic bases for "rising," "falling," or "drifting" of China. Because of their background, most European scholars have always emphasized this point and perhaps moreso than their American colleagues. This was also Gerald Segal's assumption, and I find it useful to reconsider, if not to the question whether "China matters?" It clearly does, but we must ask *how* this new relevance can be translated into strategy. In this context, the "China rise" debate has been forced on Europeans by the Trans-Pacific protagonists without paying due consideration to underlying misperceptions, power asymmetries, and diverging ideologies. Common misperceptions relate to a failure by both Beijing and Washington to understand how globalization affects aggregate national power. In spite of its unique military strength, the U.S. cannot hope to contain most traditional and non-traditional risks in the world at the same time and as a consequence has engaged in selective nation-building exercises. China's supposed "rise" is basically a bluff because a country of the PRC's size cannot be centrally administered and has, in fact, been run by overlapping local networks and lobbies rather than by one monolithical hierarchy.[84]

At first sight, such a system would appear to be rather well suited to a globalizing world that itself has in many respects been disaggregating, but not if it wants to produce the innovation and sustainable and equitable development it will need to "rise" as a state. China's Janus-faced character – Shanghai versus Guizhou, external economy versus domestic economy, rule of law versus corruption, integration versus revisionism – rather than signaling a necessary intermediate stage of development could be the inherent quality of a country that is too big to be efficiently governed without an institutional division of powers, yet due to its cultural disposition and third parties' encouragement believes that it might get away with the bluff.

There is some circumstancial evidence to support this hypothesis: a banking crisis that does not seem any closer to a solution; a lack of macro-economic tools; persistent market distortions (land is too cheap; energy is too cheap; credit and the currency are too cheap;) problems with the adaptation – let alone the indigenous development – of modern technologies; problems with the education system; half-hearted overseas strategies of PRC companies; half-hearted approaches to both "Third Worldism" and regionalism.

For movement to occur away from the intermediate stage towards either global revisionism or global integration, China would have to opt for an expansionist commercial and military strategy at the expense of internal stability and thus at the expense of the main pillar of regime legitimacy, or it would have to share sovereignty as a matter of principle and not as a matter of tactics. Either movement requires cognitive social learning, something that seems to be difficult in an oversized network-country run by civil engineers.

What remains is a big new player who – partly because of size, partly because of third parties buying the bluff – has begun making an impact on the international order in spite of a weak and arguably further weakening state capacity. Under such circumstances, the conclusions drawn by the PRC leadership (concerting with other big powers to preserve the status quo in the immediate neighbourhood, letting the U.S. overstretch itself in the rest of the world) have been sensible ones – albeit hardly adequate to address global issues such as poverty, climate change, WMD-proliferation, or human rights.

It is at this point that Europe comes in. Given a greater overlap on such global interests, the hope that Washington, contrasting with major Asian players, does not reject multilateralism as a matter of principle, and signs of surviving common values, the Transatlantic relationship could after all turn out to be the most important one in the world. For this to happen, the U.S. would have to emphasize further nation-building (and in the same context, regionalism) at the expense of power-balancing. Europe would have to complete its political union, reaffirm its commitment to international institutions and norms, turn its experience in nation-building, regionalism, and Common Security into foreign policy tools while refraining from making bold statements on situations such as the one in the Taiwan Strait or Korean Peninsula where it cannot make a difference. At the same time, Europe should not allow Washington or Beijing, or both, to dictate its Asian agenda.

Notes

1 E.g. Klaus Mehnert, *Peking und Moskau* (*Peking and Moscow*), (Stuttgart: Deutsche Verlagsanstalt, 1962).
2 E.g. Jacques Guillermaz, *Le parti communiste chinois au pouvoir* (*The CCP in Power*), (Paris: Payot, 1972).
3 Simon Leys, *Ombres chinoises* (*Chinese Shadows*), (Paris: Union générale d'éditions, 1974)."
4 Gerald Segal, "China and the Great Power Triangle," *The China Quarterly*, No. 83 (September 1980).
5 ECAN was initially organized by SOAS in London and will soon be resumed by the European Institute of Asian Studies in Brussels.
6 E.g. Helmut Schmidt, *Die Mächte der Zukunft* (*The Powers of the Future*), (Munich: Siedler, 2004).
7 One could also name a few examples of Europeans contributing to respective U.S. scholarship such as Franz Michael in the 1960s and Michael Yahuda more recently.
8 http://www.asia-alliance.org/.
9 David Shambaugh, "The New Strategic triangle: U.S. and European Reactions to China's Rise," *The Washington Quarterly*, Vol. 28, No. 3 (Summer 2005), pp. 7–25 (18).
10 http://www.soas.ac.uk/.
11 http://www.lse.ac.uk.
12 http://www.sant.ox.ac.uk.
13 http://www.seas.ac.uk/.
14 http://www.dur.ac.uk/sgia/.
15 http://www2.warwick.ac.uk/fac/soc/csgr/.
16 In this context, I should mention Marie-Luise Näth in Saarbrücken, Gottfried-Karl Kindermann and Peter J. Opitz in Munich, Hanns Maull in Trier, and François Joyaux in Paris, all of whom are retired. Italy's leading scholar on China's foreign and security policies has been Marta Dassù who is currently director of policy programs at the Aspen Institute in Rome.
17 http://orient4.orient.su.se/cpas/.
18 http://www.hhs.se.
19 http://www.helsinki.fi/hum/renvall/aps/.
20 http://www.ps.au.dk/.
21 http://www.cbs.dk/arc.
22 http://www.nias.ku.dk.
23 http://www.polchina@zedat.fu-berlin.de.
24 http://www.ruhr-uni-bochum.de/oaw.
25 http://www.uni-tuebingen.de/sinologie/.
26 http://www.tcc.leidenuniv.nl/.
27 http://www.utl.pt/.
28 Shambaugh, "The New Strategic Triangle," p. 18.
29 Exceptions to the latter rule would be foundations sponsored by political parties that serve as platforms for intellectual debate rather than research. Among the latter I should name the British Labour Party's Foreign Policy Centre that in 2004 launched a programme called "China and Globalisation" (http://fpc.org.uk), and German foundations such as the (Christian Democrat-sponsored) Konrad Adenauer Stiftung (http://suche.kas.de/), (Social-Democrat leaning) Friedrich Ebert Stiftung (http://www.fes.de/), (Green Party-linked) Heinrich Böll Foundation (http://boell.de/), (Liberal-sponsored) Friedrich Naumann Stiftung (http://www.fnst.de/), and (Christian Social-sponsored) Hanns Seidel Stiftung (http://www.hss.de/).
30 http://www.iiss.
31 http://www.crisigroup.org/.

32 http://www.eias.org.
33 http://www.theepc.be/.
34 http://www.cer.org.uk/world/china.html.
35 See Katinka Barysch with Charles Grant and Mark Leonard, *Embracing the Dragon: The EU's Partnership with China* (London: Centre for European Reform, 2005).
36 http://www.riia.org/
37 In this context, one should mention Foreign Office analyst Rod Wye who has been associated with RIIA.
38 http://www.rusi.org/.
39 http://www.ifri.org/.
40 http://www2.cnrs.fr/.
41 http://www.cefc.com.hk.
42 http://www.ceri-sciences-po.org/.
43 http://www.frstrategie.org.
44 http://www.iris-france.org/fr/.
45 http://www.duei.de/ifa/.
46 Among Giese's predecessors, Oskar Weggel stands out as one of the most prolific writers on China's foreign policies.
47 http://swp-berlin.org.de.
48 http://www.dgap.org.
49 http://www.ui.se/.
50 http://www.sipri.org.
51 http://www.upi-fiaa.fi/.
52 http://hei.unige.ch/marc.
53 http://www.realinstitutoelcano.org/.
54 http://www.ieei.pt/.
55 http://www.ispionline.it/.
56 Kay Möller, "Diplomatic Relations and Mutual Strategic Perceptions: China and the European Union," *China Quarterly* special issue No. 2 (2002), pp. 10–32 (13).
57 E.g. Philip Snow, "China and Africa: Consensus and Camouflage," Thomas W. Robinson and David Shambaugh (eds), *Chinese Foreign Policy: Theory and Practice* (Oxford: Clarendon, 1994), pp. 283–321.
58 Michael B. Yahuda, "China and Europe: The Significance of a Secondary Relationship," ibid., pp. 266–82 (281).
59 Joachim Glaubitz, "Changing Power Constellations in East Asia: Cooperation of Conflict?" Klaus Becher/Reinhard Schlagintweit (eds) *China and Germany – Different Answers to Strategic Change* (Bonn: Deutsche Gesellschaft für Auswärtige Politik, 1995), pp. 95–9 (97).
60 "A Long-Term Policy for Relations Between China and Europe," *Bulletin Quotidien Europe*, No. 1954/1955 (12 October 1995).
61 Sebastian Heilmann, "Making Human Rights Work in China", *China's International Role: Key Issues, Common Interests, Different Approaches* (Brühl: Friedrich Ebert Stiftung, 6–9 March 1997), pp. 156–6 (158).
62 This relative detachment of European academia from policymaking can also be attributed to the former's institutional isolation, when compared with the U.S., from governments.
63 Rosemary Foot, "Thinking Globally from a Regional Perspective: Chinese, Indonesian, and Malaysian reflections on the Post Cold-War Era," *Contemporary Southeast Asia*, Vol. 18, No. 1 (June 1996), pp. 17–35 (30).
64 Christoph Müller-Hofstede, "Von der Peripherie ins Zentrum: Die Volksrepublik China als Weltmacht neuen Typs" ("From Periphery to Center: The PRC as a New Type of Global Power"), *KAS-Auslandsinformationen*, Vol. 11, No. 9 (1995), pp. 92–111 (110), my translation.

65 *Building a Comprehensive Partnership with China* (Brussels: EU Commission, 25 March 1998).

66 Christoph Müller-Hofstede and Rüdiger Sielaff, "Introduction," *China's International Role*, pp. 1–4.

67 Hanns Maull, "Reconciling China with International Order," ibid., pp. 5–16 (13).

68 ECSCAP was founded by the late Gerald Segal, Hanns Maull, Tom Hart and François Godement in 1995. Its present convenors are Tom Hart, François Godement, and Frank Umbach. The Waldbröl Group was founded by Kay Möller in 1998 (cf. the Asia page on SWP's website).

69 For the purpose of this analysis, I shall include non-Europeans with a long European career-background as constituent parts of the network.

70 Gerald Segal, "Does China Matter?" *Foreign Affairs*, Vol. 78, No. 5 (September/October 1999), pp. 24–36.

71 Gerald Segal, "Sino–Soviet Relations," idem (ed.), *Chinese Politics and Foreign Policy Reform* (London: Kegan Paul, 1990), pp. 161–79 (177/8).

72 Adam Ward, "China and America: Trouble Ahead?" *Survival*, Vol. 45, No. 3 (Autumn 2003), pp. 35–56 (52/3).

73 Lawrence Freedman, "China as a Global Strategic Actor," Barry Buzan and Rosemary Foot (eds), *Does China Matter? A Reassessment* (London/New York: Routledge, 2004, pp. 21–36 (35).

74 Peter J. Opitz, *China – Der Aufstieg des Drachens: Sicherheit und Frieden zu Beginn des 21. Jahrhunderts* (*China – The Dragon's Rise: Security and Peace in the Beginning of the 21st Century*), (Munich: Bayerische Landeszentrale für politische Bildungsarbeit, 2002), pp. 203–45 (242).

75 Volker Stanzel, "A World of Warring States: China's Perception and Possibilities of Its International Role," *China's International Role*, pp. 203–17 (215).

76 Frank Umbach, "The Debate over Lifting the EU Arms Embargo on China and its Transatlantic Implications, *Conference Report: Renewing the Transatlantic Partnership* (Washington D.C.: Center for Strategic and International Studies, October 2004), pp. 45–50 (50).

77 Barry Buzan, "How and to Whom Does China Matter?", idem/Foot, *Does China Matter?* pp. 143–64 (160/1).

78 Michael Minkenberg, "Zwischen Weltpolitik und Innenpolitik: Die amerikanisch-chinesischen Beziehungen nach dem Kalten Krieg,"("Between Global and Domestic Politics: U.S.–China Relations after the End of the Cold War"), *Zeitschrift für Politikwissenschaft*, Vol. 9, No. 1 (1999), pp. 73–100 (97), my translation.

79 Valérie Niquet, "La Chine face aux défis stratégiques de l'àpres 11 septembre" ("China Facing Strategic Challenges after September 11"), *Perspectives chinoises*, No. 67 (October 2001, online), my translation.

80 Jean-Pierre Cabestan, "Sino–European Relations," in Robert Ash (ed.), *China's Integration in Asia. Economic Security and Strategic Issues* (Richmond: Curzon, 2002), pp. 214–20 (227); Michael Yahuda, "Chinese Dilemmas in Thinking about Regional Security Architecture," *The Pacific Review*, Vol. 16, No. 2 (2003), pp. 189–206 (203/4).

81 François Godement, "Chinese and Asian Concepts of Conflict Resolution," Ash, *China's Integration in Asia*, pp. 246–56 (253–5).

82 Karl Kaiser, "Strategischer Partner China" ("China as a Strategic Partner") *Internationale Politik*, Vol. 57, No. 2 (February 2002), pp. 17–18.

83 *A Maturing Partnership – Shared Interests and Challenges in EU-China Relations* (Brussels: EU Commission, 10 September 2003).

84 Segal made a similar point in 1994, although he overstimated the resulting impacts of neighbouring countries most of which have suffered from the same institutional weaknesses. Gerald Segal, "China's Changing Shape," *Foreign Affairs*, Vol. 73, No. 3 (May/June 1994), pp. 43–58.

9 Studies of China's Foreign and Security Policies in Japan

Seiichiro Takagi

When one takes stock of the state of a field, it is customary to first consult the field's representative journal such as *China Quarterly,* in case of Chinese studies, where one can safely assume that many articles worth commenting on are published. In the case of Japanese studies on China in general, and Chinese foreign and security policy in particular, neither condition is easy to obtain.

First of all, there is no equivalent of *China Quarterly* in Japan. There are some journals which exclusively publish articles on contemporary China but they are hardly representative of Japanese scholarship on the subject. For example, there is the *Chugoku Kenkyu Geppo* (*Monthly Review of China Studies*) published by the Institute for Chinese Studies, a private research institute which was established by former staff of the research department of the famous Southern Manchurian Railroad Company. But its circulation is limited to a small number of China scholars and is far from a "compulsory" reading for the specialists in the field. The *Gendai Chugoku Kenkyuu* (*Studies on Contemporary China*) is the journal published by the Association for Contemporary China Studies but membership of this association is rather limited. Many major scholars on contemporary China are not members. The *Mondai to Kenkyu* (*Issues and Studies*) is the Japanese language version of the *Wenti yu Yanjiu* and *Issues and Studies* published in Taiwan and authors used to be ideologically limited to anti-communist and pro-Guomindang intellectuals. With progress in democratization in Taiwan it increasingly published articles by mainstream China scholars but is still far from being the major journal on contemporary China. In 1997 the Association of Contemporary China of Aichi University started the journal called *Chugoku 21* (*China 21*) with the ambitious goal of making it a medium for the intellectual exchanges with China on a broad range of issues. Because of its broad coverage of issues it rarely carries articles on foreign and security policies of China.

The major articles on contemporary China are published in journals with a broader scope. The scholarly analyses on foreign relations and security problems of China are most likely to be found in journals on international relations. As such, three journals need to be mentioned. The *Kokusai Seiji* (*International Relations*) is the quarterly journal of the Japan Association of International Relations.[1] The *Kokusai Mondai* (*International Affairs*) is the monthly journal of the Japan Institute of International Affairs. Articles in *Kokusai Mondai* tend to be somewhat shorter and more policy oriented than the ones in the *Kokusai Seiji*, but many of them are of at least equal scholastic value as the ones in the latter. The *Kokusai Anzen Hosho* (*Journal of International Security*) (*Shin Boei Ronshu*) (*Journal of National Defense*) is the journal of Japan Association of International Security (Japan Association for Defense Studies until March 2001). It used to publish many articles with questionable scholarly quality, but it has improved remarkably since about the time when it changed its title because the change of name of the association encouraged many new young members to join it.

As for the scholarly journals which cover the whole of Asia two are noteworthy for their occasional publication of articles on China. One is the *Ajia Kenkyu* (*Asian Studies*), which is the journal of the Japan Association for Asian Studies. The other is the *Ajia Keizai* (*Asian Economy*) issued monthly by the Institute of Developing Economies. Although the articles in the latter are not limited to economic analyses in spite of its name, the articles on China published in them tend to be on domestic issues rather than on foreign relations and security problems.

Unfortunately just surveying these journals and books, which are easier to identify, is not sufficient to grasp the state of studies on China in Japan. Many scholars, especially young ones, publish their research in the journals published by departments of the universities they belong to. Although most university libraries have many of them, it is not worth trying to go over a large portion, if not all, of them. They come in huge numbers, but the quality of the articles varies widely. Most of these journals have almost no quality control mechanism. This situation makes the circulation of the research product much more difficult than in the United States where there are several journals which deal with more specific aspects of China or "second or third class" comprehensive journals on China.

In order to deal with this situation it is possible to use the ready-made bibliography as the starting point. The National Diet Library issues the monthly *Zasshi Kiji Sakuin* (*Index to Articles in Magazines and Journals*), which is the most comprehensive list of articles available in Japan and it is accessible on the Internet from most university libraries. However, this approach has an inherent difficulty in another characteristic of Japanese social science in general and the studies on contemporary China in particular, namely that the demarcation line between academia and journalism is very thin. Some scholars often write articles of a journalistic nature for news/opinion magazines and some journalists write articles of a more scholastic nature in some magazines. The monthly magazine *Toa* (*East Asia*), in which most articles are on China, publishes articles of substantial length both by scholars and journalists. The major opinion magazines such as *Chuo Koron* (*Central Public Views*) and *Sekai* (*The World*) sometimes carry articles which contain sound scholastic analysis. The *Zasshi Kiji Sakuin* lists all of them. It is still very time-consuming to go over them and select articles of scholarly merit. The current review is based on the body of literature identified mostly through a rough checking of the *Zasshi Kiji Sakuin*.[2]

Japanese Reviews of the Field

Generally speaking, in clear contrast to the U.S. studies on contemporary China, very little effort has been made to survey the field of contemporary Chinese studies in Japan. A welcome exception appeared in 2005 in the *Ajia Keizai*. Ebihara Tsuyoshi of Toyama Special High School of Commercial Shipping,[3] where one does not expect to find a China scholar, reviewed the studies on Chinese foreign policy in Japan since 1990 with focus on economic diplomacy.[4] He examined Japanese works on overall foreign policy, perception of the international situation, China's bilateral relations with Japan, the United States, Russia, the Korean peninsula, and ASEAN, the Third World, economic foreign policy and China's accession to the WTO.

As an observation on the existing works he made the following five points. First, as the object of study, there are many works on perceptions of the international situation and bilateral relations and relatively few works on overall foreign policy. Second, in terms of the period of time and the object of Chinese foreign policy, most of the works are on the contemporary situation and China's relationship with Japan and the United States. Third, in terms of methodology, most studies are based on careful examination of the official documents and leaders' statements. But there are few studies based on interviews. He also notes at the outset that there are almost no studies of the hypothesis-verification type. Fourth, in terms of the issue area, the bias toward national security was corrected in reflection of changes in Chinese foreign policy in the era of reform and opening up toward multilateralism, multi-dimensionality, and broadness of the issue area. However, studies on economic diplomacy, party-to-party diplomacy, and people-to-people diplomacy are insufficient. Fifth, studies on China's WTO accession are mostly on the negotiations with the United States, but there were no studies on the negotiations with Japan. The current review tries to reexamine and build on this useful effort.

As a reflection of the general internationalization of Japanese society, an increasing number of Japanese scholars are publishing their research in foreign languages, especially in English, and increasing number of foreigners work with the Japanese research community and publish their work in the Japanese language. Needless to say, in the case of contemporary China studies the foreigners are almost exclusively Chinese nationals residing in Japan. Because of this situation, two clarifications are necessary for the specification of the objects of review. In this survey, I include all the studies on contemporary China published in the Japanese language, regardless of the nationality of the author. At the same time I excluded all the works by Japanese authors published in other languages. Also excluded from the list of objects for examination are the studies on policies and behavior of some countries toward China, such as Japanese and the U.S. China policies.

The following review is divided into two parts, historical and contemporary studies. With admitted arbitrariness I use the advent of the reform and opening policy in late 1978 as the dividing line.

Historical Studies

Contrary to the second point in Ebihara's assessment mentioned above, some important books were published in the category of historical studies in the past decade. Okabe Tatsumi's *Chugoku no Taigai Senryaku* (*The External Strategy of China*) is the culmination of the author's scholarship of over 40 years and his monumental study of Chinese images of its international environment and foreign policy.[5] Although the book contains a chapter on the period of reform and openness, since it is rather weak compared with the other chapters I decided to introduce the book in this section. The rest of the book is a detailed systematic study of the evolution of the external perception and foreign policy of the People's Republic on China.

One of the interesting points the author makes is the argument that all three images which can be regarded as the prototypes of later policies appeared in rapid succession since the last phase of the Second World War. First is the notion of "peace and democracy" under the concert of powers which was spelled out in Mao's "On Coalition Government" of 1945. With the outbreak of the civil war it was replaced by the theory of the "intermediate zone," which was first explained by Mao in 1946. Okabe points out that its central thesis that the principal contradiction is that between American imperialism and the people in the "intermediate zone" implies the sidelined role of the Soviet Union and is motivated by the need to justify the civil war in spite of the Soviet reluctance to approve it. With the intensification of the Cold War this image gradually lost persuasiveness and is replaced by the "two-camp" theory, which led to the policy of leaning toward the Soviet Union.

Okabe also makes a clear distinction between the official ideology of Marxism–Leninism and the operational ideology, which is heavily colored by the notion of national interest and functioned as the guide for actual policy-making. Starting from this assumption he explains the Sino–Soviet dispute as a clash of national interest in the guise of ideological dispute and the Sino-U.S. rapprochement as Chinese power play. These conclusions may not sound particularly novel to the Western readers but it was necessary to reach them through careful analysis, which Okabe conducted in an exemplary manner, in Japan. The research community there tended to be divided into those who took the official ideology at face value and those who totally disregarded it as propaganda and understood Chinese behavior simply as pursuit of selfish goals or long-term plots.

Concerning the relationship between domestic politics and foreign relations Okabe makes some interesting points. For example, he argues that Chinese development of nuclear weapons and support for the national liberation struggle abroad were closely related to the Cultural Revolution because they constituted the security policies to ensure that its launch would not provoke an attack by the U.S. which was engaged in the war in Vietnam.

Although Okabe's work only used documentary sources, both primary and secondary, Shu Ken'ei (Zhu Jianrong) contributed a detailed and multifaceted study of Chinese involvement in the Vietnam War from summer 1964 to the end of 1965,[6] using both source materials made available in the 1990s by the Cold War

International History Project (CWIHP) and interviews with some key Vietnamese and Chinese persons. In this extensive study Shu examines the evolution of China's relationship with Vietnam, the United States, and the Soviet Union as well as Chinese military strategy and domestic politics, and tries to trace interactions among these five lines of development. Some of his interesting conclusions are first, that the seed of the deterioration of China's relationship with Vietnam was sown when it faced the escalation of the U.S. war and the Soviet Union decided to provide massive military assistance to Vietnam; second, that the Vietnam War led to deterioration of China's dispute with the Soviet Union in this period up to the stage when China contemplated a two-front war, which also led to the revision of China's military strategy; and third, that the initial steps toward the rapprochement with the United States, which resulted in Nixon's historic trip to China, were taken in 1966; and fourth, that there was a "mini-cultural revolution" in 1964 and the Vietnam War and the deterioration of the relationship with the Soviet Union were external conditions for its transformation into the "Great Cultural Revolution" in 1966. Shu also made heavy use of materials made available after the collapse of the Soviet Union and some interviews with Chinese informants to revise his earlier study on the Chinese involvement in the Korean war published in 1991 and published the revised version in the period under review.[7] His main conclusions on the decision-making process leading to Chinese participation in the war are the following:

- Chinese leaders were aware of Kim Il-Song's preparations, with Stalin's approval, for the "liberation" of the South.
- After the Truman statement of July 27 Beijing judged that the United States started to implement the policy directed against China and started preparation for the war.
- Mao thought of participating in the war in September but faced much opposition.
- After participation the initial plan of a short-term decisive war was adjusted to the more prudent one of prevention of U.S. aggression on China.

Based on these points, Shu argues that the main purpose of Chinese participation in the war was prevention of U.S. aggression against China.

On a smaller scale, Mori Kazuko analyzed the negotiations between China and the U.S. in the 1971–1972 period, in an analytical background for the translation of the transcripts of Nixon's meetings Mao Zedong and Zhou Enlai in 1972.[8] She draws on the statements made by Mao and Zhou in the transcripts as well as other English and Chinese language materials to elucidate Chinese perceptions and calculations behind the rapprochement.

The study of the Japan–China negotiations of diplomatic normalization and the peace and friendship treaty between China and Japan, edited by Ishii Akira and others,[9] is a compilation of records of Japanese government obtained by using the Japanese version of the "Freedom of Information Act" and the "testimonies" obtained by interview with politicians and diplomats involved in the negotiations, followed by analyses based on these materials. Although most of the analyses are on the Japanese side, Soeya Yoshihide analyzes the views of Japan held by the Chinese and points out that the deep-seated suspicion expressed both by the Chinese and the Americans involved in the Sino–U.S. rapprochement continued to color the Chinese approach to Japan.[10]

Izumikawa Yasuhiro reexamined the second Taiwan Strait crisis of 1958 with materials made available by the CWIHP and others,[11] and he challenges the dominant view that China caused the crisis because of Mao's radical ideology and the need for domestic mobilization. He argues that Chinese foreign policy was radicalized since mid-1957 because of the changes in the U.S. military policy in East Asia, which meant the tightening of containment against China, that China became concerned about the Soviet shift toward the peaceful co-existence with the United States in this period because of its effect of isolating China, and that the Chinese decision to bomb Jinmen was made for the purpose of checking these moves by the U.S. and the Soviet Union. In conclusion, he also argues that the Chinese decision can be explained by the theory of asymmetrical conflict and that his findings are consistent with neo-classical realist arguments.

Contemporary Studies

Overall Characterizations of Chinese Foreign Policy

In the mid-1990s, which is the beginning of the coverage of this review, there were some noteworthy attempts to capture the overall characteristics of primarily contemporary Chinese foreign policy. Mori Kazuko raises the question whether China in the near future would be a radical revisionist actor or a moderate reformist actor with regard to the existing regional order or world system.[12] She tries to answer this question by examining Chinese perceptions and the PRC's concrete diplomatic behavior in the field of international politics and security. She starts with the examination of the adjustment of the foreign policy since 1982 ("independent foreign policy") and points out China's rejection of the inevitability of the world war thesis, the recognition of the one global market and the adoption of capitalism, and increased participation in international institutions, as key features of Chinese diplomacy during this period. She then examines the new national strategy after 1992 and argues that China managed to cope with the shock caused by the collapse of the socialist system in Eastern Europe and the Soviet Union by strengthening the economic marketization and dictatorship, and that the disintegration of the Soviet Union removed the threat form the north. She also notes China's reexamination of the notion of national interest and positivism toward multilateral dialogue on political and security issues. In conclusion Mori argues that the collapse of the socialist system in Eastern Europe and the Soviet Union led to the intrinsic change in China in the world. China's approach to the world system has changed from criticism to adaptation, and that China's interest in the existing system is now transformed into interest-based functionalism.

Takahara also begins with the change in Chinese foreign policy in 1982 into that of independence and autonomy, which he sees as being motivated by recognition of the costs of continuing hostility toward the Soviet Union and the pseudo-alliance with the United States.[13] He argues that the epoch-making aspect of this change was in China's departure from the assumption of the existence of the dialectical notion of the "principal enemy" and the need to counter it, which is the point made by Okabe Tatsumi earlier in early 1980s.[14] But, unlike Mori, Takahara argues that the Chinese view of international politics as a power game among major powers has not changed, that China's defense expenditure of 1988 was three times that of ten years before, and that China was pursuing a hard-line policy with regard to its maritime interest (which he sees as reflection of the influence of the PLA). His conclusion is that the policy of reform-and-opening led to an appeasement-type foreign policy for the sake of securing the peaceful environment for economic development.

Unlike these two, Nakai Yoshifumi's do not start with 1982, but ten years later.[15] Drawing on Foreign Minister Qian Qichen's speech in 1992, he characterizes the contemporary Chinese diplomacy as that of evading regime crisis and argues that it involves three orientations:

- evasion of the regime crisis which includes such measures as compromise with the U.S., friendly relations with the periphery, and ideology-free omni-directional diplomacy;
- the creation of an environment for economic development which includes such measures as participation in international cooperation and regionalism;
- trilateral balancing among the U.S., Japan, and China.

However, he argues that since the status-quo orientation became increasingly challenged by North Korean nuclear development, Taiwan's democratization, and other pressures from the U.S., Chinese diplomacy came to assume a nationalistic character – which is oriented to the strategic realignment of foreign relations, the adamant assertion of sovereignty, and seeking perfection in its security environment. His assessment is that, since the evasion of the regime crisis has not totally disappeared, Chinese diplomacy in the twenty-first century will exhibit a duality of international cooperation and patriotism.

The omni-directional orientation of Chinese foreign policy mentioned above is examined in more detail by Kojima Tomoyuki.[16] He points out that it has four characteristics:

- It is based on the perception that the world is moving from tension to détente and that peace and development is the main current.
- The objective of the external strategy is securing a peaceful environment for the pursuit of domestic economic development.
- In terms of concrete policy, Asia is given high priority.
- The United States is even more important.

However, Kojima rejects the notion that omni-directionality constitutes the totality of Chinese foreign policy. He argues that it also has a hard-line "hegemonistic" aspect, which has the following six characteristics:

1   The perception of the international situation is still based on the extension of the Cold War.
2   The Cold War framework of power politics is not abandoned.
3   The objectives of external strategy is establishment of prestigious status as one of the poles in the multipolar system.
4   The general posture is more oriented toward the transformation of the status quo.
5   The United States is the principal adversary.
6   Concrete diplomacy is conducted as the power game to check U.S. dominance.

Kojima argues that the apparent contradiction in Chinese diplomacy, in which these two tendencies co-exist, means the possible existence of division within the leadership. Both omni-directionality and hegemonism constitute the totality of Chinese foreign policy in which each has its own place.

These analyses are all based on careful readings of Chinese public and sometimes internal documents as well as conventional observation on Chinese external behavior. Their judgments on Chinese foreign policy are all basically sound. However, their characterizations of Chinese foreign policy suffer from the problems of ad hoc conceptualization. The effort to build on others' work and to seek improved or alternative conceptualization which can capture the substance more effectively is not found in any of them. Because of this, even though different "concepts" are used, their analyses of Chinese foreign policy are not so different from each other.

General Policies Toward Major Powers

One of the characteristics of Chinese foreign policy, according to many analysts, is the importance China attaches to its relationship with major powers. There are some works which deal with this aspect in a more focused manner. In another work, Kojima argues that China gradually departed from its emphasis on the Third World and turned to prioritizing its relationship with major powers in its pursuit of a multi-polar world around 1997,[17] which he characterizes as the transformation of the foreign policy of independence and autonomy. On this basis, he analyzes the formation of partnership – strategic and otherwise – with major powers.

China's attempts to form "strategic partnerships" with major (and minor) powers are analyzed in more detail by Masuda Masayuki.[18] He also argues that the center of gravity of Chinese diplomacy became the relationship with major powers and the "strategic partnership" is one of the principal frameworks for the relationship. He traces the evolution of the use of the notion of partnership in the context of China's relationships with Russia, Brazil, France, India, Pakistan, Japan and the United States. He argues that the notion of partnership, which originally was meant to be the indicator of the depth of any bilateral relationship, came to imply the "new type" of international relationship among major powers when it was applied to Russia in 1996 as the "strategic partnership." It further evolved into the "partnership of strategic cooperation" with Russia in 1997, which implied the resistance to the U.S. unipolar dominance. As China sought to apply the concept to the relationships with the United States and Japan it went back to "strategic partnership." According to Masuda's analysis, the "strategic partnership" among major powers means the long-term relationship with global significance covers multiple issues.

Kokubun Ryosei approaches the same subject through examination of summit diplomacy.[19] He notes the central role summit diplomacy plays in confidence-building in a world that is becoming multi-polar. He argues that summit diplomacy can bring about a breakthrough in the bilateral relationship, dissolve misunderstanding and build confidence among top leaders and promote mutual understanding among the peoples – but requires a long time and effort for the relationship to recover if it fails. On this basis, he analyzes summit diplomacy with the United States, Russia, and Japan and concludes that it was successful with the U.S. and Russia, but failed with Japan.

The "New Security Concept"

China's security policy did not receive much attention from the specialists on China's foreign relations and was considered to be primarily the subject for military specialists until China came up with the "New Security Concept" (NSC) in the late 1990s. Mori Kazuko was the first in Japan to publish a substantive article on the concept.[20] She notes that the Chinese concept of security was going through a marked change in the late-1990s and argues that cooperative security (which she characterizes as soft and comprehensive) was in the ascent – rather than the security policy which depends on alliances and military strength. She does recognize China's continued dependence on military power, but does not explain the relationship between it and the NSC.

Asano Ryo tries to answer the question of whether Chinese security policy, as embodied in the NSC, has changed after the 9/11 terrorist attacks and the subsequent Iraq question.[21] He traces the evolution of the NSC since its appearance as a "prototype" in the Sino–Russian Joint Communiqué of April 1996 and argues that its presentation represented a fundamental shift in China's approach to the ASEAN Regional Forum (AEF) from passivity to activism. He points out that the factors which led to the formation of the NSC are the need to counter the China threat theory (both military and in terms of comprehensive national strength), and Jiang Zemin's assertion of leadership made possible by Deng Xiaoping's exit. Through the examination of China's response to 9/11, the following conflict over Iraq, and the Shanghai Cooperation Organization (SCO), he argues that China was increasingly concerned with energy security but its security strategy maintained the basic feature of the NSC.

Building on these and other foreign studies on the NSC, Takagi Seiichiro tries to be as comprehensive as possible.[22] He traces the evolution of the concept from its initial presentation to the ARF meeting in 1996, through expansion to include economic security after the Asian currency crisis of 1997 to its full-fledged formulation in the position paper presented to the ARF meeting in 2002. Based on the analysis of the position paper he characterizes the NSC as the amalgamation of the Western concept of cooperative security and common security with Chinese concerns. He argues that its presentation in 1996 was motivated by the needs to counter the strengthening of the U.S. alliance systems and to refute the "China threat" theory, but also functioned as the conceptual foundation for China's involvement in the multilateral security cooperation. Concerning the multilateral security cooperation, Takagi compares China's involvement in the ARF and the SCO and points out its passivity in the former and activism in the latter. Noting that little is said about the role of the military strength in the NSC, he argues that it cannot represent the totality of China's security policy and he tries to examine the relationship between the two. Drawing on the articles written by the virtual author of the NSC,[23] he argues that the total security strategy consists of the NSC and the military strategy – with the former promoting peace and reducing potential adversarys' motivation to attack China, and the latter intended to deter possible attacks and defeating enemies outside of the border.

The "China Threat" Theory

The notion of the "China threat" was hotly debated in some opinion magazines and TV shows, but the academic world largely evaded the issue. But there are some exceptions. Hiramatsu Shigeo, who has been publishing painstaking research on various aspects of the Chinese military for almost 40 years, is a persistent advocate of the danger of Chinese military power. Coincidentally, the book he published in the first year of the last decade, 1995, was on this very subject.[24] On the basis of careful documentary research, he argues that China's military is pursuing qualitative development in its nuclear arsenal, navy, and air force, as well as in organization. He also believes that China's defense expenditure should be considered higher than officially issued numbers because the procurement is based on controlled prices and development and production costs are hidden in other budget items, that China is conducting an aggressive campaign of arms sale in the developing world, and that China is making advances its ocean-going capacity. Hiramatsu's China threat perception is increasingly focused on the last point. Since 1995 he published no fewer than three books on Chinese maritime strategy. The latest one,which is entitled *China's Strategic Advance into the Ocean*,[25] is based on detailed documentary research. In it, he first traces the evolution of the leadership system of China's navy, and points out that China's maritime activities for resource exploration and investigation are expanding in the East China Sea, that China is establishing effective control in South China Sea, that China is now trying to control the deep sea bed, and that China is approaching Japanese waters. With all the alarm Hiramatsu sounds, however, it should be noted that what he is concerned most with is not the possibility of military attack on Japan. The principal threat that China poses, he argues, is in the possibility that it would succeed in asserting, with the backing of its military strength, its interest further and further away from its border at the expense of another actor – including Japan – or in establishing a "Sinocentric world" to put it simply.

Amako Satoshi edited a book which tried a more broad-based examination of the notion of the China threat.[26] Based on Amako's argument in the book's introduction that threats China can pose to the outside world come from both its external aggressiveness and internal disorder, the authors of the chapters of the book examine both possibilities as well as the China threat perception by external actors and its meaning for Japan. Three authors examine different aspects of possible external danger. Kato Hiroyuki examines the economic aspects.[27] He argues that the threat caused by China's economic growth has two sides. One is the possibility of dominance by a great economic power. The other is the threat posed by China's possible aggressive procurement of food and energy in the international market, by disturbance in the international market caused by China's enormous export capability, and by environmental degradation. He also notes that China's failure in economic growth can also cause a threat of spilling over of the resultant domestic disturbances. He tries to assess these possibilities by examining the course of China's economic development and China's developmental strategy. He argues that China's further development requires the shift in developmental strategy from comparative advantage to what he calls "developmentalism," which would face many obstacles. Thus his conclusion is that China's future development would be slow, which refutes the possibility of the China threat caused by its economic strength. He also points out that China's developmental strategy has been basically sound, which refutes the possibility of domestic economic disturbances.

In the same book, Kayahara Ikuo examines China's military capability and defense policy.[28] Unlike Hiramatsu, noted above, Kayahara characterizes Chinese military policy as basically promoting relaxation of China's strategic environment, secondary to economic development, shifting from quantity to quality, and adding new missions such as public works and the protection of maritime rights and interests. He argues that Chinese military capability is far behind the United States and Russia in terms of quality and is incapable of modern warfare because of its lack of the command-control-communication-intelligence capability. But he also says that its rapid response capability is improving and is already sufficient to make neighboring countries feel pressure. He does note, as does Hiramatsu, that China's military exercises in the area of Taiwan, nuclear tests and development, lack of transparency, rapid increase of defense expenditure, advance to the ocean, and the arms sales are all worrying signs. At the same time, he also notes constraints on the development of China's military capability and its effort for confidence-building in Asia. Kayahara's overall judgment is that the "China threat" has no substance from the military point of view (at least at this point in time) and is the result of psychological amplification in the context of lack of transparency.

Asano examines China's foreign policy with the focus on the security policy (broadly defined) and reaches similar conclusions to Kayahara's.[29] Although the overall orientation of this book is more balanced than Hirahatsu's, the problem is that it has no chapter or section which pulls these three chapters together to make an overall assessment of the extent to which China is a threat and, if it is conditional, identify conditions with which China becomes a threat.

Assessing Chinese Perceptions of the International Environment

As was indicated in many of the articles and books introduced so far, one of the central concerns for Japanese researchers is to figure out how China perceives the international situation as the basis of understanding Chinese foreign policy. Emphasizing the importance of researchers in think tanks to provide the leadership with the analysis and noting their increased freedom of expression in public media, Asano analyzes their perceptions of the disintegration of the Soviet Union and the end of the Cold War.[30] Through detailed examination of their writings he points out that analysts disagreed publicly about the significance of the Soviet collapse, some arguing that it meant a serious setback for socialism and the other arguing that it had nothing to do with socialism. He also shows how totally opposite views were held on the causal relationship between the Soviet collapse and the end of the bipolar system. He argues that the focal issue for Chinese analysts around the beginning of the 1990s was the extent to which tension in the international situation was being reduced. Even with generally welcomed reduction of tension, he points out, there is some cause to worry about its effect of weakening overall China's strategic position.

Based on similar assumptions and methodology, Takagi traced the evolution of China's perception from late 1989 to mid-1990.[31] He traces how the initial expectation for the transition from the bipolar system to multipolar system was dashed by the Gulf War, which demonstrated that the United States is the only superpower capable of massive deployment and warfighting and was replaced by the notion of "one superpower, several strong powers" ("yi chao shu qiang"). He notes that this power structure was characterized as the "primary stage of development toward multipolar structure (multipolarization), which implied its long-term existence. Then, he analyzes an interesting debate in open media between those who took almost polar opposite positions, with one side arguing that the process toward a multipolar structure was being accelerated, with another arguing that the "one superpower, several strong powers" was stable and became the post-bipolar international power structure. He notes that both coexisted and the official pronouncement took the former position while following the prescription based on the latter, much reminiscent of Mao' famous dictum on guerrilla warfare, strategically despise and tactically respect the enemy.

Diplomatic Thought and International Studies

Some scholars try to go beyond the assessment of the contemporary situation and reach ideas at the base of China's management of international relations. For example, Mori Kazuko tried to examine diplomatic thought in the reform and opening era.[32] She characterizes the transformation of Chinese foreign policy since the 1980s to the early 1990s as the departure from the notion of the "great triangle" to the "independence and autonomy" in early 1980s, then to full-fledged participation in the international economy in late 1980s, and then to active involvement in the creation of regional order in early 1990s. As the basis of transformation she examines Chinese "diplomatic thought" in four aspects: diplomatic goals, definition of China's own international roles, views on national interests, and the perceptual framework of international politics. In terms of diplomatic goals, she argues that with the shift of national goal to "socialist modernization," China's diplomacy was transformed to include construction of the stable international environment and formation of the relationship with countries for the sake of economic development in addition to conventional need to protect sovereignty. As such, the importance of international influence became lower than in the Maoist era when China saw itself as the leader of the Third World. She also points out that the new set of diplomatic goals indicates the status-quo orientation and that the transformation was not complete until mid-1980s.

Concerning China's own definition of its international role, Mori points out that China got out of the "false notion" of itself as a potential big power with a huge population and rich resources and came to perceive itself as a weak, developing country in mid-1980s – which led to a reexamined the notion of the "great triangle" and abandonment of the role of the leader of the Third World. However, she also notes that since around 1992 the perception that China was an important force in the balance and stability of the Asia-Pacific region was emerging and that China's role definition could change after it achieved its goal of economic development.

Concerning China's national interests, Mori's focus was on tracing the process in which its full-fledged pursuit became legitimate from late 1980s to early 1990s. She also notes that some Chinese recognize that national interests of countries are completely mutually exclusive and interests of some countries could be intertwined. Concerning Chinese perceptual framework for international politics, she argues that the main current since the 1980s is to hold the ideal that international society should consist of equal sovereign nations and yet to judge that the decisive role in concrete international politics is played by powerful sovereign nations.

Elaborating this last point Okabe makes a much more critical assessment of Chinese studies on international politics and relates it to the conduct of Chinese foreign policy.[33] He first argues that since modern times, the Chinese have made no contribution to progress in the study of international politics for three reasons.

First, Chinese study of international politics, including Marxism-Leninism, is learned from the West; second, in a society where freedom of expression is constrained, social sciences cannot develop as disciplines independent of politics. Lastly, the international studies is mainly concerned with the system of sovereign nation-state, which developed in Western Europe and expanded throughout the rest of the world.

He then analyzed the worldview of Chinese leaders and argues that they are classical realists and nationalists. He points out that China encountered the modern international system in the middle of nineteenth century and had no choice but to be absorbed in it. China has tried ever since to learn the logic and rule of this system and to develop capabilities to cope with stronger powers in order to survive, to catch up with the advanced nations, and then to surpass them. Chinese leaders have tried to manipulate the rules such as non-interference in internal affairs to their own benefit. Okabe then argues that Chinese foreign policy is based on a nationalistic and classical view of power politics. He says that Chinese ideological statements are nothing but assertion of national interests in China's own way, that the Five Principles of Peaceful Coexistence are nothing but a codification of classical rules of the nineteenth-century Western international system, and that the omni-directional diplomacy represents only a stylistic change.

He argues that international relations after the Second World War, especially after the 1970s and the end of the Cold War, changed dramatically – in that industrialization is no longer the indispensable condition for national independence, that effectiveness of military power has decreased, and that the homogeneity expected of nation-states can not be maintained any longer.

On this basis, Okabe criticizes Chinese conduct based on classical realism such as actual or threatened use of force, preoccupation with territory and sovereignty, and the desire to form a homogenous nation-state as anachronistic. He also points out that China's perception of its own conduct diverges seriously from others' perceptions of it, and that China's powerful memory of national humiliation since the nineteenth century is responsible for the misjudgment. In conclusion, he argues that China is preoccupied with the past self-image of a weak nation, in spite of the achievement of the major power status, and is unwilling to fulfill the corresponding obligations to provide ammunition to the advocates of the "China threat" theory.

Both Okabe and Mori are senior specialists who have been engaged in the study of China for decades. Their analyses, introduced above, are both relatively short, but they are full of intriguing insights and are the crystallization of their many years of research.

China–U.S.–Japan Relations

As the Cold War system collapsed in the early 1990s, the trilateral (or triangular in some analysts' characterization) relationship among China, Japan, and the United States increasingly attracted attention as the key dynamics in the international relations of the Asia-Pacific region.[34] Although most of the writings on this subject are of a journalistic nature, there are some scholarly works worthy of note.

Kokubun Ryosei wrote a prescriptive study trying to establish the necessity of the cooperation among China, Japan, and the United States.[35] He argues that in order for the Asia-Pacific region to create a truly affluent society it is necessary to deepen interdependence and to establish a check-and-balance mechanism in it, and that in the transition period before the full establishment of the regional confidence-building mechanism, the three countries should play such a central role. He argues that the composition of contemporary relations among the three is unclear because regional security is maintained basically by the bilateral alliances of the United States. He points out that the cooperation among the three is possible because of three reasons:

1– All three assign high priority to the relationship with the other two.
2– Interdependence is strengthening among the three.
3– There is an orientation toward concert of powers in the region.

Kokubun also notes three obstacles to the cooperation:

1– The clash of national interests caused by the development of globalization based on nation-states.
2– The internationalization of domestic politics.
3– The uncertainty surrounding China.

His prescription for cooperation involves agenda-setting and network formation. For the former he notes the central importance of involving China in the cooperative system of interdependence and proposes to start with seeking cooperation on such issues as regional income gaps, environment, and energy problems rather than security and territorial issues to avoid stimulating nationalism. In the field of security he proposes to deal with the third country issues. For the latter he argues that the government-to-government channels are important but need to be buttressed by grass-roots and "Track II" channels.

Generally speaking, inherent in any trilateral relationship is the danger of its assuming the two-against-one structure. The China–U.S.–Japan relationship is no exception, especially given the existence of the Japan–U.S. security alliance. Partly because of this concern China's view of and response to the Japan–U.S. alliance is one of the primary issues in the study of this trilateral relationship. Takagi analyses China's response to the reaffirmation of the Japan–U.S. alliance in the Joint Communiqué on Security in April 1996,[36] and points out that they saw it as the manifestation of strengthening and expansion of the area of application, as well as of enhancement of Japan's military role. He also points out that there were more fundamental concerns beneath these critical perceptions. He argues that their fundamental concerns included the perception that Japan was turning to the right and becoming a military power in its own right, and that the emergence of the regional multipolar power structure, on which they had placed their hope in early 1990s, was being critically stalled by the reaffirmation. In another article Takagi examined China's response to the strengthening of the Japan–U.S. alliance ties after the Joint Communiqué with reference to the theories of security dilemma.[37]

Japan–China Relations

Naturally, among China's bilateral relationships, the most extensively studied is the one with Japan. Japanese scholars try to use various perspectives to grasp the essence of Chinese policy toward Japan. Ishii Akira examines how the notion of the "Japan–China relationship in the world,"[38] which had been first put forward by

Prime Minister Toshiki Kaifu in August 1991, was received in China. He comes up with the judgment that China was coming to accept Japan as a "political great power," the "ambition" for which had been seen as an ominous sign that Japan was on course to become a militaristic power. He argues that the reason for acceptance was that they considered that Japan needed China's cooperation and support to become a "political great power." However, he also points out that China was still opposed to Japan's attempt to become a permanent member of the UN Security Council and continued to see Japan as its rival in the Asia-Pacific region and that Chinese military still held an antiquated view of Japan and was worried about the revival of Japanese militarism.

Kojima,[39] extending his earlier works,[40] pointed out simultaneous progression of exchanges on the surface and frictions and conflicts underneath, and examines mutual perceptions at popular level as the cause of the friction and conflict. Kokubun also starts with mutual popular images and points to the vicious circle between the deterioration of mutual images and the downturn in the bilateral relationship.[41] He argues that behind this vicious circle is the transformation of the stable structure formed after the normalization of the diplomatic relationship, which he calls the "1972 regime," existed since the late 1980s. He then analyzes the transformation from four perspectives: the structural change of the Cold War system, deepening interdependence, generational change, and the democratization of Taiwan.

The outbursts of anti-Japanese sentiment in China in recent years drew attention to Chinese public opinion and its impact on China's policy toward Japan. One of the earliest systematic examinations of the issue was made by Tsuji Kogo.[42] He traces the evolution of Chinese communist treatment of public opinion since the 1930s and points out how the government controlled the media and imposed the uniformity on public opinion after 1949. He argues that the effort to impose uniformity continued after the shift to the reform and opening policy, but its effectiveness is significantly reduced.

On this basis, he examines some polls on Japan conducted in China. Drawing on the poll conducted by the Institute of Japanese Studies of Fudan University in 1995, he points out that the peasantry and the youth are most uninformed about Japan and are most anti-Japanese, while urban residents, office workers, and those with foreign contacts have relatively objective views on Japan. He then points out that the Communist Party control of media and continued efforts to contain public opinion within an "officially approved" range, led to divergence of public reputation from publicized public opinion. And on this basis he argues that the treatment of Japan in officially approved media is quite prudent but the public reputation of Japan is emotional and biased.

Aoyama Rumi examines public opinion on Japan at two levels: the researchers in universities and think tanks and the masses.[43] The opinions of researchers, she examines, include those expressed in mass media, such as television and newspapers, and she notes the controversies on whether historic issues should be put aside, whether Japan as a military great power should be accepted, and how to understand the bilateral relations in China's Asia strategy. For mass opinion, she examines views expressed on the Internet, and points out that the opinions which record high readership deal with the issues which evoke negative images of Japan, such as its history, the Senkaku (Diaoyu) Islands, the bullet train (*Shinkansen*), the consumer service of Japanese enterprises in China, Japan's response to anti-Japanese nationalism in China, comparison of future national strength, and Japanese contempt for China. Her conclusion is that among researchers the opinion to accept Japan as a "normal state" is gradually being formed but the opinions on the Internet are still highly negative.

Ki Keiei (Qi Jingying) attempts an ambitious analysis of Chinese discourse on Japan on the Internet,[44] although in a somewhat confused way, it makes an interesting comparison of accounts of Prime Minister Koizumi's visit to the Yasukuni Shrine in the *People's Daily* (*Renmin Ribao*) and in "Strong Nation Forum" ("Qiangguo Luntan"). These research projects are obviously still at preliminary stages – but this is the subject which will receive increasing attention by the research community in Japan.

United States–China Relations

China's relationship with Japan's only ally, the United States, naturally received very high attention from Japanese scholars, second only to the relationship with Japan itself. However, analyses of the bilateral relationship tend to be focused on the U.S. side. For example, Hamamoto Ryoichi examines the evolution of the notion of "strategic partnership" in the bilateral relations to elucidate China's posture *vis-à-vis* the United States.[45] He argues that its origin was in Jiang Zemin's statement at the bilateral summit in 1993 but that it was the U.S. that proposed to form a "strategic partnership." The Chinese finally agreed to it only after securing the addition of the adjective "constructive" in the text. But although he provides a detailed analysis of U.S. motives, the reason for Chinese acceptance was not fully explained. Ito Go analyzes the bilateral relationship after 9/11.[46] His research is centered on the Taiwan problem, but also pays attention to the fluctuation of the U.S. stand between the "China threat" theory and the effective use of Chinese cooperation. Takagi analyzes Chinese responses to the evolving U.S. China policy from the George H.W. Bush to the Clinton administrations.[47] For the Chinese side, he argues that the relationship with the United States has an inherent dilemma for China, and this is made even more intractable by the U.S. engagement policy.

Russia–China Relations

The studies on China's relationship with Russia in the period covered by this review tend to be subsumed under the broader examination of the Chinese approach to the "strategic partnership." No significant enough studies on the bilateral relationship per se were found.

Other Bilateral Relationships in Asia

Some studies on Chinese policies toward the Korean peninsula provide fresh perspectives on this issue in particular and the study of Chinese foreign relations in general. For example, Masuo Chisako examines China's approach to the Korean peninsula from 1980 to 1992 to elucidate the background of the establishment of diplomatic relationship with the Republic of Korea.[48] She argues that the Chinese approach to the peninsula shifted from one based on the personal relationship with the leaders of the Socialist Party to one based on the definition of the situation and the national interest; she calls the process "Westphalianization." The unique contribution of this study is that she analyzed the party-to-party "diplomatic relationship" along with the government-to-government relationship.

Nakai analyzes the Yang Bin affair,[49] as a case study of Chinese policy toward North Korea, using the "fragmented authoritarianism" model developed by Kenneth Lieberthal and David Lampton.[50] He carefully examines the divergent definitions of the problems inherent in the North Korea question for the Beijing government and Liaoning Province. He argues that Beijing's support for the North Korean plan to establish a "special administrative district" in Shinyiju collapsed because of its conflict with local interests, which were behind the arrest of Yang Bin, who had been named by the North Korean authority as governor of the district.

Kurata Hideya analyzes China's involvement in the Four-Party Talks formally proposed in 1996 going all the way back to their embryonic form in the Kissinger's proposal in the mid-1970s.[51] He examines the Chinese response to the interaction between the North Korean attempts to negotiate the peace system on the peninsula exclusively with the United States and the U.S. attempts to create a multilateral mechanism to ensure peace on the peninsula. His argument is that China was opposed to the North Korean attempts because it enhanced U.S. influence in the sub-region and got involved in the Four Party Talks reactively.

Sato Koichi argues that ASEAN is important for China for economic and diplomatic reasons.[52] For one thing, ASEAN is important because of the economic influence of overseas Chinese. For another, the strong relationship with ASEAN strengthens China's diplomatic hand and helps ward off the Western pressure on human rights issues. He then examines three problems in China's relationship with ASEAN: the Spratly islands, economic frictions, and Taiwan's advance in ASEAN. Most other works on China's relationship with ASEAN or its member countries treat the subject in the context of regional cooperation developed around ASEAN.

Soeya Yoshihide has analyzed the Chinese approach to the ASEAN Regional Form (ARF).[53] His starting point is that there is a dual structure in the Asia-Pacific region in terms of the approach to security: the balance of power among Japan, the United States, Russia and China with the central role played by the U.S.–Japan alliance; and the norm of cooperative security as embodied in the ARF. He then points out that China's participation in the ARF is not based on its acceptance of cooperative security, but is motivated by the balance of power calculation of countering the post-Cold War U.S. predominance.

Takagi compares China's participation in the APEC and the ARF, and points out that China was quite active and accommodating in the former and passive and almost foot-dragging in the latter.[54] He explains the difference by the nature of the issues involved and the timing of participation. He argues that when China participated in the APEC in 1991 it was still trying to overcome the post-Tiananmen international isolation – whereas when it made the decision to join the ARF in 1993 it was already in the trajectory of high economic growth, and that China thinks that security cooperation is more a sovereignty issue, on which it cannot compromise, than economic cooperation.

In his analysis of the Chinese approach to multilateralism as a part of an attempt to compare it with Japanese policies, Takahara focuses on the reason why China became more proactive.[55] He argues that, traditionally, China was mainly concerned with power politics among the major powers and tried to avoid and evade multilateralism because of its obvious advantage in bilateral negotiations with smaller nations, and the possibility of domination by other major powers and constraint on its sovereignty. But Beijing became more proactive around 1997, both in the security and economic spheres. In the security sphere, he argues that China became active in the ARF because the Mischief Reef incident of 1995 caused China's fear of isolation in the context of the redefinition of the U.S.–Japan security alliance and because the U.S. had the concept of transforming APEC into a security cooperation mechanism. In the economic sphere, he argues that China's activism caused by the recognition that globalization was inevitable and that regional cooperation could be hedged against its negative effects, the experience of the Asian currency crisis led to the acceptance of the notion of economic security and self-confidence in managing multilateralism (which was caused by the post-1992 high economic growth and international appreciation for its response to the currency crisis). He also points out that Chinese leadership came to consider multilateralism as the solution to the "China dilemma," i.e. China needs a peaceful international environment for its growth, but the rapid growth itself led to the "China threat" perception on China's periphery, which in turn lead to destabilizing responses in the international environment.

Concluding Observations

Although the above literature review is still very incomplete, it does allow some preliminary observations about the state of Japanese study on foreign and security policies of China. In terms of methodology, most of the works are based on careful examination of Chinese official statements and documents. Japanese scholars usually take very seriously such expressions as "strategic partnership" and "new security concept," and try to establish their genealogy and capture the characteristics of the context in which they evolved to figure out their exact meaning.

A second notable characteristic is that almost no work on contemporary China uses interviews as a way of obtaining information. This lacuna stands in stark contrast to American studies of the subject, which rely extensively on interviews. It is also somewhat mysterious given Japan's proximity to China.

Third, most of the works are traditional descriptive analyses. Although there are sporadic efforts by some authors to link their works to some theoretical frameworks, such as the asymmetrical conflict paradigm by Izumikawa, the fragmented authoritarianism model by Nakai, and the security dilemma by Takagi, Japanese studies of China are largely atheoretical and there are almost no studies of theory falsification and hypothesis testing types.

This tendency is related to the selection of the subjects of research. Japanese scholars devote a lot of effort to figuring out perceptions of Chinese policymakers, or at least those of policy intellectuals who are supposed to provide them with information on the international situation, either as explanation of specific policies or as the subject in itself. Because of this tendency, Japanese scholars are probably among the most serious readers of works by Chinese scholars.

Other than perceptions and general characterizations of Chinese foreign and security policy, most of the works in the field are studies of Chinese policy toward (or relations with) specific countries or area. As the objects of Chinese policy, the most frequently studied countries are, naturally, Japan and the United States. There are some works on Chinese policies toward Russia, the Korean peninsula, and ASEAN. Chinese policies on and China's approach to international institutions are not studied too much, except for APEC, ARF, SCO and the WTO. There are almost no works on Chinese policies toward the Middle East, Africa and Latin America. There are hardly any works on Chinese policies on specific international or global issues, such as non-proliferation, arms control and disarmament, global environmental problems, and other non-traditional security issues. There are many studies on China's energy problems, both internal and external, but they do not fully examine their linkage with foreign and security policies.

These characteristics of Japanese studies on Chinese foreign and security policy simultaneously point to lacunae to be filled by future works. Chinese involvement in the Middle East, Africa, and Latin America is increasing rapidly. Future studies will have to cover these areas in order to grasp the totality of Chinese foreign and security policy.

Given China's rapidly rising importance in global governance, we also need to study China's policy and position on specific global issues and locate them within the framework of China's overall external strategy. We need to enhance our efforts to seek relevant theoretical frameworks and insights to inform our study and to provide the field of general international relations with useful and usable case studies. Within the areas already fairly well covered we can identify emerging or new subjects to be studied. For example, in the study of Chinese policy toward Japan, the emerging focus is the role of public opinion and the media, especially the Internet. We will also need to develop the study of the impact of the economic interdependence on overall bilateral relationship and the interaction between the two societies. In the study of Chinese policy toward the United States, we need to overcome the drift toward focusing excessively on the U.S. side, caused by the asymmetry in availability of information, and try to look more deeply into the Chinese side. The studies of Chinese perceptions of the international and situations external should continue, but they need to be enriched by deeper understanding of the relationship between perception/strategy and action and the dynamics through which certain perceptions and ideas inform the policymaking process.

Last, but not least important, Japanese studies on China in general, and its foreign and security policy in particular, need to be further informed by increased interaction with the academic community in China and with China specialists in other parts of the world. This way we will recognize our unique strengths, which will enable us to make a unique contribution to international scholarship on China.

Notes

1 "Kokusai Seiji" means international politics but "International Relations" is the official English title of the journal. This kind of discrepancy between Japanese and English titles is quite common in Japan. Usually the English titles represent the actual character of the referents more accurately.
2 I am grateful to Ms. Mao Asukata, Ph.D. Candidate, Keio University for her assistance for this and other necessary tasks.
3 Japanese and Chinese names are written in the indigenous order, i.e. the family names first and the given names second. The full names are given only for the first reference.
4 Ebihara Tsuyosi, "1990nen iko no Nihon niokeru Chugoku Taigaiseisaku Kenkyu no Doko" ("Trends in the Study on Chinese Foreign Policy in Japan Since 1990"), *Ajia Keizai*, XLVI-2 (2005.2), pp. 54–69.
5 Okabe Tatsumi, *Chugoku no Taigai Senryaku* (*The External Strategy of China*), (Tokyo Daigaku Shuppankai, 2002).
6 Shu Ken'ei, *Motakuto no Betonamu Senso: Chugoku Gaiko no Daitenkan to Bunkadaikakumei no Kigen* (*Mao Zedong's Vietnam War: The Origin of China's Great Transformation in Diplomacy and the Cultural Revolution*), (Tokyo Daigaku Shuppankai, 2001).
7 Shu Ken'ei (Zhu Jianrong), *Motakuto no Chosen Senso* (*Mao Zedong's Korean War*), (Iwanami Shoten, 2004).
8 Mori Kazuko, "Kaisetsu: 1971–72nen no Beichu Kosho ni tuite" ("Background: On the U.S.–China Negotiation in 1971–72"), in Mori Kazuko and Mori Kozaburo, translators; *Nikuson Hochu Kimitu Kaidanroku* (*The Transcript of the Secret Meetings of Nixon's China Visit*), (Nagoya Daigaku Shuppankai, 2001).
9 Ishii Akira, Shu Ken'ei, Soeya Yoshihide, and Rin Gyoko (Lin Xiaoguang), eds, *Nicchu Kokko Seijoka/Nicchu Heiwa Yuko Joyaku Teiketu Kosho* (*The Negotiations for the Normalization of the Diplomatic Relations between Japan and China and the Conclusion of the Japan China Treaty of Peace and Friendship*), (Iwanami Shoten, 2003).
10 Soeya Yoshihide, "Beichu Wakai kara Nicchu Kokko Seijoka e-Sakusosuru Nihonzou," ("From the U.S.–China Rapprochement to the Normalization of the Japan–China Diplomatic Relationship – Intricate Images of Japan"), in ibid.
11 Izumikawa Yasuhiro, "Dainiji Taiwan Kaikyo Kiki no Saikensho: Ni-chotaikoku no hazama no Chugoku Gaiko" ("The Second Taiwan Strait Crisis Reexamined: Chinese Diplomacy between the Two Superpowers"), *Kokusai Seiji*, 134 (2003).

12 Mori Kazuko, "Sekai Sisutemu no naka no Chugoku" ("China in the World System"), *Kokusai Mondai (International Affairs)*, No. 418 (1995).

13 Takahara Akio, "Kyocho Gaikou to Haken Gaikou no Wakare-michi" ("The Crossroad of Diplomacy between Cooperation and Hegemony"), in Kojima Tomoyuki, ed., *Chugoku no Jidai: 21seiki eno Cho-Taikoku ga Umareru (The Age of China: Emergence of the Superpower of the 21st Century)*, (Mita Syuppan-kai, 1995).

14 Okabe Tatsumi, "Chugoku no Taigai-seisaku to Taigai-imeji" ("China's Foreign Policy and Its Images of the External Situation"), in Okabe Tatumi, ed., *Chugoku Gaiko – Seisaku Kettei no Kozo (Chinese Diplomacy – The Structure of Decision-making)*, (Nihon Kokkusai Mondai Kenkyujo, 1983).

15 Nakai Yoshifumi, "21seiki wo mukaeru Chugoku Gaiko: 'Taisei no Kiki' kara 'Aikoku-shugi' e" ("China's Diplomacy Reaching the 21st Century: From the 'Regime Crisis' to 'Patriotism'"), *Toa (East Asia)*, No. 354 (1996).

16 Kojima Tomoyuki, "Chugoku Gaiko no Ronri – 'Zen-hoyi' to 'Haken' no Kankei" ("The Logic of Chinese Diplomacy – the Relationship between 'Omni-directionality' and 'Hegemony'") in Kojima Tomoyuki, *Gendai Chugoku no Seiji (Politics of Contemporary China)*, (Keio Daigaku Shuppankai, 1999).

17 Kojima Tomoyuki, "Taikoku Jushi no Chugoku Gaiko – 'Dokuritu Jishu' Gaiko no Henyo" ("Chinese Diplomacy of Respect for the Great Powers – Transformation of the Foreign Policy of 'Independence and Autonomy'"), in Kojima, ibid.

18 Masuda Masayuki, "Chugoku no Taikoku Gaiko: 'Senryakuteki Patona-shippu' wo megutte" ("The Great Power Diplomacy of China: Concerning the 'Strategic Partnership'"), *Toa (East Asia)*, No. 402 (2000).

19 Kokubun Ryosei, "Shuno Gaiko to Chugoku" ("The Summit Diplomacy and China"), *Kokusai Mondai (International Affairs)*, No. 466 (1999).

20 Mori Kazuko, "Posuto-Reisen to Chugoku no Anzenhoshokan – 'Kyochoteki Anzenhosho' wo megutte" ("The Post-Cold War and China's New Security Concept – Concerning the 'Cooperative Security'"), in Yamamoto Takehiko, ed., *Kokusai Anzenhosho no Shintenkai – Reisen to Sonogo (The New Development of International Security – The Cold War and After)*, (Waseda Daigaku Shuppanbu, 1999).

21 Asano Ryo, "Chugoku no Anzen Hosho Seisaku ni Naizai suru Ronri to Henka" ("The Logic Inherent in China's Security Policy and its Change"), *Kokusai Mondai*, No. 514 (January 2003).

22 Takagi Seiichiro, "Chugoku no 'Shin-Anzenhoshokan'" ("China's 'New Security Concept'"), *Boei Kenkyujo Kiyo (The Journal of the National Institute of Defense Studies)*, (March 2003).

23 Yan Xuetong, "Xulun" (Introduction) and "Zhongguo Lengzhan hou de Anquan Zhanlue" ("China's Post-Cold War Security Strategy"), in Yan Xuetong, *et al.*, *Zhongguo yu Yatai Anquan (China and the Asia-Pacific Security)*, (Beijing: Shishi Chubanshe, 1999), pp. 1–62.

24 Hiramatsu Shigeo, *Gunji-taikoku-ka suru Chugoku no Kyoi (Threat of China that is Becoming a Military Big Power)*, (Keiso Shobo, 1995).

25 Hiramatsu Shigeo, *Chugoku no Senryakuteki Kaiyo shinshutsu (China's Strategic Advance into the Ocean)*, (Keiso Shobo, 2002).

26 Amako Satoshi, *Chugoku wa Kyoi ka (Is China a Threat?)*, (Keiso Shobo, 1997).

27 Kato Hiroyuki, "Chuchoki Hattensenryaku no Sakutei wo megutte – 'Chugoku Kyoiron' no Keizaiteki sokumen" ("Concerning Formulation of the Mid- and Long-term Developmental Strategy – The Economic Aspect of the 'China Threat' Theory") in ibid.

28 Kayahara Ikuo, "Chugoku no Gunjiryoku to Kokubo-Seisaku no Shinten," ("China's Military Capability and Development of its Defense Policy"), in Amako, op. cit.

29 Asano Ryo, "Chugoku no Taigai-Seisaku – Anzen-Hosho Seisaku wo Chuusin ni," ("China's Foreign Policy – with the Focus on the Security Policy"), in Amako, op. cit.

30 Asano Ryo, "Bren Shudan no Taigai-ninsiki no Henyo" ("Transformation of the Brain Trust's Perception of the External Situation") in Okabe Tatsumi, ed., *Greta Chaina no Seiji-henyo (Political Transformation of the Greater China)*, (Keiso Shobo, 1995).

31 Takagi Seiichiro, "Datsu-reisen-ki niokeru Chuugoku no Taigai-ninshiki – 'Wahei Enpen'-ron kara 'Katoki Shuryou'-ron made" ("China's Perception of the External Situation in the Post-Cold War Period – From the Theory of 'Peaceful Evolution' to the Theory of 'the End of the Transition Period'"), in Takagi Seiichiro, ed., *Datsu-reisenn-ki no Chugoku Gaikou to Ajia-Taiheiyou (Chinese Diplomacy in the Post-Cold War Period and the Asia-Pacific)*, (Nihon Kokusaimondai Kenkyujo, 2000).

32 Mori Kazuko, "Kaikaku-Kaiho Jidai no Chugoku Gaiko – Gaiko Shiso wo Chusin ni" ("Chinese Diplomacy in the Era of Reform and Opening – with the Focus on the Diplomatic Thought"), in Okabe, op. cit.

33 Okabe Tatsumi, "Kokusai-seijigaku to Chugoku Gaiko" ("International Politics and Chinese Diplomacy"), *Kokusai Seiji (International Politics)*, No.144 (1997).

34 In the work published just prior to the period covered by this review I have examined the concept of the triangle and argued that it had only limited applicability to the Japan–U.S.–China relationship. See Takagi Seiichiro, "Ajia niokeru Datu-reisen-katei to Nichi-Bei-Chu-kankei" ("The Ending Process of the Cold War in Asia and the Japan–U.S.–China Relations"), in Hirano Ken'ichiro, ed., *Koza Gendai Ajia 4 – Chiiki Shisutemu to Kokusai Kankei (Contemporary Asia 4 – The Regional System and the International Relations)*, (Tokyo Daigaku Shuppankai, 1994).

35 Kokubun Ryosei, "Naze Ima Nichibeicyu ka – Kyocho eno Kadai to Tenbo" ("Why (do we need to consider) the Japan–U.S.–China (relations) Now? – Tasks for and the Prospect of Cooperation"), in Kokubun Ryosei, *Nihon/Amerika/Chugoku: Kyocho eno Shinario (Japan/U.S./China: the Scenario for Cooperation)*, (TBS Buritanika, 1997).

36 Takagi Seiichiro, "Reisengo no Kokusai Kenryoku-kouzou to Chugoku no Taigai Senryaku – Nichibei Anpo Saikakunin wo megutte" ("The Post-Cold War International Power Structure and China's External Strategy: Concerning the Reaffirmation of the Japan-U.S. Security Treaty"), *Kokusai Mondai* No. 454 (1998).

37 Takagi Seiichiro, "Reisen-go no Nichibei-domei to Hokuto-Ajia – Anzenhosho Jirenma no Shiten kara" ("The Post-Cold War Japan–U.S. Alliance and Northeast Asia – From the Viewpoint of the Security Dilemma"), *Kokusai Mondai*, No. 474 (1999).

38 Ihii Akira, "Shiren ni tatsu 'Sekai no naka no Nicchu Kankei'" ("'Japan–China Relations in the World' in the Moment of Truth"), *Kokusai Mondai*, No. 418 (1995).

39 Kojima Tomoyuki, "1990 nendai no Nicchu Kankei – 'Zenrin Yuko' kara 'Kyoryoku Patonashippu' e" (Japan–China Relations in the 1990s – From "Good Neighborliness and Friendship" to "Cooperative Partnership"), in Kojima, *Gendai Chugoku no Seiji*.

40 Kojima Tomoyuki, "Gendai Nicchuu Kankeiron" (On Contemporary Japan-China Relationship), in Hirano Ken'ichiro, ed., op. cit., 1994.

41 Kokubun Ryosei, "Reisen Shuketsu- go no Nicchu Kankei – '72nen Taisei' no Tenkan ("The Japan–China Relations after the Cold War: The Transformation of the '1972 Regime'"), *Kokusai Mondai*, No. 490 (2001).

42 Tsuji Kogo, "Chugoku ni okeru Yoron Keisei to Tainichi Yoron Kozo" ("The Process of the Public Opinion Formation in China and the Structure of the Public Opinion on Japan"), *Kokusai Mondai*, No. 492, 2001

43 Aoyama Rumi, "Futatsu no Kukan de Keisei sareru Chugoku no Tainichi Yoron - tome-rareru Nihon no 'Paburikku Gaikou'" ("Chinese Public Opinion on Japan Formed in the Two Spheres – The Necessity of Japan's 'Public Diplomacy'"), *Kokusai Mondai*, No. 527, 2004.

44 Ki Keiei (Qi Jingying), *Chugoku no Intanetto niokeru Tainichi Genron Bunseki – Riron to Jissho no Mosaku (The Analysis of Chinese Discourse on Japan on the Internet – In Search of Theory and Empirical Analysis)*, (Nihon Kyoho sha, 2004).

45 Hamamoto Ryoichi, "'Beichu Senryaku Patona-shippu' ni mirareru Chugoku no Gaikou Sisei" ("China's Diplomatic Posture as Seen in the 'U.S.–China Strategic Partnership'"), in Kokubun Ryosei, ed., *Grobaru-ka Jidai no Cyuugoku (China in the Age of Globalization)*, (Nihon Kokusai Mondai Kenkyu-jyo, 2002).

46 Ito Go, "911 go no Beichutai Kankei: Chugoku 'Kyoui-ron' to 'Katsuyou-ron' no Hazama de ("The U.S.–China–Taiwan Relations after the 911: Between the China 'Threat' and the China 'Utilization'"), *Kokusai Mondai*, No. 527 (2004).

47 Takagi Seiichiro, "Beikoku no Ajia Taiheiyo Seisaku to Chugoku" ("The American Policy Toward the Asia-Pacific and China"), in Takagi Seiichiro, ed., *Datsu Reisen-ki no Chugoku Gaiko to Ajia Taiheiyo*.

48 Masuo Chisako, "Toshohei-ki Chugoku no Tai-Chosen Hantou Gaikou: Chugoku Gaiko 'Uestofaria-ka' no Katei" ("China's Diplomacy toward the Korean Peninsula in the Deng Xiaoping Era: The Process of 'Westphalianization'"of China's Diplomacy"), *Ajia Kenkyu (Asian Study)*, No. 48, Vol. 3 (2002).

49 Nakai Yoshifumi, "Chugoku no Kitachousen Seisaku – You Hin Jiken wo megutte" ("Chinese Policy Towards DPRK – The Case of the Yang Bin Affair"), *Kokusai Seiji*, Vol. 135 (2004).

50 Kenneth G. Lieberthal, "Introduction: The 'Fragmented Authoritarianism' Model and Its Limitations," in Kenneth G. Lieberthal and David M. Lampton, eds, *Bureaucracy, Politics, and Decision Making in Post Mao China* (Berkeley, CA: University of California Press, 1992).

51 Kurata Hideya, "Chosen Hanto Heiwataisei Juritu Mondai to Chugoku – Hokuto Ajia Chiiki Anzenhosho to 'Takokukan Gaiko'" ("China's Approach to the Establishment of the Peace System on the Korean Peninsula – The Northeast Asian Regional Security and the 'Multilateral Diplomacy'") in Takagi Seiichiro, ed., *Datsu-Reisenki no Chugoku Gaiko to Ajia-Taiheiyo*.

52 Sato Koichi, "Chugoku Gaiko to ASEAN" ("China's Diplomacy and ASEAN"), in Ako Satoshi, ed., *Chugoku wa Kyoui ka*.

53 Soeya Yoshihide, "ASEAN Chiiki Foramu to Chugoku" ("The ASEAN Regional Forum and China") in Takagi Seiichiro, ed., *Datsu Reisen-ki no Cyugoku Gaiko to Ajia Taiheiyo*.

54 Takagi Seiichiro, "Chugoku to Ajia Taiheiyo Chiiki no Takokukan Kyoryoku" ("China and the Multilateral Cooperation in the Asia-Pacific Region"), in Tanaka Kyoko, ed., *Kokusai Kankei – Ajia Taiheiyo no Chiiki Chitsujyo (International Relations – The Regional Order in the Asia-Pacific)*, (Tokyo Daigaku Syuppan-kai, 2001).

55 Takahara Akio, "Higashi Ajia no Takokukanshugi – Nihon to Chugoku no Chiikishugi Seisaku" ("Multilateralism in East Asia – Japanese and Chinese Policies toward Regionalism"), *Kokusai Seiji*, Vol. 133 (2003).

10 Studies of China's Foreign and Security Policies in the United States

David Shambaugh

This chapter is a survey of the state of the field of China's foreign relations and security policy/military affairs in the United States. These have become a growth field in contemporary China studies in recent years. This is true for academics in universities, but also for researchers in private sector think tanks and consulting firms (some of which receive government contracts for such research on these subjects). No such survey can do full justice to such a diverse and dynamic field. As such, several preliminary caveats are in order.

First, given the volume of publications in this field in the U.S., the assessment is intentionally limited by three criteria: (a) studies completed over the last decade 1995–2005 (a previous assessment of Chinese security studies by Robert Ross and Paul Godwin, published in 1993,[1] adequately surveyed the literature up to that time); (b) published *books* (the periodical literature is just too voluminous to survey);[2] and (c) this is more of a *survey* than a critical assessment of these books and studies. The survey also disaggregates the study of China's foreign relations from the study of China's security/military affairs. This is because those who research China's foreign relations tend not to work on China's security/military affairs, and vice versa. There are some exceptions to this rule, but this is generally the case. Therefore, as they are really distinct sub-fields, it is logical to treat these two communities, and their publications, separately. Finally, no attempt has been made to consider those working in the U.S. government intelligence community who research these subjects. There is indeed a large cohort of such individuals, but since their work is not published in the public domain they are not included in this survey.

Before surveying the published literature in the field, it is useful to ask who contributes to the literature that comprises the field? As noted above, those who work on China's foreign relations tend not to work on Chinese security/military affairs and vice versa – hence we will first examine these two groups sequentially.

The China Foreign Relations Community

Those who write about China's foreign relations and teach in universities in the United States are generally political scientists specializing in Chinese affairs, although gradually scholars of international relations are beginning to integrate China into their comparative and systemic studies. Reflecting the increased interest in China's global behavior and importance, departments of political science in American universities and colleges are beginning to create faculty positions devoted to the study of China's external behavior – whereas prior to the last few years junior faculty searches were almost entirely for comparativists. Once hired, such faculty were possibly asked to teach a course on Chinese foreign policy. But this past tendency is beginning to change, as departments are increasingly recognizing that specialists in China's foreign relations are needed in their own right and that those trained in the study of Chinese domestic politics are not necessarily prepared to teach or conduct research on foreign affairs (and vice versa). This trend is fairly new in civilian U.S. universities, although the National Defense University and armed services' "war" colleges have had Chinese foreign and security policy specialists on faculty for a number of years. Even U.S. business schools are beginning to add China specialists to their faculties, to teach about China's global economic role, domestic economy, negotiating styles, and behavior in international organizations.

Such university-based scholars actively researching and publishing on China's foreign relations in U.S. universities and colleges include (from east coast to west coast): Alastair Iain Johnston (Harvard); Robert Ross (Boston College); Taylor Fravel (MIT); Samuel Kim (Columbia); Allen Carlson (Cornell); Chen Jian (Cornell); Avery Goldstein (Pennsylvania); Thomas Christensen (Princeton); Andrew Scobell (U.S. Army War College); Jonathan Pollack (U.S. Naval War College); Wang Hongying (Syracuse); Hao Yufan (Colgate); David M. Lampton (Johns Hopkins SAIS); Robert Sutter (Georgetown); Nancy Bernkopf Tucker (Georgetown); Margaret Pearson (Maryland); Shu Guang Zhang (Maryland); Warren Cohen (Maryland-Baltimore County); David Shambaugh (George Washington); Harry Harding (George Washington); Michael Yahuda (George Washington); Mike Mochizuki (George Washington); Phillip Saunders (National Defense University); Yong Deng (U.S. Naval Academy); Quansheng Zhao (American University); Ming Wan (George Mason); Liu Guoli (College of Charleston), Wang Fei-ling (Georgia Tech); John Garver (Georgia Tech); Li Hongshan (Kent State); Qiang Zhai (Auburn); Yu Bin (Wittenberg); Thomas Moore (Cincinnati); June Dreyer (Miami); Kenneth Lieberthal (Michigan); Ed Friedman (Wisconsin); Wang Jianwei (Wisconsin-Steven's Point); Suisheng Zhao (Denver); Peter Hayes Gries (Colorado); Li Xiaobing (Central Oklahoma); Allen Whiting (Arizona); Susan Shirk (California-San Diego); Robert Scalapino (California-Berkeley); Lowell Dittmer (California-Berkeley); and Mel Gurtov (Portland State).

Quite evident from this list is the fact that Chinese émigrés have joined and infused the field in growing numbers in recent years. Their native perspectives and linguistic fluency provide obvious advantages which they bring to their research and publications.

While the bulk of political scientists working on China in U.S. universities still focus on domestic Chinese affairs, those working in think tanks or consulting firms are, in fact, weighted more heavily toward the study of external China than internal China. Virtually every think tank in Washington, D.C. possesses one or more staff members who specialize (fully or partly) in China's foreign and security policy. This includes Michael Swaine and Minxin Pei (Carnegie Endowment); Alan Romberg (Henry L. Stimson Center); Richard Bush, Jing Huang, and Jeffrey Bader (Brookings Institution); Nicholas Lardy (Institute of International Economics); Bates Gill, Bonnie Glaser, Kurt Campbell, and Derek Mitchell (Center for Strategic and International Studies); Banning Garrett (Atlantic Council); John Tkacik, Larry Wortzel, and Peter Brookes (Heritage Foundation); Dan Blumenthal (American Enterprise Institute); David M. Lampton (Nixon Center); Evan Medeiros and Murray Scot Tanner (Rand Corporation); and David Finkelstein (CNA Corporation). Outside of Washington, this includes Elizabeth Economy and Adam Segal (Council on Foreign Relations in New York), Jing-dong Yuan (Monterey Institute of International Studies), and Denny Roy (Center for Asia-Pacific Security Policy Studies in Honolulu).

The capital city buzzes with a never-ending series of think tank-sponsored seminars, workshops, conferences, and speakers discussing one or another aspect of China's role in the world. Many, if not most, are geared to discussing current events and recent developments – without a great deal of intellectual depth or historical perspective. *Policy relevance* is the *sine qua non* of such events, as scholarly presentations without policy implications are a rarity. Precious few think tank fellows publish books and publishing articles in peer-reviewed academic journals is not an outlet for their work. Their preferred medium is the op-ed, policy brief, and articles in policy journals such as *Foreign Affairs*, *Foreign Policy*, *The National Interest*, or *The Washington Quarterly*. This has not always been the case. Over the past decade, Washington think tanks have moved increasingly away from in-depth research in favor of shorter analyses. Even the venerable Brookings Institution, long known for the definitive book-length manuscripts published by their senior fellows, has increasingly succumbed to the prevalent model pioneered originally by The Heritage Foundation: the *policy brief*, the *op-ed*, the current events seminar, and pseudo-lobbying. Instead of recruiting from the Academy, Brookings senior fellows now are almost all ex-government officials, whereas those who had come to Brookings from more academic backgrounds and possessed substantial scholarly standing have all departed (e.g. Ed Lincoln, Mike Mochizuki, Harry Harding, Nicholas Lardy, and Bates Gill).

Taken together, though, those in academe and think tanks have catalyzed the field of Chinese foreign policy studies. Just a decade ago the number of those active in this field was not even half as large as at present. Not only has the increased supply of scholars stimulated the field, but so too has the demand. China's emergence on the world scene, its growing "hard power" and developing "soft power," its proactive peripheral diplomacy in Asia, its voracious search for energy, its increased involvement in regional and global multilateral institutions, its occasional involvement in problem-solving (e.g. the North Korean nuclear issue), its growing transparency and increased sophistication in articulating its foreign policy – these developments have all created a sharply increased demand by the public, media, and policy community in the United States to understand better the inputs and outputs of China's foreign relations. Academic and think tank analysts have done well in answering the call and responding to the increased demand for knowledge.

The China Security Studies Community

Studies of Chinese security and China's military are somewhat different. While there has also been sharply increased demand for data, knowledge, and assessments, those who do research in this area are generally not academics. Very few scholars based in civilian universities publish about the People's Liberation Army (PLA): David Shambaugh (George Washington), Mel Gurtov (Portland State), Tom Bickford (Wisconsin-Oshkosh), Li Xiaobing (Central Oklahoma), Robert Ross (Boston College), Yu Bin (Wittenberg), Thomas Christensen (Princeton), June Dreyer (Miami), and Taylor Fravel (MIT).

Why so few? Unlike the study of China's foreign relations, where professional incentives are beginning to stimulate faculty hires and the growth of the sub-field, to date there have been few, if any, incentives in universities to go into Chinese military/security studies. It is a vicious circle: there are few professors knowledgeable and interested enough in the Chinese military/security affairs to supervise doctoral dissertations on the subject, political science departments frown upon this field as atheoretical, and there are no university teaching jobs for a graduate specializing in this subject area. This vicious circle is truly regrettable, but is a fact of academic life in the United States. Particularly puzzling is why political scientists specializing in China have long shunned PLA studies – an inexplicable peculiarity considering the pivotal role the military has played in the political life of modern and contemporary China.[3] More broadly, military and security studies still have an uneasy place and identity within the political science and international relations disciplines in the Academy (ironically, the leading journal in the field, *International Security*, has been moving in the opposite direction in recent years, by publishing increasing numbers of articles on China). Yet, one hardly ever finds panels or papers presented on Chinese military or security studies at the two leading professional association meetings, the American Political Science Association or the Inter-University Seminar on the Armed Forces and Society, much less the Association for Asian Studies. Studies of the Chinese military are just not viewed by mainstream political scientists or Asianists as fertile ground for theoretical or comparative analysis.

If the academic members of the Chinese security/military studies community remain small, then who comprise the majority? The bulk of such specialists today work in private sector research institutes, corporations, and consultancies, e.g.: Michael Swaine (Carnegie Endowment); James Mulvenon, Kevin Pollpeter, and Michael Chase (Center for Intelligence Reform and Analysis); Murray Scot Tanner, Evan Medeiros, and Roger Cliff (Rand Corporation); Bates Gill, Derek Mitchell, and Kurt Campbell (Center for Strategic and International Studies); Richard Fisher (International Assessment and Strategy Center); Larry Wortzel (formerly of The Heritage Foundation); David Finkelstein, Ken Allen, Dean Cheng, Kristen Gunness, and Maryanne Kivlehan-Wise (CNA Corporation); Ed O'Dowd and John Corbett (Centra Technologies); and Roy Kamphausen (National Bureau of Asian Research). These individuals spend much of their time, but by no means all, researching Chinese security issues and the PLA. Other members of the China security field work in U.S. government institutions (many in war colleges) – such as Jonathan Pollack (U.S. Naval War College); Andrew Scobell (U.S. Army War College); Lawrence Grinter (Air War College); Bernard Cole, Philip Saunders, and Cynthia Watson (National Defense University); Chris Twomey (Naval Postgraduate School); Denny Roy (Asia-Pacific Center for Security Studies); and Harlan Jencks (Lawrence Livermore Laboratories). Finally, there are individually-employed researchers and consultants, each of whom have contributed a great deal to the field: Eric McVadon, Dennis Blasko, Susan Puska, and Michael Pillsbury.

Included in the aforementioned is a cohort of retired U.S military officers (many former U.S. Army Foreign Area Officers or FAOs), such as Lonnie Henley, John Corbett, David Finkelstein, Mark Stokes, Roy Kamphausen, Dennis Blasko, Ed O'Dowd, Susan Puska, Eric McVadon, and others. Many of these individuals have previously served as either military attachés in China and/or in the Department of Defense. This distinguished group has made an important mark on the field of PLA studies. They have brought obvious expertise and a "feel" for understanding the PLA that academics lack. They have benefited from first-hand exposure to the highest reaches of the PLA command structure down to basic units and training facilities. There is just no replacement for this experience. But the real value-added of this group is that they have spent their entire adult professional lives as military officers, and concomitantly bring a comprehension of the weapons systems, technologies, training regimens, operations and maintenance routines for militaries that academics are hard-pressed to understand. The addition of this cohort to the PLA studies community is relatively recent (although there have always been some in the field), and it has provided an incredible boost to the field. Curiously, though, unlike the Chinese foreign policy field, to date the PLA studies field has not benefited from the addition of Chinese émigrés (particularly former PLA officers). Three exceptions to this are You Ji, Bi Jianxiang, Nan Li, but all work outside of the United States (in Australia, Canada, and Singapore respectively).

Since the mid-1990s, there are encouraging signs of a new generation of young scholars entering the field who have received their Ph.Ds in recent years: James Mulvenon from UCLA, Thomas Bickford from California-Berkeley, Evan Feigenbaum and Taylor Fravel from Stanford; Andrew Scobell from Columbia, Huang Jing from Harvard, and Evan Medeiros from the London School of Economics and Political Science. Although Mulvenon and Medeiros have opted for careers outside academe in the consulting world, Huang Jing joined the Brookings Institution, and Feigenbaum has gone into government service, Scobell and Fravel entered academe. This new generation is armed with solid social science training, a sound base in China area studies, and good Chinese language skills.

Thus, the field of Chinese security and military studies has enjoyed substantial growth in recent years. As is discussed below, the research foci have evolved, as have the available data. Also, the field is no longer as insular as in the past, as there is a much more diverse range of consumers for the field's research.

Trends in Recent Scholarship on China's Foreign Relations

The published literature on China's foreign relations has grown rapidly over the past decade. The periodical literature alone is voluminous, but we shall concentrate here on published books. These can be divided into eight general categories.

First, there are *edited compendia and synthesized overviews* of China's foreign relations; in both cases these volumes are primarily intended for use as university-level textbooks. Suisheng Zhao, Samuel Kim, and Guoli Liu have all put together very fine compendia.[4] In the case of the Kim volume, all of the essays were specially commissioned for inclusion, whereas the Zhao and Liu volumes contain previously published articles (in the case of the Zhao volume most previously appeared in the *Journal of Contemporary China*, edited by Zhao). I have found that the Kim and Liu volumes are better texts for teaching purposes, whereas the Zhao volume lacks coherence. The Kim volume, now in its fourth edition, is still a fine general reader, but even this latest edition is now eight years out of date (and many of the individual chapters have not been updated from the first edition in 1989) and Kim tells me that there will be no follow-on editions. Thus, a new and updated general reader is needed.

In addition to these compendia already published, Alastair Iain Johnston and Robert S. Ross have edited a stimulating volume entitled *New Directions in the Study of China's Foreign Policy*, published in 2006.[5] Containing chapters by many of the leading senior and rising junior scholars in the field, this volume is organized around three themes: the impact of domestic public opinion, perceptions, and identity on foreign policy; the impact of globalization of Chinese foreign policy and vice versa; and several case studies in China's regional security policy. Johnston and Ross also join with Thomas Christensen in writing a stimulating concluding chapter on future directions of the field.

In addition, four single-authored overviews have been published – which were also largely intended as teaching texts. The one by Quansheng Zhao is the least useful for this purpose.[6] The other three volumes, one by Andrew Nathan and Robert Ross, one by Denny Roy, and one by Robert Sutter cover a lot of ground and do so very effectively.[7] The Roy and Nathan/Ross books include chapters on the history of PRC foreign policy, foreign policy decision-making, China's relations with regional neighbors, China's international economic relationships, China's military and security, and China's role in international governance, as well as some specialized topics. The Nathan and Ross volume is more intellectually rich and empirically dense, and is thus more effective for graduate level teaching, but the Roy volume is a very effective first-time introduction to the subject for uninitiated undergraduates. Despite the title, the Sutter volume is primarily focused on China's relations with Asia.

The second category is the new genre of books concerning the "rise" of China. In fact, many of these volumes include the term "rise" in their title. Indeed, many of these volumes are also intended as university level teaching texts, although they are aimed equally at popular and specialist audiences. Some, such as Richard Bernstein and Ross Munro's *The Coming Conflict with China*, have generated considerable public attention and debate.[8] As the sensationalist title suggests, the authors see China's rise as an inherent challenge to the United States and other nations. Bernstein and Munro's volume was the first example of an emerging genre of "China threat" volumes that have appeared in recent years. These volumes are very polemical bearing sensationalist titles and should not be considered scholarly studies in any sense, yet they deserve mention here. This genre includes books by Bill Gertz, Edward Timberlake and William C. Triplett, Steven Mosher, and Ted Galen Carpenter.[9] A more thoughtful, yet still polemical, example is Ross Terrill's *The New Chinese Empire*.[10]

Michael Swaine and Ashley Tellis have authored a thoughtful study of China's "grand strategy," which wrestled with questions associated with the security implications of China's rise.[11] To probe this, they looked back in history to deduce China's ancient "grand strategy" and imperial statecraft. Not surprisingly, they found that China historically had employed and adopted a variety of stratagems – thus revealing the flexible and pragmatic essence of Chinese behavior. Nonetheless, they also argued that "an assertive China is likely to appear over the long haul," largely because the United States, as the established hegemon, will [appear to] frustrate China's rise."[12] This prediction awaits empirical validation.

One other recent volume by Avery Goldstein adopts a strongly theoretical approach by examining the applicability of various international relations theories to different aspects of China's rise and integration into the international order.[13] Goldstein further argues that China has a *de facto* "grand strategy" for managing its own rise and navigating the challenges that may challenge it. Goldstein's is a sophisticated and nuanced study that reflects the author's thorough reading of the literature (the footnotes alone are very worthwhile) as well as much careful thought that he gives to the various components of the issue.

Another recent example is the jointly authored and edited volume *China: The Balance Sheet*, a collaborative project by China specialists at the Center for Strategic and International Studies (Bates Gill and Derek Mitchell) and the Institute of International Economics (Nicholas Lardy).[14] This is a broad-gauged, detailed, forward-looking, and policy-relevant volume – *just* the kind of research that Washington D.C. think tanks *should* be doing instead of the superficial output described above that most now engage in.

The other volumes in the "China rise" category are all edited compendia. One contains articles previously published in the journal *International Security*,[15] and is one in a series of "readers" on different themes published jointly by the journal and MIT Press. It contains a series of high-quality contributions that focus both on China's elite perceptions and military capabilities, but also policy prescriptions for how the international community should handle China's rise. A second compendium, edited by Yong Deng and Fei-ling Wang, focuses primarily on the internal variables that will shape China's behavior in the international arena.[16] These include issues of identity and status, nationalism, perceptions, incentives, and other domestic "drivers" that shape and mediate China's external behavior. This is a very useful set of essays, many authored by Chinese scholars resident in the United States. The third, commissioned by the Cato Institute is a much less coherent and scholarly volume.[17]

A third category is *histories of Chinese Communist foreign policy*. There are five published studies in this category: one written by Michael Hunt, one co-edited by him,[18] one by Liu Xiaoyan, one by Xiaohong Liu, and one by Michael Sheng.[19] The edited volume by Hunt contains assessments by three PRC scholars of the three main actors in early Chinese Communist Party (CCP) foreign policy: Mao Zedong, Zhou Enlai, and Chen Yi. Three other chapters are interpretive in nature and attempt to draw predictive lessons from historical case studies for contemporary CCP foreign policy. Hunt's own monograph is a masterful overview of late imperial, republican, and communist era foreign relations. It excels in revealing the linkages between the domestic political and intellectual milieu and the reactions of successive Chinese regimes to external pressures and policy choices. The Liu volume is a study of China's ambassadorial corps since 1949, and is a fascinating inside account of the Chinese Foreign Ministry and its diplomats, but it also sheds light on a number of events as well.

A fourth category, related but distinct, is the vibrant sub-field of the *history of China and the Cold War*. Stimulated by the recently available materials emerging from the former Soviet Union and Eastern Europe, but also from China itself, this sector of the Chinese foreign policy field has been particularly active in recent years. The Cold War International History Project, based at the Woodrow Wilson International Center for Scholars, in conjunction with the National Security Archive at George Washington University, have done much to pioneer and catalyze this sub-field of scholarship. Several *émigré* scholars from China, now teaching in American universities, have been particularly active: e.g. Chen Jian,[20] Shu Guang Zhang,[21] and Qiang Zhai.[22] Their studies are all extremely rich and careful histories, full of new empirical evidence and fresh interpretations. The new Cold War data and histories have also afforded fruitful collaboration among scholars in China and those in the United States (and Europe). One fine example is a volume co-edited by Robert Ross and Jiang Changbin.[23] This is a very useful volume that pairs Chinese and American assessments of similar periods and subjects. This volume follows on to a similar earlier effort, edited by Harry Harding and Yuan Ming.[24] These kinds of collaboration among Chinese and foreign scholars that have occurred in the Cold War history sub-field is a model that could be fruitfully extended to other branches of Chinese foreign relations studies.

Other American scholars have been very active in the sub-field of China/Cold War studies. John Garver's excellent study of the U.S. relationship with the Chinese Nationalists (ChiNats) and their various joint operations against the Chinese Communists (ChiComs) is one such example. Another sterling example of what can be done with oral history is Nancy Bernkopf Tucker's *China Confidential*.[25] In it, Tucker skillfully interweaves her own astute analysis with interview transcripts with virtually all the key diplomats that have dealt with China issues over a half century. The result is a rich and novel reference volume that should be mandatory reading for all in the field of Sino-American relations. Similarly, Thomas Christensen's study of Sino-American relations from 1947–1958 is the key study of this period.[26]

A fifth category concerns the *policy making process of China's foreign policy*. The signal contribution in this category is David Lampton's edited volume *The Making of China's Foreign and Security Policy*.[27] This thick volume (500+ pages) contains chapters on the roles and influence of central-level institutions, provinces, the military, the "third generation" of party leaders, public opinion, international regimes, as well as several case studies (World Trade Organization accession, nonproliferation, Taiwan, and Korea policy). This is a commendable volume, suitable for graduate-level teaching, which updates previous studies by A. Doak Barnett and Lu Ning,[28] but it is curiously lacking in its consideration of the role of Chinese think tanks and research institutes in the foreign and security policy process (which are known to play an increasing role). This was the subject of a symposium of articles in *The China Quarterly* (September 2002),[29] as well as a chapter by Quansheng Zhao in an edited volume on *China's Foreign Policy Making: Societal Forces and China's America Policy*. This volume, published in 2006 and edited by Yufan Hao and Lin Su, has a less institutional focus than the Lampton volume, and contains interesting chapters by Chinese émigré authors on Chinese elite perceptions, the role of the Chinese media, the role of the internet, the role of nationalism, the impact of civil society, the role of intellectuals, think tanks, the influence of coastal provinces, and other domestic societal factors that in part shape and condition the making of China's foreign policy today.[30]

The sixth category of studies is *Chinese perceptions of international affairs in general, and the United States in particular.* Yong Deng and Fei-ling Wang edited a very useful general survey of Chinese perceptions of world affairs, with contributions written by émigré scholars in the U.S.,[31] which updates a previous effort edited by Yufan Hao and Guocang Huan.[32] Peter Gries has also authored a fine study of the impact of nationalism and national identity on China's worldview and foreign relations, particularly with respect to Japan and the United States.[33] Finally, Allen Carlson has authored a fascinating study of changing Chinese perceptions of, and policy approaches to, sovereignty in its foreign relationships.[34] Through a variety of case studies, Carlson shows how much China's most sacred and cherished national value has evolved as a result of contact with the international community.

The bulk of perception studies over the past decade have focused on mutual images of the U.S. and China. On the American side of the dyad, two studies have been published over the past decade. Richard Madsen's study exposes what he describes as the "liberal myth" that Americans have long adopted in their perceptions of China, i.e. the attempt to remake China in the American image, to project this aspiration on to China, and thus to view events in China against this transposition. As such, Madsen's astute study shows that such perceptions reveal more about America and Americans than about China and Chinese.[35] T. Christopher

Jesperson reveals similar themes in his study of American images of China during the Republican era (1931–1949) and particularly the role played by the American media and Henry Luce.[36] While not specifically about contemporary Chinese foreign relations, Jesperson's study is quite germane to understanding later and current U.S. perceptions of China.

The remaining books in this category examine Chinese and American images of each other interactively. Carola McGiffert has recently edited two companion conference volumes – one dealing with U.S. images of China and the other vice versa.[37] Oddly, the latter is the only book to appear on Chinese perceptions of America since my *Beautiful Imperialist* (a subject that remains ripe for updated research).[38] These twin volumes are very useful for teaching purposes and contain a number of insightful essays. Li Hongshan and Zhaohui Hong edited a volume with contributions written by émigré scholars, which lacks thematic coherence but nonetheless contains a number of interesting essays on U.S. media coverage of China.[39] Finally, Wang Jianwei has undertaken the most sophisticated and scholarly assessment of mutual images. Using survey research and focus group interviews, and informed by cognitive psychology, his work is a methodological model for subsequent studies.[40]

The seventh category is studies of *China's role in international institutions and regimes*. There are not many books recently published on this subject, although the periodical literature is larger. There is one fine study by Wendy Frieman of China's participation in arms control regimes (which is discussed below in the next section), while part of the Lampton volume on decision making (discussed above) contains some case studies and two general essays, but the broadest study is one edited by Elizabeth Economy and the late Michel Oksenberg.[41] This excellent volume contains chapter case studies on China's behavior in the United Nations, arms control institutions, international human rights agencies, international trade and investment regimes, and international financial institutions (IFIs).

The final category is studies of *China's bilateral and regional relationships*. This is the largest of all the categories, with studies of China and Asia;[42] China and the Koreas;[43] China and Vietnam;[44] China and India;[45] China and Russia;[46] the China–Japan–U.S. triangle;[47] and China and Taiwan.[48] By far, the greatest number of studies in this category has concerned U.S.–China relations. Several fine edited volumes have appeared,[49] while major monographs have been authored by Robert Ross, James Mann, David M. Lampton, Robert Suettinger, and Patrick Tyler.[50]

As is evident from the above survey, the study of China's foreign relations is thriving. This is even truer if one includes journal articles. Cumulatively, they reveal that the field has begun to move in some new directions over the past decade. Three of the eight categories surveyed above are relatively new: studies of China's "rise," the role of China in the Cold War, and China's behavior in international institutions. The other five categories have continuity with pre-1995 studies, although they are more recent and based on new materials.

To be sure, the literature has generated and reflected debates and controversy in the field. Examples include: the degree to which China is assimilating into international society and organizations; whether its participation in international regimes is tactical or represents real socialization and "learning"; whether China's nationalism is becoming more "confident" or more acerbic and "defensive"; whether China's diplomatic engagement of Asia is motivated by short-term tactics to pacify the periphery or long-term strategy to establish regional hegemony; whether China is a "status quo" or "revisionist" power; whether other nations (particularly in Asia) are "balancing against" or "bandwagoning with" China; whether China understands and uses "soft power" in its foreign relations; whether China will use its "hard (military) power" to coerce its neighbors; whether domestic society influences foreign policymaking or whether the process remains controlled by government organs and senior leaders; whether China–Japan relations are in an inexorable downward spiral or can be stabilized; whether the U.S.–China relationship is strategically cooperative or competitive; and whether China is a "threat" or not? These and other issues have animated debates in the Chinese foreign policy field in recent years.

Where might the field go in coming years? What needs to be done? Thomas Christensen, Iain Johnston, and Robert Ross have contributed a very thoughtful essay that calls for a number of new possible areas of inquiry.[51] They note, in particular, that the field should further explore:

- China's use of force;
- Chinese crisis behavior;
- the impact of the "security dilemma;"
- Chinese attitudes towards spheres of influence;
- the impact of public opinion on Chinese foreign policy and decision making (an area that Johnston himself is pioneering);
- Decision making strategies and habits;
- the personalities of the individuals who make foreign policy decisions, and their "rationality;"
- the impact of nationalism;
- the impact of economic interdependence on the potential for conflict (presumably as a constraint);
- the evolution of China's interaction with international institutions over time;
- the impact of domestic political change (or lack thereof);
- the role of energy security on China's foreign relationships;
- the impact of demographic changes;
- the internalization of international norms;
- the effect of the Chinese *diaspora*;
- the effects of China's regions and provinces;
- the impact of race and ethnicity;
- the impact of identity, status concerns, and belief systems;
- explicit comparisons with the foreign relations of other similar developing and newly-industrialized nations;
- the use of new and various social science methodologies to the study of Chinese foreign relations.

This is a valuable and thoughtful list of topics to explore, with which I largely concur and to which I have little further to add. I would only offer the following additional suggestions:

- Produce a compendium of key primary documents on Chinese foreign policy (White Papers, leadership speeches, Foreign Ministry statements, etc.) in recent years. This would be very useful for teaching purposes, as students are insufficiently exposed to such primary materials, and how the Chinese government views and articulates its own foreign policy, and they are overexposed to Western interpretations of Chinese foreign policy.
- Undertake additional and detailed monographic studies of China's regional relationships with Europe, Africa, the Middle East, Latin America, and Africa. There have been fine book-length studies published on China–Asia published in 2005,[52] but no studies of China's interactions with these other regions have been undertaken for many years (although there are some journal articles available).[53] Fortunately, there are several excellent recently completed or soon to be published studies of China's key bilateral relationships with South Korea,[54] India,[55] Iran,[56] Russia,[57] Vietnam,[58] and the United States,[59] but similar focused monographs are needed on China–Japan, China–UK, and China–Canada relations.
- Undertake a book-length study of the Chinese Foreign Ministry, foreign embassy operations, and current diplomatic corps.
- Undertake an updated study of the Chinese intelligence system.[60]
- Undertake a new and updated study of China's behavior and roles in the United Nations, updating Samuel Kim's book of 26 years ago.[61]
- Push China/Cold War studies out of the 1950s and more into the 1960s–1980s.
- Using newly available Chinese materials and interviews, offer retrospective explanations (in article length assessments) of key "strategic debates" in China, e.g. the 1978 decision to attack Vietnam; the 1982 "independent foreign policy" decision; the 1985–86 decision to seek *rapprochement* with the Soviet Union; the post-June 4, 1989 decision on how to deal with the United States; the 1991 decision on to approach the new post-Soviet governments in Russia and Central Asia; the early-1990s decision to open and build relations with South Korea; a host of decisions on dealing with Taiwan post-1995; the 1997–98 decision on the proactive engagement of ASEAN and Asian multilateral institutions; the 1999 "peace and development" debate; the 2003–05 "peaceful rise" debate; the 2004 decision to become more involved in U.N. peacekeeping operations (PKO); the 2004–05 decisions on how to handle North Korea and the Six Party Talks; the 2005 decision on how to handle the anti-Japan demonstrations and relations with Japan; and other such key decision points in China's foreign relations.

- More assessments of the role and influence of think tanks, universities, and other non-governmental actors in the Chinese foreign policy deliberation and policy making process.
- Undertake "cognitive mapping" studies of Chinese political and foreign policy elites.
- Assessments of misperceptions and miscalculations by Chinese leaders, in which they have misread international situations and acted irrationally.[62]
- Assessments of the role of the PLA in foreign policy (even if greatly diminished, it still presumably exists at some levels);
- Assessments of the role of economic and energy interests in China's foreign policy calculations and relations.
- Assessments of the utility (or non-utility) of international relations and comparative foreign policy theories to the study of Chinese foreign policy.
- Assessments of China's human rights diplomacy.
- Assessments of the role of public health in China's foreign policy.
- Assessments of China's impact on the Asian regional system *qua* system.[63]
- Synthesized overviews of China's foreign relations to supplement those recent studies noted in footnote 7 and the 1994 volume edited by the late Thomas Robinson and myself.[64]

Given this menu and the aforementioned list of suggestions offered by Christensen, Johnston, and Ross, the future research agenda for the field is both rich and varied. This is a sign both of the varied nature of China's interactions with the world today, but also the scholarly health of the field. Much important work has been done over the past decade (even more so if one includes the periodical literature and studies done outside the U.S.), but there are clearly many new promising subjects and areas of China's foreign relations left to be explored. Many of the above suggested topics could be fruitfully undertaken in collaboration with scholars in China.

Trends in Recent Scholarship on Chinese Security and Military Affairs

Chinese security and military studies have come a long way. More progress has been made over the past decade than in the previous four combined. More and more work is being done on China's security (regional security, energy security, security calculus, etc.), and the general knowledge and information base among specialists on the People's Liberation Army (PLA) is very impressive. Several assessments of China's security calculations have been published. There have also been several comprehensive studies of the PLA published, as well as informed studies of all services (ground, air, naval, and nuclear); civil–military relations; the officer corps; doctrine and strategy; defense policy decision making; the organization of the PLA High Command; China's national security environment and threat perceptions; military finance and budgeting; the military-industrial complex; arms sales and purchases; a wide variety of weapons systems and capabilities; logistics and various "software" issues; and other subjects. Books published on the PLA and Chinese security fall into three general categories: conference volume compendia, comprehensive studies, and specialized studies.

The *conference compendia* that have emanated from the annual U.S. Army War College Strategic Studies Institute/American Enterprise Institute/Heritage Foundation partnership,[65] the Rand/CNA,[66] and Rand/CAPS partnerships,[67] have been particularly important boosts to the field. The Institute for National Strategic Studies of the National Defense University a published a similar conference volume,[68] as did *The China Quarterly*.[69] These are difficult volumes to summarize because, as is the case with all edited conference volumes, they contain multiple chapters on various topics. Nonetheless, the organizers of these conferences and editors of these volumes are to be credited with thematically organizing each year's conference volume (the themes are evident in footnotes 65–67). In general, the Rand/CNA and Rand/CAPS volumes have been more tightly focused and more thoroughly vetted and edited – as a result the overall quality of these volumes are higher. The *People's Liberation Army as Organization* is a particularly noteworthy accomplishment, as the internal organization of the PLA has never before been dissected and discussed in such detail. The *Seeking Truth from Facts* volume is also an excellent state-of-the field of PLA studies retrospective assessment. The individual chapters and commentaries therein represent not only the most thorough overview of the field that has been done, but also offers a critical self-reflection and self-assessment of what the field got right and why, and where it went wrong in its assessments of the PLA from the 1970s–1990s. Both of these are model volumes, and owe their authoritativeness in no small part to the conceptualization and editorship of James Mulvenon. As previously noted, the SSI/AEI/Heritage volumes have been more eclectic and wide-ranging in their coverage. While each of the ten volumes in the series (to date) has tried to focus on a single broad theme, the coverage of the individual chapters has been more wide-ranging. Taken together, these conference volumes have literally pushed the field into new directions and have contributed a great deal to forging the field itself. They have also produced extremely enjoyable (if sometimes contentious) retreats and debates, and have helped to foster collegiality in the field.

The second category has been *comprehensive studies of the Chinese military*, three of which have been published over the last decade: one by myself, one by Mel Gurtov and Byong-Moo Hwang, and one by a team of Rand Corporation researchers.[70] These three volumes have many similarities, but also some differences.

Both the Shambaugh and Gurtov/Hwang volumes have chapters on civil–military relations, military expenditures and the role of the military in business, the military-industrial establishment, military doctrine and strategy, and China's national security environment. My study also examines patterns in PLA training, command and control in the armed forces, PLA force structure and the individual services (ground, air, naval, and missile forces), and China's military exchanges with the United States. Its principal value is in the detailed depictions of PLA organization, finance, weaponry, and the impact of professionalism on the entire institution. While focusing on the Chinese military, Gurtov and Hwang's study is more broadly focused on China's broad security environment and policy. It also links security policy to foreign policy, and even contains an analysis of China's arms control policies. For its part, the Rand study concentrates on the financial and industrial dimensions of PLA modernization. It contains a sophisticated discussion of the military expenditure conundrum, but also links this to broader trends and expectations in China's national economic development. The chapter on defense industrial development is also rich in detail and judicious in its assessments. More than the other two studies, the Rand volume is more forward-looking in nature, as it tries to assess and predict what financial and industrial resources will be available to the PLA in the future and how these resources match potential contingencies. All three studies draw on a range of sources, although the Shambaugh and Rand studies use more Chinese materials.

In addition to these three monographs, the Council on Foreign Relations produced a short but significant study in 2003 that assesses the overall state of PLA modernization.[71] The task force was comprised of the leading experts on the Chinese military and security affairs in the United States, who met over the course of a year to explore and debate the modernization of the Chinese military. The resulting CFR task force report examined the underlying sources and drivers of the program, the observable consequences of the program, and a series of indicators to monitor and evaluate future progress in military modernization.

All of these comprehensive studies come to similar conclusions about the state of PLA modernization:

- That military modernization begins from a relatively low base.
- It is making incremental and steady progress, and is not engaged in a "crash program" or buildup.
- It remains 10–20 years behind European, American, or Russian standards in most conventional weaponry.
- It has achieved a strong "niche capability" in ballistic missiles.
- It is building capabilities particularly with Taiwan (and the U.S.) in mind.
- It is placing as much, if not more, emphasis on "software" professionalism (recruitment, training, logistics, education, etc.) than "hardware" modernization (weaponry).
- It is investing significant financial resources in the military.
- It is working to overcome bottlenecks and impediments in the military-industrial complex.

All three volumes offer good "one-stop shopping" overviews of the Chinese military today.

The final category is *specialized studies of different aspects of Chinese security and military affairs*. These, in turn, fall into eight separate sub-categories.

The first are studies of the PLA's *use of force*. Several scholars have undertaken to study how the PLA has historically employed force, both before and after 1949. Two volumes, one single-authored by Andrew Scobell and one edited by Mark Ryan, David Finkelstein, and Michael McDevitt, examine multiple case studies in an attempt to identify patterns of Chinese crisis management and warfighting.[72] Both of these are particularly strong volumes, using comparative analysis of multiple conflicts, and taken together offer a comprehensive assessment of how the PLA has prosecuted wars under different conditions with different adversaries since 1949. Both are extremely well researched and detailed in their data (much of it coming from Chinese sources). Gary Bjorge has also contributed a detailed assessment of the PLA's strategy and tactics in the famous Huai Hai campaign of 1948.[73] A team of Rand Corporation researchers has also contributed a short study of China's potential use of force based on past "patterns" (although the emphasis of the volume is more on the future than the past).[74] Needless to say, no single and predictable "pattern" emerges from these various case studies – if anything they find that the PLA was quite flexible and adaptable in both strategy and tactics depending on the campaign and enemy.

A second, and related, category concerns Chinese "strategic culture." To a limited extent the Scobell book just discussed engages this subject, as does the Swaine/Tellis volume noted in the previous section,[75] but by far the most significant study of this kind is Alastair Iain Johnston's *Cultural Realism*.[76] Strong in theory, methodology, and data, Johnston's sophisticated study attempts to draw contemporary lessons from the classic texts of Chinese strategic thought (*bing shu*) from the Ming period; it is truly path-breaking and his findings are indeed sobering. He finds, in the data he examined, what he describes as "a *parabellum* or hard *realpolitik* strategic culture that, in essence, argues that the best way of dealing with security threats is to eliminate them through the use of force." But, he continues, "This preference is tempered by an explicit sensitivity to one's relative capacity to do this."[77] As capabilities increase, Johnston argues, so too does the propensity to use force to resolve differences among Chinese or with outsiders. While the past is never a precise guide to the present or the future, Johnston's study does give one pause when considering China's increasing military capabilities and its possible use of force in the future.

A third set of specialized studies examines China's *military-industrial complex*. Two of the studies examine China's strategic weapons (i.e. nuclear weapons) programs. Building on their earlier study of China's atomic bomb program,[78] John Lewis and Xue Litai co-authored a study of China's strategic nuclear submarine (SSBN) program.[79] Both studies are extremely rich and detailed assessments of how the PLA concentrated resources in order to achieve these two key strategic breakthroughs in weapons development, against the backdrop of a military-industrial complex that was otherwise backward and bureaucratic. The combination of concentrated resources, high-level political support, and a protected research environment that produced the breakthroughs portrayed in the Lewis and Xue volumes is also the theme of Evan Feigenbaum's study of what he describes as China's "techno-warriors."[80] Feigenbaum was Lewis' Ph.D. student at Stanford, and their three studies are reinforcing assessments. All three combine a political scientist's instincts for a political/bureaucratic story with a China specialist's feel for the data (much of the data is very unique) and security specialists' understanding of military equipment. These are commendable studies that establish a high standard for others who work on China's defense industries and the politics of military modernization.

Two other monographs that fall into this general category is the study by Bates Gill and Taeho Kim of China's arms purchases abroad,[81] and the study by James Mulvenon of the commercialization of China's military-industrial complex.[82] These monographs are all pioneering case studies. The former offers a detailed inventory of China's purchases from the former Soviet Union, Russia, Israel, and other sources. While they note that China has engaged in such imports in order to offset dire deficiencies in its own indigenous defense industries, they also reveal much about the assimilation (and difficulties therein) of foreign weaponry and defense technologies into the PLA. This volume offers a good counterpart to Gill's earlier study of China's own arms transfers abroad.[83] Mulvenon's study, like that done by British scholar Tai Ming Cheung,[84] offers a thorough and engaging exposé of the progressive commercialization of the Chinese military – what he describes as the "military-business complex." Starting from its involvement in tertiary industries and growing its own grain during the 1950s–1970s, the PLA expanded its commercial tentacles and interests into virtually every significant sector of the economy during the 1980s–1990s, prior to the divestiture order of 1998. Mulvenon (and Cheung) traces this extraordinary story in great detail, exposing activities and linkages probably unknown even to the Chinese military itself!

A fourth set of specialized studies concerns *China's arms control policies and behavior*. Two monograph-length assessments have been completed on this subject. The first was a task force report undertaken by the Council on Foreign Relations,[85] which focused particularly on how the United States and China's interests in this area intersected. The other, by Wendy Frieman, was considerably more detailed and scholarly.[86] Frieman's study is a real *tour d'force* and *tour d'horizon* of the subject. Its comprehensive approach contains individual chapters on China's participation and behavior in the Nonproliferation Treaty, International Atomic Energy Agency, Comprehensive Test Ban Treaty, Biological Weapons Convention, Chemical Weapons Convention, Missile Technology Control Regime, U.N. Register of Conventional Arms, and Convention on Conventional Weapons. It also includes an illuminating and careful assessment of China's internal bureaucracy and decision-making process concerning these issues, based on her considerable interaction with this community. Frieman finds considerable evidence of adaptation and learning on China's part, as it grows more and more comfortable participating in, and becoming a stakeholder of, such regimes. It is a commendable study that shows expertise not only on China's roles in these regimes, but also in the regimes themselves. A third careful study of China's arms control policy is forthcoming by Evan Medeiros.[87]

A fifth set of specialized PLA studies are of *the individual services: ground, air, naval, and missile forces*. A decade ago, Kenneth Allen (the dean of PLA Air Force studies), Glenn Krumel, and Jonathan Pollack provided a detailed assessment of the PLAAF for the Rand Corporation.[88] While now dated, this study still provides a thorough history and contemporary assessment of the PLAAF as an institution (including training, education, leadership, and force modernization). In 1999 U.S. Air Force Lt. Colonel Mark Stokes wrote a very detailed and dense study of China's missile forces – the Second Artillery – and aerospace program.[89] Not a study for the casual observer interested in Chinese missiles, Stokes' mastery of his subject and sources could hardly be more thorough. Bernard Cole has authored an equally definitive account of the PLA Navy (the PLAN).[90] Written more accessibly than the Stokes study, Cole's study is more of a parallel to the aforementioned study of the PLA Air Force. It offers a judicious assessment and up-to-date information on the PLAN's inventory (both surface and sub-surface); its personnel, training, and education infrastructure; its doctrine and maritime strategy; and the strategic interests and rationale for building up the naval forces. While the PLAN is one of the fastest changing of the military services, Cole's study provides a comprehensive baseline by which to measure future growth and modernization. It will be the standard in the field for some time to come. Finally, Dennis Blasko has authored a similarly thorough study of the PLA ground forces.[91] While being the definitive study of PLA ground forces, Blasko's study illuminates numerous other aspects of China's military modernization program. In all four cases – Allen, Stokes, Cole, and Blasko – these authors bring years of professional knowledge, as well as careers in the United States military, to bear on their subjects. None know their subjects better and their books provide important benchmarks for the field in the future.

A sixth category of studies are Michael Pillsbury's companion volumes *Chinese Views of Future Warfare* and *China Debates the Future Security Environment.*[92] Pillsbury has done the field of Chinese security studies a great service by exposing internal PLA debates concerning these two subjects. The former is a compendium of translated writings by Chinese military officers with no annotation or analysis by Pillsbury (excepting a preface and prologue). Pillsbury allows PLA officers to speak for themselves, and their perspectives on the "revolution in military affairs" are both prescient and illuminating. Almost a decade later, we see the PLA pursuing many of the capabilities outlined in the writings in this volume. In the latter volume, Pillsbury brings his own interpretive analysis to bear on a broad spectrum of writings by Chinese security specialists – both military and civilian. This assessment probes deeply into the Chinese internal discourse and brings to light some disturbing ideas that circulate in that community: the United States and Russia are seen as in progressive decline, the potential threats from Japan and India are rising, while the trend towards global multipolarity is in abeyance. Pillsbury also argues that three schools of thought exist within the PLA: people's war, local war, and the RMA schools. Pillsbury sees the latter as in the ascent and advocating the acquisition of various types of asymmetrical weapons.

The seventh category concerns *civil–military relations.* Two forthcoming volumes fall into this category.[93]

The eighth and final category of studies concerns the *PLA's foreign relations and U.S.–China strategic relations.* Ken Allen and Eric McVadon authored the first such study of China's military diplomacy.[94] This long-neglected subject deserves attention and the authors explore, in considerable detail, the PLA's rapidly growing involvement in both bilateral military exchanges as well as in multilateral activities. Two other studies, also carried out under the auspices of the Henry L. Stimson Center, examine security exchanges with China. One is focused exclusively on the issue of bilateral U.S.–China strategic dialogue, particularly concerning missile defense issue,[95] while the other examines U.S.–China–Japan strategic dialogue and interactions.[96] Finally, one recent Rand study takes account of the U.S.–China military exchange relationship.[97]

While the above survey is a good indication of how far the China security and PLA studies field in the United States has come over the past decade, the knowledge base is far from sufficient and there is still much work to be done. Moreover, the field is "shooting at a moving target" that is evolving and changing rapidly. Yet certain gaps in knowledge can be identified and certain suggestions can be offered for future research. What needs to be done?[98] There are a number of possibilities.

In my view, despite the very useful and generally comprehensive volume edited by James Mulvenon and Andrew N.D. Yang,[99] a careful "institutional mapping" of key PLA organizations and command and control procedures is still needed. We really do not have a clear sense of how the general departments, group armies, and regional commands are internally organized, function, and interrelate with each other. We also need to know more about how battlefield training and tactics are evolving, and how the services are adapting to the new doctrine of "the RMA with Chinese characteristics."

Notwithstanding two recently published edited volumes,[100] civil–military relations remain a "black hole" for researchers. The dynamics of post-Deng civil–military relations are not well understood. We work with woefully inadequate data, and are forced to speculate often beyond what hard evidence can sustain. Nascent signs of increased state control over the armed forces, with concomitant autonomy from the party, needs to be monitored carefully. With wholesale turnover in the officer corps and in the High Command taking place in recent years, we are confronted with a completely new generation about whom we are very poorly informed. Much more information needs to be gained about the socialization, training, and interrelationships in the upper echelons of this new generation of officers and military leaders. We may have a relatively clear understanding of the PLA's perceptual worldview and strategic outlook, but that is not the same as understanding intentions and how a military will act in a given crisis. Hence, we need to know how the PLA prepares for certain contingencies involving North Korea, Japan, Taiwan, India, the United States, and the South and East China Seas.

We know that the military-industrial complex has been handicapped historically, but it seems to be making significant progress in several areas since the creation of the General Armaments Department in 1998, and subsequent reforms undertaken by the GAD. We also have a very poor sense of the linkage between research and development, exactly why certain systems never make it to or past the prototype stage, and a whole range of issues related to systems integration and assimilation of technology. Indeed, we need to gain a clearer sense of the interaction of technology, procurement, doctrine, and strategy. Does doctrine drive procurement decisions, or how do technological impediments constrain doctrine and strategy? How are decisions made on what to buy abroad, and what assimilation problems are the PLA experiencing in the systems it has bought from Russia and other sources?

Is strategy driven by threat perception and possible contingencies, or do a wider set of variables affect the calculus? How does doctrine affect strategy, and vice versa? What is the PLA's "calculus of deterrence" (to borrow Allen Whiting's original phrase), and what is its real warfighting doctrine? What role, if any, do tactical nuclear weapons and other forms of WMD play in warfighting doctrine and exercises? Is China reconsidering its nuclear policy of "No First Use" and moving towards a doctrine of "launch on warning" (LOW)? What will the force structure look like in five years' time, after further downsizing, equipment retirement, and demobilizations? Is there a clear vision on where the PLA seeks to be five, ten, fifteen, and twenty years into the future?

In terms of the PLA's foreign relations, we need to gain a much better grip on where the PLA is going, why, what they learn abroad, and what foreign military delegations come to China. While foreign military exchanges perform important symbolic functions, as part of China's general diplomacy, they are increasing geared to substantive learning and exchanges. This needs to be much better understood, with perhaps an international data base compiled (by SIPRI or IISS?) on such exchanges.

These questions are just the tip of the iceberg. There is much that we need to know. In particular, the field needs to benefit from cross-fertilization with others, i.e.:

- more input from the government intelligence and military communities and cross-fertilization with non-government scholars and analysts;
- more and continued input from retired military, particularly those with first-hand experience in China;
- more input from, and interaction with, PLA "scholars" and officers in China;
- more Chinese émigrés to enter the field;
- more doctoral dissertations being written and young scholars being encouraged into the field;
- more comprehensive assessments of the PLA that begin to piece back together the pieces of the puzzle that have been disaggregated in recent years;
- more attempts to theorize about the PLA based on *comparative* studies of other militaries;
- more thought to be given on how to "engage" the PLA and shape a coherent long-term strategy for coexisting with the PLA.

As noted above, the PLA studies field also tends to operate in a vacuum – even from mainstream studies of Chinese security studies. It needs to be much better integrated with other academic sub-fields:

- wed PLA studies to the broader study of Chinese bureaucratic politics and institutional culture;
- wed PLA studies to broader theories of technological innovation, change, and diffusion;
- wed PLA studies to the study of the military during the Republican period (1911–49) and in some areas to the imperial period, and engage in dialogue with historians of these periods;
- wed PLA studies to comparative military studies and the study of civil–military relations, particularly in East Asian and communist systems, where there are multiple instructive comparisons to be made;
- wed PLA studies better to debates in post-Cold War strategic studies, e.g. the impact of globalization, technology and information diffusion, economic security, and a variety of aspects of non-conventional security;
- wed PLA studies to development theory, particularly in the area of technology absorption, specialization and role differentiation.

I stress that these are just some random suggestions, but their thrust is that the field is too insular and can benefit from some comparative perspectives.

The study of Chinese security and the PLA is a dynamic field, growing rapidly intellectually and analytically. We may complain about the lack of PLA transparency (rightfully so), but we can no longer grumble about insufficient data and research materials. But we need to learn how to better exploit these new materials and gain bibliographic control over them. We also need to reflect collectively on our past scholarship and analysis, to ascertain where we were right and where we were wrong and why.

Conclusion

It should be apparent from the above survey that the study of China's foreign relations and security/military policy is alive and thriving in the United States. There has been much progress made in each of these sub-fields over the past decade and, as the aforementioned suggested future research agendas reflect, there is much promising work still to be done. The demand for such informed analysis is high and growing in the United States, but fortunately so too is the supply of trained and knowledgeable experts. While there has been an influx of new younger scholars entering the field over the past decade, there will be keen demand for more (particularly in Chinese security studies) in years to come.

As has been evident in some of the Chinese foreign policy studies that have emerged over the past decade, this sub-field is beginning to communicate and interact better with mainstream international relations theorists.[101] This is healthy, and we may begin to see IR theorists increasing using China as a case study in their broader work – as has increasingly been the case for political scientists studying comparative politics over the past decade.

As noted at the outset, political science departments across the United States are beginning to create distinct faculty positions for specialists in China's foreign relations. This too is healthy, although a parallel effort needs to be made with respect to those specializing in Chinese security and military studies. This, however, is part and parcel of the identity of security policy studies and role of area studies in this sub-field. Although *International Security*, *Security Studies*, and *Survival* have all begun to publish increasing numbers of articles on China in recent years (a trend that is to be warmly welcomed), unfortunately the academic field more broadly in the United States remains very ambivalent about area sub-system and country-specific security studies. This needs to change.

We have also witnessed an influx of Chinese émigré scholars in the field. This too is healthy (although more are needed in the security/military sub-field).

Another heartening trend is in the publishing industry, as a number of leading university and trade publishers are seeking out and publishing books in these sub-fields. Stanford University Press, University of California Press, University of Washington Press, Columbia University Press, Cornell University Press, and others have all published major studies in the field in recent years. Trade publishers, such as Rowman & Littlefield, M.E. Sharpe, W.W. Norton, and RoutledgeCurzon, have done the same. However, these publishers (particularly university publishers) are increasingly making decisions about accepting manuscripts for publication based primarily on their (financial) bottom line: potential sales. Unfortunately, the reality is that scholarly erudition is not a key criterion in their calculations – they are under enormous and increasing pressure to be profitable in a shrinking and highly competitive marketplace. This is an important point for authors (and Ph.D. supervisors) to bear in mind, i.e. the study must have broad public, policy, and student appeal. Publishers simply cannot recoup their investments based on hardback sales, and require one or more paperback printings to turn a (modest) profit.

Finally, I noted at the outset that the sub-field of Chinese foreign policy studies and the sub-field of Chinese security and military studies are really quite separate communities of scholars and analysts – in terms of those involved in each, the analytical questions being posed, the empirical data being used, and the theoretical perspectives being drawn upon. If I can conclude this assessment with one clarion call, it is for these two sub-field communities to enter into real dialogue with each other. They are "first cousins" and should be communicating with one another. Moreover, those working in each sub-field needs to "cross over" and undertake some studies in the other area. This is not actually as easy as it sounds, because each has its own paradigms, data sets, predispositions, and peculiarities. For example, as I personally had to learn (quite literally), the study of the Chinese military requires deep grounding in understanding military weapons systems, technologies, strategies and doctrines, training regimens, theories of civil–military relations, and so on. PLA studies is *not* a field that can easily be "parachuted" into and easily mastered; it takes years of exposure and learning to master the generic (i.e. non-China) intricacies of these issues. Similarly, the study of China's foreign relations has its *lacunae* that require mastery. But it is time that these two communities began a direct dialogue, organize conferences together, and cross over to do research (even collaborative) in the other sub-field – thus reducing over time, and eventually eliminating, the divide that currently exists between the study of Chinese foreign and security/military policy in the United States.

Notes

1 Paul H.B. Godwin and Robert Ross, "New Directions in Chinese Security Studies," in David Shambaugh (ed.), *American Studies of Contemporary China* (Armonk, NY: M.E. Sharpe, 1993).
2 Apologies in advance to colleagues for any inadvertent oversights and mischaracterizations. Comments and reactions are most welcome.
3 One can survey many of the major monographs on Chinese politics over the years – from Franz Schurmann's *Ideology and Organization in Communist China* to Roderick MacFarquhar's edited *Chinese Politics* – and find scant attention paid to the PLA either as an actor in the political process or as an institution worthy of attention in its own right. I have attempted to rectify this in our understanding of the pre-Cultural Revolution period; see David Shambaugh, "The Building of the Civil-Military State in China, 1949–1965: Bringing the Soldier Back In," in Timothy Cheek and Tony Saich (eds), *The Construction of State Socialism in China, 1949–1965* (Armonk, NY: M.E. Sharpe, 1997).
4 Suisheng Zhao (ed.), *Chinese Foreign Policy: Pragmatism and Strategic Behavior* (Armonk, NY: M.E. Sharpe, 2004); Guoli Liu (ed.), *Chinese Foreign Policy in Transition* (New York: Aldine DeGruyter, 2004).
5 Alastair Iain Johnston and Robert S. Ross (eds), *New Directions in the Study of China's Foreign Policy* (Stanford, CA: Stanford University Press, 2006).
6 Quansheng Zhao, *Interpreting Chinese Foreign Policy* (Hong Kong: Oxford University Press, 1996).
7 Andrew Nathan and Robert S. Ross, *The Great Wall and the Empty Fortress: China's Search for Security* (New York: W.W. Norton, 1997); Denny Roy, *China's Foreign Relations* (Lanham, MD: Rowman & Littlefield, 1998); Robert G. Sutter, *Chinese Policy Priorities and Their Implications for the United States* (Lanham, MD: Rowman & Littlefield, 2000).
8 Richard Bernstein and Ross H. Munro, *The Coming Conflict with China* (New York: Knopf, 1997).
9 Bill Gertz, *The China Threat: How the People's Republic Targets America* (Washington, D.C.: Regnery, 2000); Edward Timberlake and William C. Triplett II, *Red Dragon Rising: Communist China's Military Threat to America* (Washington, D.C.: Regnery, 1999); Timberlake and Triplett, *Year of the Rat: How Bill Clinton Compromised U.S. Security for Chinese Cash* (Washington, D.C.: Regnery, 1998); Steven W. Mosher, *Hegemon: China's Plan to Dominate Asia and the World* (San Francisco, CA: Encounter Books, 2000); Ted Galen Carpenter, *America's Coming War with China* (London: Palgrave Macmillan, 2006).
10 Ross Terrill, *The New Chinese Empire and What it Means for the United States* (New York: Basic Books, 2003).
11 Michael D. Swaine and Ashley J. Tellis, *Interpreting China's Grand Strategy: Past, Present, and Future* (Santa Monica, CA: Rand Corporation, 2000).
12 Ibid, p. 233.
13 Avery Goldstein, *Rising to the Challenge: China's Grand Strategy and International Security* (Stanford, CA: Stanford University Press, 2005).
14 CSIS and Institute of International Economics (eds), *China: The Balance Sheet – What the World Needs to Know About the Emerging Superpower* (New York: Public Affairs, 2006).
15 Michael E. Brown *et al.* (eds), *The Rise of China* (Cambridge, MA: MIT Press, 2000).

16 Yong Deng and Fei-ling Wang (eds), *China Rising: Power and Motivation in Chinese Foreign Policy* (Lanham, MD: Rowman & Littlefield, 2005).

17 Ted Galen Carpenter and James A. Dorn (eds), *China's Future: Constructive Partner or Emerging Threat?* (Washington, D.C.: Cato Institute, 2000).

18 Michael Hunt and Niu Jun (eds), *Chinese Communist Foreign Relations, 1920s–1960s* (Washington, D.C.: Asia Program of the Woodrow Wilson International Center for Scholars, n.d.); Michael Hunt, *The Genesis of Chinese Communist Foreign Policy* (New York: Columbia University Press, 1996). Also see Liu Xiaoyan, *Frontier Passages: Enthnopolitics and the Rise of Chinese Communism, 1921–1945* (Stanford, CA: Stanford University Press, 2004); and Michael Sheng, *Battling Western Imperialism: Mao, Stalin, and the United States* (Princeton, NJ: Princeton University Press, 1997).

19 Xiaohong Liu, *Chinese Ambassadors: The Rise of Diplomatic Professionalism Since 1949* (Seattle, WA: University of Washington Press, 2001).

20 Chen Jian, *China's Road to the Korean War: The Making of the Sino-American Confrontation* (New York: Columbia University Press, 1994); *Mao's China and the Cold War* (Chapel Hill, NC: University of North Carolina Press, 2001).

21 Shu Guang Zhang, *Deterrence and Strategic Culture: Chinese–American Confrontations, 1949–1958* (Ithaca, NY: Cornell University Press, 1993); *Mao's Military Romanticism: China and the Korean War, 1950–1953* (Lawrence, KS: University of Kansas Press, 1995); *Economic Cold War: America's Embargo Against China and the Sino-Soviet Alliance 1949–1963* (Stanford, CA: Stanford University Press, 2001); Zhang and Chen Jian, *Chinese Communist Foreign Policy and the Cold War in Asia: New Documentary Evidence, 1944–1950* (Chicago, IL: Imprint Publications, 1995).

22 Qiang Zhai, *China and the Vietnam Wars, 1950–1975* (Chapel Hill, NC: University of North Carolina Press, 2000).

23 Robert S. Ross and Jiang Changbin (eds), *Re-examining the Cold War: U.S.–China Diplomacy, 1954–1973* (Cambridge, MA: Harvard University Press, 2001).

24 Harry Harding and Yuan Ming (eds), *Sino-American Relations, 1945–1955: A Joint Reassessment of a Critical Decade* (Wilmington, DE: Scholarly Resources, 1989).

25 Nancy Bernkopf Tucker (ed.), *China Confidential: American Diplomats and Sino-American Relations, 1945–1996* (New York: Columbia University Press, 2001).

26 Thomas J. Christensen, *Useful Adversaries: Grand Strategy, Domestic Mobilization, and Sino-American Conflict, 1947–1958* (Princeton, NJ: Princeton University Press, 1996).

27 David M. Lampton (ed.), *The Making of Chinese Foreign and Security Policy in the Era of Reform* (Stanford, CA: Stanford University Press, 2001).

28 A. Doak Barnett, *The Making of Foreign Policy in China: Structure and Process* (Boulder, CO: Westview Press, 1985); Lu Ning, *The Dynamics of Foreign Policy Decision-Making in China* (Boulder, CO: Westview Press, 1995 and 2000).

29 See Murray Scot Tanner, "Changing Windows on a Changing China: The Evolving 'Think Tank' System and the Case of the Public Security Sector," David Shambaugh, "China's International Relations Think Tanks: Evolving Structure and Process," Bonnie S. Glaser and Phillip C. Saunders, "Chinese Civilian Foreign Policy Research Institutes: Evolving Roles and Increasing Influence," Bates Gill and James Mulvenon, "Chinese Military-Related Think Tanks and Research Institutions," Barry Naughton, "China's Economic Think Tanks: Their Changing Role in the 1990s," *The China Quarterly*, No. 171 (September 2002).

30 Yufan Hao and Lin Su (eds), *China's Foreign Policy Making: Societal Forces and China's America Policy* (Burlington, VT: Ashgate, 2006).

31 Yong Deng and Fei-ling Wang (eds), *In the Eyes of the Dragon: China Views the World* (Lanham, MD: Rowman & Littlefield, 1999).

32 Yufan Hao and Guocang Huang (eds), *The Chinese View of the World* (New York: Pantheon Books, 1989).

33 Peter Hayes Gries, *China's New Nationalism: Pride, Politics, and Diplomacy* (Berkeley, CA: University of California Press, 2004).

34 Allen Carlson, *Unifying China, Unifying with the World: Securing Chinese Sovereignty in the Reform Era* (Stanford, CA: Stanford University Press, 2005).

35 Richard Madsen, *China and the American Dream: A Moral Inquiry* (Berkeley, CA: University of California Press, 1995).

36 T. Christopher Jesperson, *American Images of China, 1931–1949* (Stanford, CA: Stanford University Press, 1996)

37 Carola McGiffert (ed.), *China in the American Political Imagination* (Washington, D.C.: CSIS Press, 2003); *Chinese Images of the United States* (Washington, D.C.: CSIS Press, 2005).

38 David Shambaugh, *Beautiful Imperialist: China Perceives America, 1972–1990* (Princeton, NJ: Princeton University Press, 1991).

39 Hongshan Li and Zhaohui Hong (eds), *Image, Perception, and the Making of U.S.-China Relations* (Lanham, MD: University Press of America, 1998).

40 Jianwei Wang, *Limited Adversaries: Post-Cold War Sino-American Mutual Images* (Oxford: Oxford University Press, 2000).

41 Elizabeth Economy and Michel Oksenberg (eds), *China Joins the World: Progress and Prospects* (New York: Council on Foreign Relations, 1999).

42 David Shambaugh (ed.), *Power Shift: China and Asia's New Dynamics* (Berkeley, CA: University of California Press, 2005); Robert Sutter, *China's Rise in Asia: Promises and Perils* (Lanham, MD: Rowman & Littlefield, 2005); Carolyn Pumphrey (ed.), *The Rise of China in Asia: Security Implications* (Carlisle Barracks, PA: U.S. Army War College Strategic Studies Institute, 2002); Alastair Iain Johnston and Robert S. Ross (eds), *Engaging China: The Management of an Emerging Power* (London: Routledge, 1999); Mark Burles, *Chinese Policy Toward Russia and the Central Asian Republics* (Santa Monica, CA: Rand Corporation, 1999). Also see M. Taylor Fravel, *The Long March to Peace: Explaining China's Settlement of Territorial Disputes* (forthcoming).

43 Chae-Jin Lee, *China and Korea: Dynamic Relations* (Stanford, CA: Hoover Institution Press, 1996).

44 Brantly Womack, *China and Vietnam: The Politics of Asymmetry* (Cambridge: Cambridge University Press, 2006).

45 John W. Garver, *Protracted Contest: Sino-Indian Rivalry in the Twentieth Century* (Seattle, WA: University of Washington Press, 2001); Waheguru Pal Singh Sidhu and Jing-dong Yuan, *China and India: Cooperation or Conflict?* (Boulder, CO: Lynne Reinner, 2003); Francine Frankel and Harry Harding (eds), *The China-India Relationship: What the United States Needs to Know* (New York: Columbia University Press, 2004).

46 Jeanne Wilson, *Strategic Partners: Russian-Chinese Relations in the Post-Soviet Era* (Armonk, NY: M.E. Sharpe, 2004); Elizabeth Wishnick, *Mending Fences: The Evolution of Moscow's China Policy from Brezhnev to Yeltsin* (Seattle, WA: University of Washington Press, 2001); Sherman W. Garnett (ed.), *Rapprochement or Rivalry: Russia–China Relations in a Changing Asia* (Washington, D.C.: Carnegie Endowment for International Peace, 2001).

47 Ezra Vogel, Yuan Ming, and Tanaka Akihiko (eds), *The Golden Age of the U.S.–China–Japan Triangle, 1972–1989* (Cambridge, MA: Harvard University Press, 2002); Susan Maybaumwisniewski and Mary Sommerville (eds), *Blue Horizon: United States–Japan–PRC Tripartite Relations* (Washington, D.C.: National Defense University Press, 1997); Ming Zhang and Ronald Monteperto, *A Triad of Another Kind: The United States, China, and Japan* (New York: St. Martins, 1999); Morton Abramowitz, Funabashi Yoichi, and Wang Jisi (eds), *China–Japan–U.S.: Managing*

the Trilateral Relationship (New York: JCIE, 1998); Abromowitz, Funabashi, and Wang (eds), *China–Japan–U.S. Relations: Meeting New Challenges* (New York: JCIE, 2002); volume forthcoming by Mike Mochizuki.

48 Richard Bush, *Untying the Knot: Making Peace in the Taiwan Strait* (Washington, D.C.: Brookings Institution Press, 2005); Nancy Bernkopf Tucker (ed.), *Dangerous Strait: The U.S.–Taiwan–China Crisis* (New York: Columbia University Press, 2005); Alan D. Romberg, *Rein In at the Brink of the Precipice: American Policy Toward Taiwan and U.S.–PRC Relations* (Washington, D.C.: The Henry L. Stimson Center, 2003); Donald Zagoria (ed.), *Breaking the China-Taiwan Impasse* (Westport, CT: Praeger, 2003);

49 Ramon H. Myers, Michel C. Oksenberg, and David Shambaugh (eds), *Making China Policy: Lessons from the Clinton and Bush Administrations* (Lanham, MD: Rowman & Littlefield, 2001); Robert S. Ross (ed.), *After the Cold War: Domestic Factors and U.S.-China Relations* (Armonk, NY: M.E. Sharpe, 1998); Ezra Vogel (ed.), *Living with China: U.S.–China Relations in the 21st Century* (New York: W.W. Norton, 1997); Jonathan D. Pollack (ed.), *Strategic Surprise? U.S.–China Relations in the Early Twenty-First Century* (Newport, CT: Naval War College Press, 2003)

50 Robert S. Ross, *Negotiating Cooperation: The United States and China, 1969–1989* (Stanford,CA: Stanford University Press 1995); James Mann, *About Face: A History of America's Curious Relationship with China, From Nixon to Clinton* (New York: Knopf, 1999); David M. Lampton, *Same Bed, Different Dreams: Managing U.S.–China Relations, 1989–2000* (Berkeley, CA: University of California Press, 2001); Robert L Suettinger, *Beyond Tiananmen: The Politics of U.S.-China Relations, 1989–2000* (Washington, D.C.: Brookings Institution Press, 2003); Patrick Tyler, *A Great Wall: Six Presidents and China* (New York: Public Affairs, 1999).

51 Thomas Christensen, Alastair Iain Johnston, and Robert Ross, "Conclusion," in Alastair I. Johnston and Robert Ross (eds), *New Directions in the Study of China's Foreign Policy*, op. cit.

52 See, in particular, Sutter and Shambaugh studies cited in footnote 42.

53 A new study of China–Europe relations will be published in 2007: Eberhard Sandschneider, David Shambaugh, and Zhou Hong (eds), *China and Europe* (London: Routledge, 2007).

54 See Jae-ho Chung, *Between Partner and Ally: Korea–China Relations and the United States* (New York: Columbia University Press, 2006).

55 John Garver, *Protracted Contest*, op. cit.

56 John Garver, *China and Iran: Ancient Partners in a Post-Imperial World* (Seattle, WA: University of Washington Press, 2006).

57 Elizabeth Wishnick, *Mending Fences*; Jeanne Wilson, *Strategic Partners*, op cit.

58 Brantly Womack, *China and Vietnam: The Politics of Asymmetry*, op. cit.

59 See footnote 49–50, op cit.

60 Nicholas Eftimiades, *Chinese Intelligence Operations* (Annapolis, MD: Naval Institute Press, 1994).

61 Samuel Kim, *China, the United Nations, and World Order* (Princeton, NJ: Princeton University Press, 1979).

62 I am indebted to John Garver for this suggestion.

63 In addition to Shambaugh (ed.), *Power Shift: China and Asia's New Dynamics*, op. cit., see forthcoming volume by David Kang (Columbia University Press).

64 Thomas W. Robinson and David Shambaugh (eds), *Chinese Foreign Policy: Theory and Practice* (Oxford: Clarendon Press, 1994).

65 See C. Dennison Lane, Mark Weisenbloom, and Dimon Liu (eds), *Chinese Military Modernization* (London and Washington: Routledge, Kegan Paul and American Enterprise Institute, 1996); James Lilley and Chuck Downs (eds), *Crisis in the Taiwan Strait* (Washington, D.C.: National Defense University Press and American Enterprise Institute, 1997); James Lilley and David Shambaugh (eds), *China's Military Faces the*

Future (Armonk, NY: M.E. Sharpe, 1999); Larry Wortzel (ed.), *The Chinese Armed Forces in the 21st Century* (Carlisle Barracks, PA: U.S. Army War College Strategic Studies Institute, 1999); Susan Puska (ed.), *The PLA After Next* (ibid., 2000); Andrew Scobell (ed.), *The Costs of Conflict: The Impact of China on a Future War* (Carlisle Barracks, PA: U.S. Army War College Strategic Studies Institute, 2001); Andrew Scobell and Larry Wortzel (eds), *China's Growing Military Power* (Carlisle Barracks, PA: U.S. Army War College Strategic Studies Institute, 2002); Laurie Burkitt, Andrew Scobell, and Larry Wortzel (eds), *The Lessons of History: The Chinese PLA at 75* (Carlisle Barracks, PA: U.S. Army War College Strategic Studies Institute, 2003); Andrew Scobell and Larry Wortzel (eds), *Civil-Military Change in China: Elites, Institutions, and Ideas After the 16th Party Congress* (Carlisle Barracks, PA: U.S. Army War College Strategic Studies Institute, 2004); Andrew Scobell and Larry Wortzel (eds), *Chinese National Security Decisionmaking Under Stress* (Carlisle Barracks, PA: U.S. Army War College Strategic Studies Institute, 2005).

66 See David Finkelstein and James Mulvenon (eds), *China's Revolution in Doctrinal Affairs: Emerging Trends in the Operational Art of the Chinese People's Liberation Army* (Washington, D.C.: Beaver Press, 2005).

67 See James Mulvenon and Andrew N.D. Yang (eds), *A Poverty of Riches: New Challenges and Opportunities in PLA Research* (Santa Monica, CA: Rand Corporation, 2003); James Mulvenon and Andrew N.D. Yang (eds), *The PLA as Organization* (Santa Monica, CA: Rand Corporation, 2002); James Mulvenon and Andrew N.D. Yang (eds), *Seeking truth From Facts: A Retrospective on Chinese Military Studies in the Post-Mao Era* (Santa Monica, CA: Rand Corporation, 2001); James Mulvenon and Richard H. Yang (eds), *The People's Liberation Army in the Information Age* (Santa Monica, CA: Rand Corporation, 1999).

68 Stephen J. Flanagan and Michael Marti (eds), *The People's Liberation Army and China in Transition* (Washington, D.C.: National Defense University Press, 2003); Andrew Scobell and Larry M. Wortzel, cf. 65.

69 David Shambaugh and Richard H. Yang (eds), *China's Military in Transition* (Oxford: Clarendon Press, 1997).

70 David Shambaugh, *Modernizing China's Military: Progress, Problems and Prospects* (Berkeley, CA: University of California Press, 2003); Mel Gurtov and Byong-Moo Hwang, *China's Security: The New Roles of the Military* (Boulder, CO: Lynne Reinner, 1998); Keith Crane, Roger Cliff, Evan Medeiros, James Mulvenon, and William Overholt, *Modernizing China's Military: Opportunities and Constraints* (Santa Monica, CA: Rand Corporation, 2005).

71 Council on Foreign Relations, *Report of an Independent Task Force on Chinese Military Power* (New York: Council on Foreign Relations, 2003).

72 Andrew Scobell, *China's Use of Military Force: Beyond the Great Wall and Long March* (Cambridge: Cambridge University Press, 2003); Mark A. Ryan, David M. Finkelstein, and Michael A. McDevitt (eds), *Chinese Warfighting: The PLA Experience Since 1949* (Armonk, NY: M.E. Sharpe, 2003).

73 Gary J. Bjorge, *Moving the Enemy: Operational Art in the Chinese PLA's Huai Hai Campaign* (Fort Levenworth, KS: Combat Studies Institute Press, 2004).

74 Mark Burles and Abram N. Shulsky, *Patterns in China's Use of Force* (Santa Monica, CA: The Rand Corporation, 2000).

75 Michael Swaine and Ashley Tellis, *China's Grand Strategy*, op. cit.

76 Alastair Iain Johnston, *Cultural Realism: Strategic Culture and Grand Strategy in Chinese History* (Princeton, NJ: Princeton University Press, 1995).

77 Ibid., p. x.

78 John W. Lewis and Xue Litai, *China Builds the Bomb* (Stanford, CA: Stanford University Press, 1988).

79 John W. Lewis and Xue Litai, *China's Strategic Seapower: The Politics of Force Modernization in the Nuclear Age* (Stanford, CA: Stanford University Press, 1994).

80   Evan Feigenbaum, *China's Techno-Warriors: National Security and Strategic Competition from the Nuclear to the Information Age*, (Stanford, CA: Stanford University Press, 2003).

81   Bates Gill and Taeho Kim, *China's Arms Acquisitions from Abroad: A Quest for 'Superb and Secret Weapons'* (Oxford: Oxford University Press, 1995).

82   James Mulvenon, *Soldiers of Fortune: The Rise and Fall of the Chinese Military-Business Complex, 1978–1998* (Armonk, NY: M.E. Sharpe, 2001).

83   Bates Gill, *Chinese Arms Transfers: Purposes, Patterns, and Prospects in the New World Order* (Westport, CT: Praeger, 1992).

84   Tai Ming Cheung, *China's Entrepreneurial Army* (Oxford: Oxford University Press, 2001).

85   Robert A. Manning, Ronald Monteperto, and Brad Roberts (eds), *China, Nuclear Weapons, and Arms Control: A Preliminary Assessment* (New York: Council on Foreign Relations, 2000).

86   Wendy Frieman, *China, Arms Control, and Nonproliferation* (London: Routledge, 2004).

87   Evan Mederios, *Shaping Chinese Foreign Policy: The Evolution of Chinese Policies on WMD Nonproliferation and the Role of U.S. Policy, 1980–2004* (Stanford, CA: Stanford University Press, forthcoming).

88   Kenneth W. Allen, Glenn Krumel, and Jonathan D. Pollack, *China's Air Force Enters the 21st Century* (Santa Monica, CA: Rand Corporation, 1995).

89   Mark A. Stokes, *China's Strategic Modernization: Implications for the United States* (Carlisle Barracks, PA: U.S. Army War College Strategic Studies Institute, 1999).

90   Bernard Cole, *The Great Wall at Sea: China's Navy Enters the Twenty-First Century* (Annapolis, MD: Naval Institute Press, 2001. Also see, Srikanth Kondapali, *China's Naval Power* (New Delhi: Institute for Defense Studies and Analysis, 2001); Peter Howarth, *China's Rising Sea Power* (London: Routledge, 2006).

91   Dennis Blasko, *The Chinese Army Today: Tradition and Transformation for the 21st Century* (London: Routledge, 2006).

92   Michael Pillsbury (ed.), *Chinese Views of Future Warfare* (Washington, D.C.: National Defense University Press, 1997); Michael Pillsbury, *China Debates the Future Security Environment*, Washington, D.C.: National Defense University Press, 2000.

93   Nan Li (ed.), *Chinese Civil-Military Relations: The Transformation of the People's Liberation Army* (London: Routledge, 2006); David Finkelstein and Kristen Gunness, (eds), *Civil-Military Relations in Today's China: Swimming in a New Sea* (Armonk, NY: M.E. Sharpe, 2006).

94   Kenneth W. Allen and Eric McVadon, *China's Foreign Military Relations* (Washington, D.C.: The Henry L. Stimson Center, 1999).

95   Alan D. Romberg and Michael McDevitt (eds), *China and Missile Defense: Managing U.S.-PRC Strategic Relations* (Washington, D.C.: Henry L. Stimson Center, 2003).

96   Benjamin Self and Jeffrey Thomson (eds), *An Alliance for Engagement: Building Cooperation in Security Relations with China* (Washington, D.C.: Henry L. Stimson Center, 2002).

97   Kevin Pollpeter, *U.S.–China Security Management: Assessing the Military-to-Military Relationship* (Santa Monica,CA: Rand Corporation, 2004).

98   The following discussion draws, in part, on my "PLA Studies Today: A Maturing Field," in James Mulvenon and Richard H. Yang (eds), *The People's Liberation Army in the Information Age*, op. cit.

99   Mulvenon and Yang (ed.), *The PLA as Organization*, op. cit.

100   Cf. 93.

101   Along these lines, see Jonathan D. Pollack, "Does the Study of Asian International Relations Require International Relations Theory?" *Issues and Studies*, Vol. 41, No. 1 (March 2005), pp. 220–4.

IV. Epilogue

11 International China Watching in the Twenty-first Century

Coping with a Changing Profession

Robert Ash, David Shambaugh, and Seiichiro Takagi

In addition to the substantive aspects of researching and understanding contemporary China, this volume also reveals that the professional world of the China specialist has changed. In large part, China watching has changed because China itself has (dramatically) changed. As China looms ever larger in world affairs, the demand for information and informed analysis about it rises correspondingly. China watching and China watchers have also been affected by developments in domestic and international politics, technological developments, research methodologies, funding for research, and other factors. China watchers thus operate today in a complex professional environment. China scholars have long been the main repository of expertise on China. But, in the early twenty-first century, the professional environment has become more competitive, the object of study (China) has become infinitely more complex, and consumers of their products have become more multiple and discerning.

Today China watchers based in universities (scholars) no longer write merely for the consumption of their Sinological or disciplinary colleagues – but also for publics, governments, corporations, banks, law firms, consultancies, and the media (all of whose thirst for knowledge about China seems insatiable). As a result the "consumer base"of China specialists' has broadened considerably, although there were always some China scholars more inclined to invest and involve themselves in public education, government advising, and media commentary. To meet the rising demand, other professional institutions have hired their own in-house China expertise. Banks, corporations, and law firms all have their own in-house expertise on China, while political risk consultancies are also strengthening their China teams.[1] Universities and research institutes are therefore no longer the only repository of expertise about China. Academic China specialists today are thus not only challenged to stay on top of their topic, but must also "compete" with non-scholarly China watchers. To be sure, many China specialists continue to only write for scholarly publications, but an increasing number are being pulled into other professional worlds. Even within the Academy, business schools, law schools, and other departments not traditionally interested in China or area studies are adding China specialists to their faculties.

Because of the different consumers of China knowledge, academic China specialists have to learn to speak to multiple audiences and translate Chinese complexities into analyses understandable by their different audiences.[2] Academic jargon and theoretical arguments frequently confuse and obscure, rather than enlighten, these audiences. Briefings and written analyses need to be tailored the specific audience. What is intelligible to a banker or businessman is not necessarily accessible in the same way to a journalist or to the general public. Government policymakers and intelligence analysts also have their own special needs and vocabulary.[3] Many academic China specialists, and university-based scholars generally, have difficulty or cannot make these analytic and semantic adjustments. Indeed, many do not care to – preferring to do what they were trained in graduate schools to do: conduct and publish theoretically-informed and empirically-grounded scholarship in academic journals and books. There is, of course, nothing wrong or reprehensible in carrying out this professional mission – indeed it is what distinguishes the Academy from those other professions. But it does mean that academically published work is often inaccessible and incomprehensible to audiences beyond the narrow confines of academia (this seems to be less of an issue in Europe or Japan than in the United States). If academics want to reach larger audiences, they need to craft their message to suit the audience. There is a *great* thirst for informed analysis of China outside the university world and, as the contributions to this volume make clear, there is much that China specialists can offer to these other communities.

Another challenge is data. As analysts confront an information-rich environ-ment and bibliographic overload, simply "staying on top" of one's area of China expertise has become a major challenge in itself. Once confronted by a shortage of information that left no alternative but to "read the tea leaves" in and outside of Beijing, today's research environment on China is fundamentally different. Although it remains difficult to research some subjects deemed sensitive by the Chinese government (e.g. elite politics and national security affairs), a lack of reliable data in other areas, and the practice of self-censorship by many Chinese intellectuals, China specialists can no longer complain that there is a dearth of data. Today there is an abundance of statistical and other information inside and outside of China. The challenge is gaining effective bibliographic control over hese different data sources.

The publishing boom of the past two decades is one factor that has contributed to this situation. Official government sources report that in 2003 2,119 newspapers and 9,074 periodicals were published in China (excluding several hundred papers and local gazetteers made available through internal, or *neibu*, circulation). In addition, 1,123 publishing houses published 190,391 books that year.[4] Meanwhile, the Internet makes it possible to conduct research on a vast range of subjects from one's desktop at home – thereby partly obviating the need to travel to China to collect information and data.

In this transformed environment, China watchers need to use multiple research strategies – some from inside China, others from outside – and cross-check multiple sources for accuracy and consistency. Hong Kong, and the Universities

Service Centre at the Chinese University in particular, remains a valuable location for research. Taiwan, however, has declined in importance as a China-watching venue. Interviewing individual Chinese when they are outside of China – scholars, researchers, and officials – is also useful, as they are often able to discuss subjects abroad that they cannot in China. Interviewing of non-Chinese who interact with China – businessmen, officials, military officers, lawyers, and other professionals – can also yield valuable information and insights.

China has also become such a complex country and society that for every well-grounded assertion and analysis, a variation of the argument – even the opposite – may equally hold true. China's size and complexity simply make it very difficult to generalize about China. Even allowing for the simplified and "bottom line" analyses frequently demanded by journalists and the general public, nuance is essential. Finding the right balance requires resolving the tension between the need, on the one hand, to aggregate our knowledge about this complex society and, on the other, the propensity of the academic China field to indulge in excessive disaggregation that leads to "knowing more and more about less and less." As the chapters in this volume illustrate, and as perusal of academic journals will confirm, the level and quality of research and knowledge about contemporary China are impressive – but they also pose a daunting challenge to a non-specialist audience, and there is a danger of being unable to see the forest for the trees. In short, as it becomes progressively more difficult to offer assured conclusions about "China" writ large, it is incumbent on academic specialists to devote some of their effort towards trying to assemble the pieces of the China puzzle.

Another challenge is to find ways of improving communication among China specialists, as well as to increase joint research with Chinese colleagues in China. To be sure, the age of the Internet has already dramatically increased communications among China watchers throughout the world. List serves such as "Chinapol" link China watchers internationally on a daily basis. Such instantaneous communication is invaluable as a means of sharing information and perspectives; it also creates a true "virtual community" among China analysts. This may be the single most important development in forging a true professional community among China watchers, as previously they were linked only by their common research interests and occasional meetings in China, Hong Kong, Taiwan, or at international conferences. In addition to daily discussions of developments in China, the Internet allows colleagues to regularly and instantly communicate and collaborate with each other in order to share ideas or drafts of work-in-progress. The Internet and email communication have also brought foreign China watchers into closer and more regular contact with their counterparts inside China. Nonetheless, institutions and individuals in China remain not well integrated with the China watching community abroad. Positive steps towards improving such interaction have been the establishment of the Contemporary China Institute under the China Academy of Social Sciences in 1990, the National History Research Association (*Guoshi Xuehui*) in 1992, and the annual World Forum on China Studies initiated by the Shanghai Academy of Social Sciences in 2005.

But despite the virtues of the electronic age and the ease of international air travel, the relative lack of interaction and collaboration among China specialists throughout the world remains striking. As the chapters by Ohashi, Kojima, and Takagi in this volume make clear, the community of China watchers in Japan is particularly isolated from the international Sinological community. There also remains peculiarly little professional interaction between China specialists in Australia, Asia, Europe, Japan, and North America. Only a relatively small cohort of the total community of China specialists in these places meet and interact with any regularity. As for Africa, the Middle East and Latin America, the field of China studies is still virtually non-existent. The Association of Asian Studies annual meeting remains dominated by scholars in the United States, and the International Institute of Asian Studies in the Netherlands draws primarily on European scholars and is not truly "international"; as its namesake would indicate. Other national associations, such as the British or Australian Associations of Chinese Studies, are useful venues within these countries, but rarely attract participants from abroad. The European Association of Chinese Studies and the Europe-China Academic Network (ECAN) perform the useful function of bringing European Sinologists together, but both remain Eurocentric in focus and membership. There are perhaps a few dozen prominent China analysts around the world who do spend their professional lives on the international conference circuit, but the rest of the field – the vast majority – still rarely interact with their colleagues from other nations.

The relative lack of international interaction among China specialists is truly regrettable, as we are all engaged in a common enterprise and can benefit greatly from interaction and cross-fertilization of perspectives, methodologies, and research strategies. In his assessment of the future for American studies of contemporary China, published in 1993, the late Michel Oksenberg observed:

> Scholarship on contemporary China in the 1990s will become a truly global enterprise; as a result, mastery of languages in addition to Chinese will be even more important than in the past. The consequences [of this developing trend] are likely to be significant. There can be no doubt that Americans – as others – study China through distinctive sets of national lenses.[5]

Thirteen years later, Oksenberg's first observation concerning the internationalization of contemporary China studies has definitely occurred, as the chapters in this volume make evident, but his call for greater awareness of differing national perspectives still requires substantially increased attention.

Funding bodies around the world could make a significant difference in this regard, by earmarking funds for explicitly cooperative research projects by China scholars in different nations or to hold conferences on defined topics that bring together China specialists from around the world. It is also odd, yet evident, that collaboration between China scholars outside of China and those inside of China remains low. Certainly there are some examples, particularly in the study of the

Chinese economy (as Penelope Prime's chapter illustrates), but one would have expected far more collaborative research projects among Chinese scholars and those outside of China. Again, foundations and funding bodies could make a real difference here by creating collaborative research initiatives.

These are some of the professional challenges facing China specialists today. There are many others. They include occasional demands associated with the agendas of foundations and government funding bodies that support research on China; resource constraints of the funding bodies more generally; commercial pressures in the publishing industry (which have resulted in publishers seeking manuscripts that will sell significant print runs rather than publishing scholarly research for its own sake); research access to specific types of data in China; and the domestic politics in various countries – often contentious – of managing relations with China.

Despite these challenges, the chapters in this volume illustrate that the international field of contemporary China studies is large, robust, and specialized. It has developed dramatically from its pre- and post-World War II antecedents. As noted above, the work of China specialists is of greater demand outside of academia, but it also has become better integrated inside of the Academy. The chapters in this volume also indicate that each subfield within Chinese studies has become more and more specialized and sophisticated.

The study of contemporary China also promises to contribute to global historiography, given the unprecedented historical nature and magnitude of modernization and social change in China. China provides a fertile testing ground for the social sciences, since China's modernizing and globalizing experiences – in all their aspects – will test, confirm, or contradict existing theories about the development of societies and institutions. From this perspective, an important new trend – most manifestly observable in the United States but in evidence elsewhere too – is the growing involvement of an increasing number of social scientists who are not China specialists in undertaking comparative research on China. It is a trend that promises to enrich various academic disciplines, shed important light on China from comparative perspectives (something China specialists tend not to appreciate), and throw into clearer relief aspects of China that are and are not *sui generis.*

In other words, the study of China is not a peripheral academic pursuit. On the contrary, it is, or should be, a critically important part of our common heritage as both human beings and scholars. It also happens to be a growing concern of governments throughout the world. One lesson that emerges from this volume is that China specialists must constantly seek not only to be adaptable, flexible, and responsive to changes taking place in China, but also to examine those changes from comparative and theoretical perspectives. That China will continue to be an intellectual and policy puzzle of substantial proportions is not in doubt. What remains to be seen, however, is whether China specialists can continue to provide sensible, educated, and dispassionate analysis and comment that can inform – not inflame – debates about China.

Notes

1 The Eurasia Group in New York is an example.
2 See Harry Harding, "The Changing Roles of the Academic China-Watcher," in *Trends in China Watching: Observing the PRC at Fifty* (Sigur Center for Asian Studies, George Washington University, 1999), available at: http://www.gwu.edu/~sigur/pubs/ SCAP7-Trends.pdf.
3 See Robert Suettinger, "We're From the Government, and We're Here to Watch: U.S. Government Observation and Analysis of China, 1949–1999," ibid.; Thomas Fingar, "Government China Specialists: Scholar Officials and Official Scholars," in David Shambaugh (ed.), *American Studies of Contemporary China* (Armonk, NY and Washington, D.C.: M.E. Sharpe and the Woodrow Wilson Center Press, 1993).
4 National Bureau of Statistics of China, *China Statistical Yearbook 2004* (Beijing: China Statistics Press, 2004), pp. 844–6, 853.
5 Michel C. Oksenberg, "The American Study of Modern China: Towards the Twenty-First Century," in David Shambaugh (ed.), *American Studies of Contemporary China*, op. cit., p. 333. Oksenberg was the leading China specialist of his generation in the United States.

Index

DATE

e

A libra

eBooks are elec
store them on you.

They have advantages
to a wide variety of publish

eBooks can help your research b
bookmark chapters, annotate text a
to find specific words or phrases. Sever
fit on even a small laptop or PDA.

NEW: Save money by eSubscribing: cheap, onli
to any eBook for as long as you need it.

Annual subscription packages

We now offer special low-cost bulk subscriptions to
packages of eBooks in certain subject areas. These are
available to libraries or to individuals.

For more information please contact
webmaster.ebooks@tandf.co.uk

We're continually developing the eBook concept, so
keep up to date by visiting the website.

www.eBookstore.tandf.co.uk